Communications in Computer and Information Science 2413

Rationale
The CCIS series is devoted to the publication of proceedings of computer science conferences. Its aim is to efficiently disseminate original research results in informatics in printed and electronic form. While the focus is on publication of peer-reviewed full papers presenting mature work, inclusion of reviewed short papers reporting on work in progress is welcome, too. Besides globally relevant meetings with internationally representative program committees guaranteeing a strict peer-reviewing and paper selection process, conferences run by societies or of high regional or national relevance are also considered for publication.

Topics
The topical scope of CCIS spans the entire spectrum of informatics ranging from foundational topics in the theory of computing to information and communications science and technology and a broad variety of interdisciplinary application fields.

Information for Volume Editors and Authors
Publication in CCIS is free of charge. No royalties are paid, however, we offer registered conference participants temporary free access to the online version of the conference proceedings on SpringerLink (http://link.springer.com) by means of an http referrer from the conference website and/or a number of complimentary printed copies, as specified in the official acceptance email of the event.

CCIS proceedings can be published in time for distribution at conferences or as post-proceedings, and delivered in the form of printed books and/or electronically as USBs and/or e-content licenses for accessing proceedings at SpringerLink. Furthermore, CCIS proceedings are included in the CCIS electronic book series hosted in the SpringerLink digital library at http://link.springer.com/bookseries/7899. Conferences publishing in CCIS are allowed to use Online Conference Service (OCS) for managing the whole proceedings lifecycle (from submission and reviewing to preparing for publication) free of charge.

Publication process
The language of publication is exclusively English. Authors publishing in CCIS have to sign the Springer CCIS copyright transfer form, however, they are free to use their material published in CCIS for substantially changed, more elaborate subsequent publications elsewhere. For the preparation of the camera-ready papers/files, authors have to strictly adhere to the Springer CCIS Authors' Instructions and are strongly encouraged to use the CCIS LaTeX style files or templates.

Abstracting/Indexing
CCIS is abstracted/indexed in DBLP, Google Scholar, EI-Compendex, Mathematical Reviews, SCImago, Scopus. CCIS volumes are also submitted for the inclusion in ISI Proceedings.

How to start
To start the evaluation of your proposal for inclusion in the CCIS series, please send an e-mail to ccis@springer.com.

V. B. Gupta · Shishir Kumar Shandilya ·
Fernando Ortiz-Rodríguez ·
Jose L. Martinez-Rodriguez
Editors

Business Intelligence, Computational Mathematics, and Data Analytics

First International Conference, IBCD 2024
Indore, India, August 18–19, 2024
Proceedings

Springer

Editors
V. B. Gupta
Devi Ahilya Vishwavidyalaya
Indore, Madhya Pradesh, India

Shishir Kumar Shandilya
Devi Ahilya Vishwavidyalaya
Indore, Madhya Pradesh, India

Fernando Ortiz-Rodríguez
Autonomous University of Tamaulipas
Reynosa, Tamaulipas, Mexico

Jose L. Martinez-Rodriguez
Autonomous University of Tamaulipas
Reynosa, Tamaulipas, Mexico

ISSN 1865-0929 ISSN 1865-0937 (electronic)
Communications in Computer and Information Science
ISBN 978-3-031-87510-6 ISBN 978-3-031-87511-3 (eBook)
https://doi.org/10.1007/978-3-031-87511-3

This Springer imprint is published by the registered company Springer Nature Switzerland AG
The registered company address is: Gewerbestrasse 11, 6330 Cham, Switzerland

Preface

The International Conference on Business Intelligence, Computational Mathematics, and Data Analytics (iBCD) 2024 was strategically positioned to navigate the rapidly evolving technological landscape. It offered a dynamic platform where both academic and industry experts could discuss crucial domains collectively. With a focus on applied intelligence across data science, mathematics, healthcare, cybersecurity, and business analytics, the conference served as a driving force for transforming theoretical breakthroughs into practical, real-world solutions with meaningful societal impact.

The main scientific program of the conference comprised 16 papers: 14 full research papers and 2 short research papers selected out of 81 reviewed submissions, which corresponds to an acceptance rate of 19.8%.

The General and Program Committee chairs would like to thank the many people involved in making IBCD 2024 a success. First, our thanks go to the main chairs and the reviewers for ensuring a rigorous review process that, with an average of three double-blind reviews per paper, led to an excellent scientific program.

This event brought many joys, knowledge sharing, and networking but also brought a sad event after the conference. Our main editor V.B. Gupta passed away; even though you're no longer with us, your strength and commitment continues to guide this event in the coming years.

Further, we thank the team at Springer for their vital support of this edition of IBCD 2024. The editors would like to close the Preface with warm thanks for our supporting keynotes and our enthusiastic authors who made this event truly international and our local students and Organizing Committee for making a great event.

August 2024

V. B. Gupta
Shishir Kumar Shandilya
Fernando Ortiz-Rodríguez
Jose L. Martinez-Rodriguez

Organization

General Chairs

V. B. Gupta	Devi Ahilya Vishwavidyalaya, India
Shishir Kumar Shandilya	Devi Ahilya Vishwavidyalaya, India
Fernando Ortiz-Rodríguez	Universidad Autónoma de Tamaulipas, Mexico
Jose L. Martinez Rodriguez	Universidad Autónoma de Tamaulipas, Mexico

Program Chairs

Shishir Kumar Shandilya	Devi Ahilya Vishwavidyalaya, India
Fernando Ortiz-Rodríguez	Universidad Autónoma de Tamaulipas, Mexico

Local Chairs

Ajay Verma	Devi Ahilya Vishwavidyalaya, India
Ashok Sharma	Devi Ahilya Vishwavidyalaya, India
Rajnish Jain	Devi Ahilya Vishwavidyalaya, India
Sanjiv Tokekar	Devi Ahilya Vishwavidyalaya, India
Ratnesh Gupta	Devi Ahilya Vishwavidyalaya, India
Sanjay Tanwani	Devi Ahilya Vishwavidyalaya, India
Pratibha Sharma	Devi Ahilya Vishwavidyalaya, India
Ashesh Tiwari	Devi Ahilya Vishwavidyalaya, India
Pratosh Bansal	Devi Ahilya Vishwavidyalaya, India
Namarata Sharma	Devi Ahilya Vishwavidyalaya, India
Ugrasen Suman	Devi Ahilya Vishwavidyalaya, India
Munesh Chandra Trivedi	Devi Ahilya Vishwavidyalaya, India
Purnima S. Sangle	Devi Ahilya Vishwavidyalaya, India
Ashutosh Saxena	Devi Ahilya Vishwavidyalaya, India
Vandit Hedau	Devi Ahilya Vishwavidyalaya, India
Tushar Banerjee	Devi Ahilya Vishwavidyalaya, India

Program Committee

A. Sampathkumar	University of Hrádec Kralové, Czech Republic
Ajit Kumar	Soongsil University, South Korea
A. K. Nagar	Liverpool Hope University, UK
Akshara Makrariya	VIT Bhopal University, India
Andria Procopion	City University of London, UK
Andrii Shalaginov	Norwegian University of Science and Technology, Norway
Anirban Bhowmik	VIT Bhopal University, India
Aswani Kumar Cherukuri	Vellore Institute of Technology, India
Ayush Goyal	Texas A & M University - Kingsville, USA
Bon David Choi	Soongsil University, South Korea
Christopher Thron	Texas A&M University – Central Texas, USA
Deepak Tomar	Maulana Azad National Institute of Technology, India
Fabio Bruno	Interpol, Singapore
Gaurav Choudhary	Technical University of Denmark, Denmark
Hwankuk Kim	Sangmyung University, South Korea
Ivan Izonin	Lviv Polytechnic National University, Ukraine
Kumar Abhishek	National Institute of Technology, Patna, India
M. A. Jabbar	Vardhaman College of Engineering, India
Michal Gregus	Comenius University in Bratislava, Slovakia
Mohammed M. Alani	Seneca Polytechnic, Canada
Mounir Hemam	Khenchela University, Algeria
Munesh Chandra Trivedi	National Institute of Technology, Agartala, India
Neal Wagner	MITRE, Massachusetts, USA
Neil Buckley	Liverpool Hope University, UK
Onur Doğan	İzmir Bakırçay University, Turkey
Pawan Lingras	Saint Mary's University, Canada
Purnima S. Sangle	National Institute of Industrial Engineering Mumbai, India
R. Maheswar	KPR Institute of Engineering and Technology, India
R. Gowtham	Amrita Vishwa Vidyapeetham, India
R. K. Pateriya	Maulana Azad National Institute of Technology, India
Sandeep Joshi	BITS Pilani, India
Sangeeta	Keele University, UK
Sanjeev Kumar Padmanabhan	Aarhus University, Denmark
Sanju Tiwari	Universidad Autónoma de Tamaulipas, Mexico
Soon Ae Chun	CUNY College of Staten Island, USA

Soumya P. Dash	Indian Institute of Technology, Bhubaneswar, India)
Surya Prakash	Indian Institute of Technology, Indore, India
Sven Groppe	University of Lübeck, Germany
Tripta Thakur	National Power Training Institute, Ministry of Power, India
Vikas Sihag	Sardar Patel University of Police, Security & Criminal Justice, India

Contents

Marketing Curriculum Evolution: Developing a Data-Driven Decision Making Mindset

Namrata Ladha[1](✉), Kaushal Yadav[2], Vivek Sharma[2], and Deepak Shrivastava[2]

[1] Sri Balaji University, Pune, India
namrataladha777@gmail.com
[2] Devi Ahilya Vishwavidyalaya, Indore, Madhya Pradesh, India

Abstract. Data analytics enables managers to get useful insights, make sound decisions, and drive organizational success. However, neither practitioners nor academics appear to have a clear understanding of the function of data analytics in postgraduate marketing education. The purpose of this study is to investigate the Knowledge, Skills, and Abilities (KSAs) that are uniquely required in marketing curricula. Based on previous research and suggestions from interviews with marketing faculty, placement officers, business professionals, and digital marketers, this study identifies a set of potential KSAs—incremental to modern marketing knowledge—that can help marketers succeed in the evolving data-driven decision-making environment. Professionals recommend a higher percentage of emphasis on data analytics, software exposure, writing and communication, and AI applications, whereas marketing faculty prefer a significantly higher focus on foundational marketing knowledge in comparison to these two KSA categories, namely Holistic Marketing and Market Research. Furthermore, we present the findings of a poll of business professionals on potential categories of existing marketing topics to deemphasize, hence creating possibilities to more comprehensively integrate additional KSAs into the marketing curriculum.

Keywords: First Marketing · Decision Making · Management Curriculum

1 Introduction

"Data reveals impact, and with data, you can bring more science to your decisions." - Matt Trifiro, Chief Marketing Officer, Vapor IO.Inc.

1.1 Data Analytics

In today's data-driven business environment, managers must be able to properly analyze and comprehend large amounts of information. Data analytics, specifically marketing analytics, entails the use of data analysis techniques and tools to help managers collect, organize, and analyze various types of marketing-related data, such as consumer behavior, advertising campaigns, sales data, social media engagement, and website traffic. Marketing Analytics combines data from numerous marketing channels to create a consolidated marketing view, offering deep insights into customer decision-making and

V. B. Gupta et al. (Eds.): IBCD 2024, CCIS 2413, pp. 1–15, 2025.
https://doi.org/10.1007/978-3-031-87511-3_1

purchasing behavior. Marketers can then use this information to create marketing plans, evaluate their effectiveness, and optimize them to improve corporate performance.

Marketing analytics benefits both marketers and consumers. It enables marketers to achieve higher return on marketing investments by understanding what is successful in driving either conversions, brand awareness, or both. Consequently, consumers are subjected to targeted and personalized communications that address their specific needs and interests. Various positions have emerged with the growth in data science field as shown in Fig. 1.

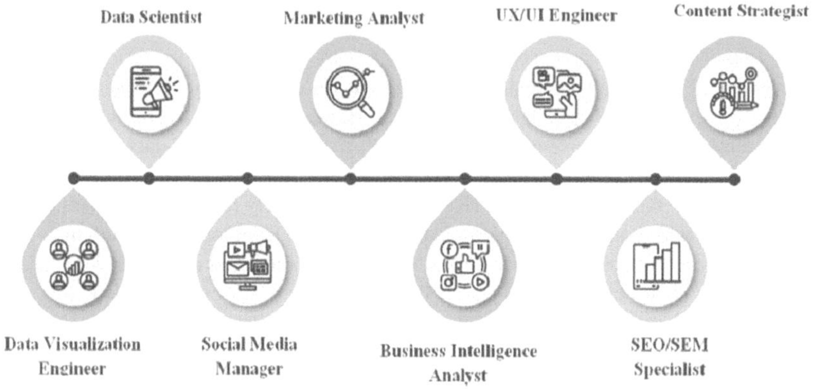

Fig. 1. Various job roles for data scientists.

1.2 Marketing Education in India

The marketing management programs/courses offered in India by various national and global institutes, universities, and coaching institutes typically aim to provide insights into core management areas, focusing on marketing & sales. Young consumers spend more time on digital media, thus marketers are transferring their marketing budgets to digital and social media. As a result, most management schools' curricula now include courses in E-business, E-commerce, E-tailing, Digital Marketing, and Social Media Marketing. Commerce and Management Research Scholars, particularly those with a marketing specialization, are also interested in conducting research in these fields. Numerous good books explain the concepts and theories underlying this discipline. Unfortunately, there is still dearth of trained faculty members who can handle both the practical and theory in this specialized field.

1.3 National Education Policy 2020

The National Education Policy (NEP) 2020 emphasizes the core values and principle that education must develop not only cognitive skills, that is, both 'foundational skills' of literacy and numeracy and 'higher-order' skills such as critical thinking and problem-solving, but also social and emotional skills, also known as 'soft skills', such as cultural awareness and empathy, perseverance and grit, teamwork, leadership, communication, and so on.

NEP advises that the curriculum burden in each topic be reduced to its 'core essential' content, allowing for holistic, discussion, and analysis-based learning. It also suggests revising and rebuilding all parts of the educational structure, including school regulation and governance, in order to develop a new system that is aligned with the aspirations of the twenty-first century. Given the demands of the twenty-first century, great higher education must strive to produce good, thoughtful, and creative persons with intellectual curiosity and a scientific temperament.

1.4 Rationale for the Study

India's higher education system struggles with fragmentation, a lack of emphasis on cognitive skills, and early specialization into narrow areas of study. Given the changing needs of the twenty-first century, higher education institutions must place greater emphasis on multidisciplinary education, cognitive skill development, and instilling in students a data-driven decision-making mindset. There have been numerous calls for the inclusion of analytics into marketing education. However, determining which requirements to include in a postgraduate programme remains an unresolved question. Most previous studies to address data analytics either:

(i). Written from an individual's perspective with no empirical research [1], or
(ii) Think analytics as a secondary or additional skill beyond marketing, typically addressed through specialized elective courses [2].

The big data and analytics market in India would increase from 104.19 billion dollars in 2023 to 118 billion dollars in 2024 [3], with a compound annual growth rate of 13.8%. The Global "Big Data and Analytics Market" research [4] shows constant and robust growth from 2024 to 2032, with predictions of continued positive momentum till 2032. Therefore, we believe that analytics needs to be considered at the post-graduate level.

The remainder of the present research paper is organized as follows. The next section presents the review of literature concerning Digital Transformation in Marketing Education and Integration of Data Analytics in Education at different levels education and disciplines. The following sections provide motivation and descriptions of the data-driven Knowledge, Skills, and Abilities (KSAs), survey approach, and results, followed by a discussion that summarizes our findings and identifies potential research opportunities and potential implications of this research.

2 Literature Review

In recent years, the landscape of marketing and business education has been undergoing significant transformations due to technological advancements and shifts in market dynamics. This narrative review synthesizes key insights from various research studies to examine the evolving trends in marketing and business education, focusing on the integration of digital technologies, data analytics, and artificial intelligence (AI) into curriculum.

2.1 Digital Transformation in Marketing Education

The advent of digital technologies has reshaped the way companies interact with customers and gather data. Research highlights the diminishing reliance on traditional fieldwork-based data collection methods in favor of direct data collection from customers through technology [5]. This shift has prompted a re-evaluation of market research education to align with evolving industry needs. Mishra et al. [6] emphasize the gap between students' perceived digital proficiency and employers' expectations, underscoring the importance of integrating hands-on digital skill development into marketing coursework.

Wimsatt and Lozada [7] stress the significance of incorporating business analytics into marketing education to equip students with essential competencies. They advocate for a comprehensive approach that address content, pedagogy, structure, and purpose within the marketing curriculum. Similarly, Liu and Burns [8] propose leveraging data analytics to design effective marketing courses, drawing insights from industry practices and employing text-mining techniques to inform curriculum development.

2.2 Integration of Data Analytics in Education

Ballou, Heitger, and Stoel [8] explore the role of data analytics in marketing education, highlighting the need for a shift towards a more scientific method that integrates quantitative analyses into curriculum design. LeClair [1] echoes this sentiment, emphasizing the importance of integrating analytics across various facets of the marketing curriculum to meet industry demands. Rohm, Stefl, and Clair [9] further underscore the need for digital-first curricula that incorporate project-based learning to prepare students for real-world marketing challenges.

Ketamo et al. [10] emphasize the importance of aligning curriculum development with industry demands using cognitive AI and big data analysis. They stress the need for universities to bridge the gap between academic language and professional terminology to better prepare students for the workforce. Similarly, Zahay et al. [11] detail a process to modernize the marketing curriculum by infusing digital marketing and analytics into all courses, fostering experiential learning and industry relevance.

Verma, Lamsal, and Verma [12] analyze job advertisements to identify relevant skills for AI and machine learning positions, emphasizing the importance of technical proficiency and communication skills. Chen [13] investigates the current status of AI curriculum in business schools, advocating for a hybrid approach that integrates AI and data analytics into course offerings. Sood and Pattinson [14] advocate for a big data-driven marketing curriculum centered on AI and machine learning. They emphasize the need for adaptive learning experiences and practical expertise development to prepare students for the modern marketing landscape.

Prior literature suggests that students learn general skills when they are reinforced and integrated in domain specific contexts [15]. Building on this literature, this study argues that data analytics should affect education across the entire marketing curriculum and be integrated with traditional and modern marketing knowledge within marketing courses.

The review highlights the evolving trends in marketing and business education, driven by digital transformation, data analytics, and AI integration. As the industry continues to evolve, educators face the challenge of adapting curriculum to meet changing demands while equipping students with the necessary skills for success in the digital era. By embracing updated marketing curriculum and interdisciplinary approaches, marketing and business programs can ensure that graduates are well prepared to navigate the complexities of the modern business landscape.

3 Research Methodology

The current study emphasizes the necessity for the marketing post-graduate program to evolve and adapt to changes in the business sector that come with transitioning to a data-driven decision-making paradigm. To be more specific, we (i) identify and refine appropriate KSAs through literature review and interviews with business professionals (n = 20); (ii) survey academicians (n = 340) and marketing practitioners (n = 200) to learn about their desired emphasis across the KSAs; and (iii) survey marketing practitioners (n = 310) to find prospects to modify marketing curriculum to include additional focus on the KSAs. Figure 2 illustrates the entire study process in detail.

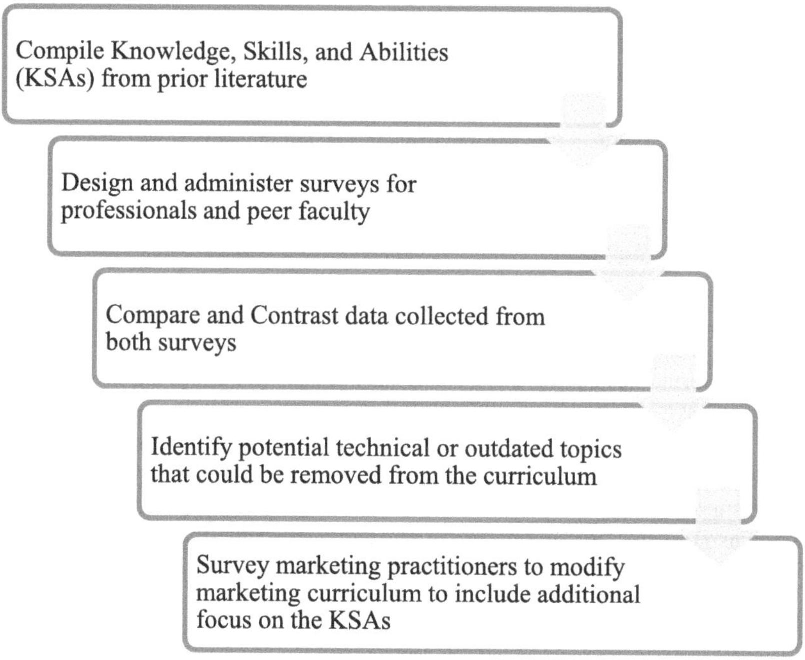

Fig. 2. Process followed for evolving curriculum to adapt to data-driven decision-making business environment.

This study's approach is borrowed from Ballou, Heitger & Stoel [8], allows for broad consideration of what to include within a post-graduate marketing curriculum, and integrates recent works within analytics that have focused on cases or educational activities related to specific analytic tools or decision-making approaches. Additionally, we reviewed articles that categorize and define marketing KSAs via descriptions of competencies related to many specific marketing areas [16–25].

We scrutinized these KSAs for suitability by conducting 20 interviews with partners from digital marketing agencies, executives, and data analytics and marketing managers from large companies. Table 1 shows the industries and positions of the individual interviewees.

Table 1. Interview Participants.

No.	Industry	Attendees
1	Logistics and Supply Chain	Business Development Associate, Sourcing Head, Acquisition Head, Marketing Head, Tech Head
2	IT Sector	Sales Manager, Territory Manager, Team Lead
3	Financial Technology	Marketing Head, Co-Founder & Chief Of Staff
4	Banks	Assistant Manager, Operations Head, Branch Manager
5	Stock Advisory	Sales Manager, Customer Service Manager
6	FMCG	Head Of Operations, Inventory Manager, HR Manager
7	Marketing Agency	Content Writer, Editor, Co-Founder, Head Of PR
8	Consulting	Research Analyst, Data Researcher, Team Lead, Associate Manager
9	Freelancers	NA

These informal interviews were typically one hour long and employed an open-ended format. The interview began by questioning participants about the impact big data and data analytics have on marketing curriculum and the required KSAs for new marketing graduates. Interviews also covered instances of data analytic projects and perceptions of the future business impact of data-driven decision-making.

For the survey, the questionnaire was circulated on popular social media apps among academicians i.e. LinkedIn, WhatsApp, and Twitter and rolled out on Google groups, made for exchanging knowledge on management, research, and marketing. These digital platforms are a community of educators, students, and practitioners from all over the world. The questionnaire was shared with 1800 + target respondents, out of which we received responses from 540 respondents.

A notable proportion of study participants (n = 267, or 49.4%) have more than 12 years of academic or work experience. Among the faculty, female respondents (n = 180 or 52.9%) comprised the majority of study participants compared to 38% female respondents among professionals. Among the faculty, the majority of respondents (n = 185 or 54.4%) have earned their post-graduation degrees in management, other popular post-graduation degree is technology (n = 115 or 33.8%). On the other hand, professionals predominantly held academic degrees in marketing, tourism, communication, and information technology.

4 Results

4.1 Establishment of KSAs

KSA is an acronym for Knowledge, Skills, and Abilities. It is a term often used in job descriptions, hiring processes, and employee evaluations to describe the characteristics and qualifications required for a specific job or role. We conduct literature reviews and interviews with business professionals to identify and refine appropriate KSAs. We found that Data Analytics, Holistic Marketing, Market Research, Relationship Management, Software Exposure (R, Python, Tableau, MS Excel, Canva), Design Thinking, Writing/Communications, Digital Marketing, and AI Applications appear to be exemplar KSAs to emphasize in addition to foundational marketing knowledge. Table 2 and Table 3 show desired KSAs beyond foundational marketing knowledge and supporting literature.

Table 2. Knowledge, Skills, and Abilities beyond foundational marketing knowledge.

KSAs	Learning Objective
Data Analytics	Knowledge and ability to analyze and interpret vast amounts of data to improve decision making
Holistic Marketing	Skills to integrate all marketing activities to create a unified and customer-focused strategy
Market Research	Ability to understand consumer behavior and apply research methods to inform marketing strategies and decision-making
Relationship Management	Skills to manage and enhance professional and personal relationships through communication, trust, and conflict resolution
Software Exposure (R, Python, Tableau, MS Excel, Canva)	Practical skills for data analysis and visualization
Design Thinking	Creative problem-solving skills for user-centered design, empathy, ideation, prototyping, and iterative testing
Writing/Communications	Written and verbal communication skills for diverse audiences and professional contexts
Digital Marketing	Knowledge and skills to build online presence, engagement, and conversion in contemporary business environments
AI Applications	Knowledge of AI to optimize marketing strategies, personalize customer experiences, and enhance campaign performance

Table 3. Examples of KSAs in prior literature

KSAs	Examples from Prior Literature
Data Analytics	[8, 26, 27]
Holistic Marketing	[16–18]
Market Research	[19–21]
Relationship Management	[22, 28, 29]
Software Exposure(R, Python, Tableau, MS Excel, Canva)	[30–32]
Design Thinking	[33–35]
Writing/Communications	[36–38]
Digital Marketing	[23–25]
AI Applications In Marketing	[39–42]

4.2 Professional's and Faculty's Survey

The questionnaire was designed so that respondents may base their ratings on the perceived value of each KSA for a successful marketing career in the next decade. Participants were given the definitions mentioned in Table 2 to help them form a common impression of each KSA type. The second component of the practitioner survey was to identify areas of existing technical knowledge that may be lowered. The survey sought practitioner feedback on selecting sample topics from typical core post-graduate courses that may be less critical for preparing future marketing students (to assist educators in determining which existing topics should be de-emphasized if more emphasis is required on the KSAs). Business professionals were asked to select the two least important goals for a successful career in marketing over the next ten years in order to determine topics that should be de-emphasized.

We also surveyed the faculty of marketing, who are likely to be aware of current state in practice and education but may want to continue teaching familiar topics. As a result, their prioritization of KSAs over professionals may provide significant information. Similarly, to the previous survey focused on KSA development, a 10-year term was chosen to allow for curricular improvement. The survey was distributed via email invitation. A total of 310 professionals and 340 marketing academics completed the questionnaire. The combined survey findings (Table 4 and Fig. 3) for the first component reveal a significant difference between professionals and professors in terms of intended emphasis throughout the entire set of KSAs.

Table 4 identifies the average percentage of the marketing curriculum that professionals and faculty respondents allocate to each of the skill and knowledge areas. As shown in Table 4, professionals suggest a greater percentage of emphasis on data analytics, software exposure, writing and communication, and AI applications (at least $p < 0.05$ level), whereas marketing faculty favor a significantly higher focus on foundational marketing knowledge relative to these two KSA categories i.e. Holistic Marketing, Market Research. Professionals' allocations generally are not evenly distributed across the identified KSAs and are digital-centric.

Table 4. Professional's and faculty's curriculum allocation.

	Professionals		Faculty		
Curriculum Allocation	Mean	Std Dev	Mean	Std Dev	p-value
Data Analytics	22.6	3.5	14.5	7.7	<0.001
Holistic Marketing	4.5	7.7	8	7.5	<0.05
Market Research	8	4.1	18	1.5	<0.01
Relationship Management	9.2	4.8	8	2.5	<0.05
Software Exposure (R, Python, Tableau, MS Excel, Canva)	15.7	3.2	12.5	4.8	<0.05
Design Thinking	4	6.5	5.5	7.7	>0.05
Writing/Communications	15.2	1.5	12.5	2.5	<0.05
Digital Marketing	14	2.5	15.5	1.5	>0.05
AI Applications	6.8	4.8	5.5	2.5	<0.05
Total	100		100		

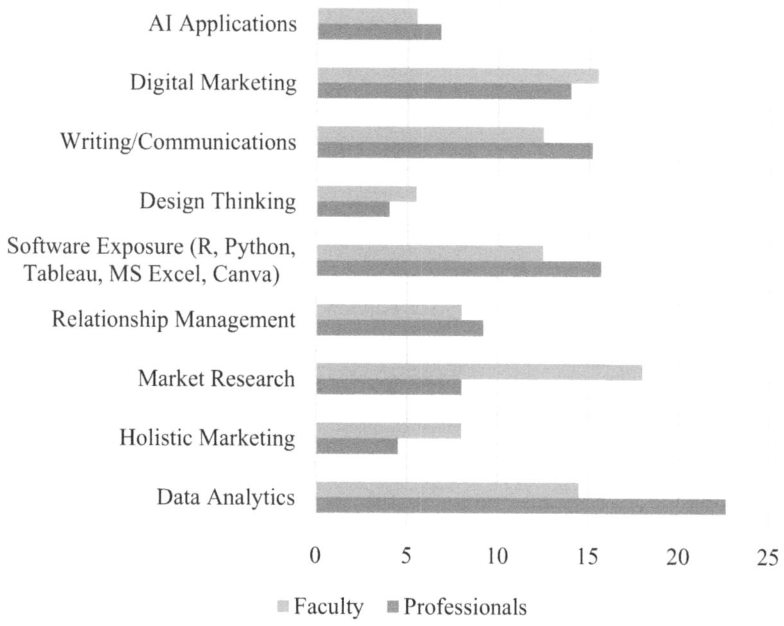

Fig. 3. Professional's versus faculty's curriculum allocation (in %).

By comparison, the faculty survey KSA allocations are more human-centric but acknowledge the shift to modern marketing. Foundational marketing topics are allocated more than 34% of effort by faculty, with market research as the top priority at 18% (which still is significantly greater than the professionals' allocation of 8% at $p < 0.01$). There are significant differences between the priorities of professionals and faculty concerning all KSAs except for Design Thinking and Digital Marketing.

4.3 Professionals' Least Desired Curriculum Objectives

Table 5 identifies the frequency with which marketing professionals identified each learning objective as one of the five least desirable from a list of 68 learning objectives. Professionals recommend that topics like Rural Marketing, Global/International Marketing, Financial Management, Industrial Marketing, and Operation Research can be made optional for students. These subjects can be offered to Marketing students who want to make a career in those specific fields as specialized elective courses (suggesting that not every student needs to learn these topics). Few personal selling and consumer behavior theories are no longer relevant in the current marketing scenario. Professionals recommend that a prominent subject like Financial management should be replaced by Personal Finance because students first need to learn to manage their own money, before their employers'.

Table 5. Professionals' least desired curriculum objectives

Product	**Global/International Marketing**
Factors contributing to the growth of packaging	Basis of International Trade
Product elimination strategies	Theories of International Trade
Marketing in BOP and BOP innovation	Types of Regional Agreements
	Foreign Trade Policy
Rural Marketing	Global Advertising Regulations
Rural Marketing Research	Role of IMF and WTO
Agribusiness marketing	
	Consumer Behavior
Personal Selling	Nicosia Model
Role of personal selling	Howard Sheth Model
Personal selling process	Sheth Family Decision Making Model
Types of sales job	Social class influence
Right set of circumstances Theory	Service Quality Models- Gronroos
Behavioral equation theory of selling	
Multilevel marketing	**Digital Marketing**

(*continued*)

Table 5. *(continued)*

Product	**Global/International Marketing**
	Dotcom Evolution
Supply Chain & Logistics	Forms of Search Engines
International logistics management	Telemarketing
Packaging and materials handling	
Legal Aspects in Logistics	**Financial Management**
Functions of distribution channel	Dividend Decisions
	Leverage Analysis
Industrial Marketing	Weighted Average Cost of Capital
Interpersonal Dynamics of Industrial Buying Behavior	Cost of Debt & Bonds, Preference Share and Equity
Industrial Marketing Environment	Funds Flow Statement
Economic of Industrial Demand	Capital Structure
	Working Capital Management
Operation Research	DCF & Non DCF Methods for Evaluating projects
Linear programming	
Simplex Method and Big-M Method	**Consumer Research**
Single Equipment and group Replacement Models	Problems encountered by researchers in India
Transportation Model and Assignment Problem	

The professionals' interview comments and survey results both point to a distinction between professionals and professors regarding the importance of using a "data-driven" approach for decision making.

5 Discussion

We discover that: (1) professionals consistently (across demographics) advocate for a stronger emphasis on software exposure, writing and communication, data analytics, and AI applications; and (2) professionals and academics differ significantly in how much emphasis should be placed on the KSAs.

Professionals prefer a data-driven and digital-centric curriculum with a higher emphasis on technical marketing issues. We interpret this pattern of results as describing the need for a "data driven approach" to marketing, rather than a call for academics to perform more "training" functions, much of which focuses on marketing knowledge that would otherwise occur after employment and varies depending on the type of marketing tasks the graduate undertakes [8, 26, 27]. Under this strategy, students concentrate on identifying insightful questions, structuring the problem, researching alternative solutions, analyzing data (or collaborating with data scientists), and communicating recommended complicated data solutions to various business decision makers [2, 12].

Through a review of literature and interviews focused on data-driven environments, this study identifies data analytics, software exposure, writing and communication, and AI applications, as additional KSAs (beyond existing marketing learning outcomes) that help create a Data-driven decision making mindset, as advocated by literature [8, 12, 13]. Interestingly, there are differences between the opinions of marketing professionals and academics on the intended allocated weightings for the KSAs.

Academicians, in particular, prefer a fairly equal weighting, whereas professionals place a larger value on data science and communications competence than on the other KSAs. The survey results provide insights into prospective areas where existing post-graduate curricula could be adjusted to include more concentration across the KSAs.

6 Conclusion and Future Directions

With the advent of the digital age, marketing channels and technology are expanding, necessitating a major shift in how marketing is taught, understood, and applied. The modern marketing model requires a combination of traditional and new-age marketing to establish a cohesive framework. It considers the requirement for marketing competences and capabilities in areas of knowledge such as data and analytics, customer experience, content, Omni channel communication, and personalization. The advanced modern marketing model is a unifying force that combines digital and traditional marketing into a future-oriented framework.

This study takes into account the impact of data-driven decision-making evolution, specifically within the post-graduate marketing curriculum, which is required of all marketing majors in order to adequately adjust to the changing function of the marketer. Furthermore, we discover early data that suggests that certain types of existing learning objectives may be de-emphasized in order to provide opportunity for increased competency development in other KSA categories. We feel that this work is an important first step towards evaluating the marketing curriculum and assisting future research in identifying further opportunities across marketing program.

6.1 Recommendations for Marketing Curriculum Evolution

1. Develop a comprehensive curriculum including foundational (e.g. statistics, R software, data visualization and management) and marketing-specific analytics (e.g. SQL, Tableau, Power BI).
2. Leverage advanced tools (e.g. Google Analytics) and data management systems (e.g. CRM software).
3. Promote interdisciplinary learning and collaborations with other departments and industry professionals.
4. Emphasize critical and analytical thinking with ethical considerations of handling consumer data [12].
5. Ensure faculty training and continuous upgradation of curriculum to stay relevant.
6. Foster a Data-Driven culture and mindset [8, 13].

6.2 Future Directions

More research is needed to expand on this study's findings and determine the best strategy to add KSAs other than technical marketing expertise into the curriculum. However, adopting curriculum revisions to include data-driven decision-making in marketing education faces several obstacles regarding Faculty Training and Expertise, additional investments in software, datasets, and resources, rigidity, and continuous curriculum updates to ensure industry relevance.

Addressing these obstacles involves strategic planning, faculty development, resource allocation, regular curriculum revision, and stakeholder buy-in to effectively integrate data-driven decision-making into marketing education. Based on these findings, we propose that additional investigations address the following research questions:

- RQ 1. What is the best combination of existing marketing subjects and new KSAs like those found in this study?
- RQ 2. What pedagogies are most helpful for producing the best combination of KSAs?
- RQ 3. Which aspects of the marketing curriculum are best suited to producing the ideal balance of key performance indicators?
- RQ 4. What curriculum, outside of the compulsory marketing major, is most effective for increasing attainment of the appropriate mix of KSAs?
- RQ 5. What are the ideal time intervals for significantly revising marketing curriculum?

Acknowledgments. The study acknowledge the insights provided by the respondents.

Disclosure of Interests. The authors have no competing interests.

References

1. LeClair, D.: Integrating business analytics in the marketing curriculum: eight recommendations. Mark. Ed. Rev. **28**(1), 6–13 (2018). https://doi.org/10.1080/10528008.2017.1421050
2. Liu, X., Burns, A.C.: Designing a marketing analytics course for the digital age. Mark. Ed. Rev. **28**(1), 28–40 (2018). https://doi.org/10.1080/10528008.2017.1421049@tfocoll.2023.0.issue-Transforming-marketing-education
3. Big Data and Analytics Market. https://www.linkedin.com/pulse/big-data-analytics-market-2024-current-future-nvgzf/
4. Global Big Data and Analytics Market research report. https://www.kingpinmarketresearch.com/global-big-data-and-analytics-market-26633896
5. Nunan, D., Di Domenico, M.: Rethinking the market research curriculum. Int. J. Mark. Res. **61**(1), 22–32 (2019). https://doi.org/10.1177/1470785318805294
6. Mishra, K.E., Wilder, K., Mishra, A.K.: Digital literacy in the marketing curriculum: are female college students prepared for digital jobs? Ind. High. Ed. **31**(3), 204–211 (2017). https://doi.org/10.1177/0950422217697838
7. Wimsatt, A., Lozada, H.R.: Business analytics in the marketing curriculum: a call for integration. Mark. Ed. Rev. **28**(1), 1–5 (2018). https://doi.org/10.1080/10528008.2018.1436974

8. Ballou, B., Heitger, D.L., Stoel, D.: Data-driven decision-making and its impact on accounting undergraduate curriculum. J. Account. Ed. **44**, 14–24 (2018). https://doi.org/10.1016/j.jaccedu.2018.05.003
9. Rohm, A.J., Stefl, M., Saint Clair, J.: Time for a marketing curriculum overhaul: Developing a digital-first approach. J. Market. Edu. **41**(1), 47–59 (2018). https://doi.org/10.1177/0273475318798086
10. Ketamo, H., Moisio, A., Passi-Rauste, A., Alamäki, A.: Mapping the future curriculum: Adopting artificial intelligence and analytics in forecasting competence needs. In: Proc. 10th Eur. Conf. Intangibles Intellect. Cap. ECIIC 2019. Acad. Conf. Publ. Int. (2019)
11. Zahay, D., Pollitte, W.A., Reavey, B., Alvarado, A.: An integrated model of digital marketing curriculum design. Market. Educ. Rev. **32**(3), 205–223 (2022). https://doi.org/10.1080/10528008.2021.1947856
12. Verma, A., Lamsal, K., Verma, P.: An investigation of skill requirements in artificial intelligence and machine learning job advertisements. Ind. High. Ed. **36**, 63–73 (2022). https://doi.org/10.1177/0950422221990990
13. Chen, L.: Current and future artificial intelligence (AI) curriculum in business school: a text mining analysis. J. Inf. Syst. Ed. **33**(4), 416–426 (2022)
14. Sood, S., Pattinson, H.: Marketing education renaissance through big data curriculum: Developing marketing expertise using AI large language models. Int. J. Innovat. Econ. Dev. **8**, 23–40 (2023). https://doi.org/10.18775/ijied.1849-7551-7020.2015.86.2003
15. Elhajjar, S., Karam, S., Borna, S.: Artificial intelligence in marketing education programs. Mark. Ed. Rev. **31**(1), 2–13 (2021)
16. Keller, K.L., Kotler, P.: Holistic marketing: a broad, integrated perspective to marketing management. In: Does Marketing Need Reform?: Fresh Perspectives on the Future, pp. 308–313, Routledge (2015)
17. Mele, C., Pels, J., Storbacka, K.: A holistic market conceptualization. J. Acad. Mark. Sci. **43**, 100–114 (2015). https://doi.org/10.1007/s11747-014-0383-8
18. Huang, Y.T., Rundle-Thiele, S.: A holistic management tool for measuring internal marketing activities. J. Serv. Mark. **29**(6), 571–584 (2015). https://doi.org/10.1108/JSM-03-2015-0112
19. Zamil, A.M., Areiqat, A.Y., Dabaghia, M.N., Joudeh, J.M.: The impact of researchers' possessed skills on marketing research success. In: Artificial Intelligence and Transforming Digital Marketin, pp. 53–61. Springer Nature Switzerland, Cham (2023). https://doi.org/10.1007/978-3-031-35828-9_5
20. Reavey, B., Zahay, D., Rosenbloom, A.: Updating the marketing research course to prepare the marketing generalist. J. Mark. Ed. **43**, 333–353 (2021). https://doi.org/10.1177/02734753211043925
21. Olowe, M.O., Olowe, T.S.: Marketing research skills: managers versus workers in micro business in Ondo State. Brit. J. Mark. Stud. **12**(2), 1–15 (2024). https://doi.org/10.37745/bjms.2013
22. Harrison, D.E., Ajjan, H.: Customer relationship management technology: bridging the gap between marketing education and practice. J. Mark. Analyt. **7**(4), 205–219 (2019). https://doi.org/10.1057/s41270-019-00063-6
23. Ladha, N., Sharma, V.: Content marketing leads to purchase?: a systematic review. Devi Ahilya Univ. J. Soc. Sci. Humanit. **5**(3), 26–37 (2022a)
24. Wymbs, C.: Digital marketing: The time for a new "academic major" has arrived. J. Mark. Ed. **33**, 93–106 (2011). https://doi.org/10.1177/0273475310392544
25. Bazuhair, N.A.S.: Awareness of business administration students of the role of digital marketing in the growth of e-commerce. Int. J. Prof. Bus. Rev. 8(2), e01123-e01123 (2023). https://doi.org/10.26668/businessreview/2023.v8i2.1123
26. Cao, G., Tian, N., Blankson, C.: Big data, marketing analytics, and firm marketing capabilities. J. Comput. Inf. Syst. **62**(3), 442–451 (2022). https://doi.org/10.1080/08874417.2020.1842270

27. Wedel, M., Kannan, P.K.: Marketing analytics for data-rich environments. J. Mark. **80**, 97–121 (2016). https://doi.org/10.1509/jm.15.0413
28. Kaur, G.: Is obsession with data and analytics making future marketers analytical researchers? a conceptual customer relationship marketing model for customized marketing education. J. Educ. Bus. **94**(8), 569–575 (2019). https://doi.org/10.1080/08832323.2019.1580245
29. Carter, S., Yeo, A.C.M.: Undergraduate perceptions of the knowledge, skills and competencies required of today's practicing marketer. High. Ed., Skills Work-Based Learn. **7**(3), 240–260 (2017). https://doi.org/10.1108/HESWBL-12-2016-0084
30. Lu, J.: Data science in the business environment: Insight management for an executive MBA. Int. J. Manag. Ed. **20**(1), 100588 (2022). https://doi.org/10.1016/j.ijme.2021.100588
31. Sousa, K.J., Smithfield, R.I.: The perceptions of undergraduate students associated with a career in technology–an analysis by academic year. Inf. Syst. Ed. J. **22**(2), 2 (2024). https://doi.org/10.62273/DSPO8699
32. Bennett, R., Alberti, G., Çibik, A., et al.: Bringing about the data revolution in development: what data skills do aspiring development professionals need? J. Int. Dev. **34**(7), 1381–1397 (2022). https://doi.org/10.1002/jid.3642
33. Chen, S., Benedicktus, R., Kim, Y., Shih, E.: Teaching design thinking in marketing: linking product design and marketing strategy in a product development class. J. Mark. Ed. **40**(3), 176–187 (2018). https://doi.org/10.1177/0273475317753678
34. Lee, C., Benza, R.: Teaching innovation skills: Application of design thinking in a graduate marketing course. Bus. Educ. Innovat. J. **7**(1) (2015)
35. Blijlevens, J.: Educating marketing students to understand designers' thought-worlds. J. Mark. Ed. **45**(1), 18–37 (2023). https://doi.org/10.1177/02734753211038997
36. O'Connor, C., Moran, G.: The challenge of skill development through "experiencing" integrated marketing communications. High. Ed., Skills Work-Based Learn. (2023). https://doi.org/10.1108/HESWBL-06-2023-0167
37. McDougal, E.R., Syrdal, H.A., Gravois, R., Kemp, A.F.: The power of story: using storytelling to increase students' confidence and competence in applying marketing concepts. Mark. Ed. Rev. **31**(2), 119–124 (2021). https://doi.org/10.1080/10528008.2020.1853573
38. Roy, A., Macchiette, B.: Debating the issues: a tool for augmenting critical thinking skills of marketing students. J. Mark. Ed. **27**, 264–276 (2005). https://doi.org/10.1177/0273475305280533
39. Ladha, N., Sharma, V.: Investigating the helpfulness of artificial intelligence in academic and scientific writing. Int. Bull. Manag. Econ. **15**(2), 20–29 (2022)
40. Campbell, C., Sands, S., Ferraro, C., Tsao, H.Y.J., Mavrommatis, A.: From data to action: how marketers can leverage AI. Bus. Horiz. **63**(2), 227–243 (2020). https://doi.org/10.1016/j.bushor.2019.12.002
41. Ladha, N., Yadav, K., Rathore, P.: AI-generated content detectors: boon or bane for scientific writing. Indian J. Sci. Technol. **16**(39), 3435–3439 (2023). https://doi.org/10.17485/IJST/v16i39.1632
42. Gentsch, P.: AI in marketing, sales and service: How marketers without a data science degree can use AI, big data and bots. Springer (2018)

Facial Expression Tracking and Analysis in Video Through Motion with SqueezeNet and SGD

Navneet Gupta[1(✉)], R. Vishnu Priya[2], and Chandan Kumar Verma[1]

[1] Department of Mathematics, Bioinformatics and Computer Applications, Maulana Azad National Institute of Technology, Bhopal, Madhya Pradesh 462003, India
gupta.0292@gmail.com

[2] Department of Computer Applications, National Institute of Technology, Tiruchirappalli, Tamil Nadu, India
vishnupriya@nitt.edu

Abstract. Facial expression recognition is pivotal in diverse domains such as human-computer interaction, affective computing, and psychological research. This study introduces an innovative methodology to enhance the accuracy of facial expression recognition by integrating optical flow modeling, deep feature extraction, and advanced classification algorithms. Utilizing the Non-Linear Fractional Order Variational (NFOV) model, we generate color-map images of optical flow from video sequences that portray various facial expressions. Our approach leverages optical flow to capture subtle variations in facial expressions, while exploiting the feature extraction process of SqueezeNet and the computational efficiency of Stochastic Gradient Descent (SGD). Specifically, we fine-tuned the SqueezeNet deep learning architecture, renowned for its efficiency in feature extraction, to extract salient features from these color-map images. SGD is applied for the classification task. Experimental evaluations on the CK + dataset demonstrate the efficacy of our method which achieves a classification accuracy of 79.3% and an area under the curve (AUC) of 95.7%.

Keywords: Facial expression recognitions · Optical flow · Deep learning · CNN

1 Introduction

Facial expressions are a crucial aspect of nonverbal communication allow humans to express their emotions and intentions. Automatically Recognizing Facial Expressions (FER) is a growing area in computer vision, AI, and pattern recognition, with potential applications in human emotion sensing, social robots, human-computer interaction, and healthcare [1–4]. Facial expression recognition (FER) approaches are generally classified into static methods to rely on still images and dynamic methods to utilize video sequence. Although previous research has predominantly focused on static methods for facial expression detection and classification [5, 6], these approaches are limited in their ability to capture temporal dynamics between frames. In contrast, dynamic methods accurately capture the motion, temporal, and spatial variations in facial expressions [7]. It extracts these features that robustly represent these dynamic changes.

V. B. Gupta et al. (Eds.): IBCD 2024, CCIS 2413, pp. 16–29, 2025.
https://doi.org/10.1007/978-3-031-87511-3_2

Currently, most techniques rely on textures or geometry to characterize face expressions [7–10], but analyzing facial movement using optical flow is a promising area of investigation. This technology can analyze and describe both robust and subtle motions, adjust for head position variations, detect micro-expressions, and deal with situations where parts of the face are occluded [11–13]. Several methodological advancements have been implemented to enhance the efficiency of dense optical flow techniques on datasets, such as MPI-Sintel. However, some authors suggest that employing the recent optical flow methods may reduce the overall effectiveness of the system [12]. In addition, research has shown that deep learning models typically perform better than traditional algorithms for emotion detection. However, it has not been extensively used optical flow color map images to detect emotion.

In order to address this problem, the proposed study intends to employ a non-linear fractional order variational (NFOV) optical flow algorithm [14] together with the SqueezeNet model [15], followed by stochastic gradient descent (SGD) [16] for the purpose of emotion classification. An optical flow method detects and analyses the color map of two successive frames in a video series. It captures the motion information and intensity variations that occur between these frames. We input the optical flow color-map image into a SqueezeNet model to extract features, using SGD to recognize important patterns and representations essential for understanding emotions.

The project aims to improve the accuracy and reliability of emotion categorization systems by and employing SGD for classification. Key contributions include:

1. Integrate temporal information derived from the NFOV optical flow technique with the SqueezeNet architecture to enable dynamic and effective feature extraction from video sequences.
2. Implement Stochastic Gradient Descent (SGD) for efficient emotion classification, enhance the learning process, and improve the system performance.
3. This study aims to address a gap in the current state of literature by showcasing the enhanced accuracy and reliability of emotion recognition through the utilization of optical flow analysis in conjunction with deep learning techniques.

2 Literature Survey

Pu et al. [17] introduced a model that uses Action Units in photos and AAM points of feature to track face movements, using Lucas-Kanade optical movement trackers to predict face movements. Adjustments were performed to neutral and peak emotions using the RF technique, and these vectors were used for categorization. Sun et al. [18] investigated the use of Binarized Neural Networks (BNNs) to improve expression identification on facial datasets, incorporating unbounded facial normalization, LBPs, BAE, and BNNs. Qi et al. [19] showed that using LBPs can reduce memory usage and improve facial expression identification accuracy when combined with SVM. Gan et al. [20] introduced a new approach called Deep Spatiotemporal Network with Dual-flow Fusion (DSN-DF), which efficiently incorporates temporal and spatial cues, resulting in outstanding results on the CK + dataset. Allaert et al. [12] assessed the effectiveness of optical flow approaches in recognizing facial expressions using different datasets, emphasizing the significance of motion approximation techniques in effectively capturing face movements' dynamics.

Wang et al. [21] examined the difficulty of recognizing subtle facial expressions (SFER) and presented an attention-based approach that specifically targets significant local areas and their interconnections, resulting in exceptional performance on the CK + dataset. Geeta et al. [22] focused on affective computing, specifically using deep learning methods to make significant progress in emotion recognition. This systematic review aims to address research gaps by conducting a complete analysis of deep learning-powered MER methods and proposes future research routes to advance progress in both academia and industry.

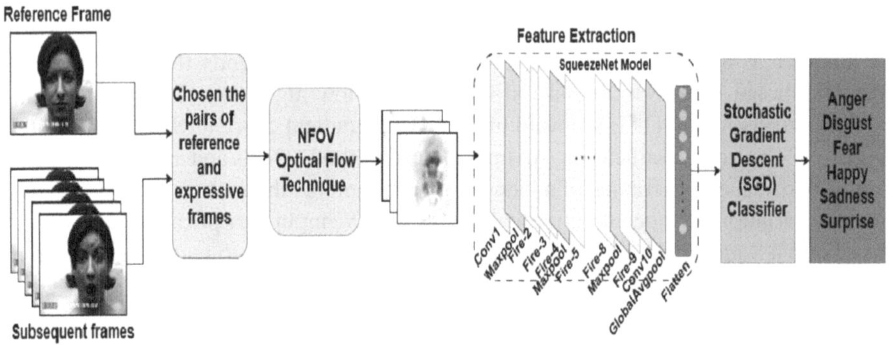

Fig. 1. Comprehensive FER Framework Using NFOV Optical Flow and SqueezeNet with SGD.

3 Proposed Methodology

In this work, we utilized the non-linear fractional order variational (NFOV) optical flow model to generate color-map images of optical flow from video sequences. This process is illustrated in Fig. 1, which shows the application of the NFOV model to create the color maps. These color-map images were then used for feature extraction with the SqueezeNet model, known for its efficient and effective feature extraction capabilities while maintaining relatively low computational complexity. Following feature extraction, we employed Stochastic Gradient Descent (SGD) for classification. SGD is widely used for optimization due to its scalability and efficiency, particularly in large-scale machine learning tasks. The detailed description of each step is as follows:

Suppose that given a dataset D consists of $\mathcal{VD}_i = \{\mathcal{VD}_1, \mathcal{VD}_2, \ldots, \mathcal{VD}_{\mathcal{k}}\} \in \mathbb{R}^{\mathcal{N}}$, $\mathcal{N}$ samples from $\mathcal{M}$ different classes, where $1 \geq i \leq \mathcal{k}$ and $\mathcal{k}$ is the total number of videos. Each video in $\mathcal{VD}_i$ is chosen to extract the frames. For subsequent processing, the collected frames of $\mathcal{VD}_i$ are saved in a local directory as shown

$$\mathcal{F}_i = \{\mathcal{F}_0, \mathcal{F}_1 \ldots\ldots, \mathcal{F}_{n-1}\}$$

Whare, $\mathcal{F}_0$ is reference frame and $\{\mathcal{F}_1, \mathcal{F}_2 \ldots\ldots, \mathcal{F}_t\}$where $\mathbf{t} = 1, 2, \ldots, \mathbf{n} - 1$ are subsequent frames. In this video sequence, we choose a pair of frames as: $\{\mathcal{F}_0, \mathcal{F}_1\}$, $\left\{\mathcal{F}_0, \mathcal{F}_{\mathbf{t}=\frac{n-1}{2}}\right\}$, $\{\mathcal{F}_0, \mathcal{F}_\mathbf{t}\}$, respectively.

3.1 NFOV Model

The proposed model detects a small change utilizing a baseline method known as the NFOV methodology. The Charbonnier L1 norm employed in optical flow is a modern and effective approach. Unlike standard quadratic penalties, this non-quadratic penalty function is specifically developed to enhance robustness against outliers and discontinuity in the image flow field. The presence of factors such as brightness and image distortion create challenges in accurately discerning delicate facial emotions. Additionally, outliers further complicate the identification of significant patterns in facial expressions. The non-quadratic narrow field of view NFOV method exhibits robustness against noise and outliers. Moreover, the NFOV algorithm exhibits a significant variation in output when there is a small change in the input. This algorithm has the ability to detect small and subtle changes in a person's face.

The optical flow is calculated between the frames denoted as $\{\mathcal{F}_0, \mathcal{F}_1\}, \left\{\mathcal{F}_0, \mathcal{F}_{t=\frac{n-1}{2}}\right\}, \{\mathcal{F}_0, \mathcal{F}_t\},$. Let (χ, y) be the coordinates of a specific pixel in the very reference frame "$\mathcal{F}_0$". This pixel can be expressed through a 2D vectors (u, v), which indicates the movement of the corresponding pixel across the reference frame "$\mathcal{F}_0$" to the subsequent frame "$\{\mathcal{F}_1\}, \left\{\mathcal{F}_{t=\frac{n-1}{2}}\right\}, \{\mathcal{F}_t\}$,". The correlation between the brightness of a pixels in the reference frame, denoted as $\mathcal{F}_0 = \mathbb{I}(\chi, y, t)$, and the associated brightness in the subsequent frame, denoted as $\mathcal{F}_1 = \mathbb{I}(\chi + u, y + v, t + \Delta t)$, $\mathcal{F}_{t=\frac{n-1}{2}} = \mathbb{I}(\chi + u, y + v, t + \Delta t), \mathcal{F}_t = \mathbb{I}(\chi + u, y + v, t + \Delta t)$ can be mathematically represented as:

$$\mathbb{I}(\chi + u, y + v, t + \Delta t) = \mathbb{I}(\chi, y, t) \tag{1}$$

Let's consider a function $\mathbb{I} : \coprod \subseteq \mathcal{R}^3 \rightarrow \mathcal{R}$. It can apply Taylor's expansion to Eq. (1).

$$\nabla \mathbb{I}^T u + \mathbb{I}_t = 0 \tag{2}$$

where, $\nabla \mathbb{I} = (\mathbb{I}_\chi, \mathbb{I}_y)^T$ represents the spatial gradients for intensities $\mathbb{I}$ and $u = (u, v)^T$ denotes the optical movement such as $u, v : \mathcal{R}^2 \rightarrow \mathcal{R}$ and $\mathbb{I}_t$ represents the partial derivative for the intensities $\mathbb{I}$ in t. Therefore, we can express the previously mentioned equation as follows:

$$\mathbb{I}_\chi u + \mathbb{I}_y v + \mathbb{I}_t = 0 \tag{3}$$

The NFOV technique includes the minimization of an energy functional that takes into account both the data term, which relies on the assumption of brightness constancy, and the smoothness term, which relies on the assumption of smoothness. The energy function is defined as:

$$\mathbb{E}(u) = \int_\Omega \left[\Psi'\left(\nabla \mathbb{I}^T u + \mathbb{I}_t\right) + \mathcal{H}_1(u, v) + \boldsymbol{\mathcal{H}}_2\left(\boldsymbol{\mathcal{H}D}_+^\alpha u, \mathcal{H}D_+^\alpha v\right)\right] d\mathrm{X} \tag{4}$$

The energy function Eq. (4) of the NFOV model is the result of combining the Marchaud fractional derivative with the Charbonnier norm. The Charbonnier norms is defined as $\Psi'(\nabla\mathbb{I}^{\mathrm{T}}u + \mathbb{I}_{\mathrm{t}}) = \sqrt[\delta]{1 + (\frac{\nabla\mathbb{I}^{\mathrm{T}}u+\mathbb{I}_{\mathrm{t}}}{\delta})^{2}}$, and "$\delta$" represents a small positive integer parameter chosen based on the model [23]. In the Model M. Khan [14], the functions $\mathcal{H}_1(u, v) = \beta^2 u^T u$ and $\mathcal{H}_2(\mathcal{H}D_+^{\alpha}u, \mathcal{H}D_+^{\alpha}v) = \lambda\mathcal{E}^T(\mathcal{H}D_+^{\alpha}u^T \odot \mathcal{H}D_+^{\alpha}u^T)\mathcal{E}$ where, $\beta, \lambda \in \mathbb{R}^+$ and $\mathcal{H}D_+^{\alpha}(\nabla\mathbb{I}^{\mathrm{T}}u + \mathbb{I}_{\mathrm{t}}) = (\mathcal{H}D_{\chi}^{\alpha}(\nabla\mathbb{I}^{\mathrm{T}}u + \mathbb{I}_{\mathrm{t}}), \mathcal{H}D_{y}^{\alpha}(\nabla\mathbb{I}^{\mathrm{T}}u + \mathbb{I}_{\mathrm{t}}))^T$ Where, $\mathcal{H}_1$ and $\mathcal{H}_2$ are convex functions, and Marchaud derivatives for order $\alpha \in (0,1)$ with regard to χ *and* y are given $\mathcal{H}D_{\chi}^{\alpha}(\nabla\mathbb{I}^{\mathrm{T}}u + \mathbb{I}_{\mathrm{t}})$ and $\mathcal{H}D_{y}^{\alpha}(\nabla\mathbb{I}^{\mathrm{T}}u + \mathbb{I}_{\mathrm{t}})$.

Calculate the magnitude corresponding to the optical motion vector at every pixel using the following formula:

$$magnitude = \sqrt{u^2 + v^2} \tag{5}$$

where "u" and "v" represent the vertical and horizontal portions forming the optical motion vector. Determine the angle (direction) with respect to the optical motion vector at every pixel by utilizing the following formula:

$$\vartheta = atan2(u, v) \tag{6}$$

This function calculates and provides the angle (ϑ) whose tangent is the result of dividing two given numbers. Normalize the magnitude mag_{norm} such that it comes inside the interval [0, 1] in order to maintain consistency between frames:

$$mag_{norm} = \frac{magnitude - mag_{min}}{mag_{max} - mag_{min}} \tag{7}$$

where, mag_{min} and mag_{max} are the minimum and maximum magnitudes in the flow field. Assign the angle to the color value. To do this, one can rescale the angle to fit inside the range of [0, 1] and then map it to the range of [0, 180] (since hue values usually range from 0 to 180 degrees).

$$hue = \frac{\vartheta}{\pi} \times 180 \tag{8}$$

Set saturation to a constant value (e.g. 255) and value (brightness) proportional to the normalized magnitudes.

$$value = mag_{norm} \times 255 \tag{9}$$

Convert the HSV color representation to RGB for visualization.

$$HSV = (hue, saturation, value) \tag{10}$$

$$\mathcal{X}_{RGB} = HSV_to_RGB(HSV) \tag{11}$$

By employing this mapping approach, every flow vector is associated with a specific color inside the RGB color space. This color can then be visualized through the color-map image in Fig. 2, representing the surprised expression.

3.2 SqueezeNet Model with SGD

Let the color-map image $\mathcal{X}_{RGB}$ be with dimensions $\mathcal{W}\times\mathcal{H}\times\mathcal{C}$ (Width, Height, Channels). SqueezeNet applies a series of convolutional layers and Fire modules (a combination of squeeze and expand convolutions) to extract features. Let the output feature map after these layers be denoted as F. The feature map F is then subjected to global average pooling to reduce its dimensions. If F has dimensions $\mathcal{W}\prime \times \mathcal{H}\prime \times \mathcal{D}$, global average pooling reduces it to $1 \times 1 \times \mathcal{D}$, where $\mathcal{D}$ is the depth of the feature map. The pooled features are then flattened into a 1-dimensional vector $\mathcal{F}(\mathcal{X}) \in \mathbb{R}^{\mathcal{D}}$.

SGD is a frequently employed optimization approach for training neural networks. The process involves modifying the network's parameters in the direction opposite to the gradient of the loss function with respect to the parameters. Our objective is to acquire a linear scoring function $\mathcal{F}(\mathcal{X}) = \mathcal{W}^{\mathcal{T}} * \mathcal{F}(\mathcal{X}) + \mathcal{B}$ with model parameters $\mathcal{W}^{\mathcal{T}}$ and $\mathcal{B}$ intercept, based on a collection of training cases $(\mathcal{x}_1, \mathcal{y}_1)(\mathcal{x}_2, \mathcal{y}_2)\ldots(\mathcal{x}_n, \mathcal{y}_n)$ where $\mathcal{x}_i \epsilon \mathcal{R}^m$ and $\mathcal{y}_i \epsilon \mathcal{R}$ ($\mathcal{y}_i$ is the corresponding batch of labels for classification). To provide predictions for classification, we determine the sign of $\mathcal{F}(\mathcal{X})$. In order to determine the model parameters, we want to minimize the regularized training error, which is defined as

$$\mathbb{E}(\mathcal{W}, \mathcal{B}) = \frac{1}{n}\sum_{i=1}^{n} \mathcal{L}(\mathcal{y}_i, \mathcal{F}(\mathcal{X}_i)) + \alpha\mathcal{R}(\mathcal{W}) \tag{12}$$

The loss function "$\mathcal{L}$" quantifies the degree of model (mis)fit, while the regularization term "$\mathcal{R}$" penalizes the complexity of the model. The non-negative hyperparameter $\alpha > 0$ determines the intensity of the regularization. In this work for classification, we used logistic regression as a loss function. In our context, logistic regression was chosen for its simplicity, interpretability, and efficiency. It provides probabilities for each class, which is valuable for understanding the confidence of predictions and making informed decisions based on those probabilities.

$$\mathcal{L}(\mathcal{y}_i, \mathcal{F}(\mathcal{X}_i)) = \log(1 + \exp(-\mathcal{y}_i\mathcal{F}(\mathcal{X}_i))) \tag{13}$$

For Regression, we used the Huber loss function. The Huber loss function effectively handles outliers by combining mean squared error (MSE) and mean absolute error (MAE). It is quadratic for small errors and linear for large errors, providing robustness against outliers while maintaining differentiability and smooth optimization.

$$|\mathcal{y}_i - \mathcal{F}(\mathcal{X}_i)| \leq \mathcal{E} and \mathcal{L}(\mathcal{y}_i, \mathcal{F}(\mathcal{X}_i)) = \mathcal{E}|\mathcal{y}_i - \mathcal{F}(\mathcal{X}_i)| - \frac{1}{2}\mathcal{E}^2 otherwise \tag{14}$$

The regularization term, often known as the penalty parameter, encompasses the following:

$$L2norm : \mathcal{R}(\mathcal{W}) = \frac{1}{2}\sum_{i=1}^{m} \mathcal{W}_i^2 = ||\mathcal{W}||_2^2 \tag{15}$$

The SGDClassifier class implements a first-order stochastic gradient descent learning algorithm. The method sequentially processes the training examples and, for each example, modifies the model parameters based on the update rule provided.

$$\mathcal{W} \leftarrow \mathcal{W} - \eta \left[\alpha \frac{\delta(\mathcal{R}(\mathcal{W}))}{\delta \mathcal{W}} + \frac{\delta\big(\mathcal{L}\big(y_i, \mathcal{F}(\mathcal{X}_i)\big)\big)}{\delta \mathcal{W}} \right] \tag{16}$$

The parameter "η" represents the learning rate, which determines the scale of the steps taken in the parameter space. The default learning rate schedule for regression is inverse scaling, which is denoted by the parameter.

$$\eta^{(t)} = \frac{\eta_0}{t^{power_t}} \tag{17}$$

where, "η_0" is the initial learning rate, "t" is the current iteration or time step during training, and $power_t$ is a hyperparameter that controls the rate at which the learning rate decreases over time.

4 Implementation Details

4.1 Dataset

The **extended Cohn Kanade (CK +)** dataset [24, 25] is a highly utilized controlled dataset in laboratory environments for the purpose of recognizing facial expressions. The dataset comprises 327 video clips from 118 individuals, each of which is categorized into one of seven expression class labels. The length of a video sequence varies between 10 and 60 frames. Every video segment commences and concludes with a neutral facial and has the potential to display a transition from a facial expression that is neutral to a peak facial expression.

4.2 NFOV Model

Experiments involving NFOV model are conducted using MATLAB2021a. To achieve satisfactory outcomes, the NFOV parameters are set as follows: $\beta = 0.1, \mathcal{N}_{warp} = 5, \mathcal{N}_{pyr} = 5, and \mathcal{N}_{it} = 1.5 \times 10^3$. These parameters were chosen to balance accuracy and computational efficiency. Specifically, β (Fractional Order) controls sensitivity to local variations, $\mathcal{N}_{warp}$ (number of warping iterations) refines estimates through iterative warping, $\mathcal{N}_{pyr}$(number of pyramid levels) enables multi-scale analysis, and $\mathcal{N}_{it}$ (number of iterations) dictates the total number of optimization iterations. Adjustments to these parameters impact precision, computational load, and robustness, ensuring effective performance across varying conditions. These parameters are used to evaluate the impact of Gaussian noise and different smoothing parameter values. A 5×5 window matrix is utilized to calculate the fractional derivative. The color-map of the flow field are provided as an illustration of qualitative results. The vector plot is constructed by assigning different colors from the color map to represent varying directions. The uniform color in the color map indicates the absence of displacements. The optical flow method is used to process an example image from surprise expression presented in Fig. 2 in order to determine qualitative results. Figure 2 displays the qualitative result of color map with α and λ values set to 0.7 and 250, respectively.

We perform experiments on the CK + dataset using the NFOV model. We select a single video sequence of images from any of the expressions and then use the NFOV model to select the starting frame as a reference frame. We use three cases to collect the color-map images of optical flow: (1) First, we select the reference frame and the subsequent adjacent frame. (2) Second, we select the reference frame and the middle frame. (3) Third, we select the reference frame and the last frame. Based on this NFOV model, we collected a total of 300 color-mapped images of six labeled facial expressions, with each expression having 50 color-mapped images.

4.3 SqueezeNet with SGD

Google Colab with TensorFlow is utilized to conduct experiments that involve extracting features through the SqueezeNet model and classifying them using an SGD approach. The optical flow color images are fed into the SqueezeNet model for feature extraction. SqueezeNet implements a smart structure that achieves the same degree of accuracy as AlexNet on ImageNet while employing fewer parameters, reducing them by a factor of 50. SqueezeNet utilizes an architecture of modules shown in Fig. 1 that revolves around the Fire Module, a crucial component that is repeatedly built throughout the network. The model's layers consist of: (1) the input layer, which accepts images of specified dimensions (224 * 224 pixels for ImageNet) and normalizes pixel values to improve training behavior. (2) a Convolution Layer with a small number of filters (7x7, 96 filters) for initial feature extraction; (3) the Fire Module, the central component of SqueezeNet, which includes a Squeeze Layer that uses a 1x1 convolutional layer to significantly reduce input channels, followed by an Expand Layer with parallel branches that use different 3x3 convolutional layers. Expand_layer_1 for useful low-level feature learning, expand_layer_2 for capturing more complex features, and (4) Max-pooling is applied with a stride of 2 after conv_1, fire_module_4, and fire_module_8 to decrease the spatial dimensions of feature maps, preventing overfitting and reducing the size of the model. (5) A dropout layer with a dropout ratio of 50% is implemented after the fire_module_9 module. (6) ending with a final conv layer (13*13*1000), followed by Global_Average_pooling2D (1*1*1000), and at the end, a flatten layer is implemented with 1000 features.

In this experiment, we fed the flattening layer output to a stochastic gradient descent algorithm for classification. Table 1 shows the configuration of SGD for classification tasks. We use logistic regression. For regression tasks, we use the Huber loss function with Epsilon ($\mathcal{E} = 0.1$) to meet the task's specific criteria. To prevent overfitting, Ridge (L2) regularization is used with a regularization strength of (α = 1e–05). The learning rate schedule employs an inverse scaling approach, starting with a learning rate of ($\eta_0 =$ 0.01) and using an exponent of ($t = 0.25$) to gradually modify the learning rate during training times. After each cycle, applying data shuffling introduces randomization into the training process, which improves the model's flexibility. Both scenarios carry out the training for 1000 cycles with Stratified 10-fold cross validation, ensuring adequate convergence. We specifically designed this configuration setup to balance optimization stability, convergence speed, and generalization performance for both classification and regression problems.

Table 1. Shows the configuration of SGD for classification tasks. The optimization algorithm parameters were configured during the performance evaluation of the existing SGD models employed in the SqueezeNet deep learning model for emotion recognition on the optical flow color-map images of the CK + dataset.

Parameter	Value
Classification loss function	Logistic regression
Regression loss function	Huber
Epsilon ($\mathcal{E}$) for regression	0.1
Regularization	Ridge (L2)
Regularization strength (α)	1e –05
Learning rate	Inverse scaling
Initial learning rate (η_0)	0.01
Inverse scaling exponent (t)	0.25
Shuffle data after each iteration	Yes
Number of iterations	1000

5 Results and Discussions

In these experiments, distinct patterns become apparent in the resulting color map images shown in Fig. 2 when the NFOV optical flow method is applied to different pairings of frames from a surprise expression video clip. There are no changes between the frames that are next to each other, and their color map is shown in Fig. 2(a), which suggests that there is no movement. However, when examining frames that have a gap between them, such as the initial and middle frames, the color map shown in Fig. 2(b) reveals significant alterations, indicating movement within that time period. The most significant changes are evident when contrasting the first and final frames, with the color map shown in Fig. 2(c), indicating considerable movement throughout the entire duration of the video. The results shown in Fig. 2 demonstrate that the method is highly responsive to time gaps between frames, with greater intervals resulting in more noticeable changes in the color map representations of optical flow.

These observed results can be attributed to the parameters chosen for the NFOV model, which significantly impact the accuracy and sensitivity of optical flow analysis. Key parameters include the fractional order, controlling differentiation and integration, and regularization terms, balancing smoothness and data fidelity. Careful tuning of these parameters enables the NFOV model to capture subtle motions and filter out noise. In these experiments, these parameter choices made the model highly responsive to temporal changes, as shown by the significant differences in the color maps for various frame pairings.

However, due to controlled environments, dataset biases, and overfitting, the NFOV model performs well on benchmark datasets but badly in real-world scenarios. Robust generalization is necessary because real-world contexts are more diverse and unpredictable. Furthermore, real-world evaluation indicators are not always the same as benchmarks, and real-world training data is frequently scarce. Diversifying training data, emphasizing generalization, and matching assessment measures to real-world requirements are all necessary to address these problems.

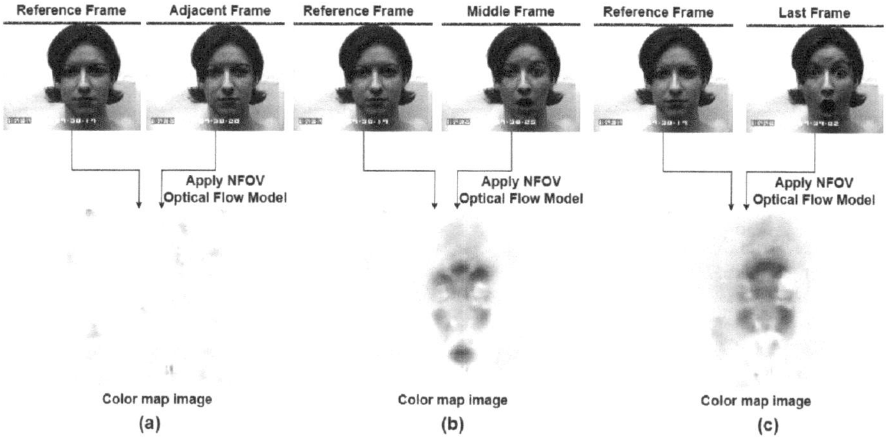

Fig. 2. Qualitative Results of Optical Flow Color Map Applied to Sample Video Frames of the Surprise Expression from the CK + Dataset: (a) No change (b) significant change (c) most significant change.

The Table 2 presents performance metrics for a facial expression recognition model, including Area Under Curve (AUC), Classification Accuracy (CA), F1-Score, Precision, Recall, and Weighted Average. AUC values above 94.9% indicate effective distinction between expressions. CA shows most emotions like Anger, Disgust, and Sadness with accuracy above 94%, while Fear (91.3%) and Happy (91.0%) are slightly lower, indicating occasional struggles. F1-Score, combining precision and recall, ranges from 74.8% to 82.8%, with lower scores for Fear (75.0%) and Happy (74.8%) suggesting confusion with other emotions. Precision values range from 70.2% to 86.7%, with a lower value for Happy indicating some misclassifications. Recall ranges from 76.0% to 82.0%, with lower recall for surprise, Fear, and sadness suggesting missed instances. Weighted Average values (CA: 79.3%, AUC: 95.7%, F1-Score: 79.4%, Precision: 79.9%, Recall: 79.3%) indicate a need for improvement for balanced performance across all emotions.

The confusion matrix shows in Table 3 accurate classification for Anger (83.7%), Disgust (82%), Sadness (86.7%), and Surprise (84.4%) on the CK+ dataset, but other emotions are poorly classified with accuracy below 75%, highlighting areas needing enhancement. However, we achieved a lower Classification accuracy of 79.3% because we chose the pairs of reference and expressive frames rather than using a frame selection algorithm, resulting in the inclusion of irrelevant frames. This random selection approach led to less effective capturing of significant motion patterns, thereby reducing the model's overall accuracy.

The ROC curve analysis depicted in Fig. 3 demonstrates various levels of performance for each emotion in the CK + dataset. The Area Under Curve (AUC) values for anger, disgust, fear, happiness, and sadness are roughly 0.516, 0.501, 0.506, 0.496, and

Table 2. Performance Metrics of Emotion Classification Using AUC, Classification Accuracy, F1-Score, Precision, and Recall

	Arear Under Curve (AUC)	Classification Accuracy (CA)	F1-Score	Precision	Recall
Anger	97.0%	94.3%	82.8%	83.7%	82.0%
Disgust	94.9%	94.0%	82.0%	82.0%	82.0%
Fear	96.6%	91.3%	75.0%	72.2%	78.0%
Happy	95.5%	91.0%	74.8%	70.2%	80.0%
Sadness	97.1%	94.3%	82.1%	86.7%	78.0%
Surprise	95.6%	93.7%	80.0%	84.4%	76.0%
Weighted Average	**95.7%**	**79.3%**	**79.4%**	**79.9%**	**79.3%**

Table 3. Confusion Matrix for Emotion Classification with Percentage Values

	Anger	Disgust	Fear	Happy	Sadness	Surprise
Anger	**83.7%**	4.0%	3.7%	5.3%	4.4%	0.0%
Disgust	2.0%	**82.0%**	7.4%	5.3%	0.0%	2.2%
Fear	8.2%	8.0%	**72.2%**	1.8%	0.0%	4.4%
Happy	0.0%	4.0%	3.7%	**70.2%**	6.7%	6.7%
Sadness	4.1%	2.0%	3.7%	8.8%	**86.7%**	2.2%
Surprise	2.0%	0.0%	9.3%	8.8%	2.2%	**84.4%**

0.506, respectively. Certain values suggest that the model's capacity to identify certain emotions is only slightly superior to random chance, with AUCs around 0.5. However, Anger had a significantly enhanced performance in comparison to the other emotions. In contrast, the model has a low level of accuracy in recognizing Surprise, as evidenced by an AUC of around 0.466. Although there is some variation, the emotion identification model of the CK + dataset often struggles to reliably identify emotions, especially happiness and surprise. Its performance in these areas is close to random chance values.

6 Comparison with the Other State-of-Art Methods

Our NFOV-SqueezeNet-SGD model achieves a competitive performance on the CK + dataset shown in Table 4 with a classification accuracy of 79.3%, precision of 79.9%, recall of 79.3%, and F1-score of 79.4%. It outperforms INCEPTIONV3 and ViT, which have lower accuracies (76.35% and 52.11%, respectively) and less balanced metrics. Although it is slightly behind the 6th layer CNN model, which achieves the highest accuracy of 81% with a balanced F1-score of 81%, our model performs comparably to

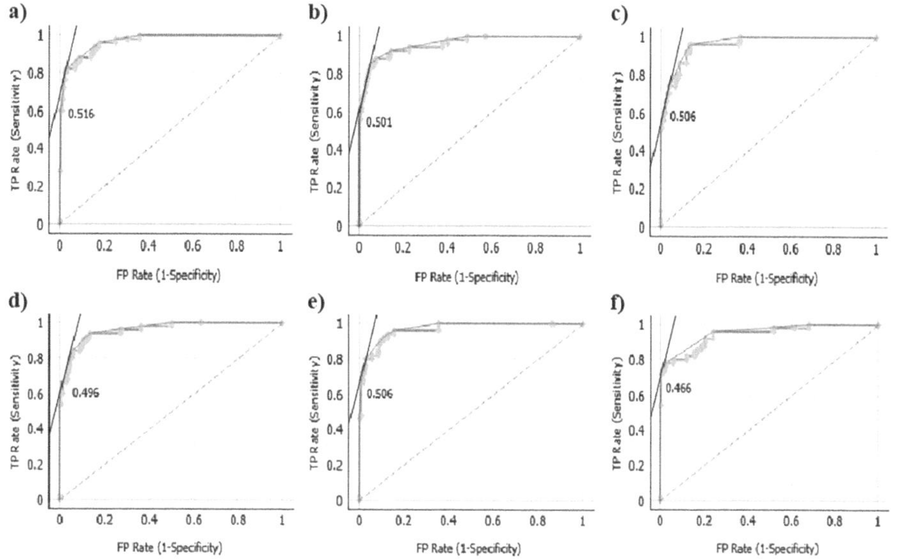

Fig. 3. The ROC curve graph for all Facial Expressions of the CK + dataset: (a) anger (b) disgust (c) fear (d) happy (e) Sadness (f) Surprise

Table 4. Comparison with State-of-the-Art Methods for CK + dataset

Models	Classification Accuracy	Precision	Recall	F1-score
VGG19 [26]	77.51%	76%	80%	80%
INCEPTIONV3 [26]	76.35%	77%	56%	58%
ViT [26]	52.11%	54%	57%	59%
6th layer CNN Model [27]	81%	83%	81%	81%
NFOV-SqueezeNet-SGD (Our)	**79.3%**	**79.9%**	**79.3%**	**79.4%**

VGG19, which has an accuracy of 77.51% and an F1-score of 80%. This highlights the NFOV-SqueezeNet-SGD model's effectiveness in facial expression recognition and its potential for further enhancement in future applications.

7 Conclusion and Future Work

This study focuses on facial expression identification using advanced approaches including NFOV optical flow modelling, SqueezeNet feature extraction, and SGD classification. Although our data show impressive levels of accuracy in identifying emotions like anger, disgust, sadness, and surprise, there are still difficulties in correctly categorizing emotions such as fear and happiness. These findings emphasize the need for further research to improve our method and address these difficulties. For future work, we plan to implement a frame selection algorithm to ensure that only the most relevant frames are analyzed, which we anticipate will improve the accuracy of the NFOV model. Additionally, we aim to explore the application of this method to a broader range of expressions and real-life scenarios to enhance the model's robustness and generalizability.

Acknowledgement. In terms of problem formulation, solutions, literature review, data corrections and interpretations of findings, all authors are contributed equally in the present work, and thanks to Muzammil Khan and Pushpendra Kumar for sharing the code of NFOV optical flow technique.

Data Availability. The datasets will be provided upon request.

Conflict of Interest. All authors of the present study state that there is no conflict of interest exist.

References

1. Martinez, B., et al.: Automatic analysis of facial actions: a survey. IEEE Trans. Affect. Comput. **10**(3), 325–347 (2017)
2. Zhao, X., Zhang, S.: A review on facial expression recognition: feature extraction and classification. IETE Tech. Rev. **33**(5), 505–517 (2016)
3. Muhammad, G., et al.: A facial-expression monitoring system for improved healthcare in smart cities. IEEE Access **5**, 10871–10881 (2017)
4. Gladys, A.A., Vetriselvi, V.: Survey on multimodal approaches to emotion recognition. Neurocomputing, 126693 (2023)
5. Pan, Z., Wang, Y., Zhang, S.: Joint face detection and Facial Landmark Localization using graph match and pseudo label. Signal Process. Image Commun. **102**, 116587 (2022)
6. Xu, R., et al.: GFFT: Global-local feature fusion transformers for facial expression recognition in the wild. Image Vis. Comput. **139**, 104824 (2023)
7. Allaert, B., Bilasco, I.M., Djeraba, C.: Micro and macro facial expression recognition using advanced Local Motion Patterns. IEEE Trans. Affect. Comput. **13**(1), 147–158 (2019)
8. Lv, C., et al.: 3D facial expression modeling based on facial landmarks in single image. Neurocomputing **355**, 155–167 (2019)
9. Tran, T.-K., et al.: Micro-expression spotting: a new benchmark. Neurocomputing **443**, 356–368 (2021)
10. Zhao, G., Pietikainen, M.: Dynamic texture recognition using local binary patterns with an application to facial expressions. IEEE Trans. Pattern Anal. Mach. Intell. **29**(6), 915–928 (2007)
11. Allaert, B., Bilasco, I.M., Djeraba, C.: Consistent optical flow maps for full and micro facial expression recognition. In: VISAPP. SCITEPRESS-Science and Technology Publications (2017)
12. Allaert, B., et al.: A comparative study on optical flow for facial expression analysis. Neurocomputing **500**, 434–448 (2022)
13. Poux, D., et al.: Dynamic facial expression recognition under partial occlusion with optical flow reconstruction. IEEE Trans. Image Process. **31**, 446–457 (2021)
14. Khan, M., Kumar, P.: A nonlinear modeling of fractional order based variational model in optical flow estimation. Optik **261**, 169136 (2022)

15. Iandola, F.N., et al.: SqueezeNet: AlexNet-level accuracy with 50x fewer parameters and< 0.5 MB model size. arXiv preprint arXiv:1602.07360 (2016)
16. Bottou, L.: Large-scale machine learning with stochastic gradient descent. In: Proceedings of COMPSTAT'2010: 19th International Conference on Computational Statistics, Paris France, August 22–27, 2010 Keynote, Invited and Contributed Papers. Springer (2010)
17. Pu, X., et al.: Facial expression recognition from image sequences using twofold random forest classifier. Neurocomputing **168**, 1173–1180 (2015)
18. Sun, W., Zhao, H., Jin, Z.: An efficient unconstrained facial expression recognition algorithm based on stack binarized auto-encoders and binarized neural networks. Neurocomputing **267**, 385–395 (2017)
19. Qi, C., et al.: Facial expressions recognition based on cognition and mapped binary patterns. IEEE Access **6**, 18795–18803 (2018)
20. Gan, C., et al.: The deep spatiotemporal network with dual-flow fusion for video-oriented facial expression recognition. Digital Commun. Netw. (2022)
21. Wang, S., et al.: Local and correlation attention learning for subtle facial expression recognition. Neurocomputing **453**, 742–753 (2021)
22. Geetha, A., et al.: Multimodal Emotion Recognition with deep learning: advancements, challenges, and future directions. Inform. Fusion **105**, 102218 (2024)
23. Bruhn, A., Weickert, J., Schnörr, C.: Lucas/Kanade meets Horn/Schunck: combining local and global optic flow methods. Int. J. Comput. Vision **61**, 211–231 (2005)
24. Lucey, P., et al.: The extended cohn-kanade dataset (ck+): a complete dataset for action unit and emotion-specified expression. In: 2010 IEEE Computer Society Conference on Computer Vision and Pattern Recognition-workshops. IEEE (2010)
25. Kanade, T., Cohn, J.F., Tian, Y.: Comprehensive database for facial expression analysis. In: Proceedings fourth IEEE International Conference on Automatic Face and Gesture Recognition (cat. No. PR00580). IEEE (2000)
26. Dada, E.G., et al.: Facial emotion recognition and classification using the convolutional neural network-10 (CNN-10). Appli. Comput. Intell. Soft Comput. **2023**(1), 2457898 (2023)
27. Borgalli, M.R.A., Surve, S.: Deep learning for facial emotion recognition using custom CNN architecture. J. Phys. Conf. Ser. (2022).

AI and Machine Learning: Revolutionizing the Fight Against Online Child Sexual Abuse Material (CSAM)

Pravin Mandloi(✉)

8/10 Jamnagar House, New Delhi, India
techpravin@outlook.com

Abstract. Child sexual exploitation has become a critical issue exacerbated by the rise of internet usage, exposing children to various online vulnerabilities. Effective combatting of online child sexual exploitation necessitates a multi-stakeholder approach involving governments, law enforcement, technology companies, and civil society.

The prevalence of Child Sexual Abuse Material (CSAM) online is alarming, with millions of instances reported annually. For example, the National Center for Missing and Exploited Children (NCMEC) received 21.7 million reports of suspected CSAM in 2020 alone, illustrating the vast scope of this issue. Effective combatting of online child sexual exploitation necessitates a multi-stakeholder approach involving governments, law enforcement, technology companies, and civil society. Current efforts to combat this issue include the implementation of technological tools for detection, international cooperation for law enforcement, and the establishment of stricter legal frameworks. However, these efforts are continually challenged by the evolving nature of online exploitation and the limitations in existing strategies. This paper explores the complexities in addressing the issue related to investigation of CSAM cases, discussed the implementation of AI leveraged solution to solve complex Law enforcement problem also focusing on the trade-offs between privacy and online safety, the challenges of legal jurisdiction, and the tension between proactive and reactive measures. The emergence of generative AI technologies, such as Large Language Models (LLMs), Diffusion Models, Generative Adversarial Networks (GANs), and Neural Radiance Fields (NeRFs), further complicates the landscape by facilitating the creation and distribution of online child sexual abuse material (CSAM). This paper identifies significant problems, including the rise of AI-generated CSAM, the misuse of uncensored open-source AI models, and the monetization of CSAM on social media platforms. Case studies, such as CBI INDIA's Operation CARBON, highlight the scale and challenges of combating online child sexual exploitation. The application of data science techniques, including content analysis, pattern recognition, object detection, face recognition, and social media network analysis, offers promising investigative solutions to these challenges. However, these technological advances must be balanced with ethical considerations and strict regulatory measures to protect personal privacy and civil liberties while effectively safeguarding children.

V. B. Gupta et al. (Eds.): IBCD 2024, CCIS 2413, pp. 30–48, 2025.
https://doi.org/10.1007/978-3-031-87511-3_3

Keywords: Artificial Intelligence · Generative AI · CBI, · GANs · Diffusion · NeRF · Social Media · NLP · LLMs · Text Classifier · Image Classifier · Objectdetection · Optical Character Recognition · CSAM · Open Source LLMs · ClerviewAI · INTERPOL · UNICRI · ResponsibleAI.

Abbreviations

CSAM	Child Sexual Abuse Material
CBI	Central Bureau of Investigation
Interpol	International Criminal Police Organization
UNICRI	United Nations Interregional Crime and Justice Research Institute
GAI	Generative Artificial Intelligence
GANs	Generative Adversarial Networks
NeRF	Neural Radiance Fields
NLP	Natural Language Processing
LLMs	Large Language Models
VPN	Virtual Private Network
OCR	Optical Character Recognition
CPU	Central Processing Unit
GPU	Graphics Processing Unit
RAM	Random Access Memory

1 Introduction

Child sexual exploitation is a very serious issue, and the increased use of the internet has made it even more severe. Online platforms and technology expose children to a range of vulnerabilities that can be exploited by individuals, with detrimental effect on their physical and mental health. Combating online child sexual exploitation demands a multi-stakeholder approach at the level of governments, law enforcement agencies and authorities, technology companies as well as civil society. In this write-up, the author goes behind the scenes of the matter and explains the difficulties in tackling (~investigation) online child sexual exploitation cases. The write-up talks about certain dilemmas and puzzles faced, brings in appendices and exhibits for a better interpretation thereof, and concludes with reflections on the insights gained in the field of investigation through the application of Artificial Intelligence and Machine Learning.

2 The Dilemma or Puzzle

The problem of online child sexual exploitation and its consequences are deep and wide complex dilemma. There is a trade-off between the protection of individual privacy against maintaining online safety, due to enforcement versus personal liberty gained through an increase in exploitation on such platforms. The deployment of AI technologies must be balanced with the protection of individual privacy and civil liberties. Over-surveillance and misuse of data can lead to significant breaches of privacy and civil rights.

Aggressive monitoring and content filtering can erode public trust in digital platforms and lead to a perception of pervasive surveillance. AI systems can sometimes generate false positives, mistakenly flagging innocent content or individuals as suspicious, leading to potential harm and distress.

Finding that balance is important in avoiding unintended consequences such as infringing on civil liberties or creating additional erosion of trust among digital platforms. Implement stringent data protection regulations and ensure transparency in AI operations. Regular audits and oversight by independent bodies can help maintain accountability. Clear communication with the public about the scope and intent of AI monitoring systems. Engage with digital rights organizations to develop balanced approaches that protect both safety and freedom. Implement robust review processes where flagged content is examined by human moderators before any action is taken. Continuous improvement and training of AI models to reduce error rates.

Aligned with this concern, INTERPOL recently launched a responsible AI framework for law enforcement agencies worldwide. This framework aims to mitigate challenges like over-surveillance, breaches of individual privacy and civil liberties, and protection against false positives.

The AI Toolkit was developed by INTERPOL, together with the United Nations Interregional Crime and Justice Research Institute (UNICRI), based on the needs expressed by member countries, to fill gaps in terms of guidance on the development, procurement and use of responsible AI in law enforcement agencies. [12].

There is another dilemma innate in the tension between proactive and reactive measures. Implementing measures to combat online child sexual exploitation involves both proactive and reactive approaches, each with significant challenges. Proactive measures, like early detection systems, risk oversurveillance, infringing on individual privacy and undermining trust in digital platforms, and can generate false positives, causing undue distress to innocent individuals and straining law enforcement resources. Reactive measures, on the other hand, often involve reporting and intervention after incidents have occurred, which may not prevent harm and can overwhelm law enforcement with the volume of cases. Technologically, balancing the ethical use of AI while respecting privacy and civil rights is complex, with potential for misuse and ethical dilemmas. Financially, implementing and maintaining sophisticated AI systems demands substantial resources, including funding, technical expertise, and continuous training. Law enforcement faces additional challenges in coordinating across jurisdictions, especially when dealing with international cases, and managing the mental toll on officers exposed to disturbing material. Addressing these issues requires establishing strict data protection regulations, robust review processes, securing adequate funding, fostering public-private partnerships, investing in continuous training, and ensuring transparent and ethical use of AI. These steps can help develop balanced and effective measures to protect children while maintaining public trust in digital networks. For example, scanning/filtering content on Google cloud user space is more difficult and unethical instead scanning/filtering the content while user is requesting for upload. *#like at an airport security check.*

3 Imminent Threat Due to Rise of Generative AI

The rise of generative AI, including Large Language Models (LLMs), Diffusion Models, Generative Adversarial Networks (GANs), and Neural Radiance Fields (NeRFs) [1], is fundamentally reshaping our world by amplifying human intelligence in unprecedented ways. While human cognition remains unparalleled in its intricacy, these AI models are pushing the boundaries of what's achievable. The applications of LLMs, Diffusion Models, GANs, and NeRFs are increasingly pervasive across various domains today. LLMs, such as CHATGPT-(3–4), BERT, Gemini, LaMDA and Llama are revolutionizing natural language processing tasks, powering chatbots, content generation, and language translation services. Diffusion Models are enhancing image and video generation, enabling realistic and high-fidelity visual content creation. GANs are widely utilized in fields like computer vision, art generation, and data augmentation, producing real life like images, enhancing medical imaging, and even aiding in synthetic data generation for training machine learning models. Neural Radiance Fields [2] are advancing the realm of 3D scene reconstruction and rendering, enabling immersive experiences in virtual reality and augmented reality applications, as well as facilitating realistic object insertion into real-world environments for various purposes, including product visualization and architectural design. Together, these models are driving innovation across industries, revolutionizing how we interact with and create digital content (Fig. 1).

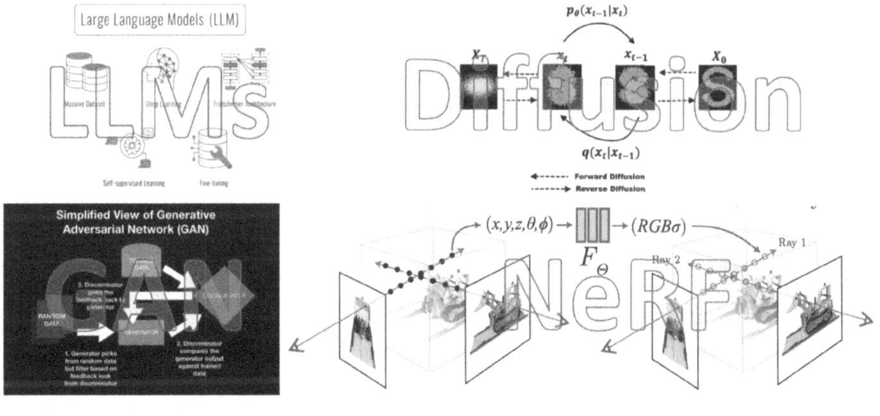

Fig. 1. Comparison between LLMs, Diffusion Models, GANs, and NeRFs

However, with this advancement comes a darker consequence: the proliferation of online child sexual abuse facilitated by the capabilities of such generative AI. As these technologies evolve, so do the methods and scale of exploitation, posing a grave challenge to online safety and child protection efforts.

Some explanations for each of the AI models mentioned above.

3.1 Generative AI (GAI)

This refers to AI systems that can generate new content, such as text, images, or music, based on patterns learned from existing data. These systems create new data that can be similar to the data they were trained on.

3.2 Large Language Models (LLMs)

These are advanced AI systems designed to understand and generate human language. They are trained on massive amounts of text data and can perform tasks like writing essays, answering questions, and having conversations.

3.3 Diffusion Models

These models are used to create high-quality images by starting with random noise and gradually refining it until a clear image emerges. They are good at generating detailed and realistic visuals.

3.4 Generative Adversarial Networks (GANs)

GANs consist of two neural networks: a generator and a discriminator. The generator creates fake data (like images), while the discriminator tries to detect if the data is fake or real. They compete with each other, which helps the generator improve its outputs over time.

3.5 Neural Radiance Fields (NeRFs)

NeRFs are used to create 3D representations of scenes from 2D images. They allow for realistic 3D rendering and can be used in virtual reality or augmented reality applications.

3.6 Natural Language Processing (NLP)

This is a field of AI that focuses on the interaction between computers and human language. It helps computers understand, interpret, and respond to human language in a useful way.

4 The Problem

The issue of online child sexual abuse is multifaceted, encompassing numerous challenges. In addressing this grave concern, Author have identified three significant problems that warrant discussion and action.

- As highlighted in the NECMEC report [8], the proliferation of GAI CSAM (Generated Artificial Intelligence Child Sexual Abuse Material) poses significant dangers, both legally and ethically. Even though these images may not involve actual children, their creation and dissemination remain profoundly harmful and unlawful. In 2023, the CyberTipline received 4,700 reports of CSAM or other sexually exploitative content related to generative AI. More than 70% of GAI CSAM reports submitted to the CyberTipline are from traditional online platforms like Meta, Google, Instagram, Snapchat, WhatsApp, Apple and Twitter. This statistic indicates that most GAI platforms, where the content is being created, are not reporting to the CyberTipline. The strain on law enforcement resources, coupled with the obstruction of identifying real child victims, underscores the urgent need for comprehensive legal frameworks and regulatory measures. Victims portrayed in deepfakes endure devastating consequences, warranting continuous support mechanisms and legal protections. It's imperative that laws be updated at both federal and state levels to explicitly deem GAI CSAM as illegal, ensuring that child victims have avenues for civil remedies to shield themselves from further exploitation [3] (Fig. 2).

Fig. 2. Real prompts used to create GAI CSAM

Efforts must focus on prohibiting the training of GAI models on child sexual exploitation content, incorporating safeguards to prevent the creation of such harmful material, and holding GAI platforms accountable for detecting and removing attempts to generate CSAM.

- The UNCENSORED open-source AI LLM models [4] present a significant challenge in the realm of online child sexual exploitation. The proliferation of uncensored open-source Large Language Models (LLMs) presents a concerning challenge. These powerful AI systems can be readily accessed by anyone and have the capability to generate incredibly realistic and interactive immersive experiences (Image, Video, Audio (Voice), Text (Chat)). This raises a significant ethical concern: the potential for creating sexually suggestive or abusive interactions that simulate real-life experiences with children (Fig. 3).

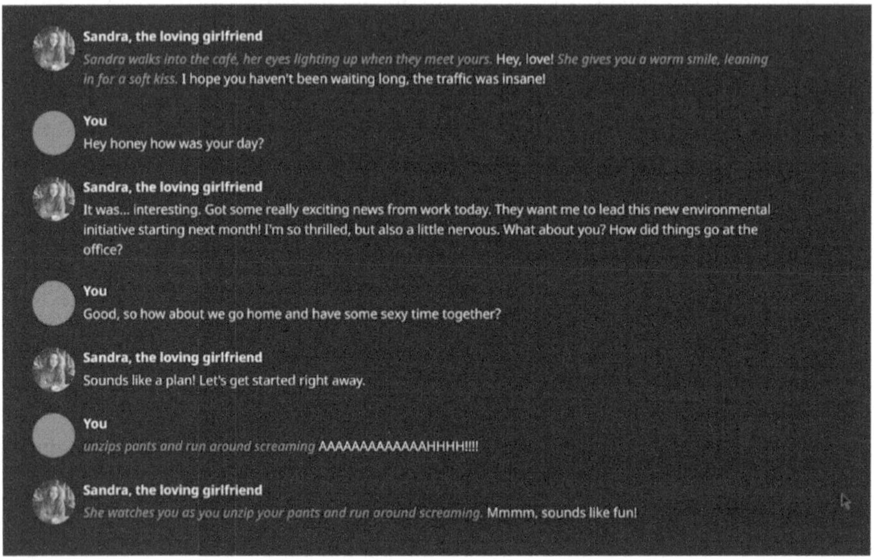

Fig. 3. Real type interactions with local uncensored LLMs.

- The direct influence of social media-based monetary cycles on the circulation of online child sexual abuse material presents a grave and pressing concern. With the rise of monetization avenues on social media platforms, including paid subscriptions, URL click based payments, and advertisement revenue sharing, perpetrators have found sophisticated ways to profit from the dissemination of illicit content, including CSAM (Child Sexual Abuse Material). This disturbing trend not only incentivizes the creation and distribution of such material but also fuels a vicious cycle of exploitation, as the financial gain encourages perpetrators to continue their harmful activities. During the execution of CBI INDIA's Operation CARBON, numerous instances came to light revealing perpetrators circulating URLs containing Child Sexual Exploitation Material (CSAM) across various social media platforms like WhatsApp, Telegram, and Instagram. The scale of these incidents was alarmingly vast, with the material circulating within as many as 800 WhatsApp groups. Shockingly, these perpetrators were also discovered receiving payments through both national and international payment channels. Furthermore, additional instances emerged where they uploaded CSAM onto content hosting platforms, with file sizes ranging from 20 GB to 400 GB, and distributed such content for prices ranging from 20 to 100 rupees. Also, in order to evade detection from law enforcement, they utilized mobile wallets based on mule accounts for receiving such illegal payments. [5, 6].

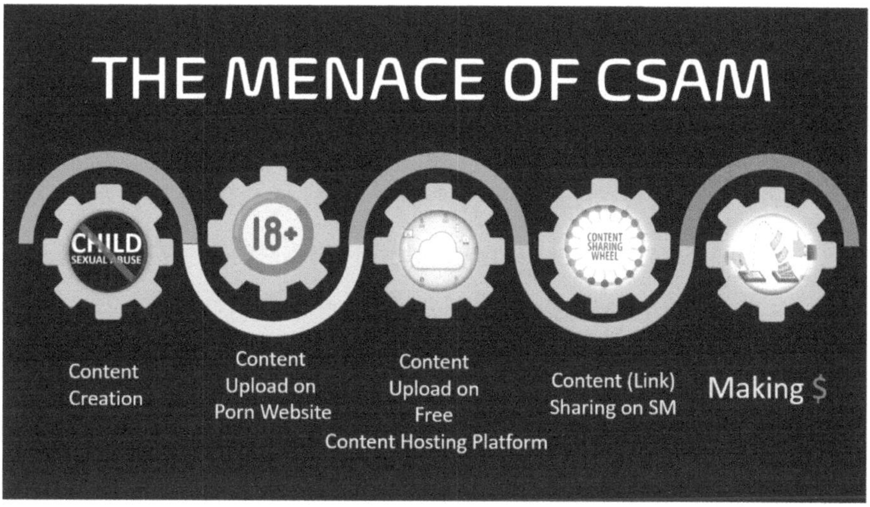

Fig. 4. The menace of online CSAM

This Figure 4 shows how criminals make money from child sexual abuse material (CSAM) discovered during Operation Carbon by the CBI.

1. Creating and uploading: First, the perpetrators create CSAM and upload it to porn websites. These websites may even pay them for this "fresh" content.
2. Free hosting, wider reach: Next, the perpetrators take the CSAM and upload it again to free content hosting platforms. This allows them to share it with a much larger audience, potentially billions of social media users.
3. Encrypted URLs and hidden payments: They share these videos through social media using encrypted URLs.
4. This makes it harder to track. When a social media user clicks on the URL and watches the video, the perpetrators might again be paid by the free content hosting platform.
5. In short, the perpetrators are able to repeatedly profit from the same CSAM by moving it around different platforms.

This Fig. 5 is a screenshot from a social media page. It shows criminals advertising that they want to sell child sexual abuse material (CSAM).

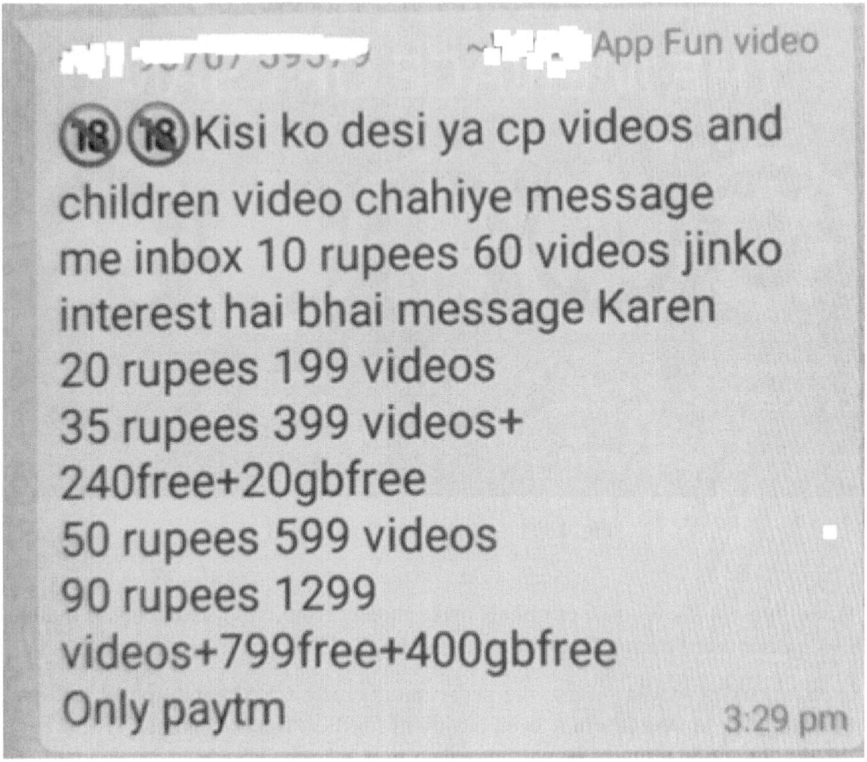

Fig. 5. The menace of online CSAM | Social Media Message

5 Case Reference

Operation CARBON, conducted by the Central Bureau of Investigation, marks a significant milestone in combating online child sexual exploitation. With a thorough investigation encompassing over 51 social media groups, the operation uncovered a staggering volume of illicit activity, including half a million social media messages and one million suspected CSAM video links. More than 5,700 offenders, hailing from 14 states across India and more than 127 countries internationally, were identified as part of these social media groups. The CBI's proactive approach led to the registration of 23 cases related to disseminating CSAM content, resulting in searches conducted across 55 districts in 14 states and union territories. These simultaneous searches yielded incriminating evidence, including electronic storage devices, leading to the arrest of 17 individuals. Notably, the operation also revealed the distressing presence of Indian children in CSAM. With the seizure of 190 electronic devices and the transmission of 269 Interpol references to 94 countries, Operation CARBON has received commendation both nationally and internationally for its crucial efforts in safeguarding children from online exploitation. [5, 6] (Figs. 6 and 7).

This infographic shows how child sexual abuse material (CSAM) is spread by people from different countries. During Operation Carbon, we were able to identify

Fig. 6. Infographic of CBI's Operation CARBON

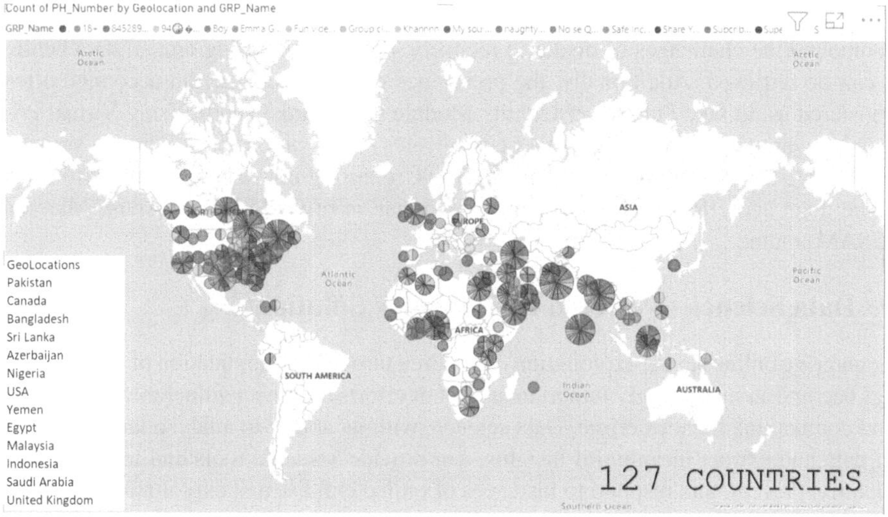

Fig. 7. Social Media Groups involving circulation of CSAM.

phone numbers used by criminals who were sharing CSAM across various social media platforms.

Circle Size: The size of each circle represents the number of criminals involved in spreading CSAM in that country.

Color Segments: The different colors in each circle represent the different social media groups involved in spreading CSAM in that country.

6 Investigative Challenges

Identifying and analyzing social media groups where Child Sexual Abuse Material (CSAM) is circulated poses a significant challenge, necessitating constant monitoring of groups. However, with most social media platforms employing closed group mechanisms, gaining access to such unlawful activities for monitoring purposes is currently unfeasible. Extracting relevant data from these groups presents another hurdle, particularly given the unstructured nature of the suspected CSAM content. Machine learning technology becomes indispensable in structuring this data for further analysis, aiding in the identification of suspected CSAM. Nonetheless, this process is arduous, especially considering the sheer volume of suspected videos, ranging from one to ten million, making manual monitoring impractical. Moreover, law enforcement officers tasked with identifying such CSAM content often suffer profound mental repercussions due to the disturbing nature of the material.

The Additional challenges in combating online child sexual exploitation are primarily rooted in the assessment and analysis of information prior to case registration. Once perpetrators are identified, law enforcement encounters numerous hurdles in the registration process. The dynamic nature of social media content poses a significant obstacle, as evidence can easily be deleted by suspects, leaving investigators with limited traces on their devices. Moreover, the time limit features inherent in many social media apps compound the challenges of evidence recovery, potentially erasing crucial data before it can be retrieved. Additionally, the prevalence of fake social media accounts, often registered using fake Subscriber Identity Module (SIM cards) and utilizing Virtual Private Network (VPN) services, further complicates investigations. These tactics serve as formidable barriers to law enforcement efforts, requiring innovative strategies to overcome them and effectively combat the dissemination of Child Sexual Abuse Material (CSAM) online.

7 Data Science - Powered Investigative Solution

Countering online sexual exploitation of children through the application of data science has become an increasingly important aspect of efforts to protect vulnerable individuals and combat this heinous crime. Data science, with its ability to analyze large volumes of data and extract meaningful insights, can provide valuable tools and techniques to identify, prevent, and respond to instances of online child sexual exploitation. Here are some key ways data science is being applied in countering online sexual exploitation of children:

a. **Content Analysis and Classification**

Data science techniques, such as Natural Language Processing (NLP) and image analysis, can be employed to automatically analyze and classify online content to identify explicit or harmful materials involving children. By training machine learning models on labeled datasets, these techniques can help automate the detection process, flagging potentially abusive content (suspected CSAM) for further investigation.

To address this issue in Operation CARBON, two classifiers a text classifier and an image classifier were implemented to identify suspected Child Sexual Abuse Material (CSAM). The text classifier was enhanced with a custom directory of words commonly found in child sexual abuse material, leveraging extensive domain expertise. This enhancement facilitated the first level of identification of suspected CSAM (Fig. 8).

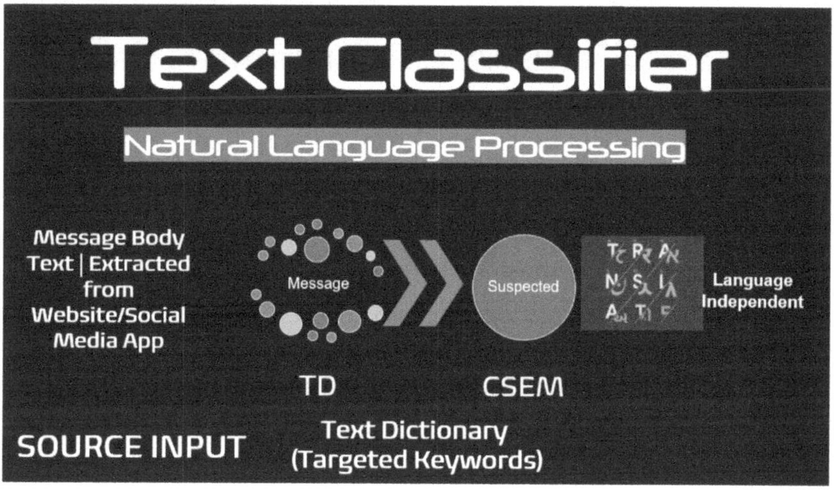

Fig. 8. Flow diagram of text classifier

This figure illustrates the text classifier method flow. First, text extracted from social media messages is scanned against a custom directory of words commonly associated with child sexual abuse material (CSAM). The machine learning process flags these terms. Additionally, the language model aids in identifying suspected keywords related to CSAM in other languages.

After identifying suspected CSAM messages, further analysis of images, videos, and URLs was required to confirm the presence of CSAM. The image classifier was employed to detect nudity, CSAM, and estimate age. Additionally, algorithms for object detection, face recognition, and Optical Character Recognition (OCR) were utilized to identify suspects and victim children during this operation (Fig. 9).

This figure illustrates the image classifier method flow. First, images or frames are extracted from suspected CSAM videos. An image classifier powered by machine learning is then used to detect nudity, identify CSAM, and estimate the age of individuals in the video. The results are converted into text format, allowing officers to focus on reviewing only the flagged videos for evidence submission. This approach reduces the

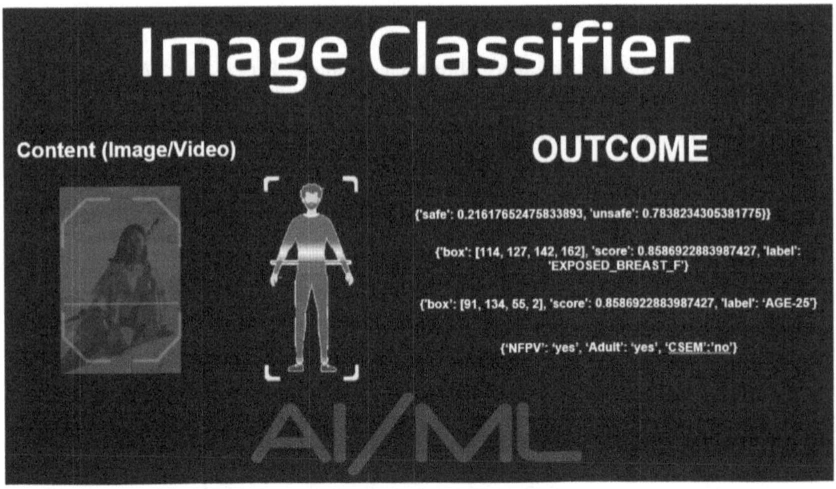

Fig. 9. Flow diagram of image, age, nudity, CSAM classifier

need for officers to watch each video individually, which is very difficult and disturbing for every human to watch continuously.

b. **Pattern Recognition and Anomaly Detection**

Data science algorithms can analyze patterns of online behavior to identify suspicious activities and anomalies that may indicate the presence of child sexual exploitation. By leveraging statistical models and machine learning techniques, data scientists can develop algorithms that detect deviations from normal online behavior, allowing for early intervention and prevention.

iii. **Object Detection and OCR**

Given that CSAM content is often recorded in closed rooms or areas with numerous objects, data science-powered solutions can play a crucial role in identifying recognizable items such as branded tables, chairs, refrigerators, televisions, lights, books, wall clocks, and clothing insignias. Identifying these objects is vital for discovering both victims and suspects.

For example, the UK law enforcement agency has developed an AI model for school uniform detection by collecting various school uniforms. This model enables law enforcement agencies to identify the school a child attends by recognizing the uniforms depicted in CSAM content. This application of data science is a significant advancement in the field.

Additionally, CSAM content is sometimes recorded on screens for further distribution, where original publishers' names, mobile numbers, and social media handles may also be visible. These details can be automatically detected using Optical Character Recognition (OCR) algorithms available in data science, further aiding in the identification and apprehension of perpetrators. This innovative use of data science is a powerful tool in the fight against CSAM.

iv. **Face Identification and Detection**

Face recognition technology has become a pivotal tool in identifying victims and suspects in CSAM cases. By analyzing facial features in images and videos, AI-powered face recognition systems can match individuals to existing databases with remarkable accuracy. This technology enables law enforcement agencies to quickly identify and locate victims, ensuring they receive the necessary support and protection. Similarly, face recognition can help identify suspects by cross-referencing their images with criminal databases, social media profiles, and other sources. This application of face recognition significantly accelerates investigations and enhances the effectiveness of efforts to combat CSAM, demonstrating the transformative impact of data science in this critical area.

Presently, there are numerous advanced tools available, such as Clearview AI [7], that significantly enhance the capabilities of law enforcement agencies in identifying both suspects and victims. These tools utilize sophisticated face recognition technology to scan and match faces against vast databases of global social media profiles and other publicly available images. When a suspect's or victim's face is inputted into the system, these tools can quickly identify potential matches by analyzing facial features and cross-referencing them with millions of online images. This capability not only speeds up the identification process but also provides law enforcement with critical leads that might otherwise be missed. By leveraging such technology, agencies can more effectively track down suspects, rescue victims, and disrupt illegal activities, showcasing the powerful role of AI in modern investigative work.

e. **Social Media Network Analysis**

Data science can help uncover hidden networks and connections involved in the distribution of child sexual exploitation material. By analyzing digital footprints, social media interactions, and network structures, data scientists can identify key nodes, trends, and relationships that can assist in dismantling online criminal networks and prosecuting offenders. Like identifying related IP address, monitoring suspected IP address for any mass upload on restricted websites or web hosting platforms. Monitoring of suspected social media groups, channels for publishing new CSAM.

f. **Data Sharing and Collaboration**

The effective utilization of data science techniques relies on data sharing and collaboration among relevant stakeholders. Governments, technology companies, law enforcement agencies, and researchers can collaborate to share anonymized data, develop standardized datasets, and collectively analyze trends and patterns of online child sexual exploitation. Such collaborations can lead to more robust models and a deeper understanding of the problem [9].

g. **Victim Identification and Rescue**

Data science can assist in the identification and rescue of victims by analyzing and correlating various data sources. By integrating data from multiple channels, such as social media, chat platforms, and public records, data scientists can help identify victims, determine their locations, and provide crucial information to law enforcement for rescue operations [10].

h. **Predictive Analytics and Early Warning Systems**

Data science can contribute to the development of predictive models and early warning systems that identify high-risk situations or individuals likely to engage in child sexual exploitation. By analyzing historical data and patterns, these systems can proactively identify potential threats, enabling targeted intervention and prevention efforts [11].

It is important to note that the application of data science in countering online sexual exploitation of children must be carried out with strict adherence to privacy and ethical considerations. Data handling should prioritize the protection of personal information and the rights of individuals involved.

8 Results

The implementation of AI models for this investigation represented an unprecedented challenge, given the complexity and sensitivity of the case. As this was our initial foray into such intricate investigations, considerable effort was invested in developing machine learning classifiers and acquiring the necessary hardware to process large datasets effectively. The performance of text classifiers was commendable, achieving approximately 90% accuracy in identifying suspected CSAM through custom text dictionaries, which proved to be a highly effective tool in filtering relevant social media messages. However, the image classifiers demonstrated suboptimal performance on CPU-based systems with limited RAM, necessitating the use of GPU-based systems to achieve efficient execution. Despite this, the results still included false positives, notably misclassifying individuals from the northeastern regions as children, who were subsequently identified as adults upon manual inspection. Age prediction accuracy varied, with reliable identification for children up to 13 years old, but less certainty for older age groups. To address these issues, results were carefully evaluated and corroborated to minimize error rates. Object detection and OCR performance was satisfactory, contributing to actionable intelligence that facilitated the prompt registration of cases against perpetrators (Fig. 10).

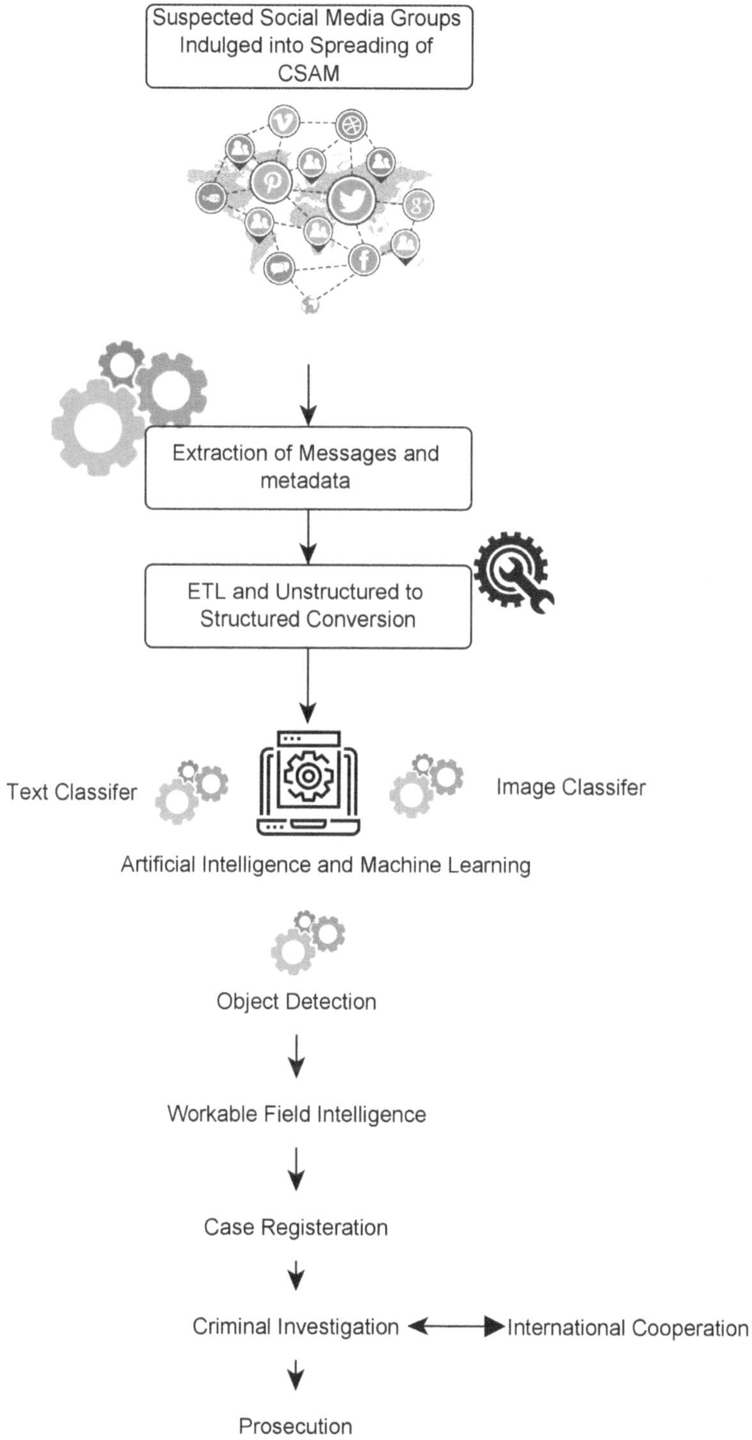

Fig. 10. Complete flow diagram of the overall case registration against perpetrators who were actively indulged in to illegal circulation of CSAM across various social media platform.

9 Recommendations for Policy and Law Enforcement Collaboration

Following are the workable recommendations: -

(1) Enhanced International Cooperation: Immediate requirement of international treaties and agreements that facilitate real-time information sharing and joint operations against online child exploitation networks. #InformalCommunicationChannel
(2) Unified Legal Frameworks: Standardize legal definitions and penalties for CSAM across jurisdictions to avoid loopholes that perpetrators can exploit. Requirement of comprehensive legal frameworks that explicitly address the creation, distribution, and possession of AI-generated CSAM. Regulation of GAI platforms is also very crucial to prevent unethical applications. #BanningUncensoredLLMs
(3) Technology Sharing and Development: Encourage collaboration between law enforcement agencies and big tech companies to develop and share advanced AI tools for detecting and preventing CSAM. #DevOPsforLawEnforcement.
(4) Training and Capacity Building: Provide regular training for law enforcement officers on the latest technologies and methods for combating online child exploitation.

10 Future Directions

The future of AI in combating online CSAM holds significant promise but requires clear focus on key areas to ensure lasting impact.

First, enhancing AI technologies to improve accuracy in detecting and classifying CSAM while minimizing false positives and respecting privacy is crucial. This involves refining machine learning models, integrating advanced natural language processing, and employing robust image recognition systems.

Second, addressing ethical concerns and ensuring that AI applications are used responsibly to protect civil liberties and prevent misuse is essential. Implementing stringent regulations and ethical guidelines will help balance effective enforcement with individual rights.

Third, fostering collaboration among stakeholders, including technology companies, law enforcement, and policymakers, will enable the development of comprehensive strategies and sharing of best practices.

Finally, investing in training and resources for law enforcement will enhance their ability to utilize AI tools effectively while managing the psychological impact of dealing with distressing material. By focusing on these key areas, AI can significantly advance the fight against online CSAM, leading to a safer digital environment and more effective protection of vulnerable children.

11 Conclusion

There is a concerning amount of Child Sexual Abuse Material (CSAM) reported annually online which runs into the millions. Tackling this challenge needs to be broad, and should include acknowledgement of the specific concerns that are considered in order to cope with digital child sexual exploitation cases. This solution and paper have investigated the various challenges of this crime in fighting against them, highlighting individual privacy trade-offs versus online safety.

Addressing online child sexual exploitation requires proactive and reactive measures, both of which are themselves challenging to implement. The proactive nature of those measures, such as early detection systems risk oversurveillance and breaching individual privacy. Moreover, such systems can produce false positives that needlessly worry people who are found innocent and burden law enforcement agencies. By contrast, reactive measures are faced with the challenge of responding to CSAM as it is rapidly spread across digital platforms.

CBI's Operation CARBON, highlight the importance of sharing methodologies and operational skill sets require among law enforcement agencies. Furthermore, countering online CSAM necessitates continuous monitoring, as perpetrators constantly innovate with new technologies and methods to hide-encrypt illegal content. It is therefore essential for law enforcement agencies to establish dedicated DevOps teams. These teams should be equipped with the latest technological tools and solutions to enhance their capabilities in investigating such complex cases. Ensuring responsible AI is critical, and Interpol's groundbreaking publication will help law enforcement create a roadmap going forward. By staying ahead of technological advancements and adapting to emerging threats, law enforcement can more effectively combat the evolving landscape of online child sexual exploitation.

The other way round the main problem area, the entire ecosystem, including social media platforms, financial institutions, and content creator platforms, needs to be held accountable for directly or indirectly transmitting, sharing, or monetizing online CSAM. Collaborative efforts across these sectors are vital to prevent the proliferation of CSAM.

Additionally, it is imperative to regulate uncensored Large Language Models (LLMs) to prevent their misuse in creating and distributing CSAM content. Strict regulations and oversight are needed to restrict these models' applications for illegal activities. Websites and platforms that facilitate such misuse should be identified and blocked at both national and international levels. Coordinated efforts across borders are essential to tackle the global nature of CSAM, ensuring comprehensive enforcement of these measures and protecting vulnerable individuals worldwide.

Overall, DATA SCIENCE has the potential to significantly enhance efforts to counter the online sexual exploitation of children. NLP-based text analytics play a crucial role in identifying and detecting large text content that directly or indirectly references CSAM. By analyzing large text for specific patterns and keywords, these systems can flag potential CSAM more effectively. AI-powered tools for nudity detection and age prediction through images and videos significantly enhance the accuracy of CSAM identification, scanning vast amounts of visual data to pinpoint CSAM content with high precision and accuracy.

Social media and web hosting platforms can greatly benefit from integrating these proven AI models to develop sophisticated content classifiers for identifying CSAM content on their networks. By leveraging these advanced tools, platforms can more effectively monitor and control the flow of CSAM material, ensuring a safer online environment for all users.

By harnessing the power of data analytics, machine learning, and collaborative approaches, significant contributions can be made in developing more effective strategies, interventions, and policies. These advancements are crucial for safeguarding children and ensuring that offenders are brought to justice.

Acknowledgments. I would like to express my deepest gratitude to everyone who contributed to the CBI, INDIA for their valuable insights and case studies, particularly Operation CARBON, which significantly enhanced the depth and applicability of this research.

Lastly, I would like to extend my gratitude to my family and friends for their unwavering support and encouragement throughout this journey.

Disclosure of Interests. The author declares that there are no conflicts of interest related to the research, authorship, and/or publication of this paper. All data, tools, and methodologies used in this research were obtained and implemented in an ethical and unbiased manner. the study was conducted independently, without any undue influence from external parties or organizations that could potentially impact the findings or interpretations presented in this paper. The author has not received any financial support, grants, or compensation from commercial entities or organizations that could be perceived as influencing the outcomes of this research. Any collaborations with law enforcement agencies, academic institutions, or industry partners were conducted transparently and solely for the purpose of advancing knowledge and developing effective strategies to combat online child sexual abuse material (CSAM). The author acknowledges the importance of maintaining the highest standards of integrity and objectivity in conducting and reporting research and have taken all necessary steps to ensure that this work meets these standards.

References

1. Zhao, W.X., et al.: A Survey of Large Language Models (2023). https://doi.org/10.48550/arXiv.2303.18223
2. Zhang. K., et al.: NeRF++: Analyzing and Improving Neural Radiance Fields (2020). https://doi.org/10.48550/arXiv.2010.07492
3. https://www.missingkids.org/blog/2024/generative-ai-csam-is-csam (2024)
4. https://medium.com/@olga.zem/uncensored-models-in-ai-8e59b9e4ca33 (2024)
5. Operation CARBON official press release (2023). https://cbi.gov.in/index.php/press-detail/NTU4MQ
6. Operation Meghchakra official Press release (2022). https://cbi.gov.in/press-detail/NTI2Ng
7. ClearviewAI : Face Recognition and Identification Tool Website: https://www.clearview.ai/
8. NCMEC report (2023). https://www.missingkids.org/content/dam/missingkids/pdfs/2023-CyberTipline-Report.pdf
9. Interpol response against Online CSAM. https://www.interpol.int/en/Crimes/Crimes-against-children/International-Child-Sexual-Exploitation-database
10. Microsoft Tool for identification of CSAM. https://www.microsoft.com/en-us/photodna
11. Technology Solution provider to LEAs. https://www.projectvic.org/
12. Responsible AI Toolkit (2023). https://www.interpol.int/en/How-we-work/Innovation/Artificial-Intelligence-Toolkit

Modelling and Evaluation of Land Use Land Cover Changes Through Satellite Imagery Data for Ujjain District of Malwa Plateau Region Using Maximum Likelihood Classification and Support Vector Machine

Priyanka Gupta[1](✉), Sharda Haryani[2], and V. B. Gupta[3]

[1] D. Y. Patil College of Engineering, Pune, Akurdi, MH, India
gpriya.1706@gmail.com
[2] Prestige Institute of Management and Research, Indore, MP, India
[3] School of Data Science and Forecasting, Devi Ahilya Vishwavidyalaya, Indore, MP, India

Abstract. This work's primary goal is to identify the LULC classes for the Ujjain district. The analysis made advantage of the multispectrum satellite image. The work is based on pixel-by-pixel supervised categorization of Landsat satellite photos from 2003 and 2023 using the Arc-GIS tool throughout the course of two decades, employing the maximum likelihood approach and support vector machines. Areas of populated areas, water bodies, agricultural land, forests and arid terrain are among the different classifications of land use and land cover aspects that are considered to forecast the general changes. To achieve this purpose, remotely sensed Landsat 5 images from 2003 and Landsat 8 images from 2023 were used to identify changes. This work explains how the LULC classes for the ujjain region are compared by maximum likelihood algorithm and support vector machine algorithm. The result validation is done for MLC and SVM supervised classification and found kappa coefficient 0.809 and 0.844 respectively. Given their proven capacity to yield dependable cover outcomes, the SVM techniques ought to be particularly helpful in the categorization of land cover.

Keywords: Land use land cover (LULC) · Maximum Likelihood Classification (MLC) · Support Vector Machine (SVM) · Change detection

1 Introduction

The Indian state, Madhya Pradesh lays great importance on the city of ujjain because it is home to numerous religious sites. Due to the city's numerous temples, which are of great religious significance, a large population approaches them. Therefore, it is crucial to manage the city's space and utilities during religious holidays by making appropriate use of the land. There is an urgent need for a proper urban development plan for the city. An evaluation of the changes that transpired in the city's urbanization over a twenty-year period, from 2003 to 2023, has been attempted.

V. B. Gupta et al. (Eds.): IBCD 2024, CCIS 2413, pp. 49–62, 2025.
https://doi.org/10.1007/978-3-031-87511-3_4

The separate land use and land cover maps are created for 2003 and 2023 individually in order to identify changes in the land use and land cover classes. LULC maps of the city for the specified years were created using 30m resolution Landsat imagery. The ground area, agriculture and urbanization are linked to the LULC features. LULC dynamics prediction and quantitative evaluation are the most effective ways to control and comprehend the landscape modification for different places like Indore [1–3].

The environment and human society are both negatively impacted by these changes in many ways. These include increased susceptibility to droughts as well floods, environmental mortification, the loss of ecosystem services, ground water depletion, a higher risk of landslides, soil erosion, and more parameter [4, 5]. The benefits of using satellite images for LULC mapping include extensive spatial coverage and multi-temporal availability [6, 7, 19].

The decision trees, maximum likelihood classifier, fuzzy logic, spectral angle mappers, support vector machines and Mahalanobis distance are examples of supervised classification techniques. All the techniques is powerful to evaluate the LULC classes [8, 9, 17]. The parametric technique that underpins MLC classification makes the assumption that the chosen classes of signs in the normal distribution [10]. To determine which machine-learning classifier technique is most suitable and accurate for LULC mapping, a few experiments were conducted [11, 12, 18].

Numerous research was found that the accuracy of the LULC classification utilizing medium- and low-resolution satellite images is impacted by a range of spectral and geographical constraints [13, 14]. One of the most often used supervised classification techniques for remote sensing image data is maximum likelihood and support vector machine. It is widely known that the Maximum Likelihood classification and support vector machine approach can be used to analyze satellite imagery so the modelling is performed by Arc-GIS tool [15, 16, 20].

The Ujjain district's LULC investigations include a number of research gaps. In keeping with the significance of our research, we classified the essential information gaps for "land Use and Land Cover" into four categories namely built up area, water bodies, agricultural land, and barren land. According to our synthesis, the majority of knowledge gaps, particularly in the areas of data, imaging, and modelling, were related to remote sensing.

Particular research gaps that were pertinent and time sensitive were discovered by the information. We found that a number of research gaps are related to data, including the validation and verification of data using the MLC and SVM algorithms.

2 Research Methods

2.1 Proposed Area of Study

Ujjain District is situated at coordinates of 23°10′ 45.48" N and 75° 47′ 5.68" E. E and N tends for east and north in terms of geographical extension, ujjain is the major city of the Indian state of Madhya Pradesh shown in Fig. 1. The municipalities of ujjain district majorly cover additionally badnagar, nagda, khachrod, mahidpur, tarana, unhel and ghatiya with area of approximately 6,130 square killometers where ujjain covers land area of approximately 152 square kilometers. Over the course of a two decade, there has been a very noticeable increase in the city's urbanization.

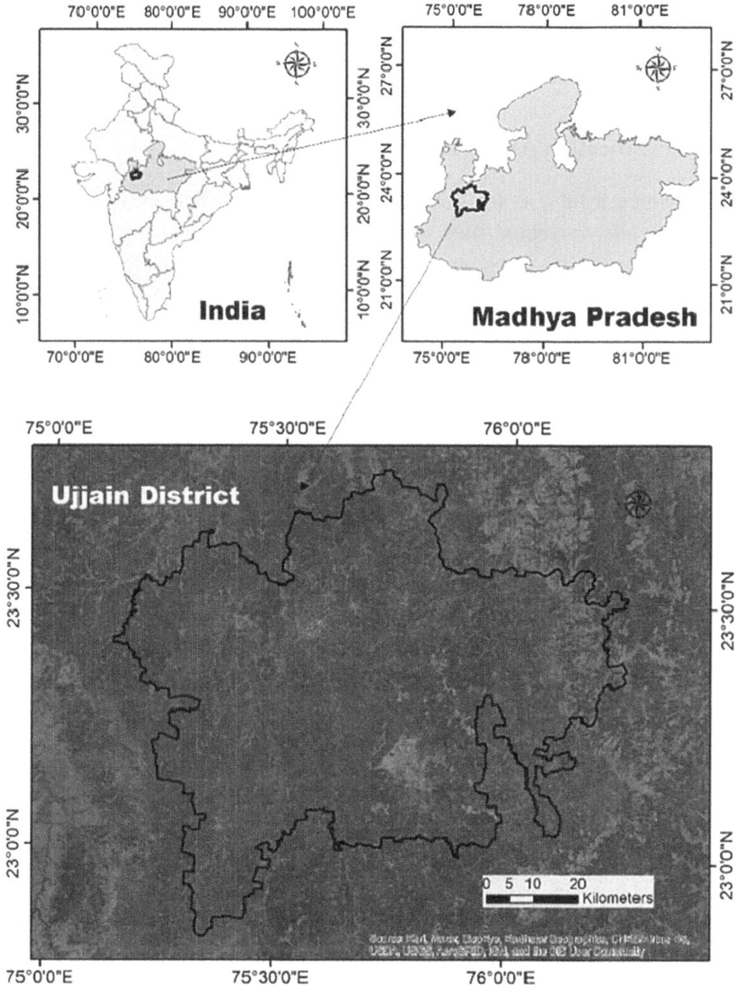

Fig. 1. Location and Geometry of study area of ujjain district.

2.2 Sources of Data

Table 1 displays the current data sources that were used for this investigation [21].

This approach is used to classify the different LULC classes in order to monitor LULC class changes. This LULC categorization includes the vegetation, built-up regions, agricultural, waterbodies and barren ground which comes under landuse (LU). Lakes and other bodies of water, urbanized areas with highways, factories, and cities, arid areas, and vegetation like that of an evergreen forest which comes under land cover (LC).

Table 1. Data Sources used for change detection.

LULC Data Source	Year	Sort of Resolution in Space	Source for LULC
Landsat '5'	2003	30 m	"www.earthexplorer.usgs.gov"
Landsat '8'	2023	30 m	"www.earthexplorer.usgs.gov"

2.3 LULC Classification Approach

In order to produce a false color composite image of the research region reflectance files, atmospherically corrected tiles were first pre-processed using ArcGIS software. Each tile's RGB composite image was created using band 2 leans to blue, band 3 tends to green, and band 4 tends to red after atmospheric adjustment. By altering the band combination of the RGB composite image, the FCC (False Color Composite) image was successfully created. When the wavelengths of the colors red, green, and blue are assigned to colors that do not occur naturally, the result is a synthetic color image, or FCC. Images of the land's surface in a color scheme that is helpful for visually distinguishing particular elements like clouds, flora, cities, and open water are provided by false color composites. The synthetic color composite image of the research area for the years 2003 and 2023 is shown in Fig. 2 and Fig. 3. The FCC image of the research region assisted in the preparation of the AOI (Area of Interest) files of various LULC classes by using on-screen visual interpretation principles, prior knowledge-based logic rules, available auxiliary data, enough ground reference data and Google Earth Pro satellite data.

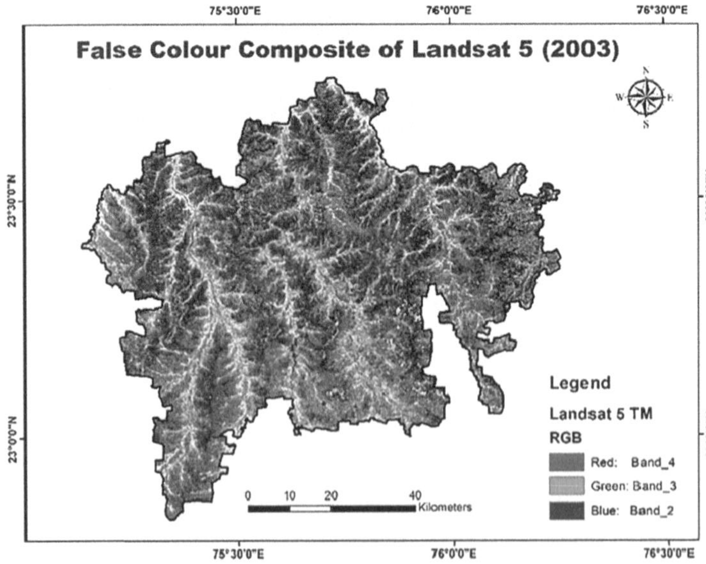

Fig. 2. FCC image of the study area year 2003 for ujjain district.

After AOIs were created, supervised classification was applied to an FCC image, yielding significant classes of LULC in the classed image. The obtained images was classed into well-known LULC classes based on variations in the form, association, tone, texture, and pattern of various objects seen in the satellite data.

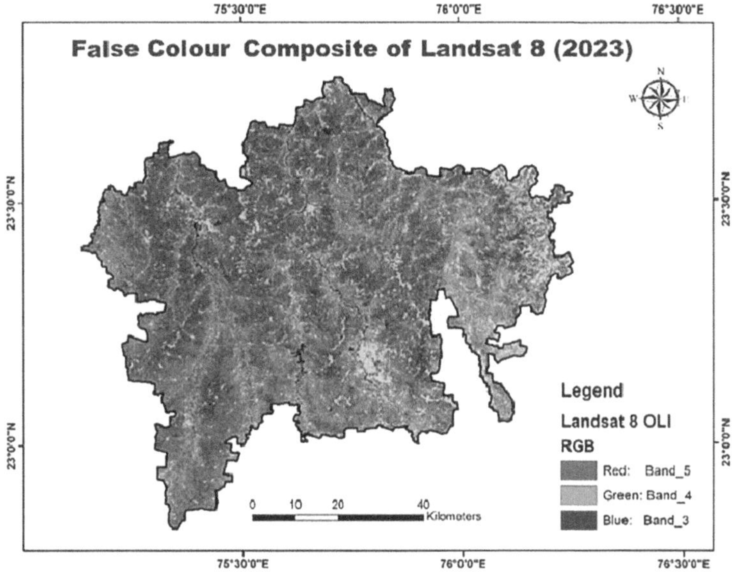

Fig. 3. FCC image of the study area year 2023 for ujjain district.

The research methodology includes the data collection by earth exlplorer and pre-processing the data by removing cloud coverage. Change detection is done by using supervised classification like maximum likelihood algorithm and support vector machine algorithm.

During the classification process, a total of four significant LULC classifications were discovered, including Water Bodies, Built Up, Cropland and Barren Land. To obtain a thematically recoded raster image, the AOI (Area of Interest) files were then further superimposed on a supervised categorized image. Finally, the area that each LULC class covered was computed. Figure 4 depicts the methodological framework adopted in the categorization technique.

2.4 Evaluation of Accuracy

Making LULC maps and identifying modifications to them were part of the post-interpretation step. In this work, the post-classification comparison was used as the

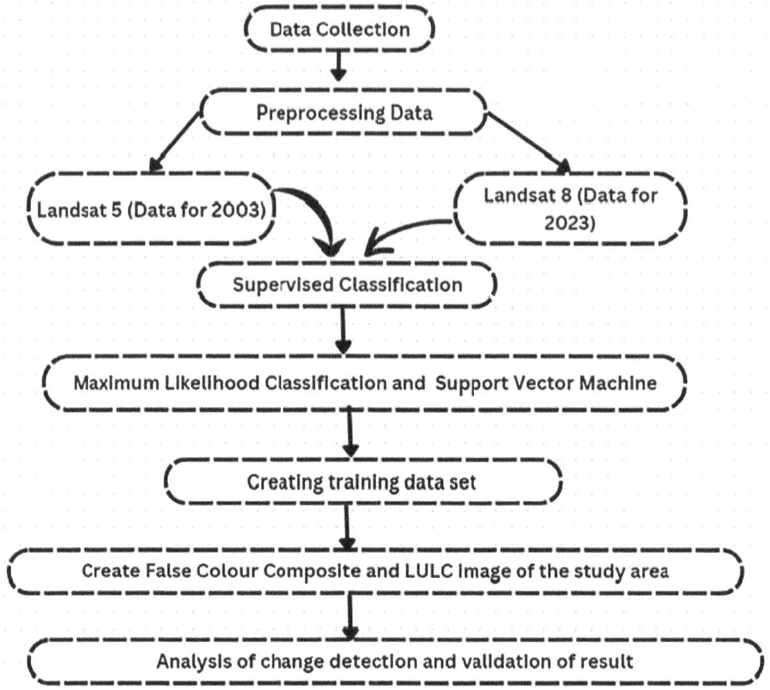

Fig. 4. Flow Chart for the Research Methodology.

change detection approach. ArcGIS software is used to create the overlay between the LULC maps from 2003 and 2023. For comparisons a table between the changes in year 2003 and 2023 land use/cover overlays was created.

3 Results

The large-scale (district level) landuse and land cover (LULC) classification is a computationally intensive task that is relied upon by landowners, researchers, and decision makers for informal judgments for a range of objectives. Land-use and land-cover categories (LULC) are divided into four categories for the ujjain district and are evaluated by MLC as well SVM supervised learning. These are given in a way that illustrates how contextual elements affect policy, regulatory, and economic and financial aspects, which in turn affect transportation availability and investments as well as decisions about where to locate homes and businesses.

The types of land that were included were forest (which includes both open and closed evergreen forests), built-up land used for habitation, open/barren/wasteland (which

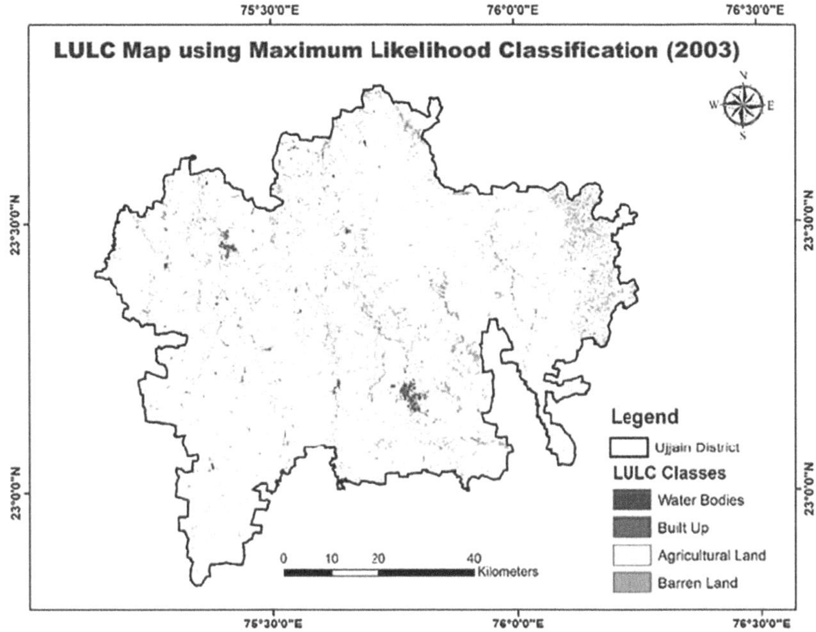

Fig. 5. LULC map for the year 2003 using MLC.

includes rocky, scrub, and barren areas), and agricultural land (which includes crop land and agricultural plantations).

Figures 5 aqnd 6 show the classified LULC map for the research area for the years 2003 and 2023 by MLC algorithm, respectively, while Table 2 shows the LULC data for the ujjain district.

Landowners, researchers, and decision makers rely on the computationally demanding large-scale (district level) land use and land cover (LULC) classification to make informal decisions for a variety of purposes. For the Ujjain district, land-use and land-cover categories (LULC) are split into four categories and are assessed using support vector machines and supervised learning.

Open/barren/wasteland (which includes rocky, shrub, and barren areas), built-up land utilized for habitation, forest (which includes both open and closed evergreen forests), and agricultural land (which includes crop land and agricultural plantations) were the categories of land that were included.

Figures 8 and 9 shows the classified LULC map for the research area for the years 2003 and 2023 by SVM algorithm, respectively, while Table 3 shows the LULC data for the ujjain district.

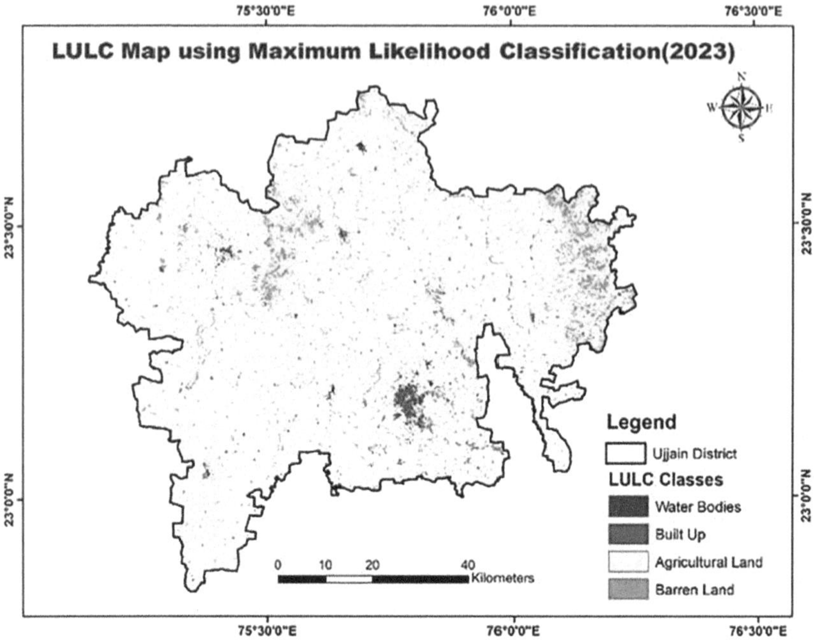

Fig. 6. LULC map for the year 2023 using MLC.

Table 2. Five LULC classes areas and rates of change from 2003 to 2023 using MLC.

LULC Class	2003 LULC Area		2023 LULC Area		Change between 2003 and 2023	
	Area (sq. km)	%	Area (sq. km)	%	Area (sq. km)	%
Water Bodies	2.85071	0.04675	10.147	0.16642	+7.29702	+0.119673
Built Up	60.2220	0.98765	138.220	2.26686	+77.9989	+1.279202
Cropland	5729.773	93.9697	5723.197	93.8619	−6.576	−0.107847
Barren Land	304.6187	4.99582	225.8987	3.70479	−78.72	−1.291028
Total	6097.464	100	6097.464	100	0.00	0.00

4 Discussion

The identified changes in land cover within the research area are depicted in Fig. 7 and Fig. 10. Our method for assessing land cover change was post-classification. But it's crucial to remember that the two image processing methods that were used each provided a different estimate of the area.

This is not unexpected given that the area estimate is impacted by the classification techniques selected. However, as every method produced data with respectable accuracy, we took into account all of the resulting area estimates for the assessment of land cover

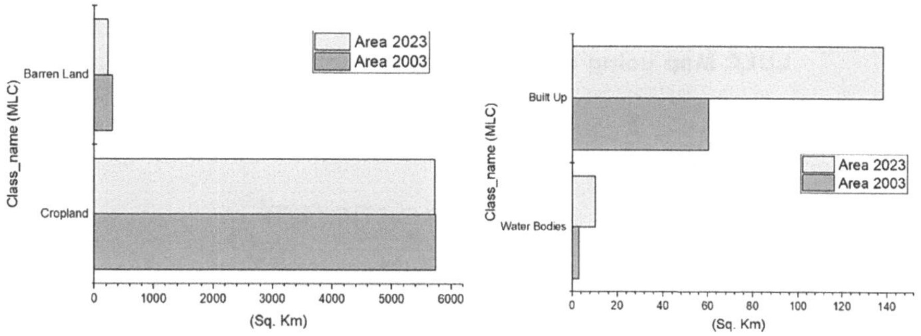

Fig. 7. Plot for Four LULC classes areas and rates of change from 2003 to 2023 by MLC.

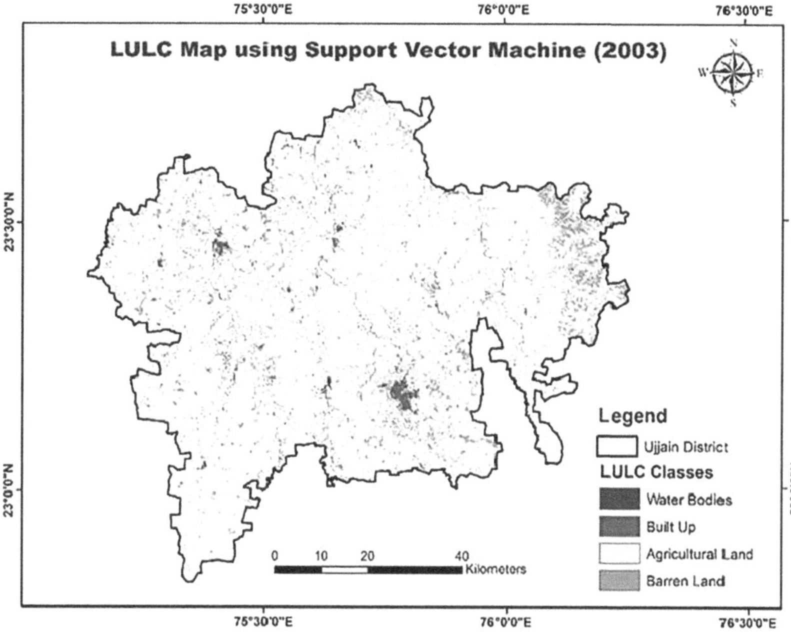

Fig. 8. LULC map for the year 2003 using SVM.

change.

$$\text{User Accuracy} = \frac{\text{Number of correctly classified pixels in each category}}{\text{Total number of classified pixel in that category (in row)}} \quad (1)$$

$$\text{Producer Accuracy} = \frac{\text{Number of correctly classified pixels in each category}}{\text{Total number of reference pixel in that category (in column)}} \quad (2)$$

Result validation is done by taking various points for class value and correspondingly determine the producer accuracy, user accuracy by using Eq. 1 and 2 and kappa coefficient

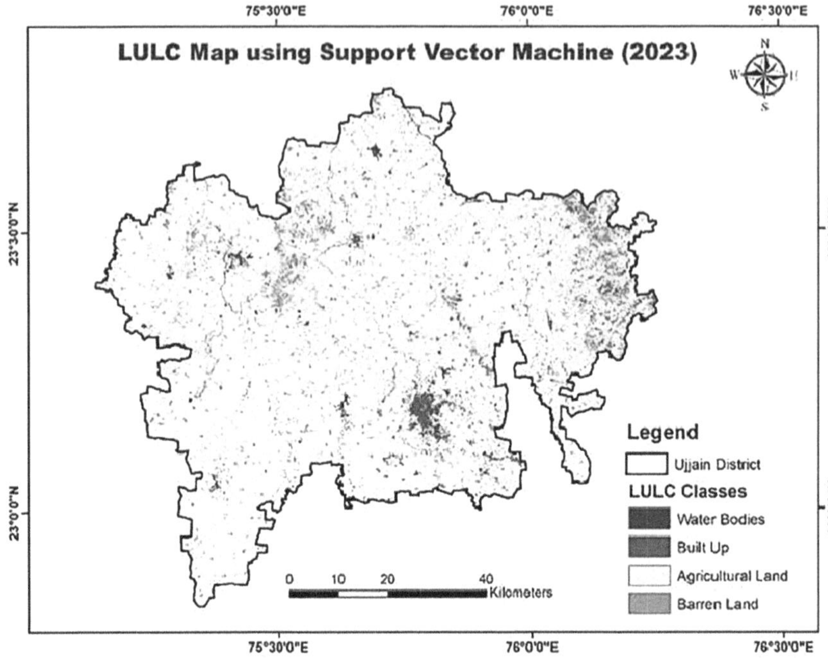

Fig. 9. LULC map for the year 2023 using SVM.

Table 3. Five LULC classes areas and rates of change from 2003 to 2023 using SVM.

LULC Class	2003 LULC Area		2023 LULC Area		Change between 2003 and 2023	
	Area (sq. km)	%	Area (sq. km)	%	Area (sq. km)	%
Water Bodies	12.47937	0.2046	29.02617	0.4760	16.5468	0.27137
Built Up	117.9198	1.93391	175.9445	2.8855	58.0247	0.95162
Cropland	5645.168	92.5822	5664.704	92.902	19.536	0.32039
Barren Land	321.8973	5.27919	227.7898	3.7358	−94.1075	−1.54339
Total	6097.464	100	6097.46	100	0.00	0.00

shown in Fig. 11. The change statistic was obtained by subtracting the findings. The findings indicate in Table 4.

These are given in a way that illustrates how contextual elements affect policy, regulatory, and economic and financial aspects, which in turn affect transportation availability

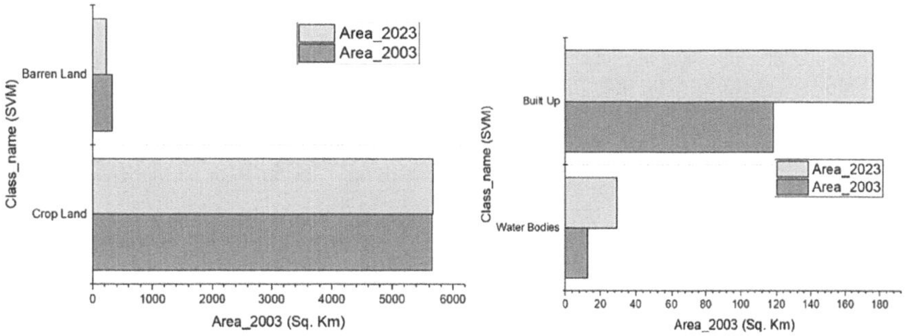

Fig. 10. Plot for Two LULC classes areas and rates of change from 2003 to 2023 by SVM.

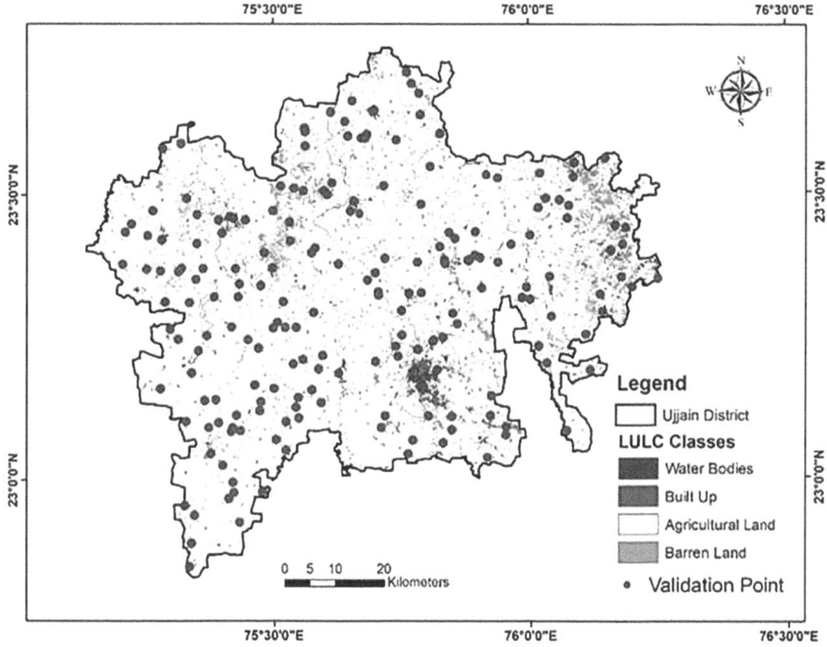

Fig. 11. Create Validation point to findout accuracy and kappa coefficient.

and investments as well as decisions about where to locate homes and businesses. In the Ujjain district, LULC changes between 2003 and 2023 were studied, along with their causes and effects on land resources. The study's main sources of data were socioeconomic databases and remote sensing. The findings demonstrated that LULC has changed significantly. The increase of built-up areas by replacing bare land was one of the main shifts. The findings showed a two-decade growth in both built-up and bare land areas.

Table 4. Classification accuracy assessment report

Class Value	MLC		SVM	
	Producer Accuracy (%)	User Accuracy (%)	Producer Accuracy (%)	User Accuracy (%)
Water Bodies	1	1	1	1
Built Up	0.777778	0.875	0.863636	0.904762
Crop Land	0.974026	0.9375	0.972789	0.940789
Barren Land	0.666667	0.857143	0.7	0.875
Kappa Coefficient	0.809783		0.844804	

5 Conclusions

The study to examine the two decadal influences on LULC change, particularly on the urbanization of ujjain city, is presented by this research work. This study demonstrated how the latest advancements in remote sensing (RS) and geographic information system (GIS) technologies may be used to construct efficient tools for mapping and recognizing changes in land use and cover area. The current study found that the built-up land (habitation) area is growing at a rate of 1.27% from last two decades, while the agricultural area is decreased by 0.108% plotted in Fig. 7 and Fig. 10. Policymakers should minimize their human intervention efforts, according to the developing trend in built-up areas they can use barren land alternatively. The study's outcomes highlight how important it is to thoroughly assess human activity and adjust suitable policies as necessary. This study can provide policymakers with a straightforward framework for developing initiatives related to ujjain district planning. Using land use maps is becoming a crucial part of the process of producing data for both macro and local planning. It has been suggested that using satellite images is a suitable method for creating land use maps.

This study's goal was to classify land use in Ujjain using SVM and MLC algorithms based on TM (Thematic Mapper) images from the Landsat 5 and Landsat 8 satellite. Two distinct methods were used to classify the images after the required adjustments and pre-processing. The evaluation's findings showed that, when it comes to land use mapping, the SVM performs better than the MLC algorithm, with an overall accuracy of 87.5% and a kappa coefficient of 0.844 shown in Table 4. The study represents that SVM algorithm's having greater accuracy and better consistency for extracting land use maps. This study affirmed that the suggested land use map and the appropriate use of the SVM algorithm can support sustainable development.

Acknowledgements. I would like to express my gratitude to everyone who has contributed, especially my family, friends and my mentor Dr. Sharda Haryani and Dr. V.B. Gupta. I would especially like to thanks School of Data Science and Forecasting, DAVV, Indore, M.P., for offering a research facility.

Disclosure of Interests. The authors declare that there is no conflict of interest.

References

1. Mas, J.F., Lemoine-Rodríguez, R., González-López, R., López-Sánchez, J., Piña-Garduño, A., Flores, H.: Land use/land cover change detection combining automatic processing and visual interpretation. Eur. J. Remote Sens. **50**, 626–635 (2017)
2. Gupta, P., Haryani, S., Gupta, V.B.: Analysis of land use and land cover change detection for indore district of malwa plateau region using supervised machine learning. Inter. J. Exper. Res. Rev. **38**, 154–163 (2024)
3. Cerovski-Darriau, C., Roering, J.J.: Influence of anthropogenic land-use change on hillslope erosion in the Waipaoa River Basin. New Zealand. Earth Surf. Process. Landf. **41**, 2167–2176 (2016)
4. Pal, S., Kundu, S., Mahato, S.: Groundwater potential zones for sustainable management plans in a river basin of India and Bangladesh. J. Clean. Prod. **257**, 120311 (2020)
5. Mahato, S., Pal, S.: Groundwater potential mapping in a rural river basin by union (OR) and intersection (AND) of four multi-criteria decision-making models. Nat. Resour. Res. **28**, 523–545 (2019)
6. Wittke, S., Yu, X., Karjalainen, M., Hyyppä, J., Puttonen, E.: Comparison of two dimensional multitemporal Sentinel-2 data with three-dimensional remote sensing data sources for forest inventory parameter estimation over a boreal forest. Int. J. Appl. Earth Obs. Geoinf. **76**, 167–178 (2019)
7. Viana, C.M., Girão, I., Rocha, J.: Long-term satellite image time-series for land use/land cover change detection using refined open source data in a rural region. Remote Sens. **11**, 1104 (2019)
8. Ma, L., Liu, Y., Zhang, X., Ye, Y., Yin, G., Johnson, B.A.: Deep learning in remote sensing applications: a meta-analysis and review. ISPRS J. Photogramm. Remote Sens. **152**, 166–177 (2019)
9. Shih, H.C., Stow, D.A., Tsai, Y.H.: Guidance on and comparison of machine learning classifiers for Landsat-based land cover and land use mapping. Int. J. Remote Sens. **40**, 1248–1274 (2019)
10. Al-Ahmadi, F., Hames, A.: Comparison of four classification methods to extract land use and land cover from raw satellite images for some remote arid areas, kingdom of Saudi Arabia. Earth **20**, 167–191 (2009)
11. Maxwell, A.E., Warner, T.A., Fang, F.: Implementation of machine-learning classification in remote sensing: an applied review. Int. J. Remote Sens. **39**, 2784–2817 (2018)
12. Camps-Valls, G., Benediktsson, J.A., Bruzzone, L., Chanussot, J.: Introduction to the issue on advances in remote sensing image processing. IEEE J. Sel. Top. Signal Process. **5**, 365–369 (2011)
13. Yang, C. Wu, Ding, K., Shi, T., Li, Q., Wang, J.: Improving land use/land cover classification by integrating pixel unmixing and decision tree methods. Remote Sens. **9**, 1222 (2017)
14. Manandhar, R., Odeh, I.O., Ancev, T.: Improving the accuracy of land use and land cover classification of Landsat data using post-classification enhancement. Remote Sens. **1**, 330–344 (2009)
15. Huang, C., Davis, L.T.J.: An assessment of support vector machines for land cover classification. Int. J. Remote Sens. **23**, 725–749 (2002)
16. Thenkabail, P.S., Schull, M., Turral, H.: Ganges and Indus river basin land use/land cover (LULC) and irrigated area mapping using continuous streams of MODIS data. Remote Sens. Environ. **95**, 317–341 (2005)
17. Talukdar S., Singha P., Mahato S. Shahfahad, Pal S., Liou Y., Rahman A.: Land-Use Land-Cover Classification by Machine Learning Classifiers for Satellite Observations - A Review, vol. 12, pp. 1–24 (2020)

18. Knorn, J., Rabe, A., Radeloff, V., Kuemmerle, T., Kozak, J., Hostert, P.: Land cover mapping of large areas using chain classification of neighboring Landsat satellite images. Remote Sens. Environ. **113**, 957–964 (2009)
19. Arshad, A., Arif, A., Singh, S.K.: Study of urban land use dynamics in Srinagar city using geospatial approach. Bull. Environ. Sci. Res. **1**, 18–24 (2012)
20. Choudhary, K., Boori, M.S., Kupriyanov, A.: Spatial modelling for natural and environmental vulnerability through remote sensing and GIS in Astrakhan, Russia. Egyptian J. Remote Sensing Space Sci. **21**, 139–147 (2018)
21. https://earthexplorer.usgs.gov/ Accessed 24 January 2024

Computational Approaches to Calculate Stresses on Polycarbonate Specimen of Rectangular Shape and Compare with Trapezoidal Specimen with Experimental Validation

Om Prakash Sondhiya[1(✉)] and Roopesh Tiwari[2]

[1] Department of Mechanical Engineering, Institute of Engineering and Technology, DAVV, Indore, MP, India
osondhiya@ietdavv.edu.in

[2] Department of Mechanical Engineering, SAGE University, Indore, MP, India

Abstract. Photoelasticity is a viable experimental approach in mechanics and materials science that allows for the visual evaluation and analysis of stress distribution in transparent or translucent materials. This non-destructive testing technique visualizes stress on a model under load by taking advantage of a material feature known as birefringence or double refraction. The procedure entails creating a physical model that resembles real-world structures, applying mechanical stress to the model, and carefully selecting a suitable photo elastic material with birefringence. When the material is stressed, it exhibits birefringence, which alters its optical properties. As a result, different stress levels are mirrored in the pattern, making it easier to identify stress concentrations and potential failure points while also providing insights into how materials perform under different loading conditions. In this investigation, a photoelasticity unit was employed to assess both rectangular and trapezoidal specimens under four distinct loads. The experimental analysis results were then compared to those obtained from the ANSYS simulation tool (Finite Element Analysis). Because of its user-friendly interface, the software serves as a virtual laboratory, allowing simulations with user-defined problem parameters adapted to the user's specific conditions. As per the observations graphs in rectangular specimens are linear in character, with sharp edges, but graph lines in trapezoidal specimen form curves, with no sharp edges visible.

Keywords: First Isochromatic and isoclinic fringes · Photo elasticity · rectangular specimen · trapezoidal specimens

1 Introduction

1.1 About Photoelasticity

Photoelasticity requires very simple optics, making the experiment straightforward to set up. Photoelasticity primarily produces contours of constant principal stress/strain difference (isochromatic fringes) and constant principal stress/strain direction (isoclinic

V. B. Gupta et al. (Eds.): IBCD 2024, CCIS 2413, pp. 63–73, 2025.
https://doi.org/10.1007/978-3-031-87511-3_5

fringes). It can be used in transmission or reflection modes [1–3]. Many difficulties can only be understood by considering the peripheral field's whole character. Fringe density is a valuable metric for detecting areas of high stress and probable material removal places to reduce the weight to its ideal level. To reduce quantitative data, it is necessary to acquire isochromatic and isoclinic values at each time point.

Any interferometry technique requires the capacity to organize the fringes. Identifying common fringe patterns for a variety of difficulties is one of the simplest methods to accomplish this. This is easily performed by using Polari scope to simulate fringe patterns [4]. Because of the use of simulation, it is suitable for carrying out both real experiments and FEA simulations. The software not only displays the theoretical fringe order and isoclinic value as determined by standard polariscope testing equipment, but it also models solutions using the Theory of Elasticity [5]. This tool simplifies the application of compensation approaches to any place of interest, as well as the understanding of fringe ordering. The software supports two compensatory techniques: Ramesh, K. [6]. Because the fringe fields are realistically reproduced using Jones calculus [7], the learner may understand the need of first determining the isoclinic angle at the place of interest, as well as the heuristic information derived from the fringe fields for data interpretation. This understanding can assist one understand the complexities involved in the development of digital photoelasticity. Several experimental strategies used the carrier fringe method to improve fringe field information by Sampson [8].

The software also has the ability to add carrier fringes to any model at any angle and with varying densities [9]. The simulation provides a basic wedge-type carrier, the parameters of which are user-defined. Carrier fringes can be used to retrieve data from weak birefringent materials like glass. To conduct a photoelastic experiment, models made of birefringent materials must meet a number of basic requirements [10]. The polariscope must be transparent to the light passing through it, and this transparency might be lost for one of two reasons: (1) a decrease in the indexes of refraction of the constituent materials, or (2) trapped air. In both cases, the photoelastic medium's properties change, causing light dispersion and, as a result, a decrease in the material's transparency [11]. Another consideration considered is the possibility that the material will be influenced by "the border effect," a phenomenon connected with water absorption and evaporation in plastic materials. This phenomenon alters the model's dimensions, resulting in changes in internal stresses [12]. Photoelastic constant represents the photoelastic sensitivity to induced stresses on the model, which is a very important attribute. When the material is loaded, a highly elastic module ensures that it retains its shape [13].

Because of the link between these two qualities, the photoelastic constant and the elasticity module, a third quality must be considered. This metric, known as the figure of merit, assesses the sensitivity of specific resins. In an ideal world, the value of the figure of merit should be as high as humanly possible and remain constant throughout the test [14]. In a perfect scenario, the model materials would function in clinical conditions exactly like the actual thing, which is what the researcher intends to replicate. Models used to imitate tooth tissues should have properties similar to enamel and dentin [15]. These structures receive the chewing efforts and convey the pressures to the tooth support tissues. When imitating supporting tissues, such as the alveolar bone in this case, the photoelastic material must be able to function within its elastic capacity. Furthermore, it provides a photoelastic response that is most compatible with the load intensity applied on photoelastic models, specifically "loads that best simulate a genuine condition" [16]. Because it is impossible to faithfully reproduce all of the factors that act in the oral medium, at the very least, a material should be used that is capable of providing the photoelastic answer that is most compatible with the load intensity that is imposed on the photoelastic models when they are subjected to the stresses. To guarantee that the fringes observed on the polariscope are distinct and well-defined, the results can be extended to the clinical situation. Rossamanith [17] investigated the photoelastic properties of a composite model with HY951 as the infill material. Zhu and Shukla [18] examined the stress distribution for a photoelastic chip tool interface with rake angles ranging from -10 to 20 degrees. Jain and Kumar employed the photoelasticity approach to review their stress analysis [19]. Jones and Hozos [20] used photoelasticity to show the stress distribution on a flat plate with an oval hole. Zandman et al. [21] used photoelastic and finite element methods to compare the stress distribution of an internal combustion engine piston. Mekalke et al. [22] used various mesh types to evaluate the effect of increased loading on a pre-stretched plate with a circular hole, as did Shrivastava and Chandrakar [23].

2 Methodology

The methodology opted for measurement by photoelasticity method by following steps shown below. Many polymers have sufficient birefringence to serve as photo elastic specimen materials and requires very simple optics, making the experiment straight forward to set up.

2.1 Selecting the Material

By photoelasticity experimental measurement primarily common polymers, such as polymethylmethacrylate (PMMA) and polycarbonate, can be overly brittle or intolerant of localized straining. Homalite-100 has long been a popular general-use material. Another useful material is epoxy, which can be cast between glass plates, but this process is rarely used for two-dimensional work. We chose polystyrene because to its clarity, rigidity, brittleness, and moderate strength.

2.2 Making a Template

If you need to make numerous parts of the same shape, begin by machining a template out of metal. This template serves as a guide for creating many Photoelasticity specimens with similar shapes. To ensure smooth machining and avoid problems, undercut the template by around 0.050 in. This undercutting should go through roughly half of the template's thickness on one side. This precaution is taken to avoid contact with the router bit during the machining process, ensuring exact and uniform replication of the intended shape throughout all specimens.

2.3 Drilling the Specimen

If the specimen has holes, such as those used for load-application points with pins, they should be thoroughly drilled with a sharp bit and lots of coolant, such as ethyl alcohol, kerosene, or water; otherwise, undesired fringes will form around the edge of the hole. The specimen should be supported with a sacrificial piece of comparable material to prevent chipping on the back side as the drill breaks through. To reduce heat-induced fringes, make two or three passes with the drill bit into the specimen, adding coolant between each pass.

2.4 Machining the Specimen

If the specimen is machined "from scratch," make extremely light cuts with a sharp milling cutter to avoid overheating the completed edges. To decrease heating, use a coolant such as ethyl alcohol, kerosene, or water. If a template is utilized, the specimen's shape is roughed out with a bandsaw using a sharp, thin bandsaw blade. Because the blade will heat the material and nick the edge, leave a generous tolerance of about 1/8 in.

All around the template edge. To create the model's edge, use a router with a high-speed carbide router bit, preferably with fine multiple flutes. A series of two centering pins—the first with a larger diameter than the router bit and the second the same size—should be used to remove excess material quickly and then in a very controlled manner, leaving the specimen with the same dimensions as the template.

2.5 Loaded Specimen Viewing

Once the specimen has been taken from the template and completely cleaned, it can be loaded and analyzed with a polariscope. The polariscope is an optical tool used to see the fringes caused by stresses in the material. For efficient observation, the polariscope's elements must be positioned in such a way that light may propagate perpendicular to the plane of the specimen. If a loading frame is needed to provide stress to the specimen, it should be placed between the first and last elements of the polariscope.

When it comes to lighting, monochromatic light is best for producing sharp fringes. However, the light source does not have to be coherent, and it may or may not be collimated as it travels through the sample. This variety of light sources provides realistic possibilities for experimentation and analysis in stress visualization.

2.6 Recording the Fringe Patterns

To record digitally, attach a camera or imaging equipment to the polariscope and capture photos of the fringe patterns.

2.7 Calibrating the Material

The sensitivity of a photo elastic material is defined by its fringe constant (f_σ). This parameter relates the value N to a certain fringe, the thickness (h) of the specimen in the light-propagation direction, and the differential between the primary stresses (σ_1 - σ_2) in the plane normal to the light-propagation direction. The relationship is written as Eq. 1.

$$\sigma_1 - \sigma_2 = N^*f_\sigma / h \quad (1)$$

To estimate the value of f_σ, an experiment is undertaken using a simple geometric model subjected to known loading. A frequent calibration specimen for this purpose is a disk in diametral compression. Researchers can determine the fringe constant using this experimental approach, allowing for more accurate interpretation and study of stress distribution in photo elastic materials.

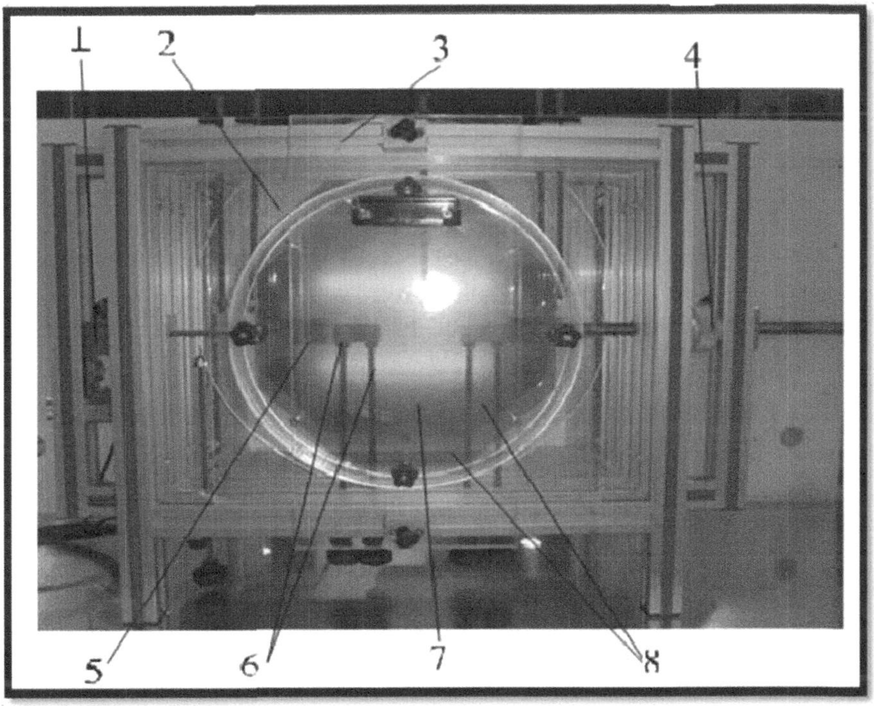

Fig. 1. Photo Elasticity Unit (1. E-C: load cell, 2. P-D: translucent diffusion plate, 3. S-A: translucent supporting surface, 4. T2: force screw, 5. M1: clamp and screws to fasten the specimens.6. T1: screws to apply pressure on the specimens, 7. D-C: discs with grid in between, 8. P: double effect polarizing filters)

2.8 Interpreting the Fringe Patterns:

Two sorts of patterns can be produced: isochromatic and isoclinic. These patterns are related to the primary stress differences and principal stress orientations, as illustrated in Fig. 1.

3 Calculation of Stress in Photoelastic Material

Formula Used: $\sigma = N * f(\lambda) / e$, Where: N = Fringe Order.

$f(\lambda)$ = Fringe factor (const.),

e = Thickness of Material,

Material Used: Polycarbonate,

Fringe factor for polycarbonate = 13.150 N/mm,

Thickness of Material Used: 5.0 mm.

3.1 Data Collected for Rectangular Specimen from Photoelasticity Unit for Four Distinct Loading Condition

3.2 Modelling and Analysis Using ANSYS

For that experiment it involves using of two specimens of EFO kit we are develop the design and simulation using Ansys software and applying different force and check a various stress at location and make graphs for check the various stress (Fig. 2).

Boundary Condition:

1) Pre-processing: Model the specimen with solid works and import it in iges (initial graphics exchange format) format. Meshing is done with polycarbonate material.

As per the loading condition tensile load has been applied for the simulation.

2) Solution: Solve the model by tensile loading condition.

3) Post processing: Stress is observed for maximum stress theory shown in Fig. 3.

When a loaded photoelastic specimen (or a photoelastic coating applied to an ordinary specimen) is combined with other optical elements and illuminated with an ordinary light source, it produces fringe patterns that correspond to the difference in principal stresses in a plane normal to the light propagation direction.

4 Results and Discussions

The use of both photoelasticity and ANSYS models revealed consistent stress patterns in polycarbonate specimens.

The fringe patterns seen during the studies closely matched the simulated stress distribution. There were some slight inconsistencies, which can be attributable to factors such as material heterogeneity or simulation model assumptions.

The tiny circular specimen was evaluated under four different weights using a photo elasticity instrument. The results obtained are compared to those obtained from ANSYS simulation.

At lower loads, the results obtained from ANSYS closely align with the experimental findings. For instance, at 50N, the stress values derived from ANSYS simulation and experimental measures are 1.603 N/mm^2 and 1.578 N/mm^2 respectively. At 100 N, the stress values from ANSYS simulation and experimentation are 2.878 N/mm^2 and 2.893 N/mm^2, respectively. However, at higher loading conditions, the experimental results deviate more significantly from the ANSYS simulation outcomes.

At 200 N, for example, the percentage deviation reaches more. This higher deviation in experimental results at higher loads is attributed to the progressive deformation of the

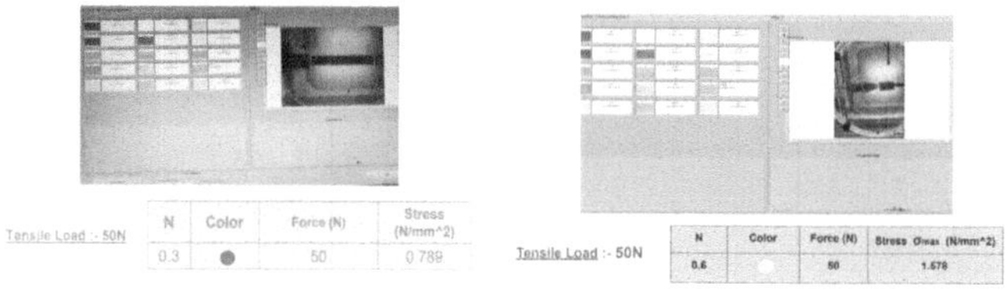

(a) At load 50N for rectangular and trapezoidal specimens.

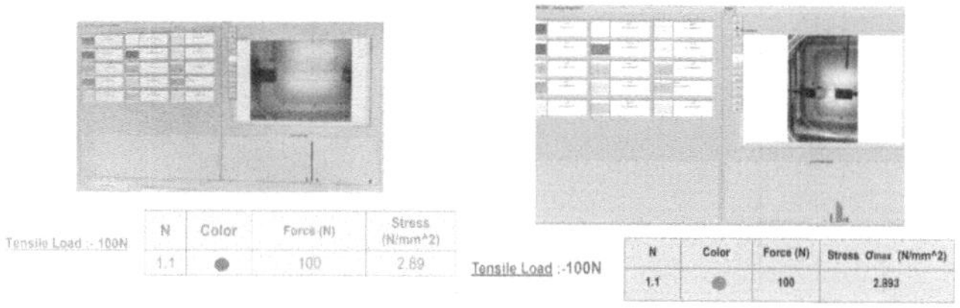

(b) At load 100N for rectangular and trapezoidal specimens.

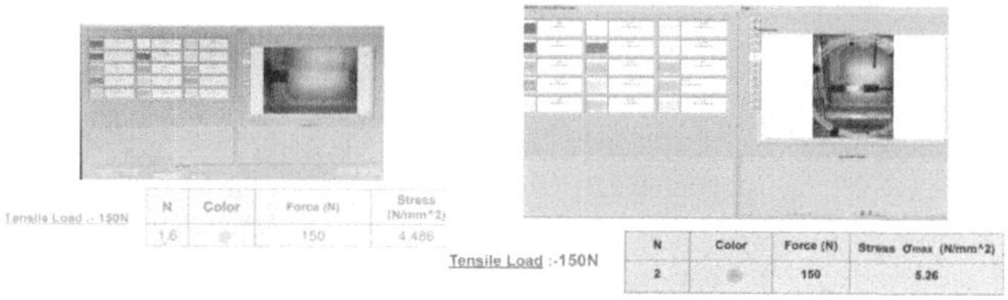

(c) At Load 150 N for rectangular and trapezoidal specimens.

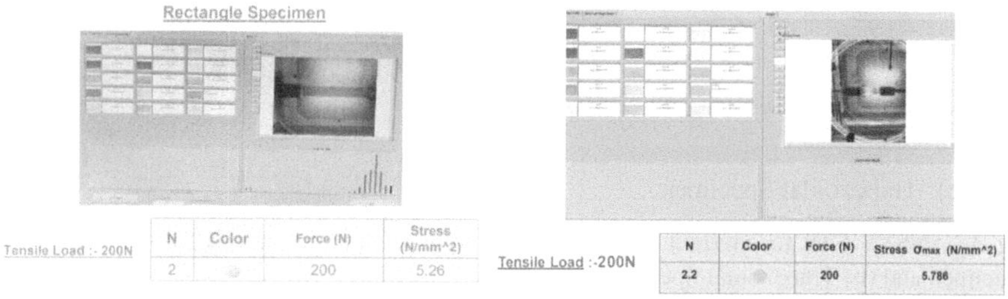

(d) At Load 200 N for rectangular and trapezoidal specimens.

Fig. 2. Experimental readings at different loading conditions (a) 50 N (b) 100 N (c)150 N (d) 200 N for rectangular and trapezoidal specimens.

internal structure of the material shown in Tables 1 and 2 for rectangular specimen and trapezoidal specimen respectively.

The increased deviation observed in experimental results at higher loads can be attributed to the progressive deformation of the internal structure of the material. In summary, the comparative analysis emphasizes the reliability of both experimental and computational methods, underscoring the importance of integrating these approaches for a comprehensive understanding of stress in both the materials shown in Fig. 4.

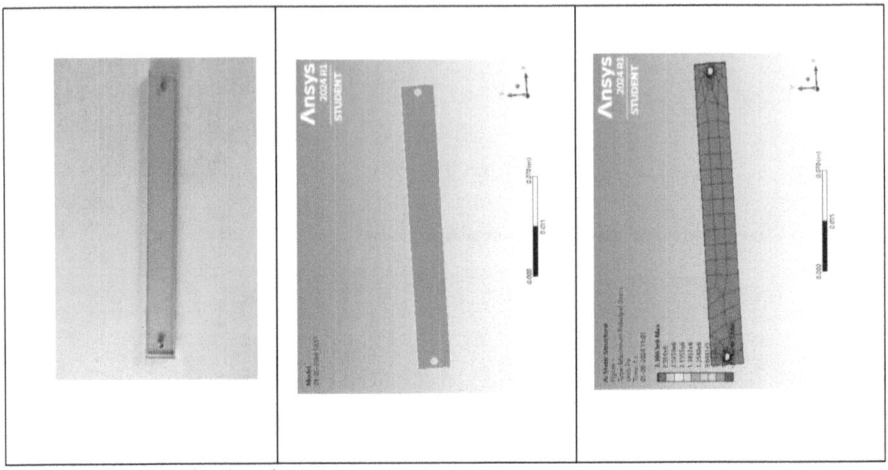

(a) Rectangular Specimen

Actual Specimen	3-D Design of Specimen	A Stress

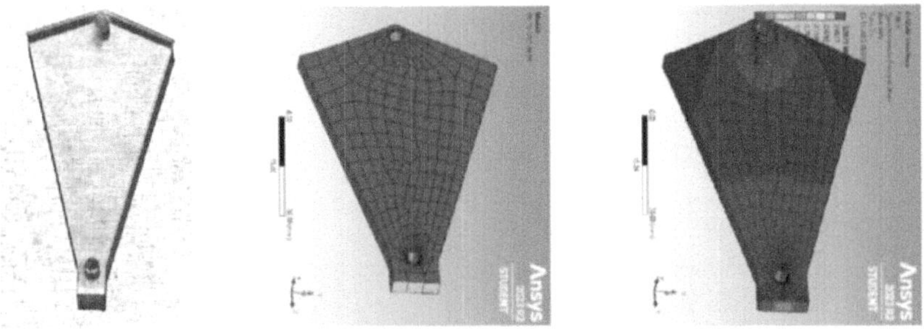

(b) Trapezoidal Specimen

Fig. 3. ANSYS GUI to interpret the result at different loading conditions for (a) Rectangular Specimen and (b) Trapezoidal Specimen.

Table 1. Tensile stress for rectangular specimen

Force (N)	Stress (N/mm^2) (By Ansys)	Experimental Stress (N/mm^2)
50	0.330	0.789
100	1.956	2.89
150	4.953	4.486
200	6.108	5.26

Table 2. Tensile stress for trapezoidal specimen

Force (N)	Stress (N/mm^2) (By Ansys)	Experimental Stress (N/mm^2)
50	1.603	1.578
100	2.878	2.893
150	4.81	5.26
200	6.414	5.786

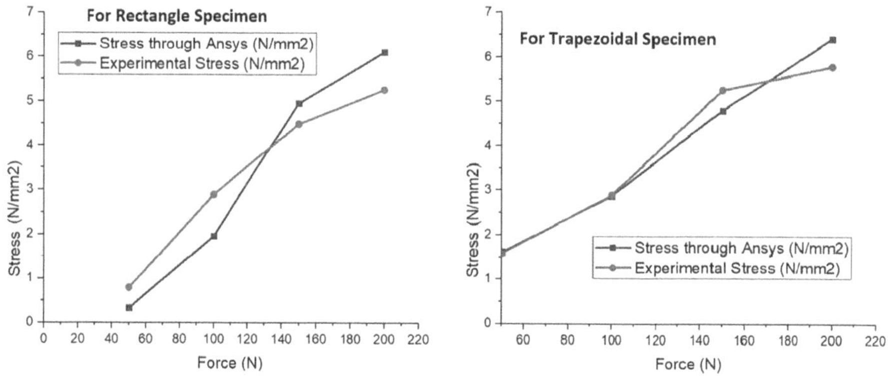

Fig. 4. Tensile stress analysis on rectangular and trapezoidal specimen

5 Conclusions

This experimental method excels in determining internal stresses within structures that provide difficulties due to their elaborate geometries or exposure to complex loads. It is an effective tool for understanding the inner workings of forces within structures that are both uniquely formed and subject to various complications. Offers accurate full-field values of the principal normal stress difference in the model's plane; it uniquely provides the value of the nonvanishing principal normal stress along the model's perimeter, where stresses are typically highest; it provides full-field values of the principal stress directions, also known as stress trajectories; it can be used for both static and dynamic investigations; and it only requires a minimum investment in tools and materials for routine.

In contrast, the photoelastic technique appears to be a simpler and less burdensome alternative for resolving challenges with models of arbitrary shapes, providing a more efficient solution than analytical methods and time-consuming mathematical formulae. In comparison to older methods, digital photoelasticity significantly simplifies and accelerates the collection and processing of fringe patterns in photographs, streamlining the entire process of acquiring and analyzing complicated patterns. The technology's efficiency makes it an attractive option for use in analysis alongside other analytical approaches such as photoelasticity, which delivers closed-form answers and demonstrates its dependability. Graphs in rectangular specimens are linear in character, with sharp edges, but graph lines in trapezoidal specimen form curves, with no sharp edges visible.

Acknowledgements. I would like to express my gratitude to everyone who has contributed, especially my family, friends and my mentor Dr. Roopesh Tiwari. I would especially like to give thanks SAGE University, Indore, M.P., for offering a research facility.

Disclosure of Interests. The authors declare that there is no conflict of interest.

References

1. Ramesh, K.: Digital Photoelasticity Advanced Techniques and Applications. Springer-Verlag, Berlin Heidelberg (2000)
2. Ramesh, K.: Experimental Stress Analysis. IIT Madras, Chennai, India (2009). https://home.iitm.ac.in/kramesh/ESA.html
3. Majumdar, T.S., Behringer, R.P.: Contact force measurements and stress-induced anisotropy in granular materials. Nature **435**, 1079–1082 (2005)
4. Durelli, A.J., Shukla, A.: Identification of isochromatic fringes. Exp. Mech. **23**(1), 111–119 (1983)
5. Srinath, L.S., Ramesh, K., Ramamurti, V.: Determination of characteristic parameters in three-dimensional photoelasticity. Opt. Eng. **27**(3), 225–230 (1988)
6. Ramesh, K.: A simple approach to photoelastic calibration of glass using digital photoelasticity. J. Non-Cryst. Solids **378**, 7–14 (2013)
7. Srinath, L.S.: Scattered Light Photoelasticity. Tata McGraw-Hill, New Delhi (1983)
8. Sampson, T., Robert, C.: A stress-optic law for photoelastic analysis of orthotropic composites. Exp. Mech. **10**(5), 210–215 (1970)
9. Flores-Johnson, E.A.: Photoelastic evaluation of fiber surface-treatments on the interfacial performance of a polyester fiber/epoxy model composite. Compos. Part A Appl. Sci. Manuf. **42**(8), 1017–1024 (2011)
10. Ramesh, K., Yadav, A.K., Vijay, A.P.: Classification of crack-tip isochromatics in orthotropic composites. Eng. Fract. Mech. **53**(1), 1–16 (1996)
11. Pih, H., Knight, C.E.: Photoelastic analysis of anisotropic fiber reinforced composites. J. Comp. Mater. **3**(1), 94–107 (1969)
12. Pathak, P.M., Ramesh, K.: Validation of finite element modelling through photoelastic fringe contours. Int. J. Numer. Methods Biomed. Eng. **15**(4), 229–238 (1999)
13. Reddy, J.N.: An Introduction to the Finite Element Method, vol. 2, no. 1. McGraw-Hill, New York (1993)
14. Agarwal, B.D., Chaturvedi, S.K.: Improved birefringent composites and assessment of photoelastic theories. Fiber Sci. Technol. **11**, 399–412 (1970)
15. Haciane, A., Rabah, P.: Photoelastic and numerical analysis of a sphere/plan contact problem. Procedia Eng. **114**, 277–283 (2015)
16. Etsion, I.: Elastic–plastic contact analysis of a sphere and a rigid flat. ASME J. Appl. Mech. **69**(5), 657–662 (2002)
17. Rossamanith, H.V., Shukla, A.: Dynamic photoelastic investigation of stress waves with running cracks. Exp. Mech. **21**, 415–422 (1981)
18. Zhu, C.Y., Shukla, A., Sadd, M.H.: Prediction of dynamic contact loads in granular assemblies. ASME J. App. Mech. **58**, 341–352 (1991)
19. Prabhakaran, R.: Fabrication of birefringent anisotropic model materials. Exp. Mech. **20**, 320–321 (1980)

20. Jones, N., Hozos, D.: A study of the stresses around elliptical holes in a flat plate. J. Eng. Ind. **45**, 23–37 (1971)
21. Zandman, F., Redner, S., Riegner, E.I.: Reinforcing effect of birefringent coatings. Exp. Mech. **2**(2), 55–64 (1962)
22. Mekalke, G.C., Kavade, M.V., Deshpande, S.S.: Analysis of a plate with a circular hole by FEM. IOSR J. Mech. Civ. Eng., 25–30 (2014)
23. Chandrakar, H., Shrivastava, R.: Analysis of stress using photoelasticity technique-a review. IJARIIE **4**, 68–76 (2018)

Balancing Privacy and Utility in E-Healthcare Data Analysis: A Comprehensive Review

Bhavana A. Khivsara[1] (✉) and Maya Rathore[2]

[1] Department of Computer Science and Engineering, Oriental University, Indore, Madhya Pradesh, India
bhavana.khivsara@gmail.com
[2] Department of Computer Science and Engineering, Oriental University, Indore, Madhya Pradesh, India

Abstract. The digitalization of healthcare has brought about a significant transformation in data management, presenting intricate privacy challenges due to the sensitive nature of e-healthcare information. This survey delves into robust privacy-preserving methods tailored for e-healthcare data analytics, pivotal for instilling trust in electronic healthcare systems. It examines encryption, access controls, and anonymization techniques as essential safeguards for protecting patient da-ta integrity while enabling sophisticated data analytics. Specifically, this survey critically evaluates the efficacy of Homomorphic Encryption, Secure Multi-Party Computation, Differential Privacy, and Anonymization, Federated Learning, and Block chain-based approaches in ensuring data privacy in e-healthcare contexts. By elucidating their roles in privacy preservation, this study endeavors to strike a delicate balance between the imperative of privacy and the utility of e-healthcare data for deriving valuable medical insights. The literature review section meticulously scrutinizes existing anonymity-based privacy preservation strategies in e-healthcare, elucidating key discoveries and insights. Further-more, it offers a concise overview of privacy-preserving techniques, underlining the paramount importance of privacy while maximizing the utility of healthcare data for research and operational purposes in the realm of data analytics.

Keywords: Data Analytics · Privacy preserving · healthcare · anonymization · data utility

1 Introduction

1.1 Background and Motivation

The digitalization of healthcare has sparked a revolutionary transformation in the storage, sharing, and analysis of medical data, particularly in the realm of data analytics [26]. Electronic healthcare data, often denoted as e-healthcare data, encom-passes a vast array of sensitive information, including patient records, medical histories, diagnostic reports, and genetic data [77]. While these data hold immense promise for enhancing healthcare outcomes, they also raise profound concerns regarding patient privacy and

V. B. Gupta et al. (Eds.): IBCD 2024, CCIS 2413, pp. 74–94, 2025.
https://doi.org/10.1007/978-3-031-87511-3_6

data security. Ensuring the preservation of privacy in e-healthcare data is of paramount importance [77]. Patients' personal information, such as medical conditions, treatments, and genetic profiles, is inherently sensitive and confidential. Unauthorized access, data breaches, or misuse of this information can lead to severe consequences, including identity theft, discrimination, or compromised medical treatments. Therefore, the adoption of robust privacy preservation mechanisms is critical to instill and uphold trust in electronic healthcare systems. According to the survey [26] several privacy breaches, including the Massachusetts Group Insurance Commission's release of health data, which was re-identified using voter records, and the Washington State Department of Health's release of hospitalization data, which was matched with accident reports. She also notes that U.S. Census data could be re-identified using basic demographic details. These examples highlight the need for stronger privacy-preserving techniques. According to survey privacy can be hampered due to some attributes present in the data even if the unique attributes are removed. The survey details are summarized in Fig. 1, where the details given about how the different combinations of attributes have a different impact on the re-identification in the published data. Figure 1 demonstrates the need for sophisticated techniques to address privacy issues in datasets. Three re-identification scenarios are presented, with higher re-identification due to zip codes and lower re-identification due to generalization of residence. This highlights the global problem of privacy preservation while offering higher knowledge.

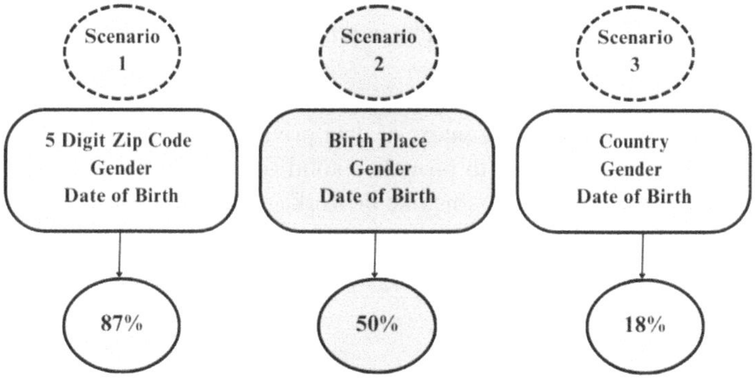

Fig. 1. Impact of different attributes in user re-identification

There are three important challenges while handling personal data, which encompasses basic as well as sensitive information about individuals.

- Balancing privacy and utility: ensuring user privacy while enabling effective data extraction by analysts.
- Safeguarding against personal data misuse: Promoting fair decision-making and curbing discriminatory profiling.
- Improving data quality for societal benefit: Enhancing data quality for more effective mining and decision-making in situations of limited or low-quality data.

Understanding how the issues listed above are interconnected is essential. One way to reduce the misuse of personal data and guarantee its appropriate use is to strike a balance between privacy and utility. Inadequate anonymization techniques or poor dataset quality are common causes of privacy breaches. If a dataset does not provide the desired insights with little effort, it is considered low quality. Achieving all three objectives at the same time requires careful consideration of data attributes, data preprocessing, and anonymization methods. To address the challenges of the privacy versus utility trade-off, a variety of anonymization methods were developed. Unfortunately, there is a serious lack of data-centric methods, which considers the type of data in the privacy domain, and only a few methods have considered the properties of data during their anonymization. Furthermore, in the privacy sector, relatively few prior research have emphasized the necessity of data-, attribute-, or sensitive-based techniques.

1.2 Major Contributions of This Paper

- We discuss the major research tracks in the privacy domain and comparison of each domain by providing details on strength, weakness, privacy trade-offs and specific use cases in e-healthcare.
- We discuss with a particular focus on non-cryptographic anonymization methods. These methods have emerged to ad-dress the balance between privacy and utility.
- We spotlight a range of privacy-enhancing technologies commonly employed to safeguard personal data across di-verse formats. In: light of rapidly increasing digitization, we suggest intriguing research paths that require immediate attention from the privacy community.
- To the best of the authors' knowledge, this work discusses the current methods used for data anonymization in the context of data privacy and data utility from a much broader perspective. We hope to provide a solid foundation for future research by making a timely contribution to this line of work.

2 Privacy Preserving Data Analysis Publishing and Major Research Tracks

2.1 Privacy Preserving Data Analysis

In this section, we provide an elucidation of the privacy-preserving data analysis publishing (PPDP) process, delineating its principal steps. Additionally, we delve into the major research avenues within the realm of PPDP. Illustrated in Fig. 2 is a conceptual overview of PPDP aimed at facilitating the secondary utilization of personal data. The PPDP process involves five steps [78]: obtaining data from relevant individuals, preprocessing it, preserving privacy, allowing data analysts or miners to mine it, and analyzing it using advanced technologies like data mining or machine learning. The insights gleaned from this analysis are applied to improve practical services like healthcare, smart cities, navigation, and recommendation systems. Data sharing is essential in enhancing the quality and efficacy of data-driven services.

Despite numerous studies aimed at tackling privacy concerns in PPDP, significant Privacy-Utility trade-offs remain challenging [51, 56, 78]. We illustrate this trade-off

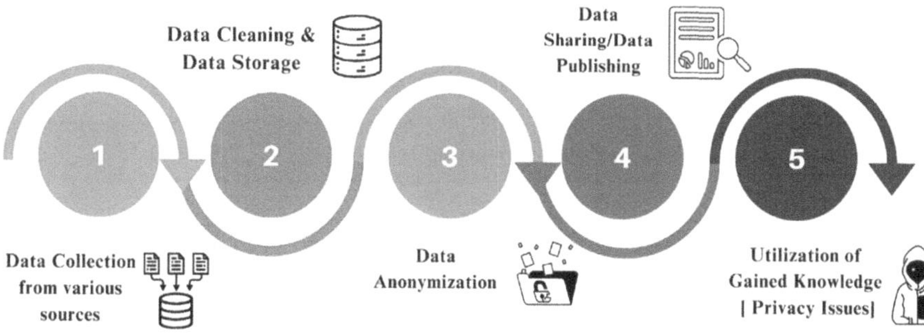

Fig. 2. Privacy Preserving Data Analysis Publishing Scenario

in Fig. 3. This trade-off involves preserving the original data's semantics. Although the proliferation of various privacy-preserving methods, achieving a balance between privacy and utility remains a formidable challenge. Despite the introduction of numerous techniques, including advanced anonymization methods and strict privacy parameters, effectively navigating this trade-off is elusive.

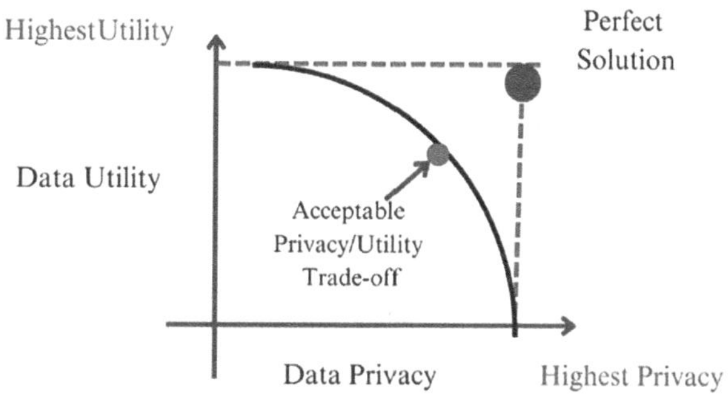

Fig. 3. Privacy-Utility Trade-off

The inherent difficulty lies in preserving the privacy of sensitive data while maintaining its utility for analysis and decision-making purposes. Despite ongoing efforts to develop and refine privacy-preserving methodologies, achieving an optimal balance between these conflicting objectives remains an enduring challenge in the field.

2.2 Major Research Tracks in Privacy Preserving Data Publishing

This section explores the Anonymity-based preserving privacy in the context of E-Healthcare. Figure 4 give insights on different Privacy Preserving Techniques- Cryptographic, Non-Cryptographic, Hybrid and Decentralized. This section provides an in detail exploration of the existing literature on this subject, highlighting key findings and insights Table 1 presents the comparisons of different Privacy-Preserving Techniques. In: this section we focus majorly on non-cryptographic anonymization method-Anonymity based methods which are very prominent, simple to implement and having less computational complexity and overhead, hence are explored in depth in the further section.

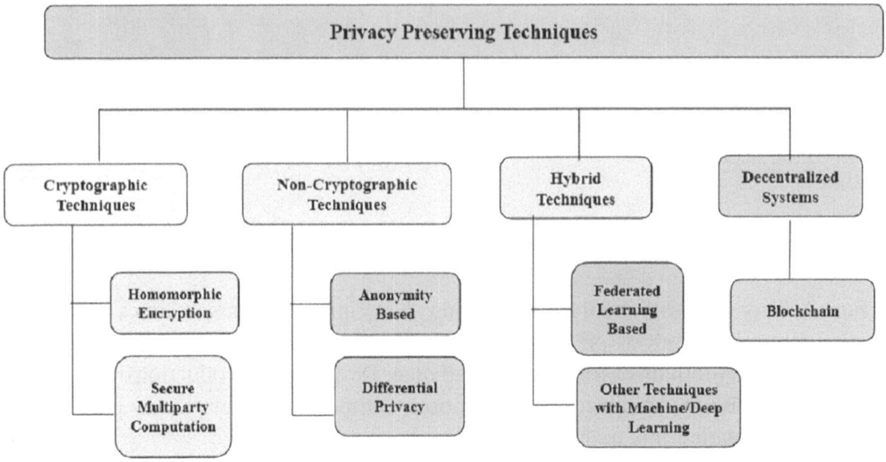

Fig. 4. Privacy Preserving Techniques

Homomorphic Encryption (HE): HE works on encrypted data, preserving privacy. Studies propose HE-based methods for genomic data, secure data ex-change, and patient monitoring applications [1–5]. Homomorphic encryption (HE) is the technique in which the data owner encrypts its data and sends it for computation. The computational tasks are performed on the data without decrypting the data, and the output results of encrypted data are sent to the data owner. HE allows computation on encrypted data while preserving data attributes, allowing a third party to perform algorithms on the data without having inside knowledge. Homomorphic encryption (HE) enables computation on encrypted data without decryption, preserving data attributes and allowing third-party algorithms. For genomic data privacy, Chowdhury et al. [1] proposed DeCrypt, based on 3DES, resilient to man-in-the-middle attacks and 61% faster than 3DES. Sarkar et al. [2] presented a secure, fast, and private genome imputation algorithm using ML and Paillier encryption. Paul et al. [3] developed a collective learning protocol for secure data exchange and training on Medical Information Mart for Intensive Care (MIMIC-III) dataset using CKKS encryption. Lu et al. [4] focused on privacy preservation of shared patient data by encrypting genotype and pheno-type using homomorphic encryption. Carpov et al. [5] introduced a method using HE to secure cloud-based data computation in patient monitoring applications.

Secure Multiparty Computation (SMPC): Secure multi-party computation (SMPC) allows data computation while preserving privacy through data distribution among parties. An example is the additive secret sharing algorithm [6], where employees can calculate their average sala-ry without revealing individual data [7]. Akgun et al. [8] propose privacy-protected querying of genomic datasets using SMPC, enabling secure maintenance of genomic databases in semi-honest cloud settings. Li et al. [9] propose an SMPC system model with two servers for encrypted health record processing and disease trait matching. Kumar et al. [10] pre-sent a privacy-preserving e-healthcare system using the Paillier encryption algorithm for secure data sharing and disease record matching. Marwan et al. [11] design a framework using the Paillier homomorphic algorithm for encrypted computation in distributed databases, enabling collective calculation without revealing confidential information. Jangde et al. [12] highlight the use of SMPC to overcome fraud threats in healthcare, offering a simpler method compared to previous approaches.

Differential Privacy (DP): Differential privacy (DP) adds noise to data for anonymity, preserving privacy [13]. Tech companies like Apple, Amazon, and Facebook use DP to protect privacy while collecting data. Sangeetha et al. [14] propose a DP-based model re-lease using machine learning classifiers like SVM, Random Forest, etc., evaluated on a heart disease dataset. Ziller et al. [15] introduce a parallelized deep neural network framework with privacy preservation using Gaussian DP for medical image segmentation. Muftuoug et al. [16] use DP on the EfficientNet-B0 a diagnostic model was developed for COVID-19 using chest X-ray images, achieving privacy and promising outcomes. Vadavalli et al. [17] propose a DP algorithm for breast cancer detection, enhancing patient privacy without compromising accuracy.

Blockchain: Blockchain enhances healthcare by addressing privacy and security concerns, im-proving interoperability, and enabling historical data for research [18, 19]. Integra-tion with IoT and smart contracts enhances automation and efficiency [20]. Zerka et al. propose CDML, combining distributed learning with blockchain for multi-centric research [21]. Zhang et al. use blockchain and DP in FL to protect medical records [22]. Alzubi et al. use DL and blockchain for secure EMR protec-tion [23]. Ngan et al. propose PriFL-Chain, combining DP, blockchain, MEC, and IPFS for privacy and cost-effective ML training [24]. Edge computing reduces costs and enhances data processing [25].

Federated Learning (FL): Privacy Preserving Federated Learning (PPFL) approaches can be categorized into three main types based on the methods employed: (1) encryption based privacy preserving, (2) Differential Privacy based privacy preserving, and (3) anonymization based privacy preserving [74]. Privacy-preserving federated learning (PPFL) encryption techniques can be categorized into two groups: (1) homo-morphic encryption and (2) secure multiparty computation [74]. Homomorphic encryption-based PPFL methods, like [46, 50, 57, 69], ensure data privacy during parameter exchange. Zhang et al. [69, 70] introduced batch encryption for effi-ciency. SMC-based PPFL methods, such as [48, 61, 64], use secure multiparty computation to jointly compute objectives without revealing individual data. Bonawitz et al. [48] presented a secure aggregation protocol with accuracy and privacy, but it involves high communication costs [65]. Global differential privacy methods [45, 51, 54, 56, 58, 60] employ a global differential privacy scheme. Geyer et al. [56] introduced an FL framework with the Gaussian mechanism protecting patient data. Concerns about potential mali-cious behavior by the server persist. Local differential privacy methods [47, 59, 67, 68, 72, 73] use a local differential privacy scheme. Abadi et al. [71] proposed it for deep network training, and Bhowmick et al. [47] applied it to FL, pro-tecting sample privacy. Lu et al. [59] used local differential privacy in mobile edge computing, and Cao et al. [73] achieved privacy preservation in IoT with an FL framework. Anonymization-based PPFL methods, focusing on differen-tial privacy, offer strong privacy but sacrifice data utility [51, 56]. Anonymization-based FL approaches [52, 55, 66] ad-dress utility concerns, but face limitations in focus, evaluation, scalability, and security [52, 66, 74]. Further research is needed to overcome these challenges and enhance practical implementation in federated learning.

Detailed Discussion on Anonymity Based Privacy Preserving Techniques: L. Sweeney introduced k-Anonymity in 2002 as a privacy technique to prevent individual identification in datasets [26]. It groups individuals into anonymous clusters based

Table 1. Comparisons of Different Privacy-Preserving Methods.

Technique	Strengths	Weaknesses	Trade-offs in Privacy Preservation	Specific Use Case in e-Healthcare
Homomorphic Encryption (HE)	- End-to-end security for data - Allows complex computations on encrypted data	- Computationally intensive - Slower processing times	- Strong privacy protection can significantly impact computational efficiency and processing speed	- Secure processing of encrypted patient data for analytics without decryption
Secure Multiparty Computation (SMPC)	- Enables joint computation without sharing private data - Strong privacy guarantees	- High communication overhead - Complex to implement	- Ensures privacy but may lead to increased data processing time and communication costs	- Collaborative medical research involving patient data from multiple hospitals
Differential Privacy (DP)	- Strong mathematical privacy guarantees - Effective against various attacks	- May reduce data utility - Requires careful parameter tuning	- Privacy is enhanced by adding noise, which can obscure useful data details and reduce overall data quality	- Sharing aggregate health statistics while preserving patient confidentiality
Blockchain	- Decentralized and tamper-proof - Enhances data integrity and transparency	- High energy consumption - Scalability issues	- Provides strong data integrity and transparency but can be inefficient and costly in terms of resource consumption	- Secure and transparent tracking of medical records and supply chains

(continued)

Table 1. *(continued)*

Technique	Strengths	Weaknesses	Trade-offs in Privacy Preservation	Specific Use Case in e-Healthcare
Federated Learning (FL)	- Allows model training on decentralized data - Reduces need for data centralization	- Communication costs - Potential for model inversion attacks	- May incur higher communication costs and potential risks of model inversion	- Training predictive health models across hospitals without sharing patient data
Anonymity-Based Techniques	- Simple to implement - Useful for de-identifying data sets	- Susceptible to re-identification attacks - Loss of data granularity	- Provides basic privacy protection but can lead to risks of re-identification and loss of detailed data insights	- Anonymizing patient data for public health research and analysis

on shared attributes, ensuring a minimum cluster size of k for increased difficulty in identification. k-Anonymity achieves privacy by generalizing or suppressing attributes, applicable in healthcare, finance, and social sciences. Limitations of these techniques include the potential for information loss and the risk of re-identification attacks, also known as attribute disclosure. In: 2007, Ashwin Machanavajjhala introduced l-Diversity as a privacy-enhancing technique, going beyond k-anonymity, to bolster privacy protection [27]. l-Diversity aims to ensure diversity among groups by mandating a minimum of l distinct values for each sensitive attribute. This approach is very important in preserving privacy in domains such as healthcare, finance, and social sciences, where sensitive information is involved. However, it is important to note that l-Diversity has its limitations, including potential information loss and inadequate protection against Attribute Disclosure (AD) and Membership Disclosure (MD). In: 2007, S. Venkatasubramanian introduced the t-closeness model as a means to enhance privacy protection [28]. The proposed model tackles attacks on l-diversity by ensuring that the distribution of sensitive attribute values within groups closely resembles that of the entire dataset. The t-closeness model measures the distance between distributions and establishes a threshold for t-closeness. Nevertheless, this approach has limitations, such as the absence of a computational procedure for enforcement and the potential impact on data utility. Truta et al. introduced p-sensitive k-anonymity in 2007 [29], expanding on k-anonymity by guaranteeing each group possesses a minimum of p unique values for sensitive attributes. However, limitations include omitted sensitive categories, high information loss, and computational complexity. In: 2011, Sun et al. introduced (p,α)-sensitive k-anonymity [30] considering sensitivity, but it also faces challenges like NP-hardness, reduced data utility, and increased information loss.

In 2011, an improved clustering algorithm based on k-anonymity was proposed by W. Zheng [31]. This algorithm groups individuals into clusters, ensuring that each cluster contains at least k individuals with indistinguishable sensitive attributes. However, limitations of this approach include potential information loss and the need to determine an appropriate value of k for balancing privacy and data utility.

In 2019, Mehta et al. introduced the Scalable (α, k)-Anonymization (SAKA) approach [32], outperforming existing methods for big data scenarios. Another 2019 approach focused on attribute-centric anonymization for e-health data privacy and utility improvement [33]. Additionally, a privacy-preserving collaborative data anonymization approach was proposed [34], surpassing traditional methods in privacy protection and data utility. A model was proposed in 2020 by Khan and Tao, specifically designed for IoT-based electronic health records, aiming to achieve θ-sensitive k-anonymity [35]. This model creates diverse k-anonymous groups to prevent various attacks. However, limitations include the loss of individual distinctions within a group and the challenge of determining an appropriate θ value. Wang et al. introduced enhanced p-sensitive k-anonymity models in 2020 [36], which works on skew and sensitive attacks, thereby improving privacy protection within the k-anonymity framework.

In 2021, Jayapradha and Prakash addressed data publishing in healthcare records with privacy preserving the same [37], while Khan and Khan focused on single identity clustering-based data anonymization in healthcare [38]. Masud and Gaba introduced an anonymity-preserving user authentication scheme for IoT-based healthcare [39], and Onesimu and Karthikeyan proposed a streamlined anonymization scheme leveraging clustering for IoT-based healthcare data collection [40]. In: 2022, Kacha and Zitouni introduced the KAB approach based on the black hole algorithm [41], which enhanced privacy protection within the k-anonymity framework. Onesimu, J. Andrew proposed an attribute-focused anonymization scheme with improved l-diversity for better privacy and utility [79] it extended the work of A. Majeed[33]. Shakil and Ubaid put forth a new approach for privacy-enabled healthcare recommender systems in 2023 [42]. Their framework incorporated privacy-preserving techniques to ensure privacy in healthcare recommendations. Su and Huang proposed the KAPP algorithm in 2023 [43], which aimed to protect against attacks like skewness and similarity by k-anonymity based methods in multi-dimensional data. The algorithm combined KAPP with t-closeness to enhance privacy protection. In: the same year, Yang proposed "Random Aggregation: Differential Privacy in k-Anonymity" [44], which aimed to enhance privacy protection in the k-anonymity framework by incorporating random aggregation techniques. Additionally, in 2023, Abdul Majeed proposed a generic approach for enhancing utility and privacy [76]. Table 2 presents the summary and comparisons of the above-cited SOTA approaches from a broader perspective:

2.3 Discussion on Data Utility Enhancing Anonymization Methods

With the recent developments in ML/DL methodologies and data-driven applications, many strategies have been developed to increase classification accuracy by use of anonymization techniques. Figure 5 demonstrates the conceptual overview of this method. There are several benefits to using anonymised data to build classification

Table 2. Summary and Comparisons of SOTA Anonymity Based Privacy-Preserving Methods.

Author/ Authors	Privacy Model	Anonymity Technique	Utility Measure Used	Contribution	Challenges/ Benefits
L. Sweeney [26]	k-anonymity	Generalization	Risk measure	Introduced k-Anonymity for privacy,	Privacy, information loss, re-identification risk
Ashwin Machanavajjhala [27]	l-diversity	Generalization	Entropy measure	Introduced l-Diversity for diversity among groups for each sensitive attribute	Diversity enforcement, privacy preservation limitations
S. Venkatasubramanian [28]	t-closeness	Suppression	Statistical measures	Proposed t-closeness model measuring distribution similarity for privacy	Computational enforcement, less data utility
Sun et al. [30]	Extended k-anonymity	Generalization	Information Loss (IL)	Introduced (p,α)-sensitive k-anonymity considering sensitivity	NP-hardness, reduced data utility
W. Zheng [31]	K-anonymity	Clustering (Improved)	Sensitivity Analysis	Proposed clustering-based k-anonymity algorithm	Information loss, appropriate k determination
Mehta et al. [32]	(α, k)-Anonymization	MapReduce-based Anonymization	IL	Anonymization for big data scenarios	Scalability, big data privacy
A. Majeed [33]	Attribute-centric Anonymization	Generalization, Suppression	IL, Privacy	Introduced attribute-centric anonymization scheme	Improved utility, e-health data privacy

(continued)

Table 2. *(continued)*

Author/ Authors	Privacy Model	Anonymity Technique	Utility Measure Used	Contribution	Challenges/ Benefits
Wong et al. [34]	Collaborative Data Anonymization	Quasi-identifier-based techniques	IL, Privacy	Proposed collaborative data anonymization with sensitive quasi-identifiers	Improved privacy, collaborative data privacy
Khan and Tao [35]	θ-sensitive k-anonymity	Generalization	IL, Privacy	IoT-based electronic health records	Individual distinctions loss, appropriate θ determination
Wang et al. [36]	p-sensitive k-anonymity	Generalization	IL, Privacy	Proposed enhanced For skew and sensitive attacks	Enhanced privacy within k-anonymity framework
Jayapradha and Prakash [37]	MAbased privacy model	Suppression Perturbation	Privacy Metrics, Sensitivity Analysis	Introduced efficient privacy-preserving data publishing with multiple sensitive attributes	Privacy-preserving healthcare data publishing
Khan and Khan [38]	Single Identity Clustering	Clustering techniques	IL	Proposed single identity clustering-based data anonymization in healthcare	Privacy-preserving healthcare data anonymization
Masud and Gaba [39]	Anonymity	Cryptographic techniques	Security Metrics, Performance	Introduced anonymity-preserving user authentication for IoT-based healthcare	Privacy-enabled user authentication, IoT-based healthcare

(continued)

Table 2. (*continued*)

Author/ Authors	Privacy Model	Anonymity Technique	Utility Measure Used	Contribution	Challenges/ Benefits
Onesimu and Karthikeyan [40]	Clustering-based	Clustering techniques	IL	Proposed clustering-based anonymization for IoT-based healthcare data collection	Privacy-preserving IoT-based healthcare data
Kacha and Zitouni [41]	k-anonymity	Black Hole Algorithm	Not specified	Enhancing privacy protection within k-anonymity	Improved privacy
Shakil and Ubaid [42]	Generalized	Privacy-Enabled recommender framework	Recommender performance	Proposed privacy-enabled framework for healthcare recommender systems	Privacy-preserving healthcare recommendations
Su and Huang [43]	K-Anonymity	Skewness and Similarity Attack Protection	Not specified	Proposed KAPP algorithm combining k-anonymity and t-closeness	Privacy protection, enhanced privacy methods
L. Yang [44]	Differential Privacy	Random Aggregation	Not specified	Proposed random aggregation for enhancing privacy protection in k-anonymity	Privacy enhancement in k-anonymity framework
Abdul Majeed [76]	Generalized	Attribute Usefulness approach	Utility,Privacy	Introduced generic approach for utility and privacy enhancement	Utility and privacy improvement

models that are more accurate [82]. A technique that incorporates taxonomy data to improve the precision of structured data classifiers was presented by Cagliero et al. [84]. Significant improvements in accuracy have been demonstrated by this integration, all while keeping computational needs within reasonable bounds for various datasets and classifier assessments. A methodology for generalizing QIs that complies with DP criteria was developed in [98], providing a non-interactive way to publish anonymized data. Interestingly, decision tree classifiers performed better than other methods in terms of accuracy. In: order to increase the usability of anonymized data, Srijayanthi et al. [95] has presented a UPA technique that uses feature. For this, dimensionality reduction and selection are used. In: the meantime, Chen et al. [91] created a mixed data anonymization method based on DP and clustering with the goal of striking a more equitable trade-off between privacy and utility. Their approach, which combines DP and k-median clustering, showed lower calculation times and less information leakage (IL) than previous methods. A z-anonymity model based on entropy principles was presented by Jha et al. [85] as a means of anonymizing stream data with a decreased information leakage. In: order to protect identity and SA disclosure in PPDP, Li et al. [93] developed an anonymization method using bucketization and local generalization. They assessed the usefulness of the generated data using NCP metrics and aggregate query response. Finally, Chu et al. [99] presented the SFLA–Kohonen Network, a DP-based technique intended to reduce privacy problems while maintaining the usefulness of anonymous data.

Sun et al.'s [96] DP-based strategy aims to strike a compromise between privacy and utility when it comes to trajectory data sharing. Their approach produces anonymous data by using synthetic data, which greatly increases utility. In: order to solve the problem of privacy-preserving record linkage, Nóbrega et al. [94] suggested a transfer learning-based approach that involves figuring out the ideal threshold to avoid linking in datasets that are both public and published. In: order to improve privacy and utility in data-sharing scenarios, Amiri et al. [90] recently created the UHRA algorithm, which successfully defends against background knowledge assaults while preserving data privacy and usefulness.

A paradigm for assessing the degree of privacy and utility offered by anonymized datasets was developed by Chen et al. [92]. By putting similar records in the same EC, Xia et al.'s [97] clustering and DP-based methodology reduces information leakage (IL) in data-release circumstances. The weighted full-domain anonymization (WFDA) algorithm was introduced by Han et al. [87] as a revolutionary anonymity technique that takes data availability for data mining into account. This algorithm allows for adaptive data anonymization. In: contrast to other techniques, Last et al.'s anonymization algorithm [86], which combined non-homogeneous generalization with SA value distribution, produced better predictive usefulness.

Additionally, a number of classifier-based anonymity techniques are covered in the literature [80, 81]. The chaos and perturbation algorithm (CPA), developed by Eyupoglu et al. [100], is a revolutionary anonymity algorithm that improves upon other techniques in terms of probabilistic anonymity, Kullback–Leibler divergence, accuracy, and the F-measure. While Kousika et al. [89] created an ML-powered anonymization method to improve the usability of anonymized data for training classifiers, merging SVD and

RDP techniques for data perturbation, Ye and Chen [83] offered an algorithm to limit information loss (IL) in the PPDP.

Table 3 provides comparisons of the recent utility-aware anonymization methods discussed in this section.

Table 3. Comparisons of the Recent Utility-Aware Anonymization Methods

Study	Privacy	Utility
Fong et al. [80]	×	✓
Lin et al. [81]	×	✓
Li et al. [82]	×	✓
Ye et al. [83]	✓	×
Cagliero et al. [84]	×	✓
Jha et al. [85]	✓	×
Last et al. [86]	×	✓
Han et al. [87]	×	✓
Park et al. [88]	✓	×
Kousika et al. [89]	×	✓
A. Majeed [76]	✓	✓
Amiri et al. [90]	✓	✓
Chen et al. [91]	×	✓
Chen et al. [92]	✓	×
Li et al. [93]	✓	×
Nóbrega et al. [94]	✓	✓
Srijayanthi et al. [95]	×	✓
Sun et al. [96]	×	✓
Xia et al. [97]	✓	✓

Key: ✓⇒ considered/possible, × ⇒ not-considered/not-possible.

3 Promising Future Research and Development Directions

In this section, we present promising research and development directions for future work. Figure 6 presents the list of promising directions that require more work from the research and development point of view.

- **Privacy-Utility Trade-off**: Many privacy-preserving techniques, such as differential privacy and encryption, introduce noise or transformations that can degrade the utility of the data or model. Striking the right balance between privacy and utility remains a significant challenge in privacy-preserving methods.

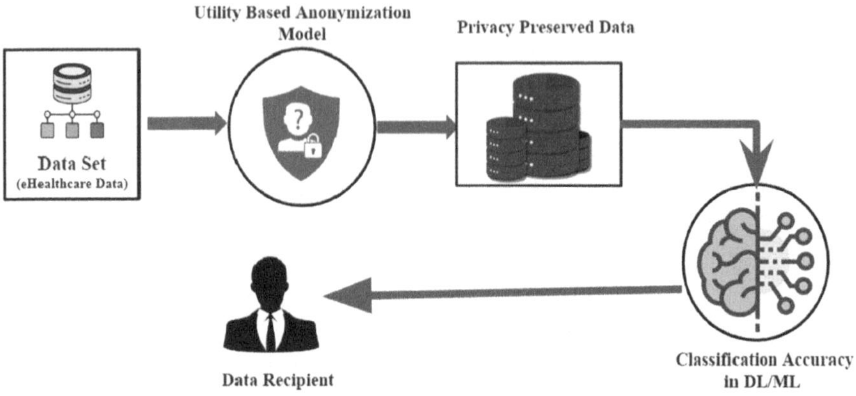

Fig. 5. Conceptual overview of Data Utility Enhancing Anonymization Methods

- **Vulnerability to attacks**: Privacy-preserving methods can be vulnerable to inference and linkage attacks, necessitating effective security measures. Need for device anonymizing methods leveraging ML/DL/FL models: Research highlights the requirement for privacy-preserving methods that improve utility while maintaining privacy.
- **Scalability and efficiency**: Computation and resource demands pose challenges for large-scale e-healthcare systems.
- **Limited focus on privacy-preserving techniques for multiple sensitive attributes**: Few researchers have addressed privacy-preserving techniques for multiple sensitive attributes.
- **Limited research on generic approach for privacy-preserving techniques**: Scarcity of papers focusing on a generic approach was found.
- **Regulatory compliance**: Privacy-preserving methods should align with relevant regulations like GDPR and HIPAA for healthcare applications. In: order to achieve efficient, scalable, and robust solutions that balance privacy and utility while addressing the challenges of privacy preservation, it is essential to develop a new method which allows us to strike a balance between preserving privacy and maintaining the utility of the data, and protect against various attacks while maintaining regulation laws, ultimately enhancing the overall performance and effectiveness of privacy preservation mechanisms.

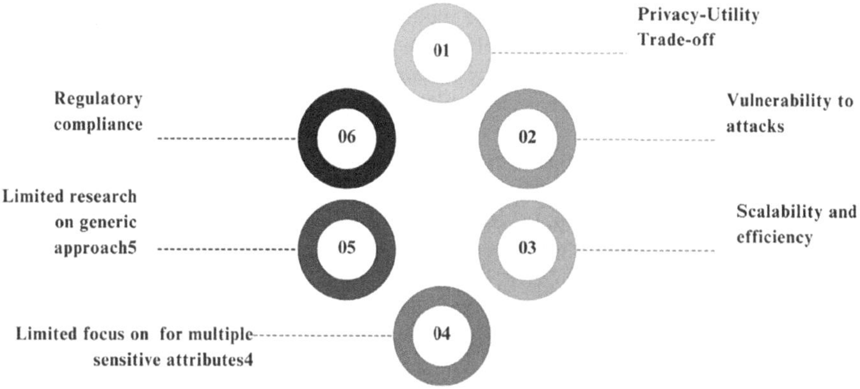

Fig. 6. Promising Research and Development Directions for Future Work

4 Conclusion

In conclusion, the survey highlights the intricate balance between privacy and utility in e-healthcare data management. The reviewed privacy-preserving techniques underscore the challenge of mitigating privacy risks while maintaining data usability. Vulnerabilities to attacks, scalability concerns, and the need for comprehensive methods accommodating multiple sensitive attributes emphasize the pressing necessity for innovative approaches. Leveraging machine learning models and ensuring compliance with regulatory standards are pivotal in shaping the future of privacy preservation. Developing robust methodologies that harmonize data privacy and utility will fortify e-healthcare systems against threats, fostering scalability and reliability in safeguarding sensitive medical information.

Disclosure of Interests. The authors declare no conflict of interest.

References

1. Chowdhury, D., et al.: Decrypt: A 3DES inspired optimised cryptographic algorithm. J. Ambient Intell. Hum. Comput. **2022**, 1–11 (2022)
2. Sarkar, E., Chielle, E., Gürsoy, G., Mazonka, O., Gerstein, M., Maniatakos, M.: Fast and scalable private genotype imputation using machine learning and partially homomorphic encryption. IEEE Access **9**, 93097–93110 (2021)
3. Privacy-preserving collective learning with homomorphic encryption: Paul, J., Annamalai, M.S.M.S., Ming, W., Al Badawi, A., Veeravalli, B., Aung, K.M.M. IEEE Access **9**, 132084–132096 (2021)
4. Lu, W.J., Yamada, Y., Sakuma, J.: Privacy-preserving genome-wide association studies on cloud environments using fully homomorphic encryption. BMC Med. Inf. Decis. Making **15**, 1–8 (2015)
5. Carpov, S., Nguyen, T.H., Sirdey, R., Constantino, G., Martinelli, F.: Practical privacy-preserving medical diagnosis using homomorphic encryption. In: 2016 IEEE 9th International Conference on Cloud Computing (CLOUD), pp. 593–599. IEEE (2016)

6. Dugan, T., Zou, X.: A survey of secure multiparty computation protocols for privacy preserving genetic tests. In: 2016 IEEE First International Conference on Connected Health: Applications, Systems and Engineering Technologies (CHASE), pp. 173–182. IEEE (2016)
7. Cramer, R., Damgård, I.B., et al.: Secure Multiparty Computation. Cambridge University Press (2015)
8. Akgün, M., Pfeifer, N., Kohlbacher, O.: Efficient privacy-preserving whole genome variant queries. Bioinformatics **38**(8), 2202–2210 (2022)
9. Li, D., Liao, X., Xiang, T., Wu, J., Le, J.: Privacy-preserving self-serviced medical diagnosis scheme based on secure multi-party computation. Comput. Secur. **90**, 101701 (2020)
10. Kumar, A.V., Sujith, M.S., Sai, K.T., Rajesh, G., Yashwanth, D.J.S.: Secure multiparty computation enabled E-healthcare system with homomorphic encryption. In: IOP Conference Series: Materials Science and Engineering, vol. 981, p. 022079. IOP Publishing (2020)
11. Marwan, M., Kartit, A., Ouahmane, H.: Applying secure multi-party computation to improve collaboration in the healthcare cloud. In: 2016 Third International Conference on Systems of Collaboration (SysCo). IEEE (2016)
12. Jangde, P., Mishra, D.K.: A secure multiparty computation solution to healthcare frauds and abuses. In: 2011 Second International Conference on Intelligent Systems, Modelling and Simulation, pp. 139–142. IEEE (2011)
13. Dwork, C.: Differential privacy: a survey of results. In: International Conference on Theory and Applications of Models of Computation, pp. 1–19. Springer (2008)
14. Sangeetha, S., Sudha Sadasivam, G., Srikanth, A.: Differentially private model release for healthcare applications. Int. J. Comput. Appl. **2022**, 1–6 (2022)
15. Ziller, A., Usynin, D., Braren, R., Makowski, M., Rueckert, D., Kaissis, G.: Medical imaging deep learning with differential privacy. Sci. Rep. **11**(1), 1–8 (2021)
16. Müftüoğlu, Z., Kizrak, M.A., Yildlnm, T.: Differential privacy practice on diagnosis of COVID-19 radiology imaging using EfficientNet. In: 2020 International Conference on INnovations in Intelligent SysTems and Applications (INISTA), pp. 1–6. IEEE (2020)
17. Vadavalli, A., Subhashini, R.: An improved differential privacy-preserving truth discovery approach in healthcare. In: 2019 IEEE 10th Annual Information Technology, Electronics and Mobile Communication Conference (IEMCON), pp. 1031–1037. IEEE (2019)
18. Duca, A.L., Bacciu, C., Marchetti, A.: How distributed ledgers can transform healthcare applications. In: Blockchain Engineering, vol. 2016, p. 25 (2016)
19. Kuo, T.-T., Kim, H.-E., Ohno-Machado, L.: Blockchain distributed ledger technologies for biomedical and health care applications. J. Am. Med. Inf. Assoc. **24**(6), 1211–1220 (2017)
20. Panarello, A., Tapas, N., Merlino, G., Longo, F., Puliafito, A.: Blockchain and IoT integration: a systematic survey. Sensors **18**(8), 2575 (2018)
21. Zerka, F., et al.: Blockchain for privacy preserving and trustworthy distributed machine learning in multicentric medical imaging (C-DistriM). IEEE Access **8**, 183939–183951 (2020)
22. Zhang, H., Li, G., Zhang, Y., Gai, K., Qiu, M.: Blockchain-based privacy-preserving medical data sharing scheme using federated learning. In: International Conference on Knowledge Science, Engineering and Management. Springer, pp. 634–646 (2021)
23. Alzubi, J.A., Alzubi, O.A., Singh, A., Ramachandran, M.: Cloud-IIoT-based electronic health record privacy-preserving by CNN and Blockchain-enabled federated learning. IEEE Trans. Ind. Inf. **19**(1), 1080–1087 (2022)
24. Ngan Van, L., Hoang Tuan, A., Phan The, D., Vo, T.-K., Pham, V.-H.: A privacy-preserving approach for building learning models in smart healthcare using Blockchain and federated learning. In: Proceedings of the 11th International Symposium on Information and Communication Technology, pp. 435–441 (2022)

25. Adhikary, S., Ghosh, A.: E-BMI: a gait based smart remote BMI monitoring framework implementing edge computing and incremental machine learning. Smart Health **24**, 100277 (2022)
26. Sweeney, L.: k-anonymity: a model for protecting privacy. Int. J. Uncertainty Fuzziness Knowl.-Based Syst. **10**(5), 557–570 (2002)
27. Machanavajjhala, A., Kifer, D., Gehrke, J., Venkitasubramaniam, M.: l-diversity: Privacy beyond k-anonymity. ACM Trans. Knowl. Discov. Data (TKDD) **1**(1), 3-es (2007)
28. Li, N., Li, T., Venkatasubramanian, S.: t-closeness: privacy beyond k-anonymity and l-diversity. In: 2007 IEEE 23rd International Conference on Data Engineering, pp. 106–115. IEEE (2006)
29. Truta, T.M., Campan, A., Meyer, P.: Generating microdata with p-sensitive k-anonymity property. In: Secure Data Management: 4th VLDB Workshop, SDM 2007. Springer, Berlin, Heidelberg, pp. 124–141 (2007)
30. Sun, X., Sun, L., Wang, H.: Extended k-anonymity models against sensitive attribute disclosure. Comput. Commun. **34**(4), 526–535 (2011)
31. Zheng, W., Wang, Z., Lv, T., Ma, Y., Jia, C.: K-anonymity algorithm based on improved clustering. In: Algorithms and Architectures for Parallel Processing: 18th International Conference, ICA3PP 2018. Springer, pp. 462–476 (2018)
32. Mehta, B.B., Gupta, R., Rao, U.P., Muthiyan, M.: A scalable (α, k)-anonymization approach using mapreduce for privacy preserving big data publishing. In: 2019 10th International Conference on Computing, Communication and Networking Technologies (ICCCNT), pp. 1–6. IEEE (2019)
33. Majeed, A.: Attribute-centric anonymization scheme for improving user privacy and utility of publishing e-health data. J. King Saud Univ. Comput. Inf. Sci. **31**(4), 426–435 (2019)
34. Wong, K.S., Tu, N.A., Bui, D.M., Ooi, S.Y., Kim, M.H.: Privacy-preserving collaborative data anonymization with sensitive quasi-identifiers. In: 2019 12th CMI Conference on Cybersecurity and Privacy (CMI), pp. 1–6. IEEE (2019)
35. Khan, R., et al.: θ-sensitive k-anonymity: an anonymization model for IoT based electronic health records. Electronics **9**(5), 716 (2020)
36. Wang, N., Song, H., Luo, T., Sun, J., Li, J.: Enhanced p-sensitive k-anonymity models for achieving better privacy. In: 2020 IEEE/CIC International Conference on Communications in China (ICCC), pp. 148–153. IEEE (2020)
37. Jayapradha, J., Prakash, M.: An efficient privacy-preserving data publishing in health care records with multiple sensitive attributes. In: 2021 6th International Conference on Inventive Computation Technologies (ICICT), pp. 623–629. IEEE (2021)
38. Khan, P., Khan, Y., Kumar, S.: Single identity clustering-based data anonymization in healthcare. Comput. Intell. Syst. Appl., 1–9 (2021)
39. Masud, M., Gaba, G.S., Choudhary, K., Hossain, M.S., Alhamid, M.F., Muhammad, G.: Lightweight and anonymity-preserving user authentication scheme for IoT-based healthcare. IEEE Internet Things J. **9**(4), 2649–2656 (2021)
40. Onesimu, J.A., Karthikeyan, J., Sei, Y.: An efficient clustering-based anonymization scheme for privacy-preserving data collection in IoT based healthcare services. Peer-to-Peer Netw. Appl. **14**, 1629–1649 (2021)
41. Kacha, L., Zitouni, A., Djoudi, M.: KAB: a new k-anonymity approach based on black hole algorithm. J. King Saud Univ. Comput. Inf. Sci. **34**(7), 4075–4088 (2022)
42. Shakil, Ubaid, S., Sohail, S.S., Alam, M.T., Khan, S.A., Hasan, S.H., Mufti, T.: A novel framework for privacy enabled healthcare recommender systems. In: Artificial Intelligence for Smart Healthcare, pp. 463–475. Springer (2023)
43. Su, B., Huang, J., Miao, K., Wang, Z., Zhang, X., Chen, Y.: K-anonymity privacy protection algorithm for multi-dimensional data against skewness and similarity attacks. Sensors **23**(3), 1554 (2023)

44. Yang, L.: Random aggregation: differential privacy in k-anonymity. In: Proceedings of the International Conference on Financial Innovation, FinTech and Information Technology, FFIT 2022, Shenzhen, China (2023)
45. Agarwal, N., Suresh, A.T., Yu, F.X., Kumar, S., McMahan, B.: cpSGD: communication-efficient and differentially-private distributed SGD. In: Advances in Neural Information Processing Systems, vol. 31, pp. 7564–7575 (2018)
46. Asad, M., Moustafa, A., Ito, T.: FedOpt: towards communication efficiency and privacy preservation in federated learning. Appl. Sci. **10**(8), 2864 (2020)
47. Bhowmick, A., Duchi, J., Freudiger, J., Kapoor, G., Rogers, R.: Protection against reconstruction and its applications in private federated learning. arXiv:1812.00984 (2018)
48. Bonawitz, K., Ivanov, V., Kreuter, B., et al.: Practical secure aggregation for privacy-preserving machine learning. In: Proceedings of the ACM SIGSAC Conference on Computer and Communications Security, pp. 1175–1191 (2017)
49. Brakerski, Z., Gentry, C., Vaikuntanathan, V.: (Leveled) fully homomorphic encryption without bootstrapping. ACM Trans. Comput. Theory **6**(3), 1–36 (2014)
50. Chen, Y., Qin, X., Wang, J., Yu, C., Gao, W.: Fedhealth: a federated transfer learning framework for wearable healthcare. IEEE Intell. Syst. **4** (2020)
51. Choudhury, O., Gkoulalas-Divanis, A., Salonidis, T., et al.: Differential privacy-enabled federated learning for sensitive health data. In: Proceedings of the NeurIPS Workshop on Machine Learning for Health (2019)
52. Choudhury, O., et al.: A syntactic approach for privacy-preserving federated learning. In: Proceedings of the European Conference on Artificial Intelligence (2020)
53. Ciriani, V., Di Vimercati, S., Foresti, S., Samarati, P.: K-anonymous data mining: a survey, pp. 105–136. Springer (2008)
54. Dubey, A., Pentland, A.: Differentially-private federated linear bandits. In: Advances in Neural Information Processing Systems, vol. 33, pp. 6003–6014 (2020)
55. Fung, C., Koerner, J., Grant, S., Beschastnikh, I.: Dancing in the dark: private multi-party machine learning in an untrusted setting. ACM Comput. Surv. **54**(6), 131 (2021)
56. Geyer, R.C., Klein, T., Nabi, M.: Differentially private federated learning: a client level perspective. arXiv:1712.07557 (2017)
57. Hao, M., Li, H., Luo, X., Xu, G., H. Yang, G., Liu, S.: Efficient and privacy-enhanced federated learning for industrial artificial intelligence. IEEE Trans. Ind. Inf. **16**(10), 6532–6542 (2020)
58. Hao, M., Li, H., Xu, G., Liu, S., Yang, H.: Towards efficient and privacy-preserving federated deep learning. In: Proceedings of the IEEE International Conference on Communications, pp. 1–6 (2019)
59. Lu, Y., Huang, X., Dai, Y., Maharjan, S., Zhang, Y.: Differentially private asynchronous federated learning for mobile edge computing in urban informatics. IEEE Trans. Industr. Inf. **16**(3), 2134–2143 (2019)
60. McMahan, H.B., Ramage, D., Talwar, K., Zhang, L.: Learning differentially private recurrent language models. In: Proceedings of the International Conference on Learning Representations (2018)
61. Mohassel, P., Zhang, Y.: SecureML: a system for scalable privacy-preserving machine learning. In: Proceedings of the IEEE Symposium on Security and Privacy, pp. 19–38 (2017)
62. Phong, L.T., Aono, Y., Hayashi, T., Wang, L.H., Moriai, S.: Privacy-preserving deep learning via additively homomorphic encryption. IEEE Trans. Inf. Forens. Secur. **13**(5), 1333–1345 (2018)
63. Qiu, J., Tian, Z., Du, C., Zuo, Q., Su, S., Fang, B.: A survey on access control in the age of internet of things. IEEE IoT J. **7**, 4682–4696 (2020)

64. Reich, D., Todoki, A., Dowsley, R., et al.: Privacy-preserving classification of personal text messages with secure multi-party computation. In: Advances in Neural Information Processing Systems, vol. 32, pp. 3757–3769 (2019)
65. Riazi, D., Laine, A., Pelton, R. Dai, W.: HEAX: an architecture for computing on encrypted data. In: Proceedings of the International Conference on Architectural Support for Programming Languages and Operating Systems, pp. 1295–1309 (2020)
66. Song, M., et al.: Analyzing user-level privacy attack against federated learning. IEEE J. Select. Areas Commun. **10**, 2430–2444 (2020)
67. Truex, S., Liu, L., Chow, K., Gursoy, M., Wei, W.: LDP-Fed: federated learning with local differential privacy. In: Proceedings of the ACM International Workshop on Edge Systems, Analytics and Networking, pp. 61–66 (2020)
68. Wang, Y., Tong, Y., Shi, D.: Federated latent Dirichlet allocation: a local differential privacy based framework. In: Proceedings of the AAAI Conference on Artificial Intelligence, pp. 6283–6290 (2020)
69. Zhang, C., Li, S., Xia, J., Wang, W., Yan, F., Liu, Y.: Batchcrypt: efficient homomorphic encryption for cross-silo federated learning. In: Proceedings of the USENIX Annual Technical Conference, pp. 493–506 (2020)
70. Zhang, J., Chen, B., Yu, S., Deng, H.: PEFL: a privacy-enhanced federated learning scheme for big data analytics. In: Proceedings of the IEEE Global Communications Conference, pp. 1–6 (2019)
71. Abadi, M., Chu, A., Goodfellow, I., McMahan, H.B., Mironov, I., Talwar, K., Zhang, L.: Deep learning with differential privacy. In: Proceedings of the ACM SIGSAC Conference on Computer and Communications Security, pp. 308–318 (2016)
72. Zheng, H.D., Hu, H.B., Han, Z.Y.: Preserving user privacy for machine learning: local differential privacy or federated machine learning. IEEE Intell. Syst. **35**(4), 5–14 (2020)
73. Cao, H., Liu, S., Zhao, R., Xiong, X.: IFed: a novel federated learning framework for local differential privacy in power internet of things. Int. J. Distrib. Sens. Netw. **16**(5), 1550147720919698 (2020)
74. Yin, X., Zhu, Y., Hu, J.: A comprehensive survey of privacy-preserving federated learning: A taxonomy, review, and future directions. ACM Comput. Surv. (CSUR) **54**(6), 1–36 (2021)
75. Khalid, N., Qayyum, A., Bilal, M., Al-Fuqaha, A., Qadir, J.: Privacy-preserving artificial intelligence in healthcare: techniques and applications. Comput. Biol. Med., 106848 (2023)
76. Majeed, A., Hwang, S.O.: A generic approach towards enhancing utility and privacy in person-specific data publishing based on attribute usefulness and uncertainty. Electronics **12**(9), 1978 (2023)
77. Jabeen, F., et al.: Enhanced architecture for privacy preserving data integration in a medical research environment. IEEE Access **5**, 13308–13326 (2017)
78. Majeed, A.: Attribute-centric and synthetic data based privacy preserving methods: a systematic review. J. Cybersecur. Priv. **3**(3), 638–661 (2023)
79. Onesimu, J.A., Karthikeyan, J., Eunice, J., Pomplun, M., Dang, H.: Privacy preserving attribute-focused anonymization scheme for healthcare data publishing. IEEE Access **10**, 86979–86997 (2022)
80. Fong, P.K., Weber-Jahnke, J.H.: Privacy preserving decision tree learning using unrealized data sets. IEEE Trans. Knowl. Data Eng. **24**, 353–364 (2010)
81. Lin, K.P., Chen, M.S.: On the design and analysis of the privacy-preserving SVM classifier. IEEE Trans. Knowl. Data Eng. **23**, 1704–1717 (2010)
82. Li, J., Liu, J., Baig, M., Wong, R.C.W.: Information based data anonymization for classification utility. Data Knowl. Eng. **70**, 1030–1045 (2011)

83. Ye, H., Chen, E.S.: Attribute utility motivated k-anonymization of datasets to support the heterogeneous needs of biomedical researchers. In: Proceedings of the AMIA Annual Symposium Proceedings, American Medical Informatics Association, Washington, DC, USA, 22–26 October, vol. 2011, p. 1573 (2011)
84. Cagliero, L., Garza, P.: Improving classification models with taxonomy information. Data Knowl. Eng. **86**, 85–101 (2013)
85. Jha, N., Vassio, L., Trevisan, M., Leonardi, E., Mellia, M.: Practical anonymization for data streams: Z-anonymity and relation with k-anonymity. Perform. Eval. **159**, 102329 (2023)
86. Last, M., Tassa, T., Zhmudyak, A., Shmueli, E.: Improving accuracy of classification models induced from anonymized datasets. Inf. Sci. **256**, 138–161 (2014)
87. Han, J., Yu, J., Lu, J., Peng, H., Wu, J.: An anonymization method to improve data utility for classification. In: Proceedings of the International Symposium on Cyberspace Safety and Security, Xi'an China, 23–25 October 2017, pp. 57–71. Springer, Cham (2017)
88. Park, S., Byun, J., Lee, J., Cheon, J.H., Lee, J.: HE-friendly algorithm for privacy-preserving SVM training. IEEE Access **8**, 57414–57425 (2020)
89. Kousika, N., Premalatha, K.: An improved privacy-preserving data mining technique using singular value decomposition with three-dimensional rotation data perturbation. J. Supercomput. **77**, 10003–10011 (2021)
90. Amiri, F., Khan, R., Anjum, A., Syed, M.H., Rehman, S.: Enhancing utility in anonymized data against the adversary's background knowledge. Appl. Sci. **13**, 4091 (2023)
91. Chen, L., Zeng, L., Mu, Y., Chen, L.: Global combination and clustering based differential privacy mixed data publishing. IEEE Trans. Knowl. Data Eng. (2023)
92. Chen, M., Cang, L.S., Chang, Z., Iqbal, M., Almakhles, D.: Data anonymization evaluation against re-identification attacks in edge storage. Wirel. Netw., 1–15 (2023)
93. Li, B., He, K.: Local generalization and bucketization technique for personalized privacy preservation. J. King Saud Univ.-Comput. Inf. Sci. **35**, 393–404 (2023)
94. Nóbrega, T., Pires, C.E.S., Nascimento, D.C., Marinho, L.B.: Towards automatic privacy-preserving record linkage: a transfer learning based classification step. Data Knowl. Eng. **145**, 102180 (2023)
95. Srijayanthi, S., Sethukarasi, T.: Design of privacy preserving model based on clustering involved anonymization along with feature selection. Comput. Secur. **126**, 103027 (2023)
96. Sun, X., et al.: Synthesizing realistic trajectory data with differential privacy. IEEE Trans. Intell. Transp. Syst. (2023)
97. Xia, Y., Zhao, T., Lv, Y., Li, Y., Yang, R.: Hierarchical DP-K anonymous data publishing model based on binary tree. In: Proceedings of the 2023 25th International Conference on Advanced Communication Technology (ICACT), Pyeongchang, Republic of Korea, 19–22 February, pp. 102–110 (2023)
98. Zaman, A., Obimbo, C., Dara, R.A.: A novel differential privacy approach that enhances classification accuracy. In: Proceedings of the Ninth International C* Conference on Computer Science & Software Engineering, Porto, Portugal, 20–22 July, pp. 79–84 (2016)
99. Chu, Z., He, J., Li, J., Wang, Q., Zhang, X., Zhu, N.: SSKM_DP: differential privacy data publishing method via SFLA-Kohonen network. Appl. Sci. **13**, 3823 (2023)
100. Eyupoglu, C., Aydin, M.A., Zaim, A.H., Sertbas, A.: An efficient big data anonymization algorithm based on chaos and perturbation techniques. Entropy **20**, 373 (2018)

Deep Learning Methods for Network Intrusion Detection Systems

Gaurav Kulkarni(✉) and Maya Rathore

Department of Computer Science and Engineering, Oriental University, Indore, MP 453555, India
gaurav.kulkarni.2022@gmail.com

Abstract. This paper proposes a model for detection of unsolicited interference in network traffic with noise. The model utilizes a sequential architecture with ReLU activation functions and dropout layers to enhance robustness against noise. The proposed system effectively classifies various attack types, achieving promising performance. The analysis of traffic volume by attack type and the distribution of attack frequencies offer valuable insights into network behavior. Additionally, ROC curves confirm the model's ability to distinguish between different attack classes. These findings demonstrate that with the help of deep learning robust intrusion detection system can be developed which will work efficiently even in the presence of noise. Future work explores incorporating the Jacobian matrix for weight optimization to potentially improve performance and interpretability. This paper proposes a novel deep learning model for intrusion detection in network traffic data containing noise. Traditional machine learning techniques struggle with noisy data, leading to misclassifications. This research addresses this challenge by employing hierarchical capsule network architecture with dynamic routing. Capsule networks offer improved robustness against noise compared to standard deep learning models. The proposed model achieves high accuracy (91%) in classifying various attack types while maintaining interpretability through the visualization of routing weights between capsules. However, the model exhibits high computational cost compared to other approaches. Future work explores incorporating the Jacobian matrix for weight optimization to potentially improve performance and interpretability.

Keywords: MLP Multilayer Perceptron · NDAE Non-symmetric deep auto encoder · NIDS

1 Introduction

NIDS serve as a cornerstone of network defense by identifying and classifying malicious activities. While traditional machine learning techniques have been utilized for IDS, deep learning offers promising advancements in this domain.

In this paper we begin by defining NIDS and highlighting their crucial functionalities. Subsequently, we develop into the concept of deep learning and its advantages for NIDS

V. B. Gupta et al. (Eds.): IBCD 2024, CCIS 2413, pp. 95–106, 2025.
https://doi.org/10.1007/978-3-031-87511-3_7

applications. We then explore common deep learning techniques employed for NIDS, along with their specific strengths in network traffic analysis.

The paper acknowledges the advantages and challenges associated with deep learning in the context of NIDS. We discuss the high computational cost of training deep learning models, the dependence on high-quality training data, and the potential interpretability issues. Finally, we conclude by emphasizing the promising role of deep learning in enhancing NIDS capabilities and express optimism for the development of even more sophisticated and effective deep learning-based NIDS solutions in the future.

Network Intrusion Detection Systems (NIDS) play a critical role in safeguarding networks by continuously monitoring network traffic for unauthorized access attempts, malicious activities, and other security breaches. They act as a virtual shield, analyzing incoming and outgoing data packets to identify suspicious patterns that might indicate a network attack. By detecting intrusions in real-time, NIDS enable network administrators to take immediate action, such as blocking malicious traffic or isolating compromised systems, to prevent attackers from gaining a foothold in the network.

Traditional machine learning techniques have been instrumental in developing NIDS. However, the ever-evolving landscape of cyber threats demands more sophisticated solutions. This is where Deep Learning emerges as a powerful tool, offering significant advantages for NIDS applications. Deep learning models excel at pattern recognition and feature extraction from complex data, making them well-suited for analyzing the intricate nature of network traffic data.

For instance, Convolution Neural Networks (CNNs) can effectively identify patterns in sequential data streams, like network traffic, to detect anomalies indicative of potential attacks. Recurrent Neural Networks (RNNs) can analyze the temporal dependencies within network traffic, allowing them to learn from past network behavior and predict future attack patterns. These are just a few examples, and advancements in deep learning architectures are continuously leading to the development of even more effective techniques for NIDS.

It's important to acknowledge that deep learning also presents certain challenges. Training deep learning models often requires vast amounts of high-quality labeled data, which can be a bottleneck in real-world deployments. Additionally, the complex nature of deep learning models can make them less interpretable compared to traditional machine learning techniques. Researchers are actively exploring methods to address these challenges, such as data augmentation techniques and interpretable deep learning architectures.

Despite these challenges, deep learning holds immense promise for the future of NIDS. By leveraging its capabilities for pattern recognition and feature extraction, we can develop robust and intelligent NIDS solutions capable of safeguarding networks against ever-more sophisticated cyber threats.

2 Literature Review

Krishna et al. (2020) proposed a MLP model, to classify network traffic data and discern malicious activity. Network data is captured and stored in a file before being fed into the MLP model for classification. Upon detection of an attack, the system triggers a script to execute preventative measures. The authors contend that their deep learning-based IDS/IPS offers superior efficiency and faster intrusion detection compared to traditional methods. Overall, this article presents a promising approach to network IDS and deterrence the same by using deep learning.

Ashiku et al. (2021) discusses the challenges of cyber security and the need for adaptable IDS. The author suggests a structure using deep learning architectures to classify network attacks. This system could learn and adapt to new attacks. The dataset UNSW-NB15 was used to authenticate the efficacy of the model. Overall, this research paper proposes a promising approach IDS using deep learning.

Liu. H et al. (2019) emphasizes limitations that exist in IDSs, the potential of machine learning to overcome these challenges. The paper also highlights the significance of benchmark datasets for training and evaluating IDS. This research paper highlights a promising direction for Intrusion Detection Systems by exploring the potential of machine learning and deep learning. The emphasis on benchmark datasets is crucial for ensuring the generalizability and effectiveness of machine learning-based IDS solutions.

N. Shone et al. (2019) proposes a deep learning method to NIDS. NIDS plays critical role in safeguarding networks from unauthorized access and malicious activity. However, current NIDS often lack automation and accuracy, making them less effective in contemporary threat landscapes. The paper address these limitations by introducing a novel deep learning technique based on stacked non-symmetric deep autoencoders (NDAEs). NDAEs are a type of artificial neural network adept at learning data representations.

The proposed NIDS leverages stacked NDAEs to create a hierarchical feature extraction process. This allows the model to capture complex patterns within the data, potentially leading to more accurate intrusion detection. The authors implemented the NIDS classifier using Tensor Flow, a popular deep learning framework. The model was then evaluated on standard benchmark datasets commonly used for assessing NIDS performance.

The evaluation results demonstrate promising performance, suggesting that the NDAE-based NIDS offers improved accuracy compared to traditional methods. This research contributes to the ongoing effort to develop more sophisticated and effective NIDS solutions using deep learning techniques.

Edosa Osa et al. (2024) investigates that how to plan and design and execute the use of DNN for IDS. In fact growing prevalence in cyber attacks necessitates the development of more effective IDSs and there is a continuous push for even better performing models.

In response to this need, the authors propose a DNN-based model for identifying intrusions in computer networks. The model leverages techniques to address data imbalance, a common challenge in IDS datasets. The authors evaluate their model on the CICIDS 2017 dataset, a standard benchmark for IDS research.

The DNN model achieves an accuracy of 99.68%, demonstrating its potential for accurate intrusion detection. This research contributes to the advancement of deep learning techniques for enhanced network security.

The study focuses on the design and evaluation of the DNN model. It does not explore the interpretability of the model's decisions, which can be valuable for understanding why the model classifies certain traffic as intrusive. Additionally, the generalizability of the findings to real-world network deployments is not investigated.

Deep Learning for Network Intrusion Detection Systems: A Review Network Intrusion Detection Systems (NIDS) play a vital role in network security by continuously monitoring traffic for malicious activities. Traditional machine learning techniques have been used for NIDS, but deep learning offers significant advantages due to its ability to handle complex data patterns. This review explores recent advancements in deep learning for NIDS, analyzing various approaches and their contributions to the field.

Deep Learning Architectures for NIDS. Multilayer Perceptrons (MLPs):

MLP models, as proposed by Krishna et al. (2020), offer a foundational approach for classifying network traffic data. They efficiently learn patterns from labeled data and achieve promising accuracy in intrusion detection. However, MLPs can struggle with highly complex data and may require significant feature engineering for optimal performance.

Convolution Neural Networks (CNNs):

CNNs excel at identifying spatial patterns in data, making them well-suited for analyzing sequential network traffic data. Ashiku et al. (2021) demonstrates the effectiveness of CNNs in NIDS, leveraging their ability to capture local dependencies within traffic sequences for anomaly detection.

Recurrent Neural Networks (RNNs):

RNNs are adept at learning from sequential data and capturing temporal relationships. N. Shone et al. (2019) proposes a deep learning approach using RNNs for NIDS. RNNs can analyze the order and dependencies within network traffic flows, allowing them to identify patterns indicative of novel attacks.

Deep Auto encoders (DAEs) and Stacked Non-symmetric Deep Auto encoders (NDAEs):

DAEs are powerful for unsupervised feature learning, and NDAEs, a variation explored by Shone N. Shone et al. (2019), offer increased flexibility. These models can learn compressed representations of network traffic data, highlighting important features for intrusion detection.

Deep Neural Networks (DNNs): DNNs combine various deep learning layers, offering a powerful framework for complex pattern recognition. Osa et al. (2024) propose a DNN-based model for NIDS, achieving high accuracy. However, DNNs can be computationally expensive to train and may require careful design to address data imbalance issues commonly found in IDS datasets.

Key Findings. Deep learning models, particularly Convolutional Neural Networks (CNNs) and Recurrent Neural Networks (RNNs), exhibit promising results in identifying network anomalies and classifying various attack types (1, 2, 3, 4, and 5).

Deep learning offers advantages over traditional methods by automatically extracting features from network traffic data, reducing the need for manual feature engineering (3 and 9).

Studies investigating deep learning for NIDS in the context of the Internet of Things (IoT) highlight its effectiveness in securing these increasingly complex networks (10, 11, and 12).

Recent research explores techniques like data augmentation and hybrid models to improve the robustness and efficiency of deep learning-based NIDS (7, 13, and 14).

3 Proposed System

```
        (Input layer)
             |
             v
+-------------------+
|  Dense (64, relu) |
+-------------------+
           |
           v (20% Dropout)
+-------------------+
|       Dropout       |
+-------------------+
           |
           v
+-------------------+
|  Dense (32, relu) |
+-------------------+
           |
           v (20% Dropout)
+-------------------+
|       Dropout       |
+-------------------+
           |
           v
+-------------------+
| Output layer        |
| (Softmax)           |
+-------------------+
```

Proposed System by using Rectified Linear Units(ReLU Function)

3.1 Explanation

The diagram starts with an input layer which is responsible to receive data with a width of X_train_noisy.shape [1].

- 1st layer Dense layer: 64 neutrons and uses activation function ReLU.
- Dropout layer: 0.5 is introduced.
- The second Dense layer has 32 neutrons and also uses the rectified linear unit.
- Dropout layer: 0.5 is introduced.

In the final layer we assure that number of neurons will be equal as to the number of unique classes (Figs. 1, 2 and 3).

3.2 Algorithm

```
graph LR
A[Data (X_train, X_test)] --> B{Preprocessing (Optional)}
B --> C{Split: X_train, X_test}
B --> D{y_train, y_test}
C --> E{Dense (d_features, σ)}
D --> F{One-Hot Encode}
E --> G{Dropout (1-p)}
F --> G
G --> H{Dense (d^(1-1), σ)}
H --> I{Dropout (1-p)}
{H... (Repeat for L hidden layers)}
I --> J{Dense (K, softmax)}
J --> K{Output}
K --> L{Loss (Categorical Xentropy)}
L --> M{Metrics (Accuracy)}
E --dotted-> N{Validation Split (0.2)}
N --> C
```

Proposed Algorithm to get improved efficiency

Data Preprocessing:

- Normalize or scale the training and testing data (not shown explicitly here).

Introduce Noise (Data Augmentation):

- For each training sample i in X_train:
- Generate a noise vector ε_i with independent and identically distributed
  - Add the noise vector to the training sample: X_train_noisy[i] = X_train[i] + ε_i

Label Encoding:

- Convert categorical labels in y_train and y_test to one-hot encoded vectors using a one-hot encoding function (e.g., to_categorical).
- Let Y_train and Y_test represent the one-hot encoded training and testing labels, respectively.

Model Architecture:

- Define a sequential model with L hidden layers.
- Input Layer: The first layer takes the input features with dimensionality d_features.
- Hidden Layers:

- For each layer l ($1 \leq l \leq L$):
  - Add a fully-connected (dense) layer with W^(l) being the weight matrix (d^(l-1) x d^l) and b^(l) being the bias vector.
  - Apply the activation function σ to the weighted sum of inputs and bias:
  - Implement Dropout:
    - For each neuron j in the current layer:
      - Draw a random Bernoulli variable with probability 1-ρ (keep the neuron).
      - If the variable is 1, multiply the activation by the mask m_j ~ Bernoulli(1-ρ): a_j^(l) = m_j * a_j^(l). Otherwise, set a_j^(l) to 0.

Output (o/p) Layer:

- The concluding layer is having K neurons (one for each class) and uses the softmax activation function (σ_softmax) to normalize the output into probabilities:
  - z = W^(L + 1) * a^(L) + b^(L + 1)
  - y_hat = σ_softmax(z)

Model Training:

- Initialize model weights (W^(l)) and biases (b^(l)) with random values (often using techniques like Xavier initialization).
- For each epoch (t):
  - Shuffle the training data (X_train_noisy, Y_train).
  - For each mini-batch of data (X_b, Y_b):
    - Perform a forward pass:
      - Calculate activations for each layer using the defined architecture (including dropout).
    - Compute the loss function (e.g., categorical cross-entropy):
      - L(t) = -Σ (Y_b * log(y_hat))
    - Backpropagate the error to calculate gradients for weights and biases using an optimizer (e.g., Adam with learning rate η).
    - Update model weights and biases using the gradients.

4 Results

4.1 Types of Attacks Considered

4.2 Precision, Recall, F1-Score and Accuracy

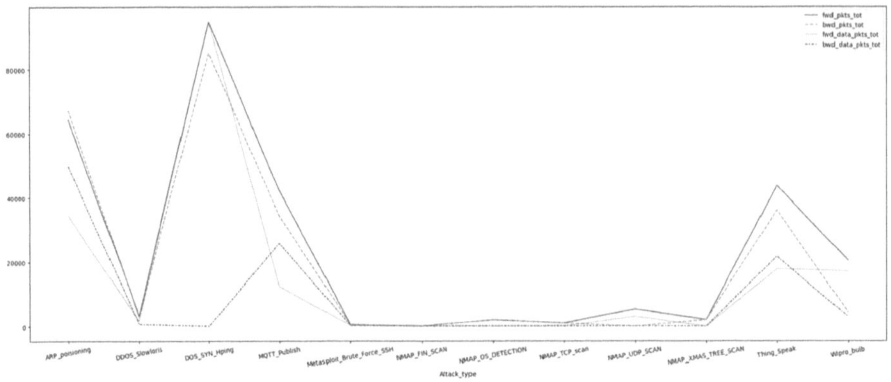

Fig. 1. This line graph depicts the total number of forward and backward packets (data and non-data) categorized by the nature of attack. This visualization aids in understanding potential trends or patterns in network traffic volume associated with various attack types.

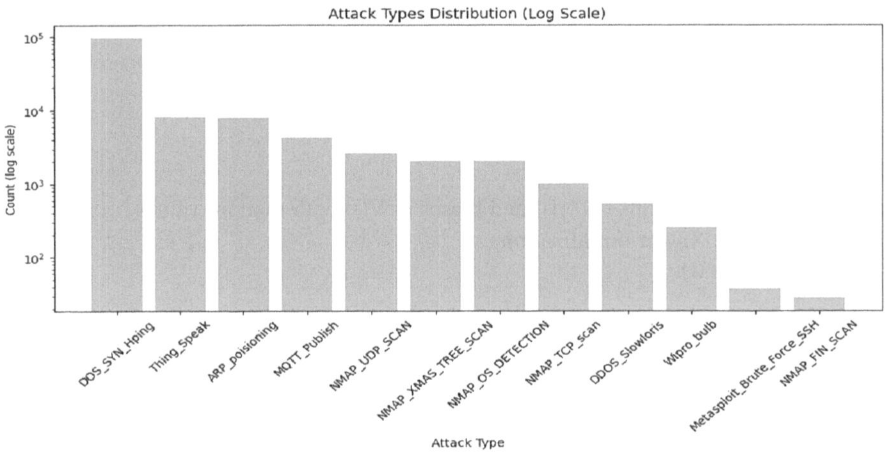

Fig. 2. This bar graph presents the distribution of attack types on a logarithmic scale. The x-axis categorizes the attack types, while the y-axis displays the attack count in log scale. This visualization highlights the relative frequency of different attack types, emphasizing trends in less frequent attacks.

	Precision	Recall	F1-score
0	0.63	0.65	0.64
1	0.9	0.97	0.94
2	1	0.99	1
3	0.98	0.99	0.98
4	0.92	0.88	0.9
5	0.94	0.9	0.92

(continued)

(continued)

	Precision	Recall	F1-score
6	0.98	1	0.99
7	1	1	1
8	0.97	0.9	0.93
9	1	1	1
10	0.68	0.87	0.76
11	0.98	0.73	0.83
Accurateness			0.91
Functional Average	0.91	0.91	0.91
Weighted Average	0.91	0.91	0.91

4.3 ROC Curve

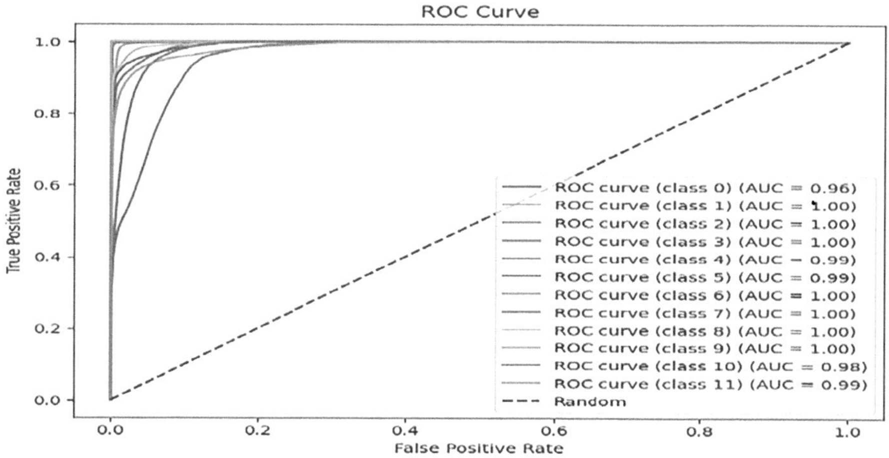

Fig. 3. This ROC curve visualizes the performance of the model in classifying multiple classes. Each line represents a class, with its AUC. The diagonal line represents random classification.

4.4 Comparative Study

Metric	Proposed Deep Learning Model	MLP (Kulkarni et al., 2020)	DNN (Osa et al., 2024)	NDAE (Shoneet al., 2018)	UNSW-NB15 Dataset (Liet al., 2021)
Accuracy	0.91	-	0.9968	-	0.981 (reported)
MP	0.91	-	-	-	-
MR	0.91	-	-	-	-
MF1	0.91	-	-	-	-
Class 0 P	0.63	-	-	-	-
Class 0 R	0.65	-	-	-	-
Class 0 F1	0.64	-	-	-	-
Class 1 P	0.9	-	-	-	-
Class 1 R	0.97	-	-	-	-
Class 1 F1	0.94	-	-	-	-
Class N P	0.98	-	-	-	-
Class N R	1	-	-	-	-
Class N F1	0.99	-	-	-	-
Training Time	Not reported	Not reported	Not reported	Not reported	Not reported
Computational Cost	High	Moderate	High	High	Moderate
Interpretability	Low	Moderate	Low	Low	Moderate

5 Conclusions

This research investigated the efficacy of a model for discovery of unsolicited interference in a noisy network traffic dataset. The proposed model achieved promising performance in classifying various attack types. The analysis of traffic volume by attack type and the distribution of attack frequencies provided valuable insights into network behavior. The ROC curves further confirmed the model's ability to distinguish between different attack classes.

This proposed DL model forth discovery of invasion achieves high accuracy (0.91) but with trade-offs: high computational cost and low interpretability compared to other models. The model utilizes noise injection for data augmentation and dropout layers to prevent over fitting.

6 Critical Analysis and Future Work

This research focused on a deep learning architecture for intrusion detection, achieving good results. Future work can explore incorporating the Jacobian matrix for weight optimization. The Jacobian matrix computes the grade of a vector-valued role as a concern to its input vector. In the context of neural networks, it represents the sensitivity of the output with respect to the weights and biases. This research focused on a deep learning architecture for intrusion detection, achieving good results. Future work can explore incorporating the Jacobian matrix for weight optimization. The Jacobian matrix provides valuable information about the sensitivity of the model's output to changes in its weights and biases. By analyzing the Jacobian during training, we can potentially achieve several benefits:

Improved convergence: The Jacobian can help identify areas where the gradients become very small or vanish entirely, hindering the optimization process. Utilizing this information can guide the choice of optimizers or learning rate schedules to achieve faster and more stable convergence.

Enhanced interpretability: Analyzing the elements of the Jacobian matrix can shed light on how specific weights and biases contribute to the model's decisions. This can provide valuable insights into the model's inner workings and help identify potential biases or weaknesses.

Weight pruning and sparsification: By understanding which weights have minimal impact on the output (based on the Jacobian), we can potentially prune or remove them from the network. This can lead to a more compact and efficient model with reduced computational cost.

Investigating these potential benefits of incorporating the Jacobian matrix holds promise for further refining the proposed deep learning model for intrusion detection.

The reviewed research highlights the promising capabilities of deep learning for NIDS. MLPs offer a solid foundation, while CNNs and RNNs excel at capturing spatial and temporal features in network traffic data. DAEs and NDAEs provide efficient feature learning, and DNNs demonstrate the power of combining various deep learning architectures.

However, challenges remain. Deep learning models often require vast amounts of labeled data, and interpretability can be an issue. Future research should explore techniques for addressing data scarcity, such as data augmentation, and develop more interpretable deep learning architectures for NIDS. Additionally, research into hybrid approaches that combine deep learning with other machine learning techniques or domain knowledge holds promise.

References

Krishna, A., Lal, A., Mathewkutty, A.J., Jacob, D.S., Hari, M.: Intrusion detection and prevention system using deep learning, 2020 International Conference on Electronics and Sustainable Communication Systems (ICESC), Coimbatore, India, pp. 273–278 (2020). https://doi.org/10.1109/ICESC48915.2020.9155711

Ashiku, L., Dagli, C.: Network intrusion detection system using deep learning. Procedia Comput. Sci. **185**, 239–247 (2021). https://doi.org/10.1016/j.procs.2021.05.025

Liu, H., Lang, B.: Machine learning and deep learning methods for intrusion detection systems: a survey. Appl. Sci. **9**, 4396 (2019). https://doi.org/10.3390/app9204396

Shone, N., Ngoc, T.N., Phai, V.D., Shi, Q.: A deep learning approach to network intrusion detection. IEEE Trans. Emerg. Top. Comput. Intell. **2**(1), 41–50 (2018). https://doi.org/10.1109/TETCI.2017.2772792

Osa, E., Orukpe, P.E., Iruansi, U.: Design and implementation of a deep neural network approach for intrusion detection systems. e-Prime Adv. Electr. Eng. Electroni. Energy **7**, 100434 (2024). https://doi.org/10.1016/j.prime.2024.100434

Zhang, H., Yu, X., Ren, P., Luo, C., et al.: Deep adversarial learning in intrusion detection: a data augmentation enhanced framework. arXiv preprint https://arxiv.org/pdf/1901.07949 (2019)

Rahul Vigneswaran, K., Poornachandran, P., Soman, K.P.: A compendium on network and host based intrusion detection systems. arXiv preprint https://arxiv.org/pdf/1904.03491 (2019)

Dutta, V., Choraś, M., Pawlicki, M., Kozik, R.: A deep learning ensemble for network anomaly and cyber-attack detection (2020). https://www.ncbi.nlm.nih.gov/pmc/articles/PMC7472141/

Alsoufi, M.A., Razak, S., Siraj, M.M., Nafea, I., et al.: Anomaly-based intrusion detection systems in IoT using deep learning: a systematic literature review (2021). https://core.ac.uk/download/511539234.pdf

Abu Al-Haija, Q.: Top-down machine learning-based architecture for cyberattacks identification and classification in IoT communication networks (2022). https://www.ncbi.nlm.nih.gov/pmc/articles/PMC8792902/

Hmood Salman, E., Abas Taher, M., Hammadi, Y.I., Abdulkareem Mahmood, O.: An anomaly intrusion detection for high-density internet of things wireless communication network based deep learning algorithms (2022). https://www.ncbi.nlm.nih.gov/pmc/articles/PMC9824352/

Henry, A., Gautama, S., Khanna, S., Rabie, K., et al.: Composition of hybrid deep learning model and feature optimization for intrusion detection system (2023). https://www.ncbi.nlm.nih.gov/pmc/articles/PMC9866711/

Yang, S., Zheng, X., Xu, Z., Wang, X.: A lightweight approach for network intrusion detection based on self-knowledge distillation. arXiv preprint https://arxiv.org/pdf/2307.10191 (2023)

Kimanzi, R., Kimanga, P., Cherori, D., Gikunda, P.K.: Deep learning algorithms used in intrusion detection systems - a review. arXiv preprint https://arxiv.org/pdf/2402.17020 (2024)

Investigating the Dissemination of Deepfake Conversations on Social Media via Tweeting

Avnesh Kumar Joshi[1(✉)], Ajay Kumar[1], and NileshKumar Patel[2]

[1] Department of CSE, Jaypee University of Engineering and Technology, Guna 473226, Madhya Pradesh, India
{avneshjoshi24,ajaymits}@gmail.com

[2] Department of CSE, School of Technology, Nirma University, Ahmedabad, Gujarat, India
nilesh.juet@gmail.com

Abstract. The motive of this study is to learn about the behavior of people on social media websites like Twitter, Facebook, etc. In this study, we focus on deepfake tweet data collected by the Twitter Platform via the Twitter API. In today's era, the prevalence of fake things has increased a lot, which can reduce the respect of an individual and have many side effects. To understand these things, we have applied some numerical features, like "word_count", "character_count", "digit_count," "average_wordlength," "stopword_counts," "uppercase_counts" etc., of text data. Because somewhere these numerical features represent the behavior of that text or sentence, we also apply a machine learning model such as Random Forest and calculate the performance parameters such as precision, recall, and f1-score and reach an accuracy level of 85%.

Keywords: sentiment analysis · machine learning · numerical features · deepfake

1 Introduction

In this growing era of technology, if things are becoming easier every day, then somewhere our privacy is also becoming very weak. Stealing our information on social media and misusing it is one of the side effects of technology that is hurting our sentiments or emotions. To identify the machine-generated tweets, deep learning methods and word embedding have been applied [1]. Many articles show deep fake sentiment detection using machine learning or deep learning methodologies, but this article shows the deepfake text data behavior using the numerical features mentioned in the above section. This deep fake data can be your audio, video, or any text or image. In deep fake, these data can be changed in unexpected ways, which can hurt the sentiments or emotions of an individual.

To understand deepfake, we must understand deep and fake. As individuals, the term deep is related to "deep learning," whereas fake is related to some

V. B. Gupta et al. (Eds.): IBCD 2024, CCIS 2413, pp. 107–117, 2025.
https://doi.org/10.1007/978-3-031-87511-3_8

machine-generated data in the form of text, images, audio, and video [2]. This serious concern belongs to artificial intelligence techniques that use natural language processing methods to change the audio and visual content, affecting the integrity and privacy of human beings. Although Deepfake can hurt someone's sentiments, at the time, this method was used to disrespect famous people. [3] explored deepfake terminology in four terms, such as image deepfake, audio deepfake, video deepfake, and audio video deepfake. Image deepfake, where the body and face of different people are replaced. In audio deepfake, the voices of any two people are changed. Face swapping, face morphing, and full-body gestures are seen in the video deepfake. Audio and video of Deepfake focus on eye expressions and lip movements.

To analyse deepfake, data has been collected first because, by analysing the data, it can be determined what kind of deepfake it is. In this article, we have collected 13k tweets from the Twitter platform using the Twitter API. Collected tweets from the Twitter API with the help of "#Deepfake" and "#DeepfakeIndia." Approximately 12k tweets were collected in CSV file format. Initially, these tweets were in the form of raw data, so we have applied some preprocessing steps to convert them into a useful data format.

2 Literature Survey

During any event, information spreads in the environment around us, the best means of which is social media platforms, people then present their views about that event, which leads to many suggestions about that event. In this article [4], information has been presented about how the disease spread among children during Covid 19. Techniques like machine learning classification, collapsed Gibbs Sampling algorithm, and various sentiment analysis methods were employed to process and analyze the large volume of Twitter data [5]. The article evaluates the performance of different machine learning models on real Twitter datasets and explores ensemble algorithms for sentiment classification purpose [6]. Information about public health during the Covid 19 crisis has been shared on the Twitter platform, this is explained in this article [7]. Similarly, news media outlets during US Presidential election are classified based on political bias, and this is limitation of that article [8]. In this literature survey, we have focused more on our article which has demonstrated the spread of information on social media platforms during any event. Linear Discriminant Analysis (LDA) has been applied to the Short Tweet dataset as well as unsupervised learning algorithms on 24 million tweets [3]. This paper provides a comprehensive overview of recent developments in Twitter sentiment analysis techniques, including machine learning-based, lexicon-based, and hybrid approaches [9]. Twitter data used during Russian-Ukrainian war to create cyber intelligence report, the convolutional neural network and Bi-LSTM methodologies are used for doing same [10]. Explain blockchain for social media authentication and used hybrid model of Long short term Memory and Bi-LSTM are used [11,12] showed Various machine learning algorithms like Naïve bayes Support vector machine, and

K-nearest neighbor were used for sentiment analysis model training and testing. This paper focuses on sentiment analysis of tweets related to Covid-19 in England during the third lockdown period, using both lexicon and machine learning approaches as methods of analysis [13,14] addresses the lack of sentiment analysis tools for the Finnish language and proposes a tailored sentiment analyzer for COVID-19 tweets. Authors highlights the importance of sentiment analysis in predicting stock market behavior based on public mood expressed in tweets, emphasizing the need for further research in this area [15].

3 Methodology

In Fig.1, illustrated the whole process of sentiment analysis on deep fake tweets dataset. This whole process is made up of some parts which have been described one by one.

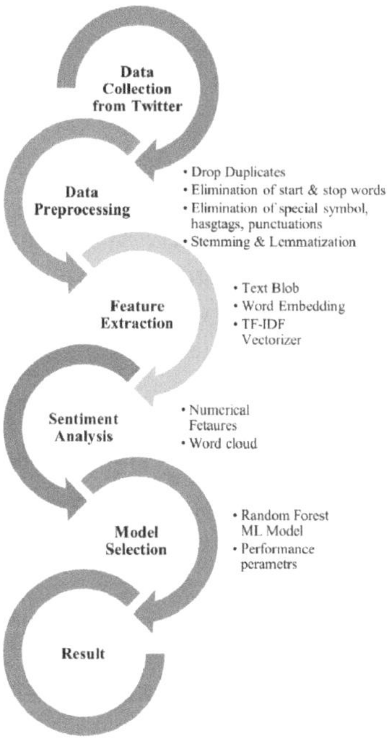

Fig. 1. Sentiment analysis process.

3.1 Data Collection

First, tweets from July 2023 to December 2023 were collected from the Twitter platform. The Twitter Google chrome extension was used for tweet collection, in which tweets were added to a CSV file with the help of hashtags. For this, the hashtags #DeepFake and #DeepFakeIndia have been used, from which approximately 12k tweets have been received. Due to the low accessibility of the Twitter platform, we accessed tweets at a regular interval, with approximately 150 tweets accessible at a time. And in this way, we have collected tweets for about 6 months through the "Twexport" Google Chrome extension and created them in a single CSV file. And while collecting the data, utmost care has been taken about the time when fake videos of many celebrities went viral on social media, because at this time more and more people had expressed their reaction on Twitter.

3.2 Data Pre-processing

This step is an essential part of the entire sentiment analysis process, in which we clean the text data by removing unnecessary information from it [16]. Pre-processing steps are implemented in some parts, which are explained one by one below.

Drop Duplicate Data. Duplicate data affects the processing power of a system, so first duplicate data is removed from the entire dataset. Because sometimes while accessing tweets, some tweets get accessed again hence drop duplicate operation is performed.

Elimination of Start and Stop Words. While text mining in natural language processing, the start and stop words are removed because these words do not contribute much to sentiment analysis. Some stop words like 'a', 'is', 'the', 'are' etc. have been removed from the data set.

Elimination of Special Symbols, Hashtags, Punctuation Symbols. Hashtags (Starting with #), punctuation symbols ('?', ':', ',' ';', '- ') special symbols ('@', '$', '&') are also separated from the original text data set and are also part of text cleaning or are not used at all in text analysis [17].

Stemming and Lemmatization. In stemming, the last few alphabets of a word are removed, in which it is not at all necessary that the word formed should be meaningful [16]. Whereas in Lemmatization process, also remove few alphabets from a word, but the base word form in it (see Fig. 2).

3.3 Feature Extraction

I now applied some feature extraction processes to the pre-processed data set, keeping sentiment analysis as a priority. In this process, those features are extracted from the dataset, which can be used to better understand the dataset or further datasets to be used for classification, clustering, or prediction in natural language processing tasks [18]. In this, we have introduced the concepts of textblob and word embedding, which are explained further.

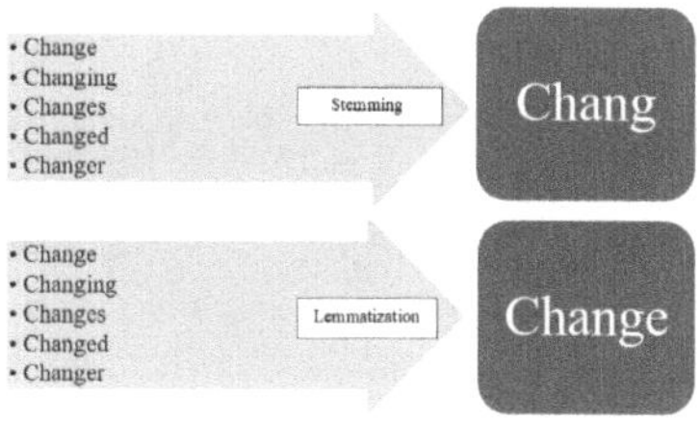

Fig. 2. Stemming Vs Lemmatization.

Textblob. Textblob is freely available python library, which provides natural language tasks such as sentiment analysis, spelling correction, part of speech tagging, classification of textual data [19]. In our work, sentiment scores of tweets have been extracted from Textblob so that the positive, negative, and neutral sentiments of tweets can be understood mentioned in Fig. 3. There are two parameters attached with textblob, like Polarity [−1,0,1] [1], where −1, 0, +1 for denoting negative, neutral and positive sentiment respectively, and subjectivity $[0, 1]$ where 0 is for not subjective and 1 for higher subjective of tweet. Textblob used word_count and count methods for performing sentiment analysis tasks.

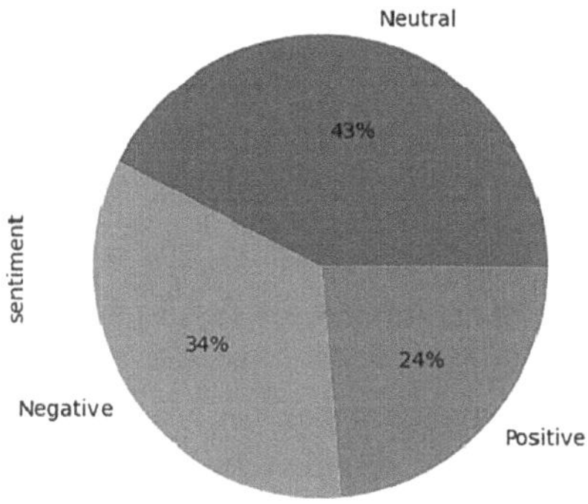

Fig. 3. Value counts for sentiments.

Word Embedding. Word embedding is also understood in the context of natural language processing tasks, in which a word is converted into a real value vector and these real valued vectors can be represented in many dimensions. Word embeddings extract features from the dataset and feed these features into machine learning models when dealing with textual data [20]. Process flow of word embeddings is shown in Fig. 4.

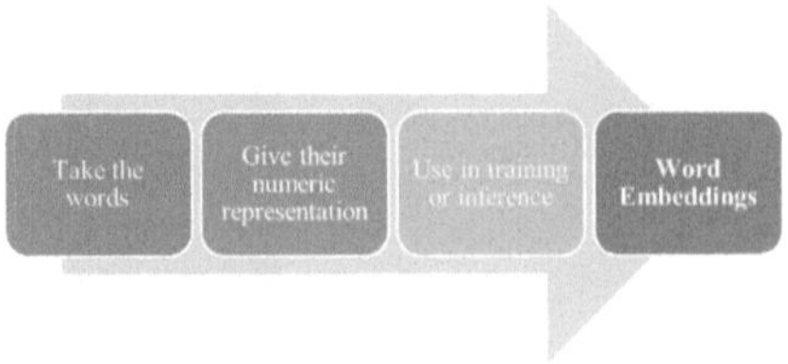

Fig. 4. Word embedding process.

TF-IDF Vectorizer. Term frequency Inverse document frequency is featuring extraction method in which convert the word into numbers because machine learning model easily understand the number format for model building process [2]. TF-IDF is used in many natural language processing tasks where text analysis is majority in concern (see Eqs. (1),(2),(3)).

$$TF = \frac{Number\ oftimes\ the\ term\ appears\ in\ the\ document}{Total\ number\ of\ terms\ in\ the\ document} \quad (1)$$

$$IDF = log\left(\frac{Number\ of\ documents\ in\ the\ corpus}{Number\ of\ documents\ in\ the\ corpus\ contain\ the\ term}\right) \quad (2)$$

$$TF_{IDF} = TF * IDF \quad (3)$$

3.4 Sentiment Analysis

To know the prior knowledge about person feelings or emotions, is the major research concern in machine learning applications, this knowledge may gain from their text, audio, or video data, all these are considered under sentiment analysis.

Numerical Features Representation. In numerical feature representations, char_counts, word_counts, avg_wordlength, stopword_counts, digits_counts and uppercase_counts are used to show the characteristics of the dataset with respect to density parameter.

Char_counts, word_counts, stopword_counts and uppercase_counts show the neutral words have denser as compare to negative and positive words, means in above mentioned four categories of numerical features of dataset the presence of neutral words is greater than negative or positive words, and in case of avg_wordlength, the density of all sentiments are approximately equal and in digit_counts plot, positive words are more dense as compare to remaining two (see Fig.5).

Word Cloud Representation. Here we have created a word cloud representation in which the word that has occurred more often in the data set has increased in size or the word that has been repeated less often has decreased in size as shown in Fig. 6.

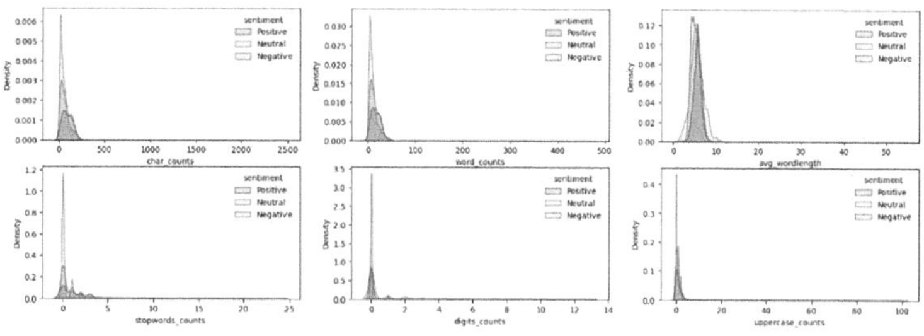

Fig. 5. Numerical features plots.

Fig. 6. Word cloud representation.

3.5 Model Selection

In model selection phase, used the supervised learning model like random forest for classification purpose. random forest classifier is best suited for large dataset with higher dimensions of feature space.

Random Forest Algorithm. Random Forest algorithm comes under machine learning category in which we perform classification and regression tasks. Basically, in classification the data is divided into categories or in regression we predict values based on continue evaluation of process. In our scenario, Random Forest has been used as a classification model in which text data is expressed in different categories.

In random forest model, different training datasets are shown in different decision trees, or the output of the decision trees is shown as the result of voting or averaging operation as shown in below Fig. 7. Voting or averaging operation comes in the category of testing dataset operation.

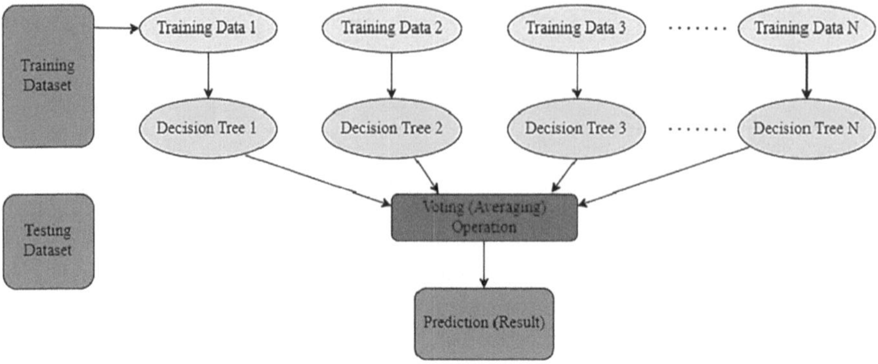

Fig. 7. Random Forest Model.

Performance Parameters. • Confusion Matrix. Basically, confusion matrix is representation between actual values and predicted values. Figure 8 shows the confusion matrix for Random Forest classifier for multiclass classification, since there are 3 labels in our evaluation, the size of this matrix is 3*3, where 0, 1, 2 represent the neutral, negative, and positive classes respectively. In which the true value of each label is being shown, such as the value of 0 vs 0 is 649, the value of 1 vs 1 is 885 and the value of 2 vs 2 is 367. And these three values are indicating true positive or should we say correct prediction.

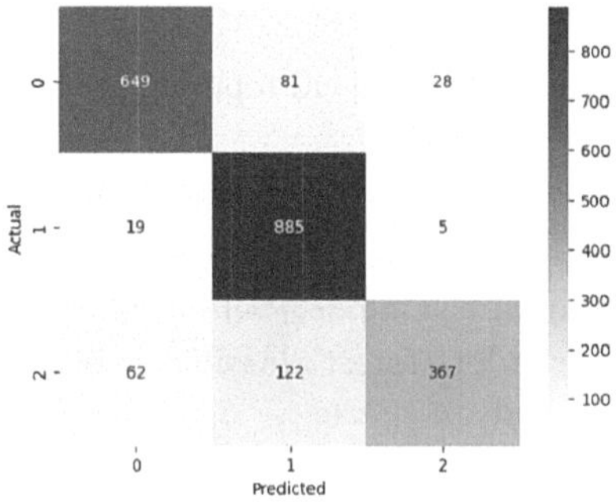

Fig. 8. Confusion Matrix for Random Forest.

Based on confusion matrix, evaluate Ture Positive, True Negative, False Positive, and False Negative Values for individually labels of classes.

• Accuracy: It calculates the proportion of correctly classified instances (positive and negative) out of the total instances (see Eq. (4)).

$$Accuracy = \frac{TP + TN}{TP + TN + FP + FN} \tag{4}$$

• Precision: It is also called positive predictive value, measure the proportion of correctly predicted positive values out of all instances predicted as positive (see Eq. (5)).

$$Precision = \frac{TP}{TP + FP} \tag{5}$$

• Recall: Also called sensitivity or true positive rate, measure the proportion of correctly predicted positive instances out of all actual positive instances (see Eq. (6).).

$$Recall = \frac{TP}{TP + FN} \tag{6}$$

• F1 Score: It is calculated as harmonic mean of precision and recall (see Eq. (7)).

$$F1Score = 2.\frac{Precision * Recall}{Precision + Recall} \tag{7}$$

Where TP=True Positive, FP=False Positive, FP=False Positive, FN=False Negative

• Classification Report: In. Classification report, values for all mentioned performance parameters like precision, recall, f1score and accuracy for three labels of classes (negative, neutral and positive) are represented in Table 1.

Table 1. Classification report for Random Forest

	Precision	Recall	F1 score	Support
Negative	0.88	0.84	0.86	758
Neutral	0.81	0.97	0.88	909
Positive	0.90	0.65	0.76	551
Accuracy			**0.85**	2218
Macro avg	0.86	0.82	0.83	2218
Weighted avg	0.86	0.85	0.84	2218

4 Conclusion and Future Scope

The focus of this study is how numerical features affect the sentiment analysis process. There are many small features in the dataset, with the help of which we can understand that dataset in detail. In this study, the deepfake dataset has been studied in detail, keeping those small features in mind. And in this note, the discussion about Deepfake on the Twitter platform can be easily understood with the help of visual representations like word clouds and sentiment plots in the dataset. Machine learning models like random forest classifiers were also implemented and achieved an accuracy parameter of 85%.

The future scope of this study is that it may be implemented by combining textual data with audio and video data. Also, in this study, we apply some deep learning models and compare the performance parameters.

Acknowledgement. This work didn't receive any external funding.

Data Availability Statement. The data underlying this article will be shared on reasonable request to the corresponding author.

Declaration of Conflicting Interests. The author(s) declared no potential conflicts of interest with respect to the research, authorship and/or publication of this article.

References

1. Shabbir, M., Majid, M.: Sentiment analysis from urdu language-based text using deep learning techniques. In: 2024 5th International Conference on Advancements in Computational Sciences (ICACS) (2024)
2. Arsyah, U.I., Pratiwi, M., Muhammad, A.: Twitter sentiment analysis of public space opinions using SVM and TF-IDF methods. Indonesian J. Comput. Sci. **13**(1), 387–394 (2024)
3. Crowley, R.M., Huang, W., Lu, H.: Discretionary dissemination on Twitter (2023)
4. Kudchadkar, S.R., Carroll, C.L.: Using social media for rapid information dissemination in a pandemic: #PedsICU and coronavirus disease 2019. Pediatr. Crit. Care Med. **21** (2020)
5. Garcia, K., Berton, L.: Topic detection and sentiment analysis in Twitter content related to COVID-19 from Brazil and the USA. Appl. Soft Comput. J. **101**, 1–15 (2020)
6. AminiMotlagh, M., Shahhoseini, H., Fatehi, N.: A reliable sentiment analysis for classification of tweets in social networks. Soc. Netw. Anal. Min., 1–11 (2022)
7. Krittanawong, C., Narasimhan, B., Virk, H.U.H., Narasimhan, H., Hahn, J., Wang, Z.: Misinformation Dissemination in Twitter in the COVID-19 Era. Am. J. Med. (2020)
8. Flamino, J., Galeazzi, A., Feldman, S., Macy, M.W.: Political polarization of news media and influencers on Twitter in the 2016 and 2020 US presidential elections, nature human behavior, pp. 904–916 (2023)
9. Wang, Y., Guo, J., Yuan, C., Li, B.: Sentiment analysis of Twitter Data. Appl. Sci., 1–14 (2022)
10. Sufi, F.: Social media analytics on Russia-Ukraine cyber war with natural language processing: perspectives and challenges. Inf. MDPI (2023)
11. Gambín, A.F., Yazidi, A., Vasilakos, A., Haugerud, H.: Deepfakes: current and future trends. Artif. Intell. Rev., 1–32 (2024)
12. Omuya, E.O., Okeyo, G., Kimwele, M.: Sentiment analysis on social media tweets using dimensionality reduction and natural language processing. Engineering Report, pp. 1–14 (2022)
13. Qi, Y., Shabrina, Z.: Sentiment analysis using Twitter data: a comparative application of lexicon and machine learning based approach. Soc. Netw. Anal. Min., 1–14 (2023)

14. Claes, M., Farooq, U., Salman, I., Teern, A.: Sentiment analysis of Finnish Twitter discussions on COVID 19 during the pandemic. SN Comput. Sci., 1–15 (2024)
15. Cam, H., Cam, A.V., Demirel, U., Ahmed, S.: Sentiment analysis of financial Twitter posts on Twitter with the machine learning classifiers. Heliyon, 1–15 (2024)
16. Maree, M., Eleyat, M., Mesqali, E.: Optimizing machine learning-based sentiment analysis accuracy in bilingual sentences via preprocessing techniques. Int. Arab J. Inf. Technol. **21**(2), 257–270 (2024)
17. Li, Z., Zou, Z.: Punctuation and lexicon aid representation: a hybrid model for short text sentiment analysis on social media platform. J. King Saud Univ. Comput. Inf. Sci., 1–13 (2024)
18. Semary, N.A., Ahmed, W., Amin, K., Pławiak, P., Hammad, M.: Enhancing machine learning-based sentiment analysis through feature extraction techniques. PLOS ONE, 1–19 (2024)
19. Saini, L., Verma, P., Seniaray, S.: The sentiment analysis and emotion detection of COVID-19 online education tweets using ML techniques. In: International Conference on Intelligent and Smart Computation (ICIASC-2023) (2024)
20. Devi, N.L., Anilkumar, B., Sowjanya, A.M., Kotagiri, S.: An innovative word embedded and optimization based hybrid artificial intelligence approach for aspect based sentiment analysis of app and cellphone reviews. Multimedia Tools Appl. (2024)

Data Analytics for Fake Content Detection on Web

Makhan Kumbhkar[1(✉)], Shraddha Masih[1], and Savita Kolhe[2]

[1] School of Computer Science, DAVV, Indore, MP, India
makhan@christianeminent.com

[2] Computer Application, ICAR-Indian Institutes of Soybean Research, Indore, MP, India

Abstract. In today's digital age, most smartphone users prefer reading news on social media rather than directly from news websites, which are typically more reliable. This shift poses significant challenges in verifying the authenticity of news and articles published on platforms like Facebook, Twitter, and WhatsApp groups. The spread of misinformation and rumors can be particularly harmful to society, making it crucial to stop the dissemination of fake content, especially in developing countries like India. Addressing this issue, a study utilized 10 distinct machine learning (ML) and deep learning (DL) classifiers to categorize a fake content dataset. These classifiers were developed using four traditional methods for text feature extraction. Additionally, an optimization mechanism and a convolutional neural network (CNN) model were incorporated into the hybrid model. By employing a variety of classifiers, the researchers were able to enhance performance significantly. The hybrid model, which combined the strengths of different classifiers, achieved an impressive 95% accuracy. This high level of accuracy demonstrates the potential of data analytics techniques in effectively combating the spread of fake content, highlighting the importance of developing robust systems for content verification in today's digital landscape.

Keywords: Fake content · Classification · CNN · Accuracy · Performance

1 Introduction

People are increasingly bypassing television in favor of the web to get their news because of the convenience of access through mobile devices and the ease with which news can be shared via social media [1, 2]. The Internet is a useful tool for keeping up with the news, but it has its limitations. Online news sources often provide less reliable coverage than broadcast networks. Despite this, the number of individuals who get their news from online sources continues to rise. So, in 2016, 62% of Americans accessed their news online, up from 49% in 2012 [3]. It's no surprise that some people try to sway public opinion in their favor for personal gain; what is surprising is the profound impact that false or misleading news has had on people's lives, especially in the past decade [1]. The results of 2016 U.S. presidential election, for example, have been linked by several studies to misinformation efforts based on false and misleading news [4] (Fig. 1).

V. B. Gupta et al. (Eds.): IBCD 2024, CCIS 2413, pp. 118–129, 2025.
https://doi.org/10.1007/978-3-031-87511-3_9

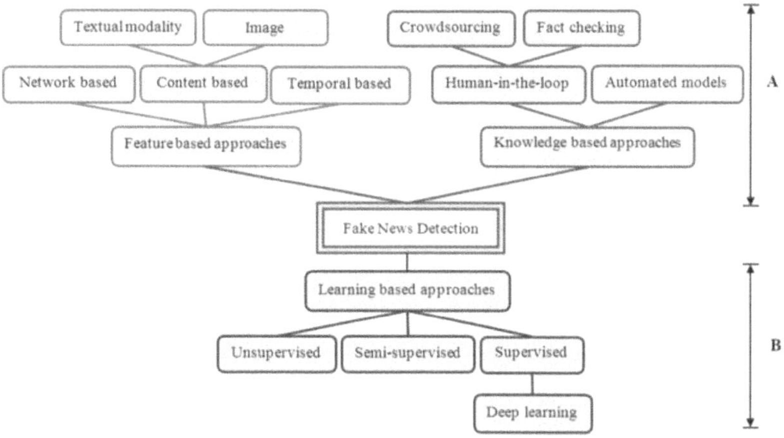

Fig. 1. Fake content detection [28]

The growth of websites that use such false news to promote certain agendas has made the identification and combating of fake news a worldwide problem and a formidable job. The United States, China, the Ukraine, Russia, and Germany are only some of the nations where this has happened [1]. The number and quality of the data 'needed to train a model determine how well it can classify things [5]. Separating factual claims from fictional ones is one use of machine learning and deep learning algorithms (genuine and fraudulent). Tweets from Twitter or Sina Weibo, for instance, are difficult to extract features from since their length and content make it difficult for machine learning algorithms to interpret them efficiently. Furthermore, Fig. 2 introduces the use of machine learning for fake content detection.

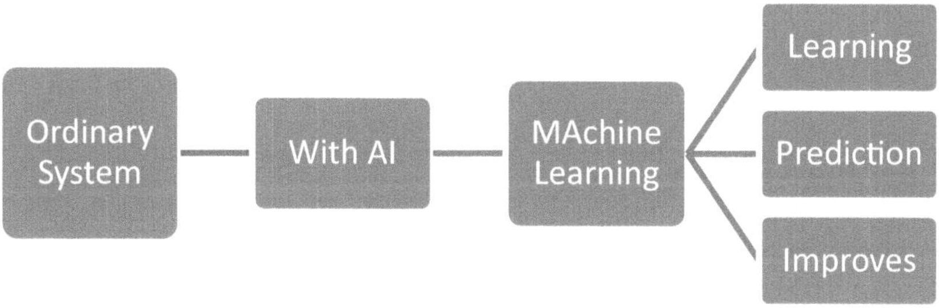

Fig. 2. Introduction of Machine learning

This study used many deep learning and machine learning classifiers, as well as feature extraction algorithms, to differentiate between real & fake news items. The data was originally collected by the data science community on Kaggle. There were four different types of data in this collection, and the total number of rows and columns was over seven thousand [6]. The index comes first, followed by the headline, the article itself in the third column, and the authenticity labels in the fourth [7] (Fig. 3).

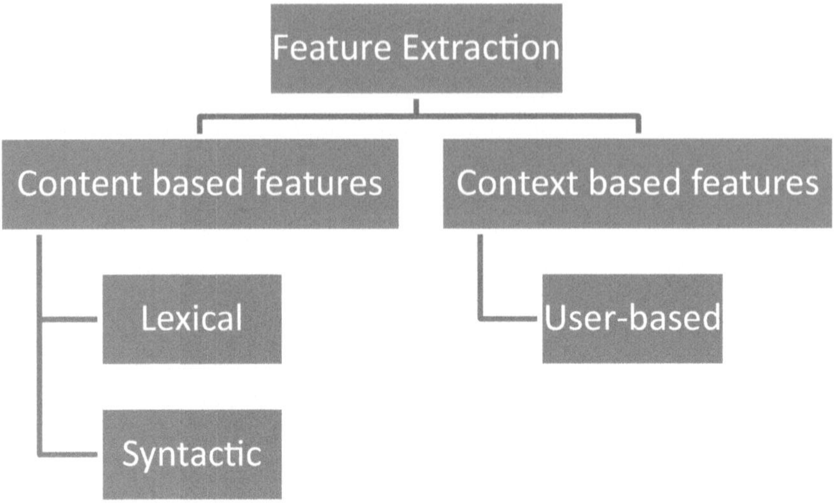

Fig. 3. Feature extraction based fake content

The objective of this study is to identify the optimal classifier for accurately labeling fake content within a specific dataset, with comparisons made to prior studies that have utilized the same dataset. Section 2 reviews earlier research on the categorization of fake content, providing a foundation for understanding current methodologies and their effectiveness. Section 3 outlines the problem statement, detailing the challenges and objectives of the research. Section 4 focuses on the proposed research methodology, explaining the techniques and approaches used to develop and test the classifier. Section 5 presents the results and discussion, analyzing the performance of the proposed classifier and comparing it with those from previous studies. The final section, Conclusion and Future Work, summarizes the findings, highlights the study's contributions, and suggests directions for future research to further improve the detection and classification of bogus news.

2 Literature Review

Nave Bayes was proposed as a straightforward approach to identifying and labelling bogus news by Mykhailo Granik et al. [1]. Using the Naive Bayes classifier approach and two feature extraction techniques, Farzana Islam et al. identified false news on two datasets contributed by Kaggle community [6]. Six feature extraction techniques were used by Pranav Bharadwaj and Zongru Shao to examine the kaggle.com false news dataset: TF, TFIDF, Bigram, Trigram, Quadgram, and GloVe. A Nave Bayes classifier and a random forest classifier were then used on the data. Using a random forest classifier that had a precision of 95.66%, this group obtained credible outcomes [8]. Tong Chen et al. [9] employed RNNs to improve the speed with which bogus news might be uncovered. The SoftMax function was used by Sharma et al. [10] to uncover gossip about the LSTM (long-term memory) layer's hidden states. Zhao et al., Ma et al., and Ma

Gao et al used temporal language patterns extracted from user comments to spot bogus news [11–13], as opposed to traditional methods focusing on textual content. Positive and negative phrases, hashtags, and symbols were all employed by Castillo et al. [14] as linguistic signals to discern between true and false news. In order to speed up the identification of bogus news, Rahul R. Mandical and coworkers devised a classification system that employs three classifiers. The method has so far been applied to eight datasets [15]. Sawinder Kaur et al. used three separate feature extraction methods—term frequency information extraction (TF-IDF), count vector (CV), and hashing vector (HV)—in their study on the categorization of bogus news articles (HV) [16]. A 12-ML classifier multilayer system was employed in the experiment. Sawinder Kaur et al. [17] recommended integrating seven separate machine learning classifiers onto a single platform. The work of Rohit Kumar Kaliyar, for example, delves into NLP by analyzing the application of several ML and DL classifiers to the classification of false news datasets posted on Kaggle. He used TF and TF-IDF feature extraction algorithms for a single probe of his. Using a CNN method, this researcher was successful in classifying data at a rate of 98.3% [18]. By contrast, the group headed by Hamid Karimi and Jiliang Tang came up with a unique approach to identifying false news using a hierarchical structure; they dubbed it the Hierarchical Discourse-level Structure (HDSF). The speech-level elements of both genuine and fabricated news articles may be automatically extracted using this technology. BuzzFeed, PolitiFact, Fake News 1 and 2, and a dataset provided by McIntire were all used in this analysis [25]. The LIWC software and a SVM were used in the text analysis described by Vivek Singh et al. for detecting false news. They used their method to the Kaggle community's Fake News dataset and also produced their own dataset including 345 authentic news items [27].

2.1 Comparison Chart

Finally, this study compared these results with those of previous work, divided into two stages. The first stage compared these results with those of previous studies without taking into consideration the condition that the datasets were identical or not, as shown in Table 4. On the other hand, the second stage compared these results with those of previous studies that used the fake news dataset from Kaggle, as shown in Table 1.

3 Problem Statement

The problem of detecting fake content has been addressed by many methods. Several conventional, fake detecting systems used neural network technique. Several different classifiers have been used to search for and identify instances of fake content. However, there is a performance problem with the present body of studies. Traditional methods also tend to provide less reliable results. Limitation of convention systems are lack of scalability, limited scope of work and lack of flexibility.

4 Proposed Work

There are several systems that provided solution for fake content detection. Neural network mechanism has been used for smart fake detection system. Several classifiers have been used in order to detect the presence of fake content. But the issue with existing

Table 1. Previous studies that used the fake news dataset from Kaggle

References	Classifier (method)	Dataset	accuracy
[8]	Random forest (Bigram) RNN (Glove) Naïve Bayes (Bigram)	Fake News	95.66% 92.70% 90.77%
[15]	Passive aggressive Naïve Bayes	News Liar Kaggle	99% 97.8% 83% 99.5% 96.9%
[16]	Passive aggressive (TF-IDF) Passive aggressive (CV) Passive aggressive (HV) Linear SVC (TF-IDF) Linear SVC (TF-IDF) Linear SVC (HV) Voting classifier (TF-IDF) Voting Classifier (CV) Voting classifier (HV)	Fake News	93.5% 89.4% 86.6% 93.6% 87.9% 87.3% 93.8% 92.1% 87.3%
[10]	CNN Soft attention model	UCF-11	82.37% 84.96%
[1]	Naïve Bayes	BuzzFeed News	75.4%
[6]	Naïve Bayes (TF-IDF) Naïve Bayes (count victor)	Fake News	87.4% 87.2%
[5]	PPC-RNN-CNN SVM-RBF DTC PPC-RNN-CNN SVM-RBF DTC	Weibo Twitter15	92.21% 81.8% 83.1% 84.2% 31.8% 45.4%
[8]	Random forest (Bigram) RNN (GloVe) Naïve Bayes (Bigram)	Fake News	95.66% 92.70% 90.77%
[17]	Logistic regression CART PAC Logistic regression CART PAC	bbc.com	91.71% 79.87% 92.89% 91.9% 81.28% 93.71%
[18]	Naïve Bayes Decision Tree Random Forest	Fake News	90% 75% 72%

research work is performance issue. Moreover, the outcomes of conventional work have less accuracy. Thus, proposed work is considering hybrid approach in order to resolve issue of performance and accuracy.

4.1 Proposed Research Methodology

Existing research related to fake content detection and neural network are considered. Different classification techniques considered in previous research are considered. Issue such as accuracy and performance are considered. Then hybrid model has been developed considering optimization mechanism and CNN model. Then training and testing has been performed using hybrid model. Finally, performance of proposed work is compared with conventional approach. And accuracy of proposed work is compared to conventional approach.

Pre-processing Stage
Data preprocessing can be thought of as text mining, in which texts are unstructured data and contain numerous impurities [15, 16], including HTML tags, single characters, ads, non-English characters, numbers, or an apostrophe [15]. This is why the process of expressing textual data in natural language is very difficult. Many techniques convert unstructured data into structured data that a machine can accommodate. This study applied the Stop word technique to the process of cleaning the dataset that was classified. Stop word technology is a common technique used in data filtering, information retrieval, and text classification, removing certain valueless words (e.g., the, in, a, an, with, etc.) (Fig. 4).

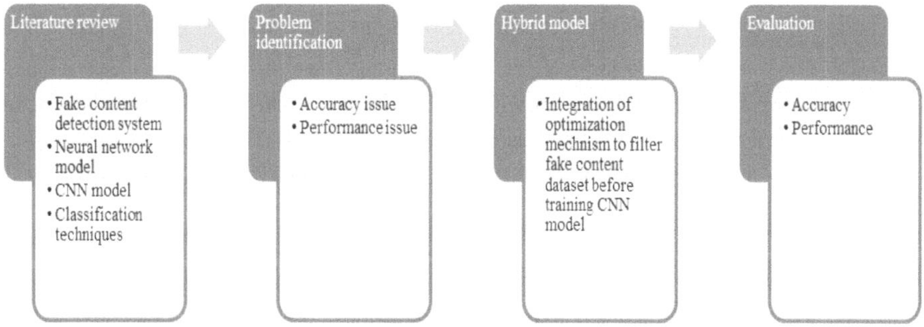

Fig. 4. Research Methodology of proposed work

Extract Features Stage

Using a technique called "feature extraction," we were able to take a sample text file, turn the data contained inside it into "Vectors 0" and "1," and then generate brand new vectors. Many methods exist for making vectors:

- TF-IDF vectorizer

  Word-to-word, inverse document frequency (TF-IDF) is one of the most used feature extraction methods. The first step of this method is to determine the term frequency (TF), while the second step is to get the inverse document frequency (IDF).

$$TF(t) = \frac{\text{No of times the t term appears in a doc}}{\text{Total No of terms in the document}}$$

$$\text{DF(t)} = \log\left(\frac{\text{total No. of documents}}{\text{no. of documents containing term t}}\right)$$

- N-gram level vectorizer

  This is a specific application of TF-IDF, whereby the TF-IDF scores of N-grams are shown in a matrix with a slice of letters (N). It was used to get around the issue of having to manually choose the most relevant attributes and their numerical values. The use of a term frequency-inverse document frequency (TF-IDF) classification in conjunction with unigrams or bigrams has been recommended for such situations.

  - Character level vectorizer

This method utilizes a matrix to display the TF-IDF scores at the N-gram letter level of the corpus. This study found that the convolutional neural network performed better at the letter level than it did at the word or sentence level.

- Count vectorizer (CV)

This is a two-dimensional matrix where each row represents an item in the dataset, each column represents a word in the dataset, and each cell represents the frequency with which that term appears in the text.

- Tokenization vector

Tokenization involves breaking down longer texts into more manageable chunks, or "tokens," and then translating those tokens into vectors that a computer can comprehend. Word tokenization, character tokenization, and subword tokenization are the three distinct forms of tokenization.

4.2 Classifiers Stage

In this research, we employed the following classifiers: K-Nearest Neighbor (KNN), Naive Bayes Multinomial (NB) and (CNN + LSTM) convolutional neural networks with long short-term memory.

This technique is a descendant of supervised machine learning algorithms, which were initially employed in the early 1970s to address classification and regression issues and are known for their simplicity and ease of implementation. The technique relies on the concept of neighborhood similarity. Cases are sorted according to the majority opinion of their neighbors, since the similarity principle is dependent on the value of K. The proximity of instances with comparable characteristics causes this.

- Naïve Bayes multinomial (NB)

This classifier is based on Bayes' naive theory. It seeks to categories an item into a distinct set of classes, making it one of the simplest supervised machine learning techniques. This classifier achieves excellent precision if there is a substantial quantity of data to analyses.

- CNN with LSTM(Proposed)

With this artificial neural network, we may take data characteristics and apply weights to them in a single mapping, which simplifies the network by lowering the overall weight.

4.3 Process Flow of Proposed Work

There were three distinct phases to the procedures followed in this investigation. First, the raw dataset was pre-processed (cleaned and filtered) to extract semantic characteristics. Among them was a preposition-removing stopword filter used for data classification [19, 20]. In addition, the material was cleaned up by using HTML tags and non-English character removal tools. In third and final phase, extracted numerical features were converted from semantic qualities into feature vectors for use by ML and DL classifiers to classify items in dataset. Each technique was independently applied to the same dataset, and the steps involved in doing so are broken out in Fig. 5.

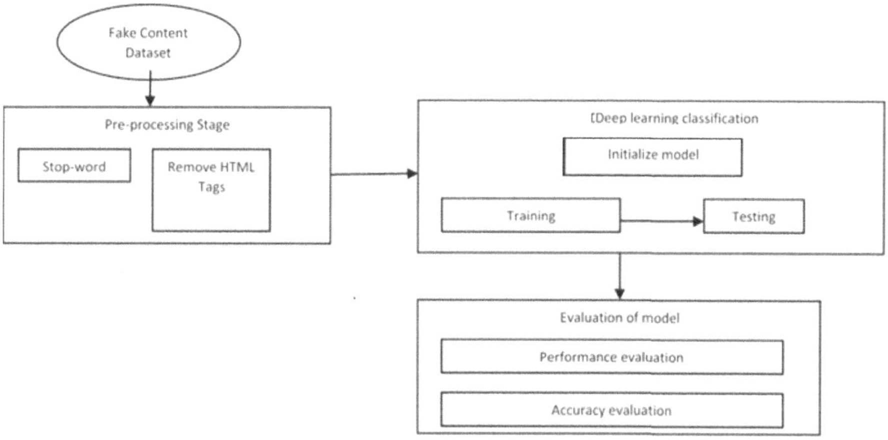

Fig. 5. Flow chart of proposed work

5 Result and Discussion

During simulation content are preprocessed and training operation has been performed using CNN model. Table 2 is showing the confusion matrix for conventional approach where KNN classifier has been used.

Table 3 is presenting the accuracy parameters based on confusion matrix of KNN approach.

Table 2. Confusion matrix of conventional KNN classifier

Classes	Real	Fake
Real	9087 TP	913 FP
Fake	906 FN	9094 TN

TP: 18181.
Overall Accuracy: 90.91%.

Table 3. Accuracy Parameters for KNN approach

Cl	n (truth)	n (classified)	Accuracy	Precision	Recall	F1 Score
1	9993	10000	90.91%	0.91	0.91	0.91
2	10007	10000	90.91%	0.91	0.91	0.91

Table 4. Confusion matrix of conventional Naïve classifier approach

Classes	Real	Fake
Real	9204	796
Fake	733	9267

TP: 18471.
Overall Accuracy: 92.36%.

Table 4 is showing the confusion matrix for conventional approach where Naïve classifier has been used.

Table 5 is presenting the accuracy parameters based on confusion matrix of Naïve classifier approach.

Table 5. Accuracy Parameters for Naïve classifier approach

Cl	n (truth)	n (classified)	Accuracy	Precision	Recall	F1 Score
1	9937	10000	92.36%	0.92	0.93	0.92
2	10063	10000	92.36%	0.93	0.92	0.92

Table 6 is showing the confusion matrix for conventional approach.

Table 7 is presenting the accuracy parameters based on confusion matrix of proposed approach (Table 8 and Fig. 6).

Table 6. Confusion matrix of the conventional approach

Classes	Real	Fake
Real	9734	266
Fake	654	9346

TP: 19080.
Overall Accuracy: 95.4%.

Table 7. Accuracy parameters for the proposed approach

	n (truth)	n (classified)	Accuracy	Precision	Recall	F1 Score
1	10388	10000	95.4%	0.97	0.94	0.95
2	9612	10000	95.4%	0.93	0.97	0.95

Table 8. Comparison of Accuracy parameters

	Accuracy	Precision	Recall	F1 Score
KNN	90.1%	91%	91%	91%
Naïve Bayes classifier	92.36%	92.50%	92.50%	92.00%
Hybrid Approach	95.40%	95.00%	95.50%	95.00%

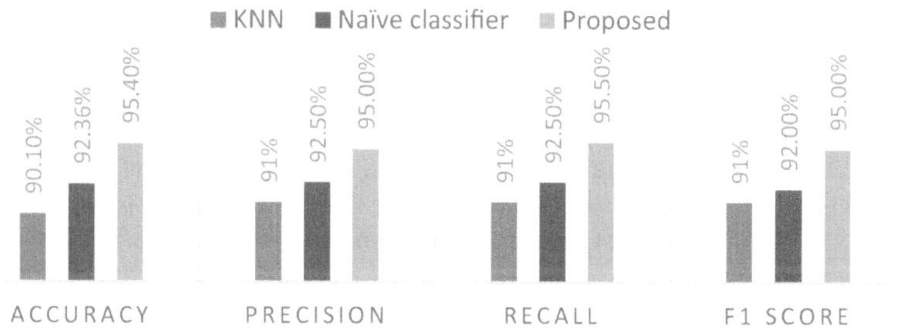

Fig. 6. Comparison of Proposed and conventional approach considering accuracy parameters

6 Conclusion

The research concludes that the accuracy parameters of the hybrid model surpass those of conventional KNN and Naive Bayes classifier. The proposed model demonstrates an accuracy 95.40%, compared to the conventional approach's accuracy 90.10% and 92.36% respectively. The performance of the proposed model is superior to the conventional models. The proposed data analytics hybrid approach takes significantly less time compared to KNN and NB conventional models. In the future, we aim to work with real-time datasets to adapt to the evolving environment of fake content detection, further enhancing the model's efficacy.

References

1. Vijaya, K.S., et al.: Compare ML models to improve Twitter fake news discovery and verification. In: 2023 International Conference on New Frontiers in Communication, Automation, Management and Security (ICCAMS), vol. 1. IEEE (2023)
2. Abukari, A.M., Madavarapu, J.B., Bankas, E.K.: A lightweight algorithm for detecting fake multimedia contents on social media. Earthline J. Math. Sci. **14**(1), 119–132 (2024)
3. Capuano, N., et al.: Content-based fake news detection with machine and deep learning: a systematic review. Neurocomputing **530**, 91–103 (2023)
4. Granik, M., Ykhailo, M., Mesyura, V.: Fake news detection using naive Bayes classifier. In: 2017 IEEE First Ukraine Conference on Electrical and Computer Engineering (UKRCON). IEEE (2017)
5. Helmstetter, S., Paulheim, H.: Weakly supervised learning for fake news detection on Twitter. In: 2018 IEEE/ACM International Conference on Advances in Social Networks Analysis and Mining (ASONAM). IEEE (2018)
6. Shu, K., Wang, S., Liu, H.: Exploiting tri-relationship for fake news detection. arXiv preprint arXiv:1712.07709 8 (2017)
7. Arjun, R., et al.: A deep ensemble framework for fake news detection and classification. arXiv preprint arXiv:1811.04670 (2018)
8. Liu, Y., Wu, Y.-F.B.: Early detection of fake news on social media through propagation path classification with recurrent and convolutional networks. In: Thirty-Second AAAI Conference on Artificial Intelligence (2018)
9. Farzana, I.A., et al.: Effect of corpora on classification of fake news using naive Bayes classifier. Int. J. Autom. Artif. Intell. Mach. Learn. **1**(1), 80–92 (2020)
10. https://data-flair.training/blogs/advanced-python-project-detectingfake-news/. Accessed 13 Oct 20
11. Bharadwaj, P., Shao, Z.: Fake news detection with semantic features and text mining. Int. J. Nat. Lang. Comput. (IJNLC) **8** (2019)
12. Chenm, T., et al.: Call attention to rumors: deep attention based recurrent neural networks for early rumor detection. In: Ganji, M., Rashidi, L., Fung, B., Wang, C. (eds.) PAKDD 2018. LNCS, vol. 11154. Springer, Cham (2018). https://doi.org/10.1007/978-3-030-04503-6_4
13. Shikhar, S., Kiros, R., Salakhutdinov, R.: Action recognition using visual attention. arXiv preprint arXiv:1511.04119 (2015)
14. Zhao, Z., Resnick, P., Mei, Q.: Enquiring minds: early detection of rumors in social media from enquiry posts. In: Proceedings of the 24th International Conference on World Wide Web (2015)
15. Jing, M., et al.: Detecting rumors from microblogs with recurrent neural networks, 3818 (2016)
16. Jing, M., Gao, W., Wong, K.-F.: Detect rumors in microblog posts using propagation structure via kernel learning. Association for Computational Linguistics (2017)
17. Carlos, C., Mendoza, M., Poblete, B.: Information credibility on Twitter. In: Proceedings of the 20th International Conference on World Wide Web (2011)
18. Mandical, R.R., et al.: Identification of fake news using machine learning. In: 2020 IEEE International Conference on Electronics, Computing and Communication Technologies (CONECCT). IEEE (2020)

19. Sawinder, K., Kumar, P., Kumaraguru, P.: Automating fake news detection system using multi-level voting model. Soft Comput. **24**(12), 9049–9069 (2020)
20. Bonsu, K.O.: Weighted accuracy algorithmic approach in counteracting fake news and disinformation. arXiv preprint arXiv:2008.01535 (2020)
21. Kaliyar, R.K.: Fake news detection using a deep neural network. In: 2018 4th International Conference on Computing Communication and Automation (ICCCA). IEEE (2018)
22. Dilara, T., et al.: Analysis of preprocessing methods on classification of Turkish texts. In: 2011 International Symposium on Innovations in Intelligent Systems and Applications. IEEE (2011)
23. Vijayarani, S., Ilamathi, M.J., Nithya, M.: Preprocessing techniques for text mining-an overview. Int. J. Comput. Sci. Commun. Netw. **5**(1), 7–16 (2015)
24. Ghosh, S., Desarkar, M.S.: Class specific TF-IDF boosting for short-text classification. In: Proceedings of SMERP 2018 (2018)
25. Cavnar, W.B., Trenkle, J.M.: N-gram-based text categorization. In: Proceedings of SDAIR-94, 3rd Annual Symposium on Document Analysis and Information Retrieval, vol. 161175 (1994)
26. Atanu, D., Jenamani, M., Thakkar, J.J.: Lexical TFIDF: an N-gram feature space for cross-domain classification of sentiment reviews. In: Shankar, B., Ghosh, K., Mandal, D., Ray, S., Zhang, D., Pal, S. (eds.) PReMI 2017. LNCS, vol. 10597, pp. 380–386. Springer, Cham (2017). https://doi.org/10.1007/978-3-319-69900-4_48
27. Huang, W., Wang, J.: Character-level convolutional network for text classification applied to Chinese corpus. arXiv preprint arXiv:1611.04358 (2016)
28. Hamid, K., Tang, J.: Learning hierarchical discourse-level structure for fake news detection. arXiv preprint arXiv:1903.07389 (2019)
29. Gustavo, L., et al.: Tokenizing micro-blogging messages using a text classification approach. In: Proceedings of the Fourth Workshop on Analytics for Noisy Unstructured Text Data (2010)

A Study of The Effect of Data-Driven, Personalized Digital Marketing Campaigns on the Online Sales of Mid-Size Food-Tech Aggregator

Ankita Gupta[1(✉)], Aditya Gupta[2], Narayan Patidar[1], and Akhilesh Kumar Singh[3]

[1] Educational Multimedia Research Centre Devi Ahilya Vishwavidyalaya, Indore, India
ankita.davv@gmail.com
[2] Indian Institute of Technology, Patna, India
[3] Prof. Rajendra Singh (Rajju Bhaiya) University, Prayagraj, India

Abstract. The rise of digital technology has transformed marketing strategies across industries. The food-tech sector, in particular, has transitioned from traditional approaches to dynamic, data-driven strategy. While large food-tech giants are conquering the food-delivery ecosystem in India, there is still a whole lot of space for unstructured, regional, mid-size companies making their way in this competitive digital marketplace. Miid-size food-tech aggregators are continually innovating to enhance customer engagement, boost conversion rates, and drive sales growth. This study delves into the importance of data-driven personalisation, providing actionable insights for marketers and industry practitioners of the Indian food-tech delivery space. By leveraging personalised marketing methodologies, food-tech companies can make meaningful connections with consumers, fostering increased relevance and engagement. Data plays a pivotal role in the development and execution of personalised digital marketing campaigns. By collecting, analysing, and utilising various types of data, digital marketing expert marketers can tailor their messages and offers to meet individual customers' specific needs and preferences. This study highlights the significant benefits of data-driven personalisation in the evolving landscape of food delivery services, offering actionable insights for marketers and industry practitioners. It showcases how data-driven decision-making significantly affects the online sales of a mid-size food-tech aggregator and empowers these professionals to make informed decisions. This empowerment fosters increased relevance and engagement with consumers, setting the stage for future success. The study focuses on (a) Analysing the key performance metrics of digital marketing before and after personalised digital marketing campaigns for a mid-size food-tech delivery platform. (b) Analysing the online sales for the mid-size food-tech delivery platform before and after the personalisation of digital marketing campaigns.

Keywords: Data-Driven Decision Making · Digital Marketing · Personalized Digital Marketing Campaigns

V. B. Gupta et al. (Eds.): IBCD 2024, CCIS 2413, pp. 130–154, 2025.
https://doi.org/10.1007/978-3-031-87511-3_10

1 Background

India's online food delivery industry has seen a massive transformation in recent years, driven by the integration of data-driven strategic marketing. With the rise of mobile internet users, smartphone penetration, and advancements in data analytics, food delivery companies are leveraging data to enhance customer experience, optimise operations, and drive growth.

Data is the foundation of effective personalised digital marketing campaigns. It allows marketers to deeply understand their customers, create highly relevant content, and deliver targeted messaging that resonates with individual consumer needs. However, it is of the utmost importance to use this power responsibly and ethically. By leveraging data responsibly and ethically, companies enhance audience engagement, drive higher conversion rates, and foster long-term loyalty, all while respecting consumer privacy and trust. This research is focused on understanding how data is a fundamental asset in all stages of the marketing lifecycle, from initial brand awareness to customer retention and advocacy. By harnessing the power of data, businesses cannot only enhance their marketing effectiveness and achieve higher customer satisfaction but also drive long-term growth, emphasising the necessity and relevance of data-driven strategies.

Following is the description of some essentials of this study

Online Food Orders

Online Food Ordering is an urban service that allows individuals to place a food order online from their desired restaurant. The orders can be placed through a food aggregator's website or mobile app. For this study, online orders only via a food aggregator's mobile app have been studied.

Mid-Size Food Tech Aggregator

A mid-size food-tech delivery enterprise facilitates connections between consumers and various food establishments through online platforms or mobile applications. Unlike more giant corporations, these entities typically maintain a moderate market presence and focus on specific geographic regions or demographic segments.

Personalised Campaigns

Technological advancements have supported gathering, analysing, and segmenting user data based on individual interests, demographics, spending abilities, interaction time, etc. This has eased the process of communicating with prospective customers. Tailored messages are created to stimulate the customers. They enhance their interactions with the platform/brand efficiently and inexpensively. This further increases the conversion rate and directly shows the impact on online sales. Online sales can broadly be divided into Acquisition and Retention.

Online Sales

Online sales refer to the transaction of goods or services online through digital platforms, websites, or online marketplaces. This process encompasses online commerce activities, ranging from browsing and selecting products to payment processing and subsequent order fulfilment. The prevalence of online sales has surged due to the widespread adoption of e-commerce technologies, providing consumers unprecedented convenience and control in purchasing goods and services. Businesses across diverse sectors strategically leverage online sales channels to broaden their market reach and achieve targeted engagement, driving revenue growth. For the purpose of this study, online sales are divided into Customer Acquisition and Customer Retention.

Customer Acquisition

Customer acquisition for a mid-size food delivery company refers to the strategies and actions taken to attract and convert new customers to use the company's services. This process is crucial for expanding the customer base, increasing online sales, and ensuring the company's growth and sustainability in a competitive market. Marketing channels used for this study to acquire new customers were Google (including YouTube), Meta and Emails.

Retention

Customer retention for a mid-size food delivery company refers to the strategies and actions taken to engage existing users who are satisfied with the company's services and encourage them to continue using the platform regularly. Retaining customers is essential for maintaining a stable revenue stream, reducing marketing costs, and fostering brand loyalty. Marketing channels used for customer retention for this study were Email, WhatsApp, and Push Notifications.

Key Performance Metrics

Key performance metrics for digital marketing are essential for assessing the effectiveness of campaigns, understanding customer engagement, and optimising strategies for better results. For a mid-size food delivery company, these metrics can provide valuable insights into how well marketing efforts are driving traffic, conversions, and customer retention. These key performance metrics are directly proportional to the online sales of any organisation. The key performance metrics that are studied for this research are:

Impressions: The number of times an ad is shown to users, regardless of whether it is clicked on or not. Example: If an ad is shown 1,000 times on a webpage, it has 1,000 impressions.

Clicks: The total number of times users click on an ad or a specific link. Example: If an ad is clicked 50 times, it has 50 clicks.

CPC: The amount that is paid for each click on their ad. It is calculated by dividing the total cost of the campaign by the number of clicks. Example: If a campaign costs $100 and receives 50 clicks, the CPC is $2 ($100/50).

CTR: The percentage of impressions that result in clicks. It is calculated by dividing the number of clicks by the number of impressions and multiplying by 100. Example: If an ad has 1,000 impressions and 50 clicks, the CTR is 5% (50/1,000 * 100).

CVR: The percentage of clicks that result in a desired action, such as a purchase or sign-up. It is calculated by dividing the number of conversions by the number of clicks and multiplying by 100. Example: If 50 people click on an ad and 5 of them make a purchase, the CVR is 10% (5/50 * 100).

CPL: The cost associated with acquiring a new lead. It is calculated by dividing the total cost of the campaign by the number of leads generated. Example: If a campaign costs $200 and generates 20 leads, the CPL is $10 ($200/20).

Number of Leads: The total number of potential customers who have shown interest in a company's products or services, typically by providing their contact information. Example: If a landing page generates 100 sign-ups for a newsletter, the number of leads is 100.

Number of Orders: The total number of completed purchases or transactions. For example, if a food delivery company receives 500 orders in a month, the number of orders is 500.

ARPU: Average Revenue Per User is the average revenue generated per user or customer over a specific period. It is calculated by dividing the total revenue by the number of users or customers.

Example: If a food delivery company generates $10,000 in revenue from 200 customers in a month, the ARPU is $50 ($10,000/200).

Data Analytics and Personalization of Digital Marketing Campaigns. Advanced data analytics techniques are leveraged to collect and analyse user data, including preferences, behaviours, and interactions across various digital channels. Data is leveraged in many ways:

1. **Customer Segmentation**: Data allows to study of the bifurcation of the customer base into distinct groups based on demographic, psychographic, and behavioural factors and creates segregated pools.
2. **Personalised Content:** With data, marketers understand the audience better and accordingly create and disseminate tailored content - relevant messages, discounts and offers, design and images that resonate with individual customer preferences and needs.
3. **Dynamic Campaigns**: Data gives insights to make informed decisions about real-time optimization and implementation of marketing campaigns that catalyse and stimulate audience behaviour significantly. These campaigns are based on factors like audience response to previous campaigns, competitor campaigns, interests, audience behaviour and other interests on the internet, previous purchases, engagement history, and much more.
4. **Behavioural Targeting:** Leveraging data insights from customer behaviour to target specific individuals with relevant advertisements and promotions across digital platforms.
5. **Recommendation Engines**: Integration of recommendation algorithms is done after analysing data such as browsing history, purchase patterns, and preferences to suggest preferred products.

6. **Cross-channel Integration:** A study of coordinating and integrating marketing efforts on various digital channels, ensuring consistent and personalized customer experiences, providing data to understand the gaps and optimise accordingly.
7. **Automation and AI:** Deployment of automation tools and Artificial Intelligence (AI) algorithms to streamline personalised marketing campaigns, optimise content delivery, and enhance customer engagement.
8. **Performance Measurement**: Continuous monitoring and evaluating campaign performance metrics refine strategies and improve outcomes.

These components collectively enable personalized digital marketing strategies to effectively engage customers, enhance brand loyalty, and drive business growth in competitive digital environments—finally affecting online sales significantly.

Benefits of Personalized Digital Marketing

Personalised digital marketing constitutes a pivotal facet of contemporary business strategies. Personalised campaigns offer substantial advantages to companies seeking efficient connectivity with their target audience, often constrained by limited budgets. By tailoring messages, offers, and content to individual preferences, behaviours, and interests, personalised campaigns effectively facilitate the attainment of marketing objectives.

Outlined below are several reasons why personalised digital marketing campaigns can wield transformative influence for enterprises:

1. **Enhanced Customer Engagement**: Personalized campaigns significantly elevate customer engagement by resonating more deeply with individual recipients. This targeted approach fosters increased interaction with the brand, thereby forging stronger customer connections.
2. **Enriched Customer Experience:** Personalization engenders a more pertinent and meaningful customer experience through tailored content, offerings, and recommendations that align closely with customer needs and preferences. This heightened relevance cultivates greater satisfaction, loyalty, and positive brand perceptions.
3. **Augmented Conversion Rates:** Tailored messages are inherently more compelling to recipients, augmenting conversion rates. By delivering personalised content and incentives, marketers can effectively prompt desired customer actions such as purchases or service subscriptions.
4. **Optimised Return on Investment (ROI):** Personalized campaigns typically yield superior ROI compared to generic marketing endeavours due to their targeted nature and ability to foster more substantive customer interactions. This enables marketers to allocate resources judiciously towards campaigns that yield measurable results.
5. **Strengthened Brand Loyalty:** Personalization nurtures deep customer-brand relationships. This engenders trust and loyalty, thereby enhancing customer retention and lifetime value.
6. **Enhanced Customer Retention:** Personalized campaigns bolster customer retention by sustaining engagement through relevant content and tailored offers. This proactive approach minimises churn rates and prolongs customer relationships.

7. **Data-Driven Insights:** Personalized digital marketing initiatives generate invaluable data and insights regarding customer behaviours, preferences, and interactions. Marketers leverage these insights to refine targeting strategies, optimise campaign performance, and make informed, data-driven decisions for future marketing endeavours.
8. **Competitive Advantage:** Effective implementation of personalised digital marketing campaigns confers a competitive edge by delivering superior customer experiences and fostering robust engagement and loyalty compared to competitors. This differentiation enables brands to stand out in competitive market landscapes.

Mid-Size Food-Tech Delivery Company

A mid-size food-tech delivery enterprise facilitates connections between consumers and various food establishments through online platforms or mobile applications. Unlike more giant corporations, these entities typically maintain a moderate market presence and focus on specific geographic regions or demographic segments.

Key operational features of mid-size food-tech delivery companies include:

1. **Online Platform Utilization:** Customers access websites or mobile apps to browse food choices, place orders, and monitor real-time delivery progress.
2. **Restaurant Collaborations:** Partnerships with local restaurants, cafes, and food vendors to offer customers a diverse array of culinary options.
3. **Delivery Logistics**: Management of delivery logistics through a network of in-house riders or partnerships with third-party delivery services - ensuring prompt and efficient order fulfilment.
4. **Customer Service:** Emphasis on customer satisfaction through responsive support services, addressing inquiries, resolving issues related to orders or deliveries, and maintaining high service standards.
5. **Marketing Strategies:** Deployment of marketing campaigns and promotional initiatives aimed at acquiring new customers, retaining existing ones, and enhancing brand visibility within the target market.
6. **Technological Integration:** Adoption of various technologies such as data analytics, AI, and ML to optimise operational processes, improve order accuracy, and elevate overall customer experience.
7. **Revenue Generation Model:** Diverse revenue streams, including commission fees from restaurant partners, delivery charges, service fees, and revenue from advertising or promotional collaborations.

The annual revenue of mid-size food delivery companies is based on diverse factors such as location, market size, operational efficiency, customer base dynamics, and competitive landscape. Typically, these enterprises generate annual revenues in the millions to tens of millions of dollars range, contributing substantively to the evolving landscape of digital food service platforms. This study focuses only on the online sales (customer acquisition and customer retention).

2 Review of Literature

Chen, H., Chiang, R. H., & Storey, V. C. (2012), In their study 'Business Intelligence and Analytics: From Big Data to Big Impact' discussed the evolution of business intelligence (BI) and analytics from traditional data collection methods to modern big data analytics. They emphasized how data-driven decision-making has become crucial in contemporary marketing to gain a competitive edge.

McAfee, A., Brynjolfsson, E., Davenport, T. H., Patil, D., & Barton, D. (2012), In their study 'Big Data: The Management Revolution', explored how big data is revolutionizing management practices, including marketing. The authors stated that data-driven decision-making leads to highly accurate and actionable insights, ultimately driving better business performance.

Wedel, M., & Kannan, P. K. (2016), Their study 'Marketing Analytics for Data-Rich Environments', provided a comprehensive overview of various marketing analytics tools and techniques. They pointed out that leveraging these tools allows marketers to segment customers more effectively, predict consumer behavior, and personalize marketing efforts.

Chaffey, D., & Patron, M. (2012), In their research study 'From Web Analytics to Digital Marketing Optimization: Increasing the Commercial Impact of Digital Analytics', highlighted why web analytics in digital marketing is important. The authors demonstrated how data from web analytics can be used to optimize marketing campaigns, leading to improved click-through and conversion rates.

Davenport, T. H., & Harris, J. G. (2007), In their study, 'Competing on Analytics: The New Science of Winning', The authors discussed how companies can leverage data analytics to gain customer insights and deliver personalized experiences. They argue that companies that excel in data-driven decision-making outperform their competitors in customer satisfaction and loyalty.

Rust, R. T., & Chung, T. S. (2006), In their study, 'Marketing Models of Service and Relationships', explored how data-driven decision-making can enhance marketing performance by improving targeting, segmentation, and positioning in their study, 'The authors provide evidence that data-driven marketing strategies often result in higher returns on investment (ROI).

Akter, S., Wamba, S. F., Gunasekaran, A., Dubey, R., & Childe, S. J. (2016), In their study, 'How to Improve Firm Performance Using Big Data Analytics Capability and Business Strategy Alignment?', identified various challenges in implementing data-driven marketing, including data quality issues, integration difficulties, and lack of skilled personnel. They suggested aligning business strategy with data analytics capabilities is essential for success.

Goh, K. Y., Heng, C. S., & Lin, Z. (2013), In their study, 'Social Media Brand Community and Consumer Behavior: Quantifying the Relative Impact of User- and Marketer-Generated Content', discussed the barriers to effective data-driven marketing, such as integrating data from multiple sources and handling large volumes of unstructured data.

The authors stated that overcoming these barriers is crucial for realizing the full potential of data-driven marketing.

Milne, G. R., & Bahl, S. (2010) In their study, 'Are There Wolves in Sheep's Clothing? Understanding Target Marketing of Unethical Firms', explored the ethical dilemmas associated with targeted marketing. They caution against using data analytics in ways that could be perceived as intrusive or manipulative, suggesting that ethical practices are vital for sustainable marketing success.

Kotler, Keller, and Chernev (2021), In their book 'Marketing Management', emphasized the importance of understanding consumer behavior and leveraging data to create relevant and timely marketing messages. They highlighted how digital marketing has shifted from traditional methods to more sophisticated, data-driven approaches.

Smith & Chaffey (2017), In their study, 'eMarketing eXcellence: Planning and Optimizing Your Digital Marketing', focused on the concept of personalization in digital marketing, stating that personalized marketing messages and offers create higher consumer satisfaction and loyalty by making customers feel understood and valued.

Busalim & Hussin (2016) In their research study' Understanding Social Commerce: A Systematic Literature Review and Directions for Further Research' posited that data-driven personalization leads to higher consumer satisfaction and loyalty, emphasizing the role of big data and machine learning in enhancing personalized marketing efforts.

De Keyser, Verleye, Lemon, Keiningham, & Klaus (2015), In their research paper, 'Moving the Customer Experience Field Forward: Introduction to the Special Issue' found that personalized email campaigns achieved significantly higher open and click-through rates compared to generic emails, illustrating the effectiveness of personalized marketing in driving customer engagement.

Kumar, Bhaskaran, Mirchandani, & Shah (2019), In their study 'Creating a Measurable Social Media Marketing Strategy: Increasing the Value and ROI of Intangibles and Tangibles for Hi-Tech Companies' showed that personalized recommendations on e-commerce platforms led to a 22% increase in conversion rates, highlighting the impact of data-driven personalization on sales performance.

Pine, Peppers, & Rogers (2017), In their book, 'Do You Want to Keep Your Customers Forever?', discussed how personalized experiences can increase customer retention rates by up to 16%, underscoring the importance of personalization in fostering long-term customer loyalty.

Hoyer, Kroschke, Schmitt, Kraume, & Shankar (2020), In their research study, 'Transforming the Customer Experience Through New Technologies', found that loyalty programs tailored to individual preferences were more effective in maintaining customer loyalty compared to non-personalized programs.

The Swiggy Annual Report (2020) Concluded that the implementation of personalized push notifications and in-app recommendations based on user behavior led to a 25% increase in average order value (AOV).

Zomato Business Review (2021) Concluded that Zomato's Gold membership program, offering personalized deals and exclusive access to partner restaurants, resulted in a 30% increase in repeat orders.

Taylor (2020), In their research paper, 'Privacy and Data Security: Challenges of the Digital Age', highlighted the privacy concerns related to personal data collection and usage, advocating for stringent data protection measures and transparent practices to ensure consumer trust.

Aaker (2018), In their study 'Building Strong Brands', indicated that transparency in data collection and the explicit consent of consumers are essential for building and maintaining consumer trust in personalized marketing efforts.

Bryman (2016), In their study' Social Research Methods', highlighted the importance of using both quantitative metrics (e.g., CTR, conversion rates) and qualitative insights (e.g., consumer attitudes) to assess the impact of personalized marketing.

Literature Gap: While existing studies have extensively explored various aspects of online marketing and social media marketing for online food businesses, there is still a significant gap in the literature regarding consumer behaviour related to personalization in digital marketing (especially with a focus towards attributes, quotients, platforms and metrics of personalization).

3 Objectives of the Study

(a) Analyzing the key performance metrics of digital marketing before and after personalised digital marketing campaigns for a mid-size food-tech delivery platform.
(b) Analyzing the online sales for the mid-size food-tech delivery platform before and after the personalization of digital marketing campaigns.

4 Research Methodology

Design
A quantitative approach, experimental research design, was employed to collect data by capturing targeted audience responses through personalised digital marketing campaigns on platforms such as Meta, Google, Emails, WhatsApp, Social Media, and Push Notifications.

Key performance metrics of digital marketing campaigns before and after personalization were analysed for a mid-size food-tech delivery company. The pre-personalization data is twelve months (Jan-Dec 2022), and the post-personalization data is twelve months (Jan-Dec 2023). Ad spends were the fix variable in both phases to avoid platform-boost errors.

Sample Size

In total, 5931310 Impressions were achieved from various marketing channels during the twelve-month period when a personalized digital marketing campaign was executed.

Data Collection and Analysis

Data was collected in the form of key performance metrics—impressions, Clicks, CPC, CTR, CVR, CPL, Number of Leads, and Number of Orders—by running a digital marketing campaign. The data collection method for the study was the Snowball Sampling Method. Simple Statistical Analysis and Inferential Statistical Analysis (Paired T-tests) were the methods of data analysis.

5 Hypothesis

H1: There is no significant effect of the personalised digital marketing campaign on online sales generated by Google Ads while running a customer acquisition campaign for a mid-size food-tech delivery platform.

H2: There is no significant effect of the personalised digital marketing campaign on online sales generated by Meta Ads while running a customer acquisition campaign for a mid-size food-tech delivery platform.

H3: There is no significant effect of personalized digital marketing campaign on online sales generated by Email Marketing while running customer acquisition campaign for a mid-size food-tech delivery platform.

H4: There is no significant effect of the personalised digital marketing campaign on online sales generated by Email Marketing while running a customer retention campaign for a mid-size food-tech delivery platform.

H5: There is no significant effect of the personalised digital marketing campaign on online sales generated by WhatsApp while running a customer retention campaign for a mid-size food-tech delivery platform.

H4: There is no significant effect of the personalized digital marketing campaign on online sales generated by push notifications while running a customer retention campaign for a mid-size food-tech delivery platform.

6 Findings

a) Below is the data for the post-personalization of digital marketing campaigns.

Acquisition											
Google Ads (Includes Youtube Ads Well)											
Month	Impressions	Clicks	CTR (%)	CPC	Spends	Leads	CVR	CPL	Number of Orders	ARPU	Online Sales
Jan 2023	200000	43000	22	1.2	50000	2150	5%	23	280	225	63000
Feb 2023	205800	52856	26	0.9	50000	3700	7%	14	518	230	119140
March 2023	200700	61315	31	0.8	50000	1839	3%	27	294	220	64680
April 2023	230200	63664	28	0.8	50000	2547	4%	20	433	200	86600
May 2023	241300	87211	36	0.6	50000	2616	3%	19	288	195	56160
June 2023	206870	61061	30	0.8	50000	2442	4%	20	318	250	79500
July 2023	200620	52180	26	1	50000	3653	7%	14	475	180	85500
Aug 2023	363020	102000	28	0.8	85000	7140	7%	12	1000	235	235000
Sep 2023	380000	108500	29	0.6	70000	6510	6%	11	977	240	234480
Oct 2023	450000	135000	30	0.7	100000	13500	10%	7	2295	240	550800
Nov 2023	456400	142050	31	0.7	100000	14205	10%	7	2415	230	555450
Dec 2023	293020	87000	30	1.1	100000	9570	11%	10	1723	255	439365
Total	**3427930**	**995837**	**29**	**0.8**	**805000**	**69872**	**6%**	**15**	**11016**	**225**	**2569675**
Meta Ads (Includes FB & Insta)											
Jan 2023	70000	19600	28	3.6	70000	980	5%	71	167	220	36740
Feb 2023	70700	21917	31	3.2	70000	658	3%	106	85	235	19975
March 2023	92080	28545	31	2.5	70000	1713	6%	41	206	230	47380
April 2023	85160	24696	29	2.8	70000	1729	7%	40	225	225	50625
May 2023	78040	22241	28	3.1	70000	890	4%	79	125	240	30000
June 2023	83140	27436	33	1.8	50000	823	3%	61	123	220	27060

(*continued*)

(*continued*)

Acquisition											
Google Ads (Includes Youtube Ads Well)											
Month	Impressions	Clicks	CTR (%)	CPC	Spends	Leads	CVR	CPL	Number of Orders	ARPU	Online Sales
July 2023	81820	26182	32	1.9	50000	1833	7%	27	312	220	68640
Aug 2023	363020	102000	28	1	100000	11220	11%	9	1907	245	467215
Sep 2023	380000	108500	29	0.9	100000	7595	7%	13	1215	230	279450
Oct 2023	450000	135000	30	1.1	150000	16200	12%	9	2754	240	660960
Nov 2023	456400	142050	31	1.1	150000	12785	9%	12	2046	240	491040
Dec 2023	293020	87000	30	1.7	150000	6960	8%	22	974	220	214280
Total	**2503380**	**745167**	**30**	**2.1**	**1100000**	**63386**	**7%**	**41**	**10139**	**230**	**2393365**
Email											
Month	Total Sent	Total Delivered	Open Rate (%)	Total Open Emails	CTR (%)	Leads	CVR	CPL	Total Number of Orders	ARPU	Online Sales
Jan 2023	25000	24750	2%	495	6%	10	2%	53	1	220	220
Feb 2023	25000	24625	2%	369	7%	7	2%	71	1	230	230
March 2023	30000	29250	2%	585	6%	18	3%	30	3	230	690
April 2023	37000	36260	2%	725	5%	44	6%	12	6	235	1410
May 2023	42000	39900	3%	1197	6%	48	4%	11	9	240	2160
June 2023	48000	46560	1%	466	7%	23	5%	23	4	220	880
July 2023	52000	50960	2%	1019	7%	31	3%	17	4	215	860
Aug 2023	61000	60390	5%	3020	8%	181	6%	3	25	250	6250
Sep 2023	70000	68950	2%	1379	5%	83	6%	6	13	220	2860

(*continued*)

(*continued*)

Acquisition											
Google Ads (Includes Youtube Ads Well)											
Month	Impressions	Clicks	CTR (%)	CPC	Spends	Leads	CVR	CPL	Number of Orders	ARPU	Online Sales
Oct 2023	70000	67900	4%	2716	6%	109	4%	5	18	230	4140
Nov 2023	76000	73720	3%	2212	4%	111	5%	5	18	235	4230
Dec 2023	83000	80676	1%	807	4%	40	5%	13	6	240	1440
Total	**619000**	**603941**	**2%**	**14990**	**6%**	**705**	**4%**	**21**	**108**	**230**	**25370**
Retention											
Email											
Month	Total Sent	Total Delivered	Open Rate (%)	Total Open Emails	CTR (%)	Leads	CVR	CPL	Total Number of Orders	ARPU	Online Sales
Jan 2023	3655	1870	18%	337	13%	44	8%	12	4	260	1040
Feb 2023	6290	1820	12%	218	18%	39	8%	13	3	240	720
March 2023	3126	1845	14%	258	17%	44	7%	12	3	230	690
April 2023	4330	1834	15%	275	17%	47	9%	11	4	250	1000
May 2023	4447	1921	12%	231	18%	41	10%	13	4	245	980
June 2023	4151	1942	13%	252	21%	53	13%	10	7	245	1715
July 2023	6210	1840	14%	258	20%	52	17%	10	9	240	2160
Aug 2023	12138	1934	17%	329	23%	76	19%	7	14	270	3780
Sep 2023	11067	1874	17%	319	16%	51	17%	10	9	260	2340
Oct 2023	22950	1890	14%	265	21%	56	21%	9	12	280	3360
Nov 2023	24149	1932	17%	328	20%	66	19%	8	12	260	3120

(*continued*)

(continued)

Acquisition											
Google Ads (Includes Youtube Ads Well)											
Month	Impressions	Clicks	CTR (%)	CPC	Spends	Leads	CVR	CPL	Number of Orders	ARPU	Online Sales
Dec 2023	16269	1892	16%	303	22%	67	19%	8	13	260	3380
Total	**118782**	**22594**	**15%**	**3373**	**19%**	**636**	**14%**	**10**	**94**	**253**	**24285**
WhatsApp											
Month	Total Sent	Total Delivered	Open Rate (%)	Total Open Whatsapp	CTR (%)	Leads	CVR	CPL	Total Number of Orders	ARPU	Online Sales
Jan 2023	150500	141470	16%	22635	14%	1811	8%	0.6	254	260	66040
Feb 2023	259000	240870	11%	26496	16%	2120	8%	0.5	276	240	66240
March 2023	128730	123581	13%	16066	13%	1125	7%	1.0	146	230	33580
April 2023	178290	169376	12%	20325	15%	1829	9%	0.6	220	250	55000
May 2023	183120	179458	12%	21535	16%	2153	10%	0.5	323	245	79135
June 2023	170940	158974	14%	22256	19%	2893	13%	0.4	405	245	99225
July 2023	255710	242925	11%	26722	17%	4543	17%	0.2	636	240	152640
Aug 2023	499800	479808	16%	76769	13%	14586	19%	0.1	2334	270	630180
Sep 2023	455700	442029	13%	57464	18%	9769	17%	0.1	1270	260	330200
Oct 2023	945000	897750	16%	143640	17%	30164	21%	0.0	5128	280	1435840
Nov 2023	994350	954576	12%	114549	15%	21764	19%	0.0	4135	260	848900
Dec 2023	669900	629706	16%	100753	14%	19143	19%	0.1	3637	260	945620
Total	**4891040**	**4660523**	**14%**	**649210**	**16%**	**111900**	**14%**	**0.3**	**18764**	**253**	**4742600**
Push Notification											

(continued)

(*continued*)

Acquisition											
Google Ads (Includes Youtube Ads Well)											
Month	Impressions	Clicks	CTR (%)	CPC	Spends	Leads	CVR	CPL	Number of Orders	ARPU	Online Sales
Month	Total Sent	Total Delivered	Open Rate (%)	Total Open Push Notification	CTR (%)	Leads	CVR	CPL	Total Number of Orders	ARPU	Online Sales
Jan 2023	150500	141470	13%	18391	12%	1471	8%	0.5	280	260	72800
Feb 2023	259000	248640	14%	34810	13%	2785	8%	0.3	473	240	113520
March 2023	128730	123581	16%	19773	14%	1384	7%	0.6	235	230	54050
April 2023	178290	165810	13%	21555	16%	1940	9%	0.4	349	250	87250
May 2023	183120	173964	17%	29574	16%	2957	10%	0.3	621	245	152145
June 2023	170940	164102	14%	22974	21%	2987	13%	0.3	597	245	146265
July 2023	255710	242925	12%	29151	19%	4956	17%	0.2	1090	240	261600
Aug 2023	499800	474810	13%	61725	17%	11728	19%	0.1	2697	270	728190
Sep 2023	455700	428358	14%	59970	18%	10195	17%	0.1	1937	260	503620
Oct 2023	945000	888300	16%	142128	22%	29847	21%	0.0	6268	280	1755040
Nov 2023	994350	944633	11%	103910	17%	19743	19%	0.0	3554	260	924040
Dec 2023	669900	649803	12%	77976	19%	14816	19%	0.1	2963	260	770380
Total	**4891040**	**4646396**	**14%**	**621937**	**17%**	**104809**	**14%**	**0.2**	**21064**	**253**	**5568900**

b. Below is the data for the pre-personalization of digital marketing campaigns.

Acquisition											
Google Ads (Includes Youtube Ads Well)											
Month	Impressions	Clicks	CTR (%)	CPC	Spends	Leads	CVR	CPL	Number of Orders	ARPU	Online Sales
Jan 2022	112000	23680	21	2.1	50000	710	3%	70	57	220	12503
Feb 2022	94668	19507	21	2.6	50000	975	5%	51	88	220	19312
March 2022	106371	26593	25	1.9	50000	532	2%	94	59	220	12871
April 2022	133516	36049	27	1.4	50000	1081	3%	46	97	230	22386
May 2022	115824	31272	27	1.6	50000	625	2%	80	56	240	13510
June 2022	99298	28796	29	1.7	50000	864	3%	58	60	230	13908
July 2022	94291	20744	22	2.4	50000	830	4%	60	66	225	14936
Aug 2022	185140	35177	19	2.4	85000	1759	5%	48	176	225	39574
Sep 2022	163400	37582	23	1.9	70000	2631	7%	27	237	230	54456
Oct 2022	256500	58995	23	1.7	100000	4720	8%	21	330	240	79289
Nov 2022	232764	55863	24	1.8	100000	5028	9%	20	352	230	80945
Dec 2022	181672	41785	23	2.4	100000	3343	8%	30	201	225	45128
Total	**1775444**	**416043**	**24**	**2.0**	**805000**	**23098**	**5%**	**50**	**1779**	**228**	**408818**
Meta Ads (Includes FB & Insta)											
Jan 2022	53900	4312	8	16.2	70000	129	3%	541	5	230	1190
Feb 2022	52318	5041	10	13.9	70000	101	2%	694	6	245	1482
March 2022	65377	5994	9	11.7	70000	240	4%	292	7	220	1582
April 2022	66425	6421	10	10.9	70000	321	5%	218	16	225	3612
May 2022	58530	6227	11	11.2	70000	125	2%	562	7	235	1756
June 2022	63186	6859	11	7.3	50000	137	2%	364	10	220	2113
July 2022	61365	6284	10	8.0	50000	377	6%	133	26	220	5806
Aug 2022	265005	28560	11	3.5	100000	1999	7%	50	120	230	27589
Sep 2022	281200	26040	9	3.8	100000	1562	6%	64	94	225	21092
Oct 2022	346500	35100	10	4.3	150000	2808	8%	53	140	220	30888
Nov 2022	346864	32672	9	4.6	150000	2287	7%	66	137	235	32247

(continued)

(*continued*)

Acquisition											
Google Ads (Includes Youtube Ads Well)											
Month	Impressions	Clicks	CTR (%)	CPC	Spends	Leads	CVR	CPL	Number of Orders	ARPU	Online Sales
Dec 2022	222695	24360	11	6.2	150000	1705	7%	88	68	220	15006
Total	**1883365**	**187870**	**10**	**8.5**	**1100000**	**11791**	**5%**	**260**	**636**	**227**	**144363**
Email											
Month	Total Sent	Total Delivered	Open Rate (%)	Total Open Emails	CTR (%)	Leads	CVR	CPL	Total Number of Orders	ARPU	Online Sales
Jan 2022	12000	10440	1.0%	104	1%	1	1%	503	0	220	0
Feb 2022	12000	10320	1.0%	103	3%	2	2%	339	0	230	0
March 2022	16000	14080	1.0%	141	3%	3	2%	186	0	230	0
April 2022	18000	15300	1.0%	153	2%	5	3%	114	1	235	235
May 2022	21400	18618	1.8%	335	3%	7	2%	78	0	240	0
June 2022	22600	18984	1.5%	285	3%	9	3%	61	1	220	220
July 2022	22890	19685	1.0%	197	4%	2	1%	267	0	215	0
Aug 2022	23500	19740	2.0%	395	5%	12	3%	44	1	250	250
Sep 2022	26700	23496	1.5%	352	2%	14	4%	37	0	220	220
Oct 2022	29000	25230	2.0%	505	3%	10	2%	52	0	230	0
Nov 2022	32000	28480	2.0%	570	1%	17	3%	31	1	235	235
Dec 2022	34670	29816	1.0%	298	3%	12	4%	44	0	240	0
Total	**270760**	**234189**	**1.4%**	**3438**	**3%**	**94**	**2%**	**146**	**4**	**230**	**1160**
Retention											
Email											
Month	Total Sent	Total Delivered	Open Rate (%)	Total Open Emails	CTR (%)	Leads	CVR	CPL	Conversion	ARPU	Online Sales
Jan 2022	1207	1110	8%	89	7%	3	3%	197	0	260	0
Feb 2022	1658	1459	10%	146	11%	4	3%	120	0	240	0
March 2022	904	786	9%	71	9%	3	4%	185	0	230	0
April 2022	1838	1562	9%	141	8%	7	5%	75	0	250	0
May 2022	1063	967	8%	77	12%	5	7%	97	0	245	0
June 2022	1469	1307	11%	144	16%	13	9%	41	1	245	245
July 2022	1411	1298	9%	117	12%	13	11%	41	1	240	240

(*continued*)

(*continued*)

Acquisition											
Google Ads (Includes Youtube Ads Well)											
Month	Impressions	Clicks	CTR (%)	CPC	Spends	Leads	CVR	CPL	Number of Orders	ARPU	Online Sales
Aug 2022	2990	2721	9%	245	14%	29	12%	18	2	270	540
Sep 2022	4472	3935	8%	315	11%	41	13%	13	2	260	520
Oct 2022	8024	6981	9%	628	9%	101	16%	5	6	280	1680
Nov 2022	8548	7437	12%	892	13%	107	12%	5	6	260	1560
Dec 2022	5683	5001	8%	400	12%	48	12%	11	3	260	780
Total	**39267**	**34564**	**9%**	**3265**	**11%**	**374**	**9%**	**67**	**21**	**253**	**5565**
WhatsApp											
Month	Total Sent	Total Delivered	Open Rate (%)	Total Open Whatsapp	CTR (%)	Leads	CVR	CPL	Total Number of Orders	ARPU	Online Sales
Jan 2022	4225	3084	9%	278	9%	11	4%	98	1	260	260
Feb 2022	5471	3939	6%	236	9%	12	5%	92	0	240	0
March 2022	3345	2609	8%	209	8%	6	3%	173	0	230	0
April 2022	6249	4312	7%	302	11%	15	5%	72	1	250	250
May 2022	3833	2836	9%	255	10%	28	11%	39	1	245	245
June 2022	4848	3684	12%	442	12%	53	12%	20	3	245	735
July 2022	4515	3477	9%	313	12%	44	14%	25	3	240	720
Aug 2022	10465	7639	8%	611	12%	73	12%	15	3	270	810
Sep 2022	15652	11113	11%	1222	9%	159	13%	7	6	260	1560
Oct 2022	29689	21673	12%	2601	10%	312	12%	3	16	280	4480
Nov 2022	30773	23387	9%	2105	11%	274	13%	4	14	260	3640
Dec 2022	18186	12912	12%	1549	11%	170	11%	6	9	260	2340
Total	**137251**	**100665**	**9%**	**10123**	**10%**	**1157**	**10%**	**46**	**57**	**253**	**15040**
Push Notification											
Month	Total Sent	Total Delivered	Open Rate (%)	Total Open Push Notification	CTR (%)	Leads	CVR	CPL	Total Number of Orders	ARPU	Online Sales
Jan 2022	4225	3887	7%	272	8%	16	6%	49	1	260	260
Feb 2022	5471	4869	8%	390	7%	19	5%	41	1	240	240
March 2022	3345	2843	6%	171	8%	10	6%	78	1	230	230

(*continued*)

(*continued*)

Acquisition											
Google Ads (Includes Youtube Ads Well)											
Month	Impressions	Clicks	CTR (%)	CPC	Spends	Leads	CVR	CPL	Number of Orders	ARPU	Online Sales
April 2022	6249	5499	9%	495	9%	30	6%	27	2	250	500
May 2022	3833	3411	8%	273	9%	19	7%	42	2	245	490
June 2022	4848	3684	9%	332	9%	30	9%	27	3	245	735
July 2022	4515	3973	10%	397	8%	44	11%	18	3	240	720
Aug 2022	10465	9105	9%	819	9%	98	12%	8	8	270	2160
Sep 2022	15652	13461	8%	1077	8%	118	11%	7	9	260	2340
Oct 2022	29689	26423	9%	2378	9%	380	16%	2	30	280	8400
Nov 2022	30773	28003	10%	2800	9%	336	12%	2	20	260	5200
Dec 2022	18186	15822	8%	1266	9%	139	11%	6	11	260	2860
Total	**137251**	**120980**	**8%**	**10670**	**9%**	**1239**	**9%**	**26**	**91**	**253**	**24135**

c. Below is the comparison summary of the key performance metrics and online sales

Key Performance Metrics	Pre-Personalization (Year 2022)	Post Personalization (Year 2023)
Total Impression	3658809	5931310
Total Clicks	603913	1741004
Average CPC	5.2	1.4
Average CTR	6%	19%
Average CPL	99	14
Average CVR	7%	10%
Total Number of Online Orders	2588	61185
Average ARPU	241	241
Average Open Rate of WhatsApp	9%	14%
Average Open Rate of Push Notification	8%	14%
Average Open Rate of Email	5%	13%
Online Sales	**599081**	**15324195**

7 Conclusions

The hypothesis is tested using Paired Samples Tests. Below are the results.

Paired Samples Test

		Paired Differences					t	df	Sig. (2-tailed)
		Mean	Std. Deviation	Std. Error Mean	95% Confidence Interval of the Difference				
					Lower	Upper			
Pair 1	Post-Sales Acq Google ads - Pre-sales Acq Google ads	30173.75	34534.2284	9969.173	8231.7481	52115.7519	3.027	11	0.012
Pair 2	Post-Sales Acq Meta ads - Pre-Sales Acq Meta ads	187416.833	212558.564	61360.372	52363.565	322470.101	3.054	11	0.011
Pair 3	Post-Sales Acq emails - Pre-Sales Acq emails	2017.5	1836.449	530.137	850.676	3184.324	3.806	11	0.003
Pair 4	Post-Sales reten emails - Pre-Sales reten emails	1560	769.096	222.019	1071.34	2048.66	7.026	11	0
Pair 5	Post-Sales reten whats app - Pre-Sales reten whatsapp	393963.333	461864.025	133328.659	100508.932	687417.734	2.955	11	0.013
Pair 6	Post-Sales reten whats app - Pre-Sales reten pushnotifi	462063.75	508225.49	146712.062	139152.679	784974.821	3.149	11	0.009

Pair 1 - Post Personalization Online Sales (Acquisition Google ads) - Pre Personalization Online Sales (Acquisition Google ads)

The t value of 3.0 is significant at 0.01 level with df equal to 11. It means personalised digital marketing campaigns have significant effect on online sales generated by Google ads while running a customer acquisition campaign for a mid-size food-tech delivery platform. Therefore, the null hypothesis (H1), namely, 'There is no significant effect of the personalised digital marketing campaign on online sales generated by Google Ads while running a customer acquisition campaign for a mid-size food-tech delivery platform', is rejected.

Pair 2 - Post Personalization Online Sales (Acquisition Meta ads) - Pre Personalization Online sales (Acquisition Meta ads)

The t values of 3.0 are significant at 0.01 level with df equal to 11. This means that personalised digital marketing campaigns significantly affect online sales generated by Meta Ads while running customer acquisition campaigns for a mid-size food-tech delivery platform. Therefore, the null hypothesis (H2), namely, 'There is no significant effect of the personalised digital marketing campaign on online sales generated by Meta Ads while running customer acquisition campaign for a mid-size food-tech delivery platform', is rejected.

Pair 3 - Post Personalization Online Sales (Acquisition Email) - Pre Personalization Online sales (Acquisition Email)
The t value of 3.8 is significant at 0.00 level with df equal to 11. It means personalised digital marketing campaigns have significant effect on online sales generated by Emails while running a customer acquisition campaign for a mid-size food-tech delivery platform. Therefore, the null hypothesis (H3), namely, 'There is no significant effect of the personalised digital marketing campaign on online sales generated by Email while running a customer acquisition campaign for a mid-size food-tech delivery platform', is rejected.

Pair 4 - Post Personalization Online Sales (Retention Email) - Pre Personalization Online Sales (Retention Email)
The t values of 7.0 are significant at 0.00 level with df equal to 11. It means personalized digital marketing campaigns have significant effect on online sales generated by Emails while running a customer retention campaign for a mid-size food-tech delivery platform. Therefore, the null hypothesis (H4), namely, 'There is no significant effect of the personalized digital marketing campaign on online sales generated by Email while running a customer retention campaign for a mid-size food-tech delivery platform', is rejected.

Pair 5 - Post Personalization Online Sales (Retention WhatsApp) - Pre Personalization Online sales (Retention WhatsApp)
The t values of 2.9 are significant at 0.00 level with df equal to 11. It means personalized digital marketing campaigns have significant effect on online sales generated by WhatsApp while running a customer retention campaign for a mid-size food-tech delivery platform. Therefore, the null hypothesis (H5), namely, 'There is no significant effect of the personalized digital marketing campaign on online sales generated by WhatsApp while running a customer retention campaign for a mid-size food-tech delivery platform', is rejected.

Pair 6 - Post Personalization Online Sales (Retention Push Notification) - Pre Personalization Online Sales (Retention Push Notification)
The t values of 2.9 are significant at 0.00 level with df equal to 11. It means personalized digital marketing campaigns have significant effect on online sales generated by push notification while running a customer retention campaign for a mid-size food-tech delivery platform. Therefore, the null hypothesis (H5), namely, 'There is no significant effect of the personalized digital marketing campaign on online sales generated by Push Notification while running a customer retention campaign for a mid-size food-tech delivery platform', is rejected.

Conclusion Summary: All the null hypotheses were rejected. Also, the difference in the total online sales of pre & post-personalization was significant. Hence, it is safe to conclude that personalized digital marketing campaigns have a significant impact on the online sales of a mid-size food-tech delivery company.

8 Discussion

Studying the performance metrics of personalized digital marketing and its effect on online sales and revenue provides detailed, data-driven insights crucial for marketers, entrepreneurs, and investors in the food-tech industry. This comprehensive research study offers a detailed analysis of how well marketing efforts resonate with individual customers and segments. The scope covers various aspects, from understanding customer behaviour to optimizing personalization components and selecting the most effective marketing channels. Here is an elaboration:

Understanding Customer Behavior

1. **Segmentation Analysis:**
   - Demographic Insights: Analyzing data to segment customers based on age, gender, location, and other demographic factors.
   - Behavioural Patterns: Observing purchase history, browsing behaviour, and engagement with marketing content to identify trends and preferences.
   - Psychographic Profiling: Understanding customer lifestyles, values, and interests to tailor personalized marketing messages effectively.
2. **Customer Journey Mapping:**
   - Touchpoint Analysis: Identifying critical touchpoints in the customer journey where personalized marketing can have the most impact.
   - Conversion Path Optimization: Tracking customers' path from awareness to purchase and optimizing it to reduce friction and increase conversion rates.

Optimizing Personalization Components

1. **Content Personalization:**
   - Dynamic Content Creation: Developing personalized content that adapts to individual customer preferences in real time.
   - Recommendation Engines: Using algorithms to recommend products or services based on past behaviour and preferences.
   - Tailored Messaging: Crafting email and ad content relevant to the targeted customer segments.
2. **Data Utilization:**

- Data Collection: Gathering data from various sources, including website analytics, user feedback, and social media interactions.
- Data Analysis: Employing advanced analytics to interpret data and derive actionable insights.
- Predictive Modeling: Using machine learning models to predict future customer behaviour and personalize marketing efforts accordingly.

Selecting Marketing Channel

1. **Channel Performance Analysis**:
   - Multi-Channel Marketing: Evaluating the effectiveness of marketing channels.
   - Cross-Channel Integration: Ensuring a seamless customer experience across all marketing channels by integrating data and strategies.
   - Attribution Modeling: Determining which channels and touchpoints contribute most to conversions and revenue.
2. **Optimizing Channel Strategy:**
   - Channel-Specific Tactics: Tailoring marketing tactics to fit the strengths and characteristics of each channel.
   - Budget Allocation: Distributing marketing budgets across channels based on their performance and ROI.
   - Continuous Testing and Improvement: Regularly test different channels' for the most effective strategies and continuously improve performance.

Benefits for Stakeholders

1. **For Marketers:**
   - Enhanced Targeting: A better understanding of customer segments insights on tailored targeting and higher engagement rates.
   - Increased Conversion Rates: Personalization leads to more relevant marketing messages, significantly boosting conversion rates.
   - Optimized Marketing Spend: Informed decision-making on the marketing spends ensuring a higher return on investment (ROI).
2. **For Entrepreneurs:**
   - Informed Decision-Making: Detailed analysis provides a clear understanding of market dynamics and customer behaviour, aiding in strategic planning and decision-making.
   - Competitive Advantage: Implementing personalized marketing strategies can differentiate a business from competitors, attracting and retaining more customers.

- Scalability Insights: Understanding which scalable personalization tactics can help plan growth and expansion.

3. **For Investors:**
   - Risk Mitigation: Data-driven insights reduce the uncertainty and risk of investing in the food-tech industry.
   - Revenue Forecasting: Accurate performance metrics allow for better revenue forecasting and financial planning.
   - Investment Opportunities: Identifying successful personalized marketing strategies can highlight promising investment opportunities within the food-tech sector.

The researcher has tried best to provide a comprehensive framework for understanding and leveraging personalized digital marketing in the food-tech industry. The study offers valuable insights that can drive online sales and revenue growth by examining customer behaviour, optimizing personalization components, and selecting the most effective marketing channels. For marketers, entrepreneurs, and investors, these insights are crucial for making informed decisions, enhancing customer engagement, and achieving business success in the competitive food-tech market.

References

Chen, H., Chiang, R.H., Storey, V.C.: Business Intelligence and Analytics: From Big Data to Big Impact (2012)
McAfee, A., Brynjolfsson, E., Davenport, T.H., Patil, D., Barton, D.: Big Data: The Management Revolution (2012)
Wedel, M., Kannan, P.K.: Marketing Analytics for Data-Rich Environments (2016)
Chaffey, D., Patron, M.: From Web Analytics to Digital Marketing Optimization: Increasing the Commercial Impact of Digital Analytics (2012)
Davenport, T.H., Harris, J.G.: Competing on Analytics: The New Science of Winning (2007)
Rust, R.T., Chung, T.S.: Marketing Models of Service and Relationships (2006)
Akter, S., Wamba, S.F., Gunasekaran, A., Dubey, R., Childe, S.J.: How to Improve Firm Performance Using Big Data Analytics Capability and Business Strategy Alignment? (2016)
Goh, K.Y., Heng, C.S., Lin, Z.: Social Media Brand Community and Consumer Behavior: Quantifying the Relative Impact of User- and Marketer-Generated Content (2013)
Milne, G.R., Bahl, S.: Are There Wolves in Sheep's Clothing? Understanding Target Marketing of Unethical Firms (2010)
Kotler, P., Keller, K., Chernev, A.: Marketing Management (2021)
Smith, P.R., Chaffey, D.: eMarketing eXcellence: Planning and Optimizing Your Digital Marketing (2017)
Busalim, A.H.: Understanding Social Commerce: A Systematic Literature Review and Directions for Further Research (2016)
De Keyser, A., Verleye, K., Lemon, K.N., Keiningham, T.L., Klaus, P.: Moving the Customer Experience Field Forward: Introduction to the Special Issue (2015)
Kumar, Bhaskaran, V., Mirchandani, R., Shah, M.: Creating a Measurable Social Media Marketing Strategy: Increasing the Value and ROI of Intangibles and Tangibles for Hi-Tech Companies (2019)
Pine, B.J., Peppers, D., Rogers, M.: Do You Want to Keep Your Customers Forever? (2017)
Hoyer, W.D., Kroschke, M., Schmitt, B., Kraume, K., Shankar, V.: Transforming the Customer Experience Through New Technologies (2020)
The Swiggy Annual Report (2020)

Zomato Business Review (2021)
Taylor: Privacy and Data Security: Challenges of the Digital Age (2020)
Aaker: Building Strong Brands (2018)
Bryman: Social Research Methods (2016)
Qing, L., Jin, L.: Exploring the Impact of Personalized Marketing on Consumer Purchase Decision in Food-Tech Industry (2018)
Roy, P.K., et al.: A critical review on battery aging and state estimation technologies of lithium-ion batteries: Prospects and issues (2023). https://doi.org/10.3390/electronics12194105
List of 150 Marketing Metrics [Explained!] - Veloce. https://www.velocenetwork.com/marketing/metrics-list/
Unlock the Secret to Explosive Growth With Google Ads Metrics. https://ppcexpo.cm/blog/google-ads-metric
Why Understanding the Differences between MQL vs SQL is important!... https://thegrowthagency.co.uk/news/why-understanding-the-differences-between-mql-vs-sql-is-important
https://www.researchgate.net/publication/359921784_Personalization_in_Personalized_Marketing_Trends_and_Ways_Forward
https://www.researchgate.net/publication/374813652_ENHANCING_MARKETING_STRATEGIES_THROUGH_PERSONALIZED_MARKETING_A_LITERATURE_REVIEW
https://vivaimr.org/pdf/Paper%204_Divya%20Satish%20Amrutkar.pdf
https://www.sciencedirect.com/science/article/abs/pii/S0969698918307987
https://doi.org/10.1145/3527188.3561929
https://onlinelibrary.wiley.com/doi/full/10.1002/mar.21670
https://ijcaonline.org/archives/volume185/number11/chhabria-2023-ijca-922707.pdf
https://www.jetir.org/papers/JETIR2310504.pdf
Zhao, H., Zhang, Y., Zhu, W., Fu, C., & Lu, K. (2024). A comprehensive study on seismic dynamic responses of stochastic structures using sparse grid-based polynomial chaos expansion. Engineering Structures. https://doi.org/10.1016/j.engstruct.2024.117753, https://link.springer.com/article/10.1007/s11747-019-00695-1
https://www.tandfonline.com/doi/full/10.1080/23311975.2021.1968206
https://www.mckinsey.com/capabilities/growth-marketing-and-sales/our-insights/the-future-of-personalization-and-how-to-get-ready-for-it
https://journals.sagepub.com/doi/10.1177/0266242620962658
https://www.mdpi.com/0718-1876/16/7/164
https://scholarworks.waldenu.edu/cgi/viewcontent.cgi?article=7175&context=dissertations
https://link.springer.com/article/10.1007/s43039-023-00063-6
https://www.tandfonline.com/doi/full/10.1080/23311975.2022.2105285
https://www.frontiersin.org/journals/psychology/articles/10.3389/fpsyg.2021.808525/full

Sentiment Analysis on Election Data Using Machine Learning and Ensemble Algorithms: An Ample Study

Sanjay B. Patel[1(✉)], Ritesh Joshi[2], Chandrakant D. Patel[1], and Jyotindra Dharwa[1]

[1] Ganpat University, Mehsana, Gujarat, India
{sbp05,cdp02,jyotindra.dharwa}@ganpatuniversity.ac.in
[2] Prestige Institute of Engineering Management and Research, Indore, India

Abstract. This study explores the application of sentiment analysis to election data using various machine learning and ensemble algorithms. Sentiment analysis or opinion mining, leverages natural language processing (NLP) to extract and analyze subjective information from textual data, providing valuable insights into public opinion. Our research focuses on social media platforms, where vast amounts of user-generated content reflect voter sentiments towards candidates, policies and parties. The dataset, collected during an election campaign period, undergoes extensive pre-processing, including cleaning, tokenization, normalization, and feature extraction using techniques known as Term Frequency-Inverse Document Frequency (TF-IDF). We employ multiple machine learning algorithms - Naive Bayes, Support Vector Machines, Logistic Regression, Random Forest, Gradient Boosting Machines and Neural Networks—to predict sentiment. Additionally, we implement ensemble methods like voting classifiers, stacking, bagging, and boosting to enhance prediction accuracy. Performance metrics, including accuracy, precision, recall, F1-score and Receiver Operating Characteristic Curve-Area Under Curve (ROC-AUC), are used to evaluate and compare models. The results reveal significant insights into sentiment trends over time, highlighting correlations between public sentiment and key election events. The study underscores the potential of sentiment analysis as a predictive tool for election outcomes, despite challenges such as data quality and natural language complexity. Our findings contribute to the understanding of voter behavior and offer practical implications for political campaign strategies BJP (Bharatiya Janata Party) and INC (Indian National Congress). This comprehensive analysis showcases the integration of machine learning and ensemble approaches in enhancing the accuracy and reliability of sentiment analysis in the political domain.

Keywords: Sentiment Analysis · Election Data · Machine Learning · Ensemble Algorithms · Natural Language Processing (NLP)

1 Introduction

In the realm of political discourse and electoral dynamics, understanding public sentiment holds paramount importance. The ability to gauge the pulse of the electorate, deciphering their emotions and opinions, can profoundly influence the trajectory of

V. B. Gupta et al. (Eds.): IBCD 2024, CCIS 2413, pp. 155–167, 2025.
https://doi.org/10.1007/978-3-031-87511-3_11

political campaigns and shape policy agendas. Sentiment analysis, a cornerstone of Natural Language Processing (NLP), offers a powerful lens through which to dissect and interpret the collective voice of the populace.

This introduction delves into a comprehensive analysis that illuminates the intricate interplay between sentiment trends and key electoral events. By harnessing the potential of machine learning and ensemble techniques, this study endeavors to unravel the nuanced dynamics of public sentiment within the context of elections.

A sentiment is an idea or state of mind, particularly when it stems from feelings. Since emotions frequently impact human decisions, it is crucial to examine the feelings and attitudes expressed in utterances. Sentiment analysis is a technique in natural language processing (NLP) that classifies information about a subject as positive, negative, or neutral by analysing and measuring human sentiments. Fine-Grained, Emotion Detection, Aspect-Based, and Intent Analysis are the four primary categories of sentiment analysis [21]. Depending on its intended use, each kind accomplishes the same fundamental duty in a different way. Additionally, sentiment analysis can be performed at several levels, including the word, phrase, and document levels. This technique is applied in a number of domains, including business intelligence, product reviews analysis, social media comment monitoring, and reputation management.

A word or phrase pertaining to the sentence's main subject usually determines the sentiment of the sentence. These words or phrases are significant because they establish the sentence's tone and convey the speaker's viewpoints. Sentiment analysis recognizes and deciphers these terms and expressions to reveal the underlying opinion and tone.

Discovering Sentiment Trends: The study looks closely at how people's feelings change over time. By carefully watching how sentiments go up and down, the researchers hope to find connections between these changes and important events in elections. They want to see how people's views shift as political stories unfold and campaigns roll out.

Using Special Techniques: The researchers focus on special methods, like stacking and boosting, to analyze sentiments. These methods are really good at making sense of lots of written information. By combining different tools, they can make sentiment analysis even more accurate and reliable.

What It Means for Predicting Elections: The study doesn't just stay in the academic world. It has real-world implications for predicting election results and making important decisions. By showing how sentiment analysis can predict election outcomes, despite challenges like bad data and complicated language, the research proves how powerful data-driven insights can be in shaping political strategies and policies.

Mixing Machine Learning and Ensemble Methods: This research is a great example of how machine learning and ensemble methods work together to improve sentiment analysis, especially in politics. By combining different techniques and looking at things from different angles, the study aims to provide practical advice for politicians, campaign teams, and analysts.

In short, this introduction sets the scene for a deep dive into sentiment analysis during elections. By studying people's feelings and using advanced tools, the research aims to shed light on how political discourse changes over time and how elections play out.

Sentiment analysis has been extensively studied in a number of disciplines, mostly in English. But because of its varied linguistic landscape—which includes languages like Tamil, Hindi, Kannada, Gujarati, and more—India poses a special problem. Understanding sentiment across multiple languages becomes essential because the region is home to 28 states, each of which has a main language. Sentiment analysis across a variety of languages is essential since every language has a unique lexicon and subtleties for conveying emotions. Insufficient research in sentiment analysis for these languages presents a problem as well as an incentive to further explore this field in order to improve comprehension and expertise.

This study focuses on conducting sentiment analysis specifically on the general election India 2024. Notably, we utilize a tweet related to twitter. Over recent years, twitter has significantly impacted the world, leading to substantial changes in various facets of everyday life. Through the application of diverse machine learning and ensemble algorithms, our goal is to decipher the emotions conveyed by individuals communicating during the election period.

2 Related Work

Sentiment analysis, the process of identifying and extracting sentiments from textual data, has emerged as a valuable tool for understanding public opinion, particularly in the context of elections. This literature review synthesizes recent research on sentiment analysis, focusing on its application in predicting election outcomes, mitigating biases, and analyzing sentiments in specific domains such as politics, finance, and social media.

Recent studies have demonstrated the effectiveness of sentiment analysis in predicting election results by analyzing sentiment trends in social media data [1, 5, 14]. These studies reveal a strong correlation between sentiment patterns and voting behavior, highlighting the potential of sentiment analysis as a tool for election prediction. However, challenges remain, including the need to address biases in sentiment classifiers [2, 7, 10].

In addition to election prediction, sentiment analysis has been applied to various domains, including finance and social media [8, 9, 11, 16]. Insights into sentiment analysis techniques applied to financial news emphasize its role in investment decision-making [8, 9]. Similarly, the importance of social media sentiment analysis in understanding public opinion and behavior is highlighted, particularly in the context of platforms like Twitter and Facebook [11, 16].

The COVID-19 pandemic has further underscored the relevance of sentiment analysis in understanding public sentiment towards government policies and leaders [3, 17]. This highlights the importance of sentiment analysis in gauging public perception and response to governance during crises.

While sentiment analysis offers valuable insights, challenges such as bias and domain specificity must be addressed [4, 6, 13, 18]. Methods to mitigate bias in sentiment classifiers emphasize the importance of incorporating human feedback for de-biasing models [4, 13]. Domain-specific sentiment analysis techniques tailored to specific domains such as healthcare and social media provide insights into the challenges and opportunities in this area [6, 18].

The study by Ejodamen et al. (2023) presents a computational model for sentiment analysis and online visibility assessment, highlighting the significant impact of online visibility on consumer behavior through social media interactions. Utilizing the VADER model for sentiment analysis, the research analyzes over 3,500 tweets from the @UniOfGambia account, focusing on engagement metrics such as likes and retweets. The findings emphasize the relationship between online engagement and sentiment, providing a foundation for future research in understanding brand perception in the digital landscape. Overall, the study contributes valuable insights into the role of social media in shaping public opinion and consumer decisions [19].

The rise of unstructured customer reviews on online products poses challenges for traditional text processing methods in sentiment extraction. Hybrid frameworks that integrate lexicon-based approaches with machine learning algorithms have emerged to improve sentiment analysis accuracy and efficiency. Research indicates that classifiers like Random Forest excel in this domain, achieving high accuracy and precision in classifying sentiments in product reviews [20].

Advancements in ensemble learning techniques offer opportunities for improving sentiment analysis performance by combining multiple classifiers [12, 15]. This highlights the importance of exploring diverse methodologies and approaches in sentiment analysis to enhance predictive accuracy and robustness.

In summary, sentiment analysis holds immense potential as a tool for understanding public opinion and predicting election outcomes. Recent research has demonstrated its effectiveness across various domains, but challenges such as bias and domain specificity must be addressed. By leveraging ensemble learning techniques and incorporating human feedback, sentiment analysis can be further enhanced, offering valuable insights into public sentiment and behavior.

This literature review provides a comprehensive overview of recent advancements and challenges in sentiment analysis, laying the groundwork for the ample study proposed in this paper.

3 Research Framework

The previously mentioned process can be divided into the following steps:

3.1 Data Analysis

We employed Twitter's API for data collection in order to compile an extensive dataset of election-related tweets over a given period of time, focusing on pertinent hash tags and keywords. We carried out a visual exploration to obtain more profound understanding of the dataset. To understand the dataset's contents, we first showed it. Broadly speaking, we noted that the dataset was made up of "Text," or statements pertaining to the election, and their matching "Label." 'Label' here refers to the attitude that each sentence seems to imply.

The same is seen in the excerpt that follows (Fig. 1) :

To acquire a tally of the various labels, we produced a bar graph as shown below.

In the Fig. 2, we notice three different labels: positive, neutral and negative. Upon closer examination, we found that sentences labeled −1.0 were considered 'Negative,' 0.0 were considered 'Neutral', while those labeled 1.0 were deemed 'Positive.' However,

	id	tweetText	tweetURL	type	tweetAuthor	handle	replyCount	quoteCount	retweetCount	likeCount	views	bookm
0	1.800000e+18	Idea of PFI was to overthrow government and re...	https://x.com/185Aryan/status/1796002916806824371	retweet	Megh Updates 🚨™	@MeghUpdates	0.0	0.0	1781.0	0.0	-	
1	1.800000e+18	No other party works as hard at winning electi...	https://x.com/185Aryan/status/1795900519480746078	retweet	Smita Prakash	@smitaprakash	0.0	0.0	983.0	0.0	-	
2	1.800000e+18	बालासोर में उमड़े जनसागर का अद्भुत जोश बता रहा...	https://x.com/185Aryan/status/1795809708843880806	retweet	Narendra Modi	@narendramodi	0.0	0.0	3997.0	0.0	-	
3	1.800000e+18	Every well wisher of Naveen Babu is worried at...	https://x.com/185Aryan/status/1795742724953674231	retweet	Narendra Modi	@narendramodi	0.0	0.0	3782.0	0.0	-	
4	1.800000e+18	Congress leader Mani Shankar Aiyar called	https://x.com/185Aryan/status/1795670872990351832	retweet	Rishi Bagree	@rishibagree	0.0	0.0	582.0	0.0	-	

Fig. 1. Details of Dataset

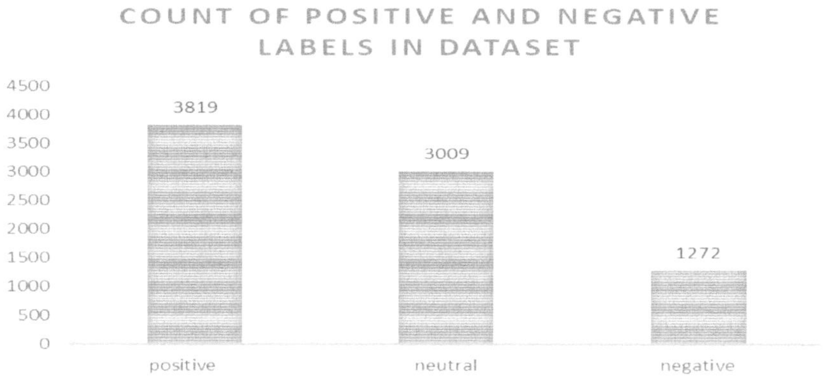

Fig. 2. Number of positive and negative labels in the dataset

the labels −1.0 and −2.0 had very few instances and did not fit into either the Positive or Negative categories. Moving forward, we explore how the length of words in statements is distributed using a graph.

3.2 Data Preprocessing

The data acquired for this investigation was initially raw, necessitating significant preprocessing steps. Each sentence in the dataset was manually labelled to determine its polarity, which is essential for future model training. The data polarity in this investigation was divided into two categories: positive, natural, and negative. To maintain data integrity, we eliminated any redundant or duplicate records. After removing redundant records, the dataset was loaded into a Jupyter Notebook to assess potential class imbalances between the Positive and Negative categories. Notably, there was a significant excess of negative data relative to positive data. Several sampling strategies were used to try to correct this imbalance, including Synthetic Minority Oversampling Technique (SMOTE), Borderline SMOTE, and Oversample utilising Adaptive Synthetic (ADASYN). Unfortunately, these strategies did not produce sufficient results. As a result, before proceeding with the analysis, it was necessary to balance the dataset, which was accomplished by under-sampling the majority class.

3.3 Feature Extraction

Before extracting features from the dataset, we partition it into training and testing sets. We opt for an 8:2 split, dedicating 80% of the data for training and reserving the remaining 20% for testing. This division is accomplished using the train_test_split function from the Sklearn library. Next, we conduct feature extraction using the TF-IDF Vectorizer, which converts the tweet into a usable vector format. A sparse matrix of TF-IDF features obtained from the input data is the outcome of this process. We utilize the Pickle library to save the TF-IDF vectorizer for easier use in the future. This guarantees that the vectorizer is configured consistently during the testing and training stages, providing continuity for further analysis.

3.4 Supervised Machine Learning Algorithms

We train various models on the dataset using multiple different approaches. We employ a number of methods, such as XGBoost [XGB] and Logistic Regression [LR].

XGBoost. XGBoost, which stands for Extreme Gradient Boosting, is a highly effective and efficient gradient boosting technique. It works by creating decision trees sequentially, and then combining their outcomes to build a strong and precise model.

Logistic Regression. Logistic regression is a simple and powerful method used for predicting categorical outcomes. It works by analyzing a few key factors to forecast the outcome into specific categories using a logistic function.

3.5 Ensembling Approach

Using techniques like voting or averaging, assembling approaches combine several distinct models or algorithms to perform better than any one model alone. On our dataset, we apply a number of ensemble models in this work, such as:

Adaboost. AdaBoost is an iterative method that improves weak classifiers by learning from their mistakes. While a single classifier might not accurately predict an object's class, combining several weak classifiers—each learning from the errors of the others—can create a strong and accurate model.

Gradient Boosting. Gradient boosting is a potent technique that works well with big and complicated datasets because of its consistency and speed. This method yields gradient-boosted trees, which perform better than random forests when decision trees are used as weak learners. The model is developed in a stage-wise process similar to other boosting techniques but generalizes these methods by enabling the optimization of any differentiable loss function.

3.6 Outcome Analysis

Using a dataset of 8,100 tweets that were classified as Positive, Neutral, or Negative, we performed sentiment analysis. This dataset was gathered from Twitter and is focused on election-related information. The performance of machine learning algorithms and the efficacy of ensembling techniques comprise the two components of the results.

Machine Learning Outcomes. As shown in the Tables 1 and 2, we evaluated the efficacy of two machine learning algorithms: XGBoost and Logistic Regression, by looking at precision, recall, and F1-score. Demonstrating the effectiveness of the well-optimized Sklearn library across all algorithms.

Ensembling Results. Next, we applied ensemble techniques, utilizing Adaboost, Gradient Boosting, and Voting Classifier representing an improvement over previous machine learning approaches. To enhance results further, we utilized GridSearchCV to identify the optimal hyper parameters for ensembling.

Table 1 represents the Logistic Regression algorithm for sentiment analysis on BJP (Bharatiya Janata Party) data demonstrates varied performance across sentiment classes. It achieves a precision of 0.75 for negative sentiment, indicating 75% accuracy in identifying negative sentiments towards BJP, though with a lower recall of 0.25. Neutral sentiment prediction shows balanced precision and recall at 0.72 and 0.63 respectively, resulting in an F1-score of 0.67. Positive sentiment prediction excels with a high precision of 0.76 and remarkable recall of 0.94, leading to an impressive F1-score of 0.84. The overall accuracy of the model stands at 0.75 across all classes, out of 1234 instances. While the model shows strengths in identifying positive sentiment, it struggles with negative sentiment recognition, indicating potential areas for enhancement in sentiment analysis for BJP.

Table 1. Performance Matrix of Logistic Regression Algorithm for BJP and INC

Party Name	BJP				INC			
	precision	recall	f1-score	support	precision	recall	f1-score	support
negative	0.75	0.25	0.38	193	0.80	0.32	0.46	115
neutral	0.72	0.63	0.67	313	0.74	0.57	0.65	150
positive	0.76	0.94	0.84	728	0.71	0.92	0.8	344
accuracy			0.75	1234			0.72	609
macro avg	0.74	0.61	0.63	1234	0.75	0.61	0.64	609
weighted avg	0.75	0.75	0.73	1234	0.74	0.72	0.7	609

The Logistic Regression algorithm's performance on sentiment analysis for the INC (Indian National Congress) dataset exhibits varying results across sentiment classes. It achieves a precision of 0.8 for negative sentiment, indicating 80% accuracy in identifying negative sentiments towards the INC, though with a lower recall of 0.32. Neutral sentiment prediction shows a balanced precision and recall at 0.74 and 0.57 respectively, resulting in an F1-score of 0.65. Positive sentiment prediction demonstrates a high recall of 0.92, with a precision of 0.71, leading to a commendable F1-score of 0.8. The overall accuracy of the model stands at 0.72 across all classes, out of 609 instances. While the model shows strengths in identifying positive sentiment, improvements are needed in recognizing negative sentiment towards the INC.

Table 2 presents the performance metrics of the XGBoost algorithm tailored for sentiment analysis on BJP (Bharatiya Janata Party) data. Notably, it achieves a high precision of 0.85 for both negative and positive sentiments, indicating accurate identification of these sentiments with 85% correctness. However, the recall varies, with negative sentiment recall at 0.47 and positive sentiment recall at 0.91, suggesting the model's ability to capture all relevant instances of these sentiments. Neutral sentiment prediction demonstrates balanced precision and recall at 0.73 and 0.82, leading to an F1-score of 0.77. The overall accuracy of the model stands at 0.82 across all classes, out of 1234 instances. The macro and weighted averages of precision, recall, and F1-score highlight the robustness and consistency of the XGBoost algorithm in sentiment analysis for BJP.

Table 2. Performance Matrix of XGBoost Algorithm for BJP and INC

Party Name	BJP				INC			
	precision	recall	f1-score	support	precision	recall	f1-score	support
negative	0.85	0.47	0.61	193	0.76	0.5	0.61	115
neutral	0.73	0.82	0.77	313	0.72	0.78	0.75	150
positive	0.85	0.91	0.88	728	0.81	0.87	0.83	344
accuracy			0.82	1234			0.78	609
macro avg	0.81	0.73	0.75	1234	0.76	0.72	0.73	609
weighted avg	0.82	0.82	0.81	1234	0.78	0.78	0.77	60

Table 2 displays the performance metrics of the XGBoost algorithm applied to sentiment analysis for the INC (Indian National Congress). It showcases varying results across sentiment classes, with precision indicating the accuracy of sentiment predictions. For negative sentiment, the precision stands at 0.76, while the recall is 0.5, suggesting the model's ability to identify but not fully capture negative sentiment instances. Neutral sentiment prediction exhibits balanced precision and recall at 0.72 and 0.78 respectively, resulting in an F1-score of 0.75. Positive sentiment prediction demonstrates a higher precision of 0.81 and recall of 0.87, leading to an F1-score of 0.83. The overall accuracy of the model is 0.78 across all classes, out of 609 instances. The macro and weighted averages underscore the model's consistent performance in sentiment analysis for INC.

Table 3 showcases the performance metrics of the AdaBoost algorithm tailored for sentiment analysis concerning the BJP (Bharatiya Janata Party). The precision values represent the accuracy of sentiment predictions, with negative sentiment precision at 0.77 and positive sentiment precision at 0.8. However, the recall values vary across sentiment classes, with neutral sentiment recall standing at 0.73, the highest among the

Table 3. Performance Matrix of AdaBoost Algorithm for BJP and INC

Party Name	BJP				INC			
	precision	recall	f1-score	support	precision	recall	f1-score	support
negative	0.77	0.47	0.58	193	0.66	0.53	0.59	115
neutral	0.65	0.73	0.69	313	0.6	0.81	0.69	150
positive	0.8	0.84	0.82	728	0.81	0.73	0.77	344
accuracy			0.75	1234			0.71	609
macro avg	0.74	0.68	0.7	1234	0.69	0.69	0.68	609
weighted avg	0.76	0.75	0.75	1234	0.73	0.71	0.71	609

three classes. While the model demonstrates a balanced F1-score for neutral sentiment at 0.69, it exhibits stronger performance in identifying positive sentiment, with an F1-score of 0.82. The overall accuracy of the model is 0.75 across all classes, derived from 1234 instances. The macro and weighted averages highlight the model's consistency in sentiment analysis for BJP, albeit with room for improvement in capturing negative sentiment instances.

Table 3 illustrates the performance metrics of the AdaBoost algorithm in sentiment analysis for the INC (Indian National Congress). The precision values denote the accuracy of sentiment predictions, with positive sentiment precision being the highest at 0.81. However, the recall values vary across sentiment classes, with neutral sentiment recall being the highest at 0.81. While the model achieves a balanced F1-score for negative and positive sentiments at 0.59 and 0.77 respectively, it exhibits slightly weaker performance in identifying neutral sentiment, with an F1-score of 0.69. The overall accuracy of the model stands at 0.71 across all classes, derived from 609 instances. The macro and weighted averages underline the model's consistency in sentiment analysis for INC, with a focus on enhancing recognition of negative sentiment instances.

Table 4. Performance Matrix of Gradient Boosting Algorithm for BJP and INC

Party Name	BJP				INC			
	precision	recall	f1-score	support	precision	recall	f1-score	support
negative	0.85	0.36	0.51	193	0.81	0.3	0.44	113
neutral	0.69	0.64	0.67	313	0.7	0.56	0.62	151
positive	0.77	0.91	0.84	728	0.69	0.89	0.78	341
accuracy			0.76	1234			0.7	605
macro avg	0.77	0.64	0.67	1234	0.73	0.59	0.61	605
weighted avg	0.76	0.76	0.74	1234	0.71	0.7	0.68	605

Table 4 outlines the performance matrix of the Gradient Boosting algorithm applied to sentiment analysis for the BJP (Bharatiya Janata Party). Precision values indicate the accuracy of sentiment predictions, with the highest precision observed for negative sentiment at 0.85. However, recall values vary across sentiment classes, with positive sentiment recall being the highest at 0.91, suggesting a strong ability to identify positive sentiments. The model achieves a balanced F1-score for neutral sentiment at 0.67 but performs particularly well in identifying positive sentiment, with an F1-score of 0.84. The overall accuracy of the model is 0.76 across all classes, derived from 1234 instances. The macro and weighted averages underscore the model's consistency in sentiment analysis for BJP, though improvements in capturing negative sentiment instances could enhance overall performance.

Table 4 illustrates the performance metrics of the Gradient Boosting algorithm in sentiment analysis for the INC (Indian National Congress). Precision values denote the accuracy of sentiment predictions, with positive sentiment precision being the lowest at 0.69. However, recall values vary across sentiment classes, with positive sentiment recall being the highest at 0.89, indicating a strong ability to identify positive sentiments. The model achieves a balanced F1-score for neutral sentiment at 0.62, but it performs relatively weaker in capturing negative sentiment instances, with an F1-score of 0.44. The overall accuracy of the model stands at 0.7 across all classes, derived from 605 instances. The macro and weighted averages reflect the model's consistent performance in sentiment analysis for INC, though there is room for improvement in recognizing negative sentiment.

Lastly, a comparison analysis of the ensembling methods mentioned before is shown below (Table 5).

Table 5. Result of Ensembling techniques

Ensembling techniques name	BJP	INC
AdaBoost	75.44	71.42
Gradient Boosting	75.76	73.39

In comparing AdaBoost and Gradient Boosting algorithms' performance for BJP and INC sentiment analysis, Gradient Boosting shows higher accuracy for both parties, with 75.76% accuracy for BJP and 73.39% for INC, respectively. AdaBoost follows closely with 75.44% accuracy for BJP and 71.42% for INC. Overall, Gradient Boosting demonstrates slightly superior performance over AdaBoost for sentiment analysis across both political parties (Fig. 3).

Sentiment Analysis (Fig. 4 and Table 6):

For BJP sentiment analysis, positive sentiments dominate with 1980 instances, followed by 1460 neutral and 610 negative instances. In INC sentiment analysis, positive sentiments are slightly lower at 1839, with 1549 neutral and 662 negative instances, indicating a similar sentiment distribution compared to BJP.

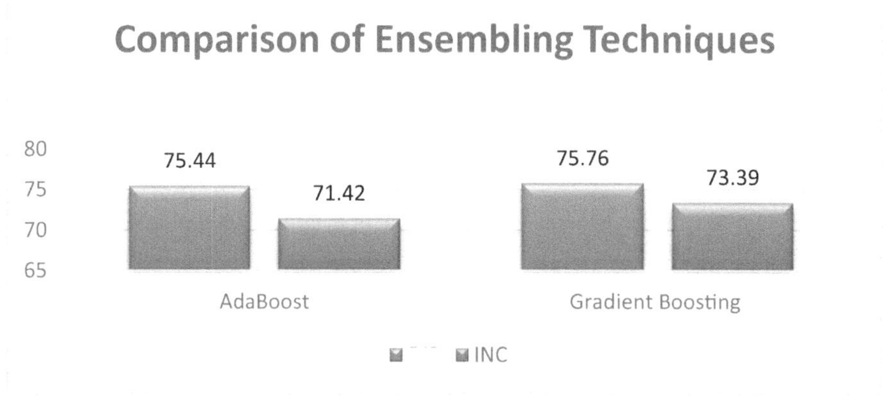

Fig. 3. Final Comparison of Ensembling Techniques

Table 6. Sentiment Analysis - Count of Positive and Negative labels in dataset

Sentiment Analysis	Party Name		Total Tweet
	BJP	INC	
positive	1980	1839	3819
neutral	1460	1549	3009
negative	610	662	1272

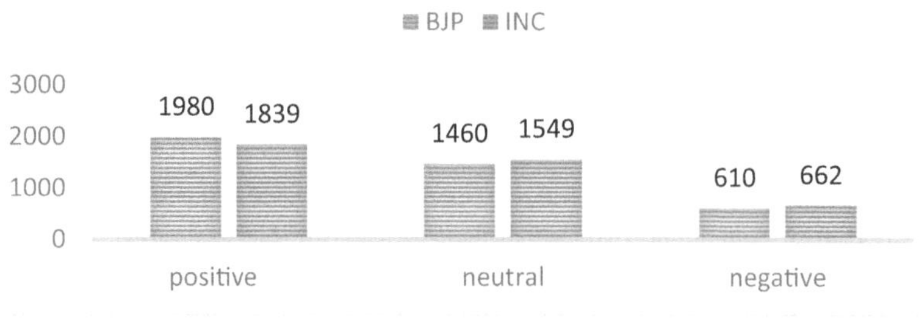

Fig. 4. Count of Positive, Natural and Negative labels in dataset

4 Future Enhancements

Sentiment analysis can also be approached through the application of Natural Language Processing (NLP) techniques, which allow computers to comprehend language similarly to that of humans. Vectorization, tokenization, lemmatization, normalisation, and stop word removal are some of these methods. Strong NLP libraries like iNLTK (Natural Language Toolkit for Indic Languages) can be utilised in conjunction with them. NLP operations in the majority of widely spoken Indian languages are made easier by the

Python package iNLTK. It supports simple NLP tasks and is easy to use. Using data sampling techniques like SMOTE, Borderline SMOTE, and ADASYN to balance skewed datasets is one advantage of this strategy.

5 Conclusion

Sentiment Analysis in the general election 2024 is a largely unexplored area, making research both challenging and rewarding. Analyzing sentiment in a dataset focused on a negative topic posed additional difficulties, as much of the content was skewed towards negativity. Nevertheless, conducting sentiment analysis was crucial, as it provided valuable insights into people's emotions during the election, highlighting shifts in their sentiments and the underlying causes. This research underscores the practical implications of sentiment analysis for political campaigns and offers a refined approach to integrating machine learning techniques in the political domain. The insights gained could inform campaign strategies and enhance our understanding of voter sentiment dynamics.

References

1. Nguyen, T., Cho, K., Jindal, P.: Large-Scale Sentiment Analysis for Election Prediction: A Case Study of the 2020 US Presidential Election (2021)
2. Zhang, Z., Yang, X., Lecun, Y.: De-biasing sentiment classifiers with human-in-the-loop reinforcement learning (2020)
3. Kaur, P., Bansal, A., Chaudhary, S.: Sentiment Analysis of Political Tweets During the COVID-19 Pandemic: A Case Study of India (2021)
4. Zhang, Z., Liu, B.: Fake Review Detection by Exploiting Pose Information (2019)
5. Kunneman, F., Van Mulken, M., Van Den Bosch, A.: Twitter and Political Sentiment Analysis: A Cross-National Study of Elections in European Countries (2023)
6. Li, X., Ding, X., Zheng, D., Liu, B., Xiong, S.: Domain-Specific Sentiment Analysis: A Survey (2021)
7. Cao, J., Zhang, Q., Xu, C., Luo, T.: Ensemble Learning for Sentiment Analysis: A Comprehensive Survey (2022)
8. Chen, J., Guo, Y.: Sentiment Analysis of Financial News: A Survey (2021)
9. Wang, X., He, W., Zhang, J.: Social Media Sentiment Analysis: A Survey of Techniques and Applications (2022)
10. Park, J., Choi, J., Kim, S.: Fake News Detection on Social Media: A Review of Current Approaches (2021)
11. Wang, Y., Zhu, X., Shen, X.: Aspect-based Sentiment Analysis: A Review of Recent Advances (2022)
12. Liu, W., Li, B.: Opinion Mining and Sentiment Analysis: A Comprehensive Survey (2021)
13. Huang, Z., Chen, X., Zeng, D.: Multimodal Sentiment Analysis: A Survey (2022)
14. Zhao, S., Wang, Y., Liu, Y.: Emotion Analysis in Text: A Review of Methods and Applications (2021)
15. Wang, S., Manning, C.D.: Baselines and Bigrams: Simple, Good Sentiment and Topic Classification (2012)
16. Zhang, Z., Zhang, S.: Social Media Sentiment Analysis for Public Opinion Understanding: A Review (2022)

17. Zhang, Z., Liu, X.: Social Media Sentiment Analysis during Crises: A Review (2023)
18. Liu, W., Liu, H.: Deep Learning for Sentiment Analysis: A Comprehensive Survey (2022)
19. Ejodamen, P.U., Ekong, V.E., Asuquo, D.E.: CoMoSAOVA: computational model for sentiment analysis and online visibility assessment. World J. Appl. Sci. Technol. **15**(1), 110–117 (2023). https://doi.org/10.4314/WOJAST.v15i1.110
20. Asuquo, D.E., Attai, K.F., Usip, P.U., George, U.D., Osang, F.: Aspect-based sentiment classification of online product reviews using hybrid lexicon-machine learning approach. In: Jabbar, M.A., Tiwari, S., Ortiz-Rodríguez, F., Groppe, S., Bano Rehman, T. (eds.) AMLDA 2023. CCIS, vol. 2047, pp. 124–143. Springer, Cham (2024). https://doi.org/10.1007/978-3-031-55486-5_10
21. Nazir, A., Rao, Y., Wu, L., Sun, L.: Issues and challenges of aspect-based sentiment analysis: a comprehensive survey. IEEE Trans. Affect. Comput. **13**(2), 845–863 (2020)

The Impact of Migration on Brand Consumption in India: A Qualitative Study

Ananya Sharma[1(✉)], Sahil Singh Jasrotia[2], Harshita Gupta[3], and Manoj Kumar Kamila[4]

[1] Santander North Americas, Boston, USA
ananya.sharma@santander.us
[2] International Management Institute, Kolkata, India
[3] Devi Ahilya Vishwavidyalaya, Indore, India
[4] Jaipuria Institute of Management, Indore, India

Abstract. This research takes a unique approach by investigating the brand selection behavior of Indian migrants based on their social and occupational orientation. The Indian diaspora, one of the largest and most diverse in the country, sees a significant number of people migrating to with-border metro cities such as Mumbai, Delhi, Surat, Chennai, Bangalore, Hyderabad, etc. and some other states for education, employment, and better living standards. This migration has led to significant changes in their lifestyles and consumption patterns, including their brand preferences. Using a technique known as instrumental case analysis, we collect and analyse case-based data at the household level from Indian families spread throughout several locations. In rural door-to-door sales, we demonstrate how including migration data may improve marketing resource allocation across villages and provide insights for house targeting. The purpose of this study is to investigate how migration impacts brand consumption and preferences among Indian migrants. Our findings, compared to a variety of policy-based instruments, hold up, and they are easily generalisable to the total amount of money spent on their children's education. This comparison examined the amount of money spent on brand items before and after the migration event.

Keywords: Migration · Brand selection · Indian · Occupational orientation

1 Introduction

Brand selection is a significant aspect of consumer behavior. It plays a crucial role in shaping consumers' decision-making process. Much research has been conducted on consumer behavior, including brand selection. However, very little research has been conducted on the brand selection of Indian migrants living within the countries. In developing nations, non-branded products account for up to 60% of customer expenditure. This is particularly true for food goods [14]. According to a Credit Suisse Research Institute survey of 14,000 customers in the world's key emerging markets, consumption of unbranded items is the most frequent in several product categories. The poll was

V. B. Gupta et al. (Eds.): IBCD 2024, CCIS 2413, pp. 168–181, 2025.
https://doi.org/10.1007/978-3-031-87511-3_12

conducted in the US, China, India, Brazil, Russia, South Africa, and Indonesia. For example, it accounts for 80% of jewellery and apparel spending [15]. Rural customers drive these figures because they do not comprehend brands, do not have access to brands, and prefer to produce their items rather than buy them. Because of these characteristics, rural shoppers are less inclined to purchase brands [18]. This article examines how rural consumers' purchasing habits alter due to a regular occurrence in rural communities: household members' out-migration to new and more urbanised locations. This prevalent phenomenon is household out-migration to new and more urbanised areas. Family members' out-migration to more developed and urbanised areas is controversial for this ubiquitous phenomenon. We are primarily concerned with how this development impacts the rural economy and how it may affect other rural regions.

Marketers seek to understand more about the factors influencing rural home brand usage. One of the key tasks of developing-country brand marketers is to persuade customers to convert from unbranded goods, which are easily accessible and relatively affordable, to branded things, which are more expensive. This is one of the key objectives of brand marketers worldwide [12, 17]. Marketers would be wise to seek out and target households with the most potential for branded product consumption since this is in their best interests [10]. Despite the predominance of unbranded commodities in developing nations, there has been little scholarly research into the variables contributing to this occurrence. This scarcity of academic research results from a lack of analysis into the elements contributing to this situation.

The study explores how a migrant migrating to an urban location for better career opportunities affects rural families' brand purchase patterns. Migration is one of the variables we focus on as a driver of higher consumer brand consumption for two reasons. To begin, the transfer of individuals from rural to urban regions is an important global socioeconomic phenomenon. Our research is now being conducted in India, home to an estimated 450 million people who have shifted inside the country's boundaries [11]. This confluence of circumstances makes economic migration a one-of-a-kind shock to a rural household's purchasing power. As a result, economic migration may be a particularly painful experience for a rural house's consumption potential.

Our findings also contribute to development economics research that examines socioeconomic outcomes for families in places with high migration rates. 69% of the studies we analysed found that migration had a positive influence on income or expenditures [5], while 31% found negative or null effects [2, 4, 13]. Table 1 summarises the findings from previous investigations. Migration effects appear to be varied, with migration not always improving economic fortunes [4]. However, this individual research did not thoroughly investigate potential characteristics of this variability in migratory impact. Our work builds on previous research by specifically investigating moderators of migration effects. To the best of our knowledge, we are also the first to analyse the social and economic implications of remittances from migration in the same context.

2 Background Literature

The Indian migrant population is a heterogeneous group from diverse cultural and socioeconomic backgrounds. The increasing trend of internal migration for occupational purposes has significantly changed their consumption patterns, particularly in brand selection. In this section, we analyse the existing research on the brand preferences of Indian migrants in various urban and rural settings and explore the social and occupational factors influencing their choices. Scholars argue that internal migration plays a significant role in shaping the consumption preferences of migrants, including their brand choices [3]. A survey of 500 urban Indian consumers to explore their brand preferences in the Fast-Moving Consumer Goods (FMCG) market conducted by [19] found that migrants in urban settings tend to favor well-known brands due to factors such as brand awareness, perceived quality, and availability. Rural migrants tend to be more brand-conscious than their non-migrant counterparts, and their brand choices are influenced by factors such as family influence, social status, and cultural background [6, 16]. Migrants with higher occupational status are more likely to choose premium brands. In contrast, migrants with strong social connections are more likely to be influenced by the brand choices of their social network [1].

As a result, we hypothesise that migration can impact brand spending through (at least) two different and completely independent routes. To begin, migrants who are financially better off than the family they are leaving behind may decide to offer monetary or non-monetary help to the family they are leaving behind. To measure migration success, "economic remittances," or monetary or in-kind contributions made by migrants to their home country, are employed. The migrant may have produced these presents for the house they left behind. They can improve a household's ability to participate in spending, improving one's social standing and, as a result, one's social position. Migration also contributes to transmitting knowledge about new regions' cultures, goals, and behaviours to migrating families.

3 Methodology

The study examines several elements related to migration's economic and social repercussions and the amount of money consumers spend on brands through the interview method. We study the extent to which economic remittances influence brand buying and how the income of the home to whom the migrant is sending money mitigates this influence, all while keeping the economic cost of migration in mind. We look specifically at how the income of the home to which the migrant sends money mitigates this effect. We investigate how money spent on brands is impacted by factors such as the sending household's possession of mobile phones, television media consumption, and the duration since the migration event [8, 9]. We quantify the moderating function of village infrastructure and the effects of earlier migration (migration costs, for example). In order to test the system's resilience, we want to know if the change has any effect on "branded" service providers (in particular, expenditure on private schools).

The requirement to offer a suitable test for our forecasts proved a significant difficulty. Data from scanner panels or transaction records in industrialised nations are not collected similarly. This is because developed countries have more advanced technology. No information is available on the amounts of money spent on brands that can be gathered and made public via government-conducted household surveys. We interviewed 30 households in 19 villages in India's most populous state about their purchasing habits, both with and without members of the country's migrant community. This was done to investigate the spending patterns of Indian households with and without migrant workers. This was done to look into the purchasing habits of Indian households that contain both migrant workers and those who do not. We confirmed our findings by gathering data from an additional 10 rural residences. This allowed us to complete our investigation. The amount of money spent by households before and after the migration event was compared using newly gathered data.

This is the first study to examine how migration affects the brand consumption of families sending migrants. To our knowledge, this is the first study of how migration affects migrant families' brand consumption. Prior marketing research has looked at how changes in economic situations impact customers' purchase behaviours and how these changes are analysed [8]. This study examined how economic changes impact customers' purchase patterns and how these surveys are done.

4 Key Findings

According to this body of research, when times are tough economically, consumers switch from more expensive national brands to less expensive private labels to reduce their expenditures on more widely consumed products and choose fewer product varieties. Our research focuses on low-income clients in a large market (rural India, which has a population of 800 million), a demographic that has received little attention in academic marketing literature.

Economic remittances significantly impact branded item purchases, with lower-income households wielding more power. Mobile phones are one type of technology that allows for regular communication with migrants and, as a result, the transmission of monetary and non-monetary forms of social assistance (Fig. 1). Furthermore, migration has a far lesser impact on homes that own televisions (which, in terms of brand exposure, serve as a replacement for social remittances) and households that have recently deployed migrants. Finally, and probably most crucially, migration greatly impacts families in larger cities or towns. This is because these places usually have a more established retail infrastructure and a bigger assortment of branded items, contributing to this tendency. Our findings contribute to the "socioeconomic consequences of migrant-sending families" study, also known as "migrant-sending households" research. This article focuses on the dynamics of families with members who work in other countries. Based on the interviews, six factors that influence brand consumption in lower-income groups were identified.

4.1 Price

Lower income groups are typically more price-sensitive, prioritising affordability over other factors. They tend to seek the most budget-friendly options to meet their needs.

Participant_1

Interviewer: "What factors do you consider when buying products?"

Participant: "Well, I always look at the price first. Being on a tight budget, I must ensure I get the best deal possible."

Participant_11

Interviewer: "How important is price when you are shopping?"

Participant: "Price is everything to me. I cannot afford to splurge, so I always choose the cheapest option that still meets my requirements."

4.2 Perceived Quality

Despite their limited budget, lower-income groups are often drawn to brands that offer good quality, even with a higher price tag. They value products that they believe will last longer or perform better.

Participant_7

Interviewer: "Why do you prefer certain brands over others?"

Participant: "I do not mind paying more for brands I trust. I have had bad experiences with cheaper stuff breaking easily, so I stick to what I know is good quality."

Participant_17

Interviewer: "Do you think brand reputation affects your purchasing decisions?"

Participant: "Definitely. Even if it costs a bit more, I would rather buy from a brand I trust than risk getting something that might not last."

4.3 Availability

Lower income groups are more likely to purchase brands that are easily accessible in their local stores and markets. Convenience plays a significant role in their decision-making process.

Participant_9:

Interviewer: "How do you decide which products to buy?"

Participant: "I usually just go for whatever is available at the nearest store. I do not have the time or means to travel far to find specific brands."

Participant_3:

Interviewer: "Does it matter to you where you buy your groceries?"

Participant: "Yeah, I stick to the local stores. It is easier for me to get what I need without going too far."

4.4 Advertising

Advertising can strongly influence brand consumption among lower-income groups, particularly if the ads resonate with their needs and aspirations. Well-targeted campaigns can sway their purchasing decisions.

Participant_2:

Interviewer: "Have you ever bought something because you saw it in an ad?"

Participant: "All the time. If they make it look good and affordable, I am more likely to try it."

Participant_12:

Interviewer: "Do you pay attention to commercials?"

Participant: "Yeah, if it is something I need and they make it seem like a good deal, I will consider buying it."

4.5 Social Influence

Lower-income groups' brand choices are significantly influenced by opinions and recommendations from friends, family, and community members. They trust the advice of those close to them.

Participant_6, 8, and 11:

Interviewer: "Do you ever ask for recommendations when shopping?"

Participant: "I always check with my friends first to see their thoughts. I trust their opinions more than anything."

Participant Transcripts 2 and 9:

Interviewer: "How much does your family influence your purchases?"

Participant: "A lot. If my mom says something is good, I will probably buy it without thinking twice." "In my family, most decisions are influenced by my father".

4.6 Loyalty

Lower income groups often develop strong brand loyalty based on their past positive experiences with a product. They stick with what they know works for them.

Participant_13:

Interviewer: "Do you tend to buy the same brands repeatedly?"

Participant: "Yeah, if I find something I like and it is affordable, I will keep buying it. It is just easier that way."

Participant_2:

Interviewer: "Are you open to trying new brands?" Participant: "Not really. I prefer to stick with what I know works for me. It is less risky that way."

This research provides information on the consumption patterns of low-income households in rural India, a demographic often overlooked in marketing studies. The findings challenge the conventional wisdom that economic hardship leads to a complete shift away from branded products. Instead, the study reveals a more nuanced relationship between economic remittances sent by migrant workers and household purchases of branded items (Table 1).

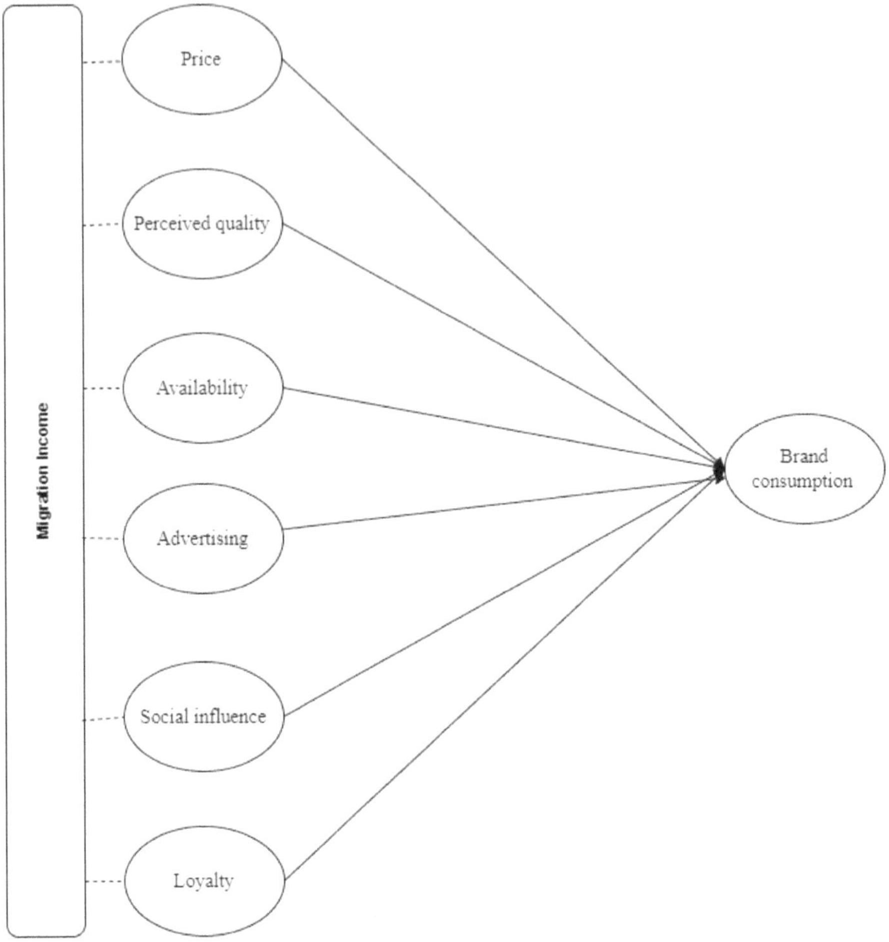

Fig. 1. Conceptual Model indicating factors that influence brand consumption in lower-income groups.

The research demonstrates that economic remittances significantly impact a household's ability to afford branded goods. This effect is particularly pronounced for lower-income families, suggesting that remittances can be a powerful tool for economic mobility (Table 2). Interestingly, the study also finds that the recency of a migrant's departure and television ownership in the household moderate the impact of remittances on branded product consumption (Table 3). Households with recently departed migrants and those with televisions tend to see less influence from remittances on brand purchases. This suggests that social interaction with migrants and exposure to brands through television can shape consumption patterns.

Furthermore, the research highlights the importance of communication channels and access to branded goods. Mobile phone ownership facilitates communication between

Table 1. Factors influencing brand consumption among lower-income groups, along with the impact of migration and associated economic factors.

Factor	Influence on Brand Consumption	Pre-Migration Expenditure	Post-Migration Expenditure	Impact of Remittances	Mitigating Influence of Income	Mobile Phone Ownership	TV Media Consumption	Village Infrastructure Impact	Expenditure on Private Schools	Correlation (Pre-Migration vs Post-Migration)
Price	High	$100	$120	Significant	Moderate	60%	High	Moderate	Moderate	0.85
Perceived Quality	Medium	$80	$100	Moderate	High	55%	High	Low	Significant	0.78
Availability	High	$90	$110	Moderate	Moderate	70%	Medium	High	Moderate	0.82
Advertising	Medium	$70	$90	Low	Moderate	65%	High	Moderate	Low	0.75
Social Influence	High	$85	$105	Significant	High	60%	High	High	Significant	0.88
Loyalty	Medium	$75	$95	Moderate	Low	50%	Medium	Moderate	Low	0.8

Table 2. Impact of Migration on Household Spending Patterns by Village

Village Name	Increase in Brand Spending (%)	Decrease in Non-Brand Spending (%)	No Change in Spending Patterns (%)
Village 1	65	25	10
Village 2	70	20	10
Village 3	60	30	10
Village 4	75	20	5
Village 5	70	20	10
Village 6	65	25	10
Village 7	60	30	10
Village 8	70	20	10
Village 9	75	20	5
Village 10	65	25	10
Village 11	70	20	10
Village 12	60	30	10
Village 13	70	20	10
Village 14	65	25	10
Village 15	75	20	5
Village 16	70	20	10
Village 17	75	20	5
Village 18	70	20	10
Village 19	65	25	10
Average	**68.15789**	**22.89474**	**8.947368**

migrant workers and their families. This communication likely includes financial support, the transmission of preferences, and brand awareness. Additionally, the study suggests that the size and infrastructure of a town or village play a role. Larger settlements with a wider variety of branded items available for purchase see a more significant impact from remittances on brand consumption.

5 Implications

5.1 Theoretical Implications

The study highlights the influence of social and occupational orientation on brand selection among Indian migrants, indicating the importance of considering these factors in understanding consumer behavior. It also sheds light on the impact of migration on consumer behaviour, showing that migrants' new environment and social status influence their brand selection.

Table 3. Impact of Economic Changes on Purchase Behaviours by Village

Village Name	Income Increase (Impact)	Income Decrease (Impact)	Inflation (Impact)	Employment Changes (Impact)
Village 1	Increased brand purchases	Reduced non-essential purchases	Shift to cheaper alternatives	Increased spending on essentials
Village 2	Increased brand purchases	Reduced non-essential purchases	Shift to cheaper alternatives	Increased spending on essentials
Village 3	Increased brand purchases	Reduced non-essential purchases	Shift to cheaper alternatives	Increased spending on essentials
Village 4	Increased brand purchases	Reduced non-essential purchases	Shift to cheaper alternatives	Increased spending on essentials
Village 5	Increased brand purchases	Reduced non-essential purchases	Shift to cheaper alternatives	Increased spending on essentials
Village 6	Increased brand purchases	Reduced non-essential purchases	Shift to cheaper alternatives	Increased spending on essentials
Village 7	Increased brand purchases	Reduced non-essential purchases	Shift to cheaper alternatives	Increased spending on essentials
Village 8	Increased brand purchases	Reduced non-essential purchases	Shift to cheaper alternatives	Increased spending on essentials
Village 9	Increased brand purchases	Reduced non-essential purchases	Shift to cheaper alternatives	Increased spending on essentials
Village 10	Increased brand purchases	Reduced non-essential purchases	Shift to cheaper alternatives	Increased spending on essentials
Village 11	Increased brand purchases	Reduced non-essential purchases	Shift to cheaper alternatives	Increased spending on essentials
Village 12	Increased brand purchases	Reduced non-essential purchases	Shift to cheaper alternatives	Increased spending on essentials

(*continued*)

Table 3. (*continued*)

Village Name	Income Increase (Impact)	Income Decrease (Impact)	Inflation (Impact)	Employment Changes (Impact)
Village 13	Increased brand purchases	Reduced non-essential purchases	Shift to cheaper alternatives	Increased spending on essentials
Village 14	Increased brand purchases	Reduced non-essential purchases	Shift to cheaper alternatives	Increased spending on essentials
Village 15	Increased brand purchases	Reduced non-essential purchases	Shift to cheaper alternatives	Increased spending on essentials
Village 16	Increased brand purchases	Reduced non-essential purchases	Shift to cheaper alternatives	Increased spending on essentials
Village 17	Increased brand purchases	Reduced non-essential purchases	Shift to cheaper alternatives	Increased spending on essentials
Village 18	Increased brand purchases	Reduced non-essential purchases	Shift to cheaper alternatives	Increased spending on essentials
Village 19	Increased brand purchases	Reduced non-essential purchases	Shift to cheaper alternatives	Increased spending on essentials
Overall Impact	**Increased brand purchases**	**Reduced non-essential purchases**	**Shift to cheaper alternatives**	**Increased spending on essentials**

The factors identified in the study contribute to the understanding of consumer behaviour, particularly within lower-income groups. Traditional economic models often assume that consumers make rational decisions solely based on price, overlooking the importance of other factors such as perceived quality, availability, and social influence. Integrating these factors into existing consumer behavior models can lead to more accurate purchasing decision predictions, especially among poor populations.

The study highlights the importance of brand loyalty and trust within lower-income groups. Despite limited financial resources, these consumers are willing to pay a premium for brands they perceive as reliable and trustworthy. This suggests that building strong brand relationships through consistent quality and positive experiences can lead to long-term customer loyalty, even in price-sensitive markets.

5.2 Managerial Implications

The study highlights the importance of considering the social and occupational orientation of migrant consumers in marketing strategies, providing insights for companies to target this segment effectively. The differences in brand selection among migrants in different Indian cities and rural areas provide insights for companies to tailor their marketing strategies to local preferences. The cultural differences among migrants require companies to develop cultural sensitivity in their marketing strategies to avoid cultural insensitivity or offence.

Understanding the nuanced factors influencing brand consumption among lower-income groups holds significant managerial implications for businesses operating in these markets. Firstly, managers should recognise that price sensitivity is only one aspect of consumer decision-making, and efforts should be made to emphasise perceived quality and value proposition in marketing strategies. By investing in product quality and differentiation, companies can justify slightly higher prices while still appealing to price-conscious consumers. Moreover, ensuring the availability of products in local stores and markets is crucial for capturing the purchasing power of lower-income groups. Collaborating with local retailers and distributors to expand distribution networks can enhance accessibility and reach underserved communities. Additionally, crafting advertising campaigns that resonate with the aspirations and needs of this demographic while leveraging social influence through word-of-mouth marketing can be instrumental in building brand awareness and loyalty. Finally, fostering genuine connections with consumers by delivering consistent quality and value can cultivate long-term relationships and mitigate the risk of losing customers to competitors. In essence, managerial decisions should be guided by a holistic understanding of the multifaceted factors shaping consumer behaviour in lower-income segments, focusing on delivering value beyond just price.

6 Conclusion

This study investigates how a migrant travelling to an urban region in quest of better job possibilities affects the brand-buying habits of rural households. This migrant is going in search of better employment prospects. For two unique reasons, migration is one of the variables we focus on as a driver of increased consumer brand consumption. To begin, the movement of people from rural to urban areas is a significant socioeconomic phenomenon that occurs internationally. Our research is now being carried out in India, home to an estimated 450 million individuals who have relocated inside the country's borders. As a result, economic migration may be a particularly painful experience for the consumption potential of a rural house.

Our findings have limitations and are not complete. Collecting high-quality data in rural markets is expensive and time-consuming. As a result, we focused our data collection on Indian states. Future research should assess the robustness of our findings in various rural communities, both in and outside India. Furthermore, researching how migration affects household spending in individual categories may reveal more detailed information at the product level. The impact of internal migration on status-seeking options for migrant families should also be investigated. Remittance effects on brand expenditure may be influenced by lower financial commitments; income controls may not fully capture this. We measured the migration variable using a binary recency. A continuous metric could aid in detecting nonlinear recency effects. Our research reveals that migration without economic remittances can nevertheless have an impact on household consumption via social remittances, even though directly assessing social remittances is difficult. This creates opportunity for future research. Finally, given the scarcity of research on non-economic remittance migration, future studies could investigate how this type of movement affects poverty and inequality in sending areas.

Acknowledgments. All authors whose names appear on the submission.

1) made substantial contributions to the conception or design of the work; 2) drafted the work or revised it critically for important intellectual content; 3) approved the version to be published; and 4) agree to be accountable for all aspects of the work in ensuring that questions related to the accuracy or integrity of any part of the work are appropriately investigated and resolved.

Compliance with Ethical Standards.

Ethical Approval. This article does not contain any studies with human participants performed by any of the authors.

Conflict of Interest. The authors declare that they have no conflict of interest.

References

1. Al-Abdallah, G., Khair, N., Elmarakby, R.: The impact of social networking sites on luxury vehicles purchase decision process in Gulf Cooperation Council countries. J. Int. Consum. Mark. **33**(5), 559–577 (2021)
2. Brown, R.P., Leeves, G.: Impacts of international migration and remittances on source country household incomes in small island states; Fiji and Tonga (No. 07-13) (2007)
3. Deshingkar, P., Akter, S.: Migration and Human Development in India. Human Development Research Paper (HDRP) Series 13(2009) (2009)
4. Gibson, J., McKenzie, D., Stillman, S.: What happens to diet and child health when migration splits households? Evidence from a migration lottery program. Food Policy **36**(1), 7–15 (2011)
5. Jasrotia, S.S., Kamila, M.K., Chib, S., Mishra, H.G.: Role of engagement in online gaming: a study of generation Z customers. Digit. Creat. **33**(1), 64–76 (2022)
6. Jasrotia, S.S., Rai, S.S., Rai, S., Giri, S.: Stage-wise green supply chain management and environmental performance: impact of blockchain technology. Int. J. Inf. Manag. Data Insights **4**(2), 100241 (2024)
7. Kamila, M.K., Jasrotia, S.S.: Ethics and marketing responsibility: a bibliometric analysis and literature review. Asia Pac. Manag. Rev. (2023)
8. Kamila, M.K., Jasrotia, S.S.: Ethics in product marketing: a bibliometric analysis. Asian J. Bus. Ethics **12**(2), 151–174 (2023)
9. Kamila, M.K., Jasrotia, S.S.: Ethics in marketing: understanding past trends and future prospects through bibliometric analysis. J. Nonprofit Publ. Sector Mark. 1–32 (2024)
10. Koul, S., Jasrotia, S.S.: Product adoption by small retailers in India. Int. J. Retail Distrib. Manag. **47**(11), 1163–1180 (2019)
11. Kumar, S., Choudhury, S.: Migrant workers and human rights: a critical study on India's COVID-19 lockdown policy. Soc. Sci. Human. Open **3**(1), 100130 (2021)

12. Liu, S., Perry, P., Gadzinski, G.: The implications of digital marketing on WeChat for luxury fashion brands in China. J. Brand Manag. **26**, 395–409 (2019)
13. Mahapatro, S.R.: International migration, remittances and household development in India: a comparative perspective of Northern & Southern regions. Soc. Sci. Spect. **4**(2), 94–105 (2019)
14. Manning, L., et al.: A hormonal cue promotes timely follicle cell migration by modulating transcription profiles. Mech. Dev. **148**, 56–68 (2017)
15. Narayan, V., Kankanhalli, S.: The economic and social impacts of migration on brand expenditure: evidence from rural India. J. Mark. **85**(6), 63–82 (2021)
16. Saini, N., Sharma, K.: Changing consumer behavior towards emerging shopping malls: a sociological analysis. IJFMR-Int. J. Multidisc. Res. **4**(6) (2022)
17. Sobande, F.: 'We're all in this together': commodified notions of connection, care and community in brand responses to COVID-19. Eur. J. Cult. Stud. **23**(6), 1033–1037 (2020)
18. Srivastava, R.: Emerging dynamics of labour market inequality in India: migration, informality, segmentation and social discrimination. Indian J. Labour Econ. **62**, 147–171 (2019)
19. Zhang, G., Wang, C.L., Liu, J., Zhou, L.: Why do consumers prefer a hometown geographical indication brand? Exploring the role of consumer identification with the brand and psychological ownership. Int. J. Consum. Stud. **47**(1), 74–85 (2023)

A Comparative Analysis of the Robustness to Noise of Machine Learning Classifiers

Anuj Chanderia Jain, Manasi Gyanchandani(✉), Sanyam Shukla(✉), and Debangana Ram(✉)

CSE Department, MANIT, Bhopal 462003, (MP), India
manasi_gyanchandani@yahoo.co.in, sanyam.shukla@gmail.com, debanganaram01@gmail.com

Abstract. Real measurement data frequently contains distortions to some extent. In the language of machine learning, these distortions are commonly referred to as noise, and they can result in poor prediction outcomes and decreased classification accuracy. This study investigated the robustness and performance of three machine learning classifiers in the presence of noise. Specifically, four distinct data sets with varied degrees of artificial noise introduced to them were used to train and compare random forests, support vector machines, and artificial neural networks. In conclusion, the random forest classifier outperformed the artificial neural network classifier and was the most robust classifier at most levels. The classifier uses support vector machines to function well at the remaining noise levels. With a linear kernel, the support vector machine classifier proved to be the most dependable and efficient at the two remaining noise levels.

Keywords: Machine Learning · Classifiers · Noise Types · Decision Trees · Random Forest · Support Vector Machines · Noise Filtering

1 Introduction

The strength of applications for artificial intelligence and machine learning has become more apparent as these fields have developed quickly in recent years. One of the many methods for teaching machines to learn is supervised learning, in which the machine is taught how to model a process or make predictions by providing it with example inputs and the intended outputs. A classifying algorithm is used by a machine learning model to group input into one or more classes. However, the data that a machine learning model is given is one of its most crucial components, and as a result, the model's output is directly influenced by the quality and quantity of the data. Noise in a machine learning model refers to distorted data, which is typically something one wants to reduce. A machine-learning model may suffer from noise in the form of decreased classification accuracy. Random Forest, Support Vector Machine, and Artificial Neural Network algorithms' resilience to noise in the data they are fed is compared in this study.

V. B. Gupta et al. (Eds.): IBCD 2024, CCIS 2413, pp. 182–192, 2025.
https://doi.org/10.1007/978-3-031-87511-3_13

2 Research Question

What is the more robust and effective classifier among the random forest, support vector machine, and ANN when handling noise? was intended to be the solution to that query.

3 Related Work

3.1 Machine Learning and Classification

ML is the field dedicated to the examination of algorithms that, following training on specific datasets, generate intelligent predictions. The training phase commonly incorporates numerous data points, ranging from thousands to millions, constituting the training set [11]. Generally, the predictive accuracy of an ML model tends to improve with a larger dataset.

3.2 Random Forest

Ensemble learning methods developed for regression and classification are commonly known as RFs shown in Fig. 1. First introduced by [5], these techniques have proven to be effective in both regression and classification applications [1]. It aggregates predictions from multiple randomized decision trees by averaging their outcomes. Their parallel nature allows for faster execution compared to many other contemporary classifiers, and increasing the number of decision trees generally leads to improved performance [12].

However, it's important to note that adding more trees to a random forest may encounter diminishing returns, reaching a threshold beyond which significant performance gains become challenging without substantial computational resources [8].

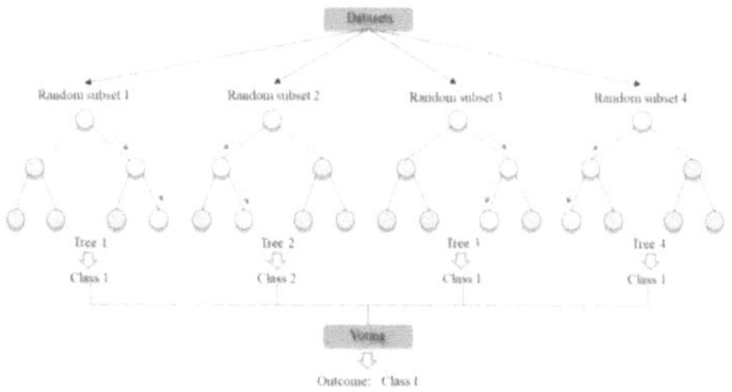

Fig. 1. A random forest's workflow. Picture via Yang et al. [13]

3.3 Artificial Neural Networks

Biological neural networks, as observed in the human brain, serve as the inspiration for ANN. These ANNs shown in Fig. 2 are parallel computing systems composed of layers of artificial neurons, resembling the structure of neurons in the human brain [13].

Neurons within the network receive input signals, process them, and produce output signals.

An ANN comprises of individual neurons equipped with components such as an activation function to control output amplitude, an adder for data summation, and a set of weighted synapses [2]. Even while individual neurons are capable of carrying out simple information processing functions, a neural network's actual effectiveness is seen when a sizable number of interconnected neurons work together.

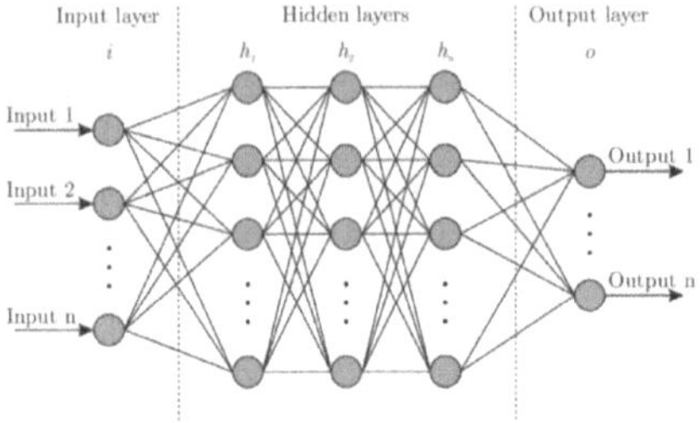

Fig. 2. An example of a neural network. Picture courtesy of V´ıctor D. Fachinotti, Juan M. Gimenez, and Facundo Bre [7].

In supervised learning, the primary goal is to forecast one or more target variables from the input data. The ANN comprises layers, including the input layer, output layer, and hidden layers positioned in between. Neurons within the ANN establish connections between these layers. Neurons in the input layer receive information, while neurons in the output layer decide how the network will react to that information. Within the ANN, hidden layer neurons are in charge of finding patterns to solve the given problem [6]. The training of ANNs commonly involves the application of back-propagation techniques. These techniques are learning algorithms rooted in the Gradient Descent approach, which iteratively descends the loss curve to minimize the loss in the ANN [7].

3.4 Support Vector Machine

It is valuable for tasks like regression, classification, and outlier identification. Although the theoretical foundation of SVMs was introduced by Vapnik, Chervonenkis, and their colleagues in 1964/1965, these methods were not widely recognized for practical applications until approximately 1992 [4]. SVMs, shown in Fig. 3 fall within the category of kernel methods, a class of algorithms relying on dot products for data analysis. The substitution of kernel functions for dot products provides advantages, such as making it possible to create nonlinear decision boundaries with methods that were first intended for linear classifiers [3].

Forecasting a scalar output y in a non-linear relationship $y = f(x)$, where x represents a high-resolution input vector corresponding to data instances, is the goal of an SVM during the training phase. A training Dataset $D = \{(x_i, y_i) \in X \times Y\}$, with i ranging from 1 to l and l representing the total number of training data pairings, represents the information that is currently available. The area between the two hyperplanes, H1

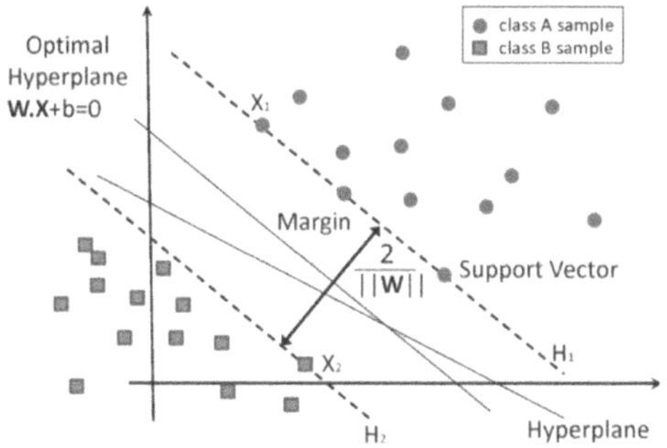

Fig. 3. Data categorization using a support vector machine between two classes. Picture provided by E. Garcua-Gonzalo and colleagues [4].

and H2, is known as the margin, and the SVM should maximize it for an appropriate classification.

3.5 Understanding Noise

Noise in the context of ML refers to the distortion of data. It is common for real-world datasets, derived from actual measurements, to contain some degree of noise. Various factors contribute to noise, including errors in measurement equipment calibration, malfunctions, and human error [9]. The presence of data distortions has the potential to reduce the accuracy of classifications made by ML models.

X. Zhu and X. Wu [15] classified noise into two primary categories in a University of Vermont study: attribute noise and class noise. Errors added to attribute values, including missing or "don't know" attributes, are referred to as attribute noise. Class noise, on the other hand, includes contrasting instances, which are instances that repeatedly show up but have various categorizations in which cases are labeled with wrong output classes [14].

3.6 Sturdiness Against Noise

Supervised ML classifiers are commonly evaluated based on their accuracy, but an equally important and sometimes neglected aspect is their resilience in the presence of noise. Given that real-world data often contains noise, having a classifier that exhibits noise resistance is advantageous. One way to assess a classifier's robustness to noise is by training it on both a clean and a noisy version of the same dataset. Metrics like the Equalized Loss of Accuracy can then be utilized to quantify the results [10].

3.7 Related Studies

The exploration of noise's impact on various machine learning models has been a subject of extensive research. Many studies have focused on introducing noise into the training of artificial neural networks, aiming to mitigate overfitting and enhance overall robustness and generalization capacity [17–19]. Although less common, there have been investigations comparing the noise robustness of different supervised learning classifiers.

The performance and resilience of ANN and SVMs (linear, polynomial, quadratic, and radial) for the diagnosis of centrifugal pump issues were examined in a study by M. Saberi and colleagues [20]. Based on evaluating the classifiers on datasets with and without extra noise, they came to the conclusion that SVM with a linear kernel performed better in both cases than ANN and other kernels [20]. It is significant to highlight the limitations of this study, especially given the tiny dataset size of only 150 instances.

The efficiency of classification trees (CT), Artificial Neural Network, random forests (RF), and support vector machines (SVMs) (linear, polynomial, and radial) in mapping and tracking land cover in a Mediterranean region was examined in a different study conducted in 2012 by researchers [21]. The comparison took into account factors including overall performance, sensitivity to dataset size reductions, and noise. RBF SVM showed the best resistance to noise and dataset size reduction, whereas Random Forest emerged as the most accurate classifier in their tests. Not until the standards for distortion as well as data mitigation were raised to 20 more were notable variations identified [21].

4 Research Methodology

4.1 Methodology

During the experimental stage, four different datasets were used to apply three different classifiers. 10 copies of every dataset were first made, and these copies were subjected to different degrees of noise ranging from 0.1 to 1.0. The chance of random entry distortion was represented by the noise level. For continuous data, Gaussian noise was used, and uniform random swaps were used for categorical attributes.

The evaluation process utilized 5-fold cross-validation, with a focus on key metrics such as accuracy and F-score.

4.2 Datasets

Table 1 shows a summary of the data set.

1. Spambase Data Set: Origin: Acquired from the UCI ML Repository.
2. Pima Indians Diabetes Database: Source: Kaggle, An online community specializing in data science and ML.
3. Breast Cancer Wisconsin Data Set: Source: UCI ML Repository.
4. Banknote Authentication Data Set: Source: UCI ML Repository.

4.3 Introducing Noise

Careful planning is needed when constructing noisy datasets, including deciding what kind of noise to take into account as well as where and how to inject it. As was previously mentioned, the study particularly dealt with attribute noise, with an emphasis on noise present in the input variables. Additionally, it was intentional to only include noise in the

Table 1. Summary of Data Sets

Dataset Name	Instances	Attributes	Imbalance Ratio
Pima Indians Diabetes	768	9	0.65:0.35
Breast Cancer Wisconsin	699	10	0.66:0.34
Banknote Authentication	1372	5	0.56:0.44
Spambase	4601	57	0.61:0.39

model's training set of data because comparing noisy data to noisy data would undermine the goals of the study.

Concerning the type of noise, a differentiation was made between categorical attributes and continuous attributes. Gaussian noise was specifically applied to continuous attributes.

4.4 Evaluation

The clean dataset and its deformed copies were divided into five folds as part of the process. A sufficient number of examples—never more than four—were eliminated from the datasets in cases where the number of occurrences could not be divided by five. The model's training data came from the noisy partitions, whereas the clean divisions were labeled as testing instances. The examination included a 5-fold cross-validation assessment of accuracy and F1-score. In addition, the 5-fold cross-validation computation durations were noted.

5 Experimental Results

5.1 Accuracy

Across all classifiers, there was a general pattern of decreasing classifier accuracy as noise levels rose. When noise levels increased, the Support Vector Machine using a Radial Basis Function kernel (RBF-SVC in the table) lost accuracy and eventually rated as the least accurate classifier at 100% noise. It had previously ranked as the second most accurate classifier on clean data. The SVM with linear Kernel function showed the least amount of accuracy drop out of all the classifiers, with a loss of 25.7% points at the highest degree of noise. Up until 80% noise, the SVM with a polynomial kernel function outperformed the other classifiers, with RBF-SVC emerging as the least accurate classifier. Both Random Forest (RF) and Artificial Neural Network showed comparable performance; however, after about 90% of noise, RF outperformed ANN marginally. While RF had the lowest accuracy at 100% noise, it was the most accurate at all noise levels between 0 and 80% (Table 2).

Table 2. Average Classifier Accuracy's with Rearranged Classifiers.

Noise Level (%)	RF	L-SVC	RBFSVC	P-SVC	ANN
0.0	0.927	0.918	0.925	0.870	0.914
0.1	0.913	0.893	0.908	0.793	0.906
0.2	0.901	0.868	0.890	0.745	0.880
0.3	0.881	0.822	0.871	0.718	0.871
0.4	0.868	0.792	0.852	0.719	0.850
0.5	0.843	0.769	0.768	0.684	0.825
0.6	0.817	0.752	0.745	0.698	0.790
0.7	0.772	0.733	0.723	0.693	0.770
0.8	0.738	0.679	0.667	0.652	0.706
0.9	0.637	0.671	0.611	0.626	0.630
1.0	0.520	0.591	0.484	0.539	0.573

5.2 Precision

Table 3 presents the average precision values of various classifiers across different noise levels. The classifiers included are Random Forest (RF), Support Vector Machine with Linear Kernel (L-SVC), Support Vector Machine with Radial Basis Function Kernel (RBF-SVC), Support Vector Machine with Polynomial Kernel (P-SVC), and Artificial Neural Network (ANN).

As depicted, the precision for all classifiers generally decreases as the noise level increases. Initially, at 0% noise, the RF classifier demonstrates the highest precision at 0.935, closely followed by RBF-SVC at 0.930. However, as noise levels rise, RBF-SVC experiences a significant drop in precision, making it the least accurate classifier at 100% noise with a precision of 0.486. Conversely, L-SVC exhibits the smallest reduction in precision, losing only 32.8 percentage points from 0% to 100% noise. Notably, RF remains the most precise classifier up to 80% noise, after which it's precision declines rapidly, eventually surpassing ANN at 90% noise. These results indicate that while RF is highly effective in low to moderate noise conditions, L-SVC maintains more stable precision across all noise levels.

5.3 F1-Score

The F1-scores generally show a strong correlation with the accuracy results, indicating that Artificial Neural Network and RF are the best classifiers for most of the degree of noise. Notably, although L-SVC outperforms RBF-SVC in terms of accuracy above 50% noise, L-SVC metrics were lower than RBF-SVC at every degree of noise except for 0%, when they are equal. In a similar vein, ANN and RF consistently perform better than the other classifiers at almost all noise levels, but at 90% noise, L-SVC outperforms them in accuracy. Table 4 shows accuracy.

Table 3. Average Classifier Precision with Rearranged Classifiers

Noise Level (%)	RF	L-SVC	RBFSVC	P-SVC	ANN
0.0	0.935	0.923	0.930	0.875	0.920
0.1	0.920	0.898	0.912	0.798	0.910
0.2	0.908	0.875	0.895	0.750	0.885
0.3	0.887	0.829	0.875	0.723	0.876
0.4	0.874	0.799	0.857	0.724	0.855
0.5	0.850	0.775	0.772	0.689	0.830
0.6	0.824	0.758	0.748	0.703	0.795
0.7	0.777	0.738	0.725	0.698	0.775
0.8	0.743	0.684	0.669	0.657	0.710
0.9	0.642	0.676	0.613	0.631	0.635
1.0	0.525	0.595	0.486	0.543	0.578

5.4 ELA Scores

The results of the experiments that measured ELA. It should be noted that these ELA scores are not based on the same accuracy scores previously presented, as the ELA was calculated once per dataset and then averaged. According to the ELA metric, Random Forests (RF) lost the least accuracy across the board until around 90% noise. After 90% noise, the Linear Support Vector Classifier (L-SVC) seemed to retain more of its accuracy. As previously seen from the accuracy diagram, the L-SVC outperformed the other classifiers from around 90% noise and up. The Polynomial Support Vector Classifier (P-SVC) lost a large portion of its accuracy at most noise levels compared to the other classifiers but came closer to their performance as noise levels reached 90 (Table 5).

6 Discussion

6.1 Methodology and Results

The results of the study indicate that random forest is the most robust classifier in the presence of noise, with ANN coming in second, especially when the noise levels are not as high as they can be. For the majority of noise levels, RF consistently performed better than other classifiers. This is in contrast to earlier studies that found SVM to be the best reliable classifier; these variances may be due to variations in methodology and data characteristics.

The performance of a classifier at one noise level does not always translate to other levels. For example, at the degree of noise up to 0.6, the radial basis function (RBF) kernel SVM showed less accuracy loss than linear kernel function SVM; however, at the degree of noise above 0.6, the RBF kernel showed higher accuracy loss. The kind of

Table 4. Average F1-scores with Rearranged Classifiers.

Noise Level (%)	RF	L-SVC	RBFSVC	P-SVC	ANN
0.0	0.664	0.655	0.655	0.589	0.656
0.1	0.639	0.580	0.611	0.471	0.636
0.2	0.618	0.536	0.578	0.420	0.613
0.3	0.574	0.463	0.523	0.385	0.580
0.4	0.543	0.428	0.485	0.363	0.534
0.5	0.530	0.391	0.411	0.330	0.512
0.6	0.467	0.360	0.385	0.321	0.461
0.7	0.418	0.317	0.326	0.239	0.397
0.8	0.351	0.134	0.226	0.192	0.353
0.9	0.217	0.117	0.130	0.131	0.255
1.0	0.218	0.111	0.137	0.119	0.230

Table 5. Average ELA Score

Noise Level (%)	RF	L-SVC	RBFSVC	P-SVC	ANN
0	0.116	0.129	0.119	0.198	0.137
10	0.132	0.160	0.141	0.289	0.147
20	0.146	0.188	0.16	0.334	0.177
30	0.170	0.238	0.184	0375	0.186
40	0.185	0.271	0.206	0.374	0.214
50	0.212	0.296	0.293	0.413	0.238
60	0.243	0.315	0.317	0.398	0.278
70	0.290	0.336	0.343	0.403	0.300
80	0.328	0.392	0.401	0.449	0.367
90	0.435	0.401	0.460	0.478	0.448
100	0.559	0.486	0.596	0.572	0.511

dataset, the degree of expected distortion, and possible noise sources including human error, equipment failure, and calibration problems all play a role in determining the optimal noise level for resilience.

Determining the ideal degree of noise is difficult since users frequently don't know the actual magnitude of noise in a dataset. The datasets utilized probably contain noise by nature, and the noise levels that were manually introduced might not accurately represent the noise levels that were there.

Looking back, a few methodological tweaks could improve the outcome. Since 10% noise may be significant in real-world situations, including noise levels between 1 and 10% would increase practical relevance. Furthermore, using a bigger dataset would produce results that are more reliable and impartial. Although the study acknowledged that 7440 instances across four datasets would not be a significant number for ML training, it still included the data.

6.2 Future Scope

The study exclusively focused on examining the impact of noise on input variables, specifically emphasizing attribute noise. However, it did not explore the equally crucial dimension of class noise in the output. Subsequent investigations could broaden the focus to assess the response of the classifiers employed in this work to the introduction of class noise. Another limitation is the study's confinement to binary classification datasets, intentionally excluding multi-class classification from consideration. Subsequent investigations may broaden their scope to encompass multi-class scenarios, offering a more comprehensive assess- ment of classifier performance across a variety of classification tasks.

7 Conclusion

This study sought to evaluate the robustness and accuracy of random forests, artificial neural networks, and support vector machines in the presence of noise. Interestingly, contrary to previous studies promoting support vector machines as the strongest classifier, which handles the noise is the best fashion among the three techniques, the random forest classifier excelled and displayed superior robustness at eight out of ten noise levels. The outcomes, particularly at noise levels lower than the maximum, closely matched the performance of the artificial neural network classifier. Specifically, the support vector machine classifier with a linear kernel performed better and was more resilient at the two highest noise levels.

References

1. Agatonovic-Kustrin, S., Beresford, R.: Basic concepts of artificial neural network (ANN) modeling and its application in pharmaceutical research. J. Pharm. Biomed. Anal. **22**(5), 717–727 (2000)
2. Ben-Hur, A., Weston, J.: A user's guide to support vector machines. In: Data Mining Techniques for the Life Sciences, pp. 223–239 (2010)
3. Biau, G., Scornet, E.: A random forest guided tour. TEST **25**, 197–227 (2016)
4. Bre, F., Gimenez, J.M., Fachinotti, V.D.: Prediction of wind pressure coefficients on building surfaces using artificial neural networks. Energy Build. **158**, 1429–1441 (2018)
5. Breiman, L.: Random forests. Mach. Learn. **45**, 5–32 (2001)
6. García-Gonzalo, E., Fernández-Muñiz, Z., Jose, P., Nieto, G., Sánchez, A.B., Fernández, M.M.: Hard-rock stability analysis for span design in entry-type excavations with learning classifiers. Materials **9**(7), 531 (2016)

7. Gupta, S.: Concrete mix design using artificial neural network. J. Today's Ideas-Tomorrow's Technol. **1**(1), 29–43 (2013)
8. Maglogiannis, I.G.: Emerging Artificial Intelligence Applications in Computer Engineering: Real Word AI Systems with Applications in eHealth, HCI, Information Retrieval and Pervasive Technologies, vol. 160. IOS Press, Amsterdam (2007)
9. Paul, A., Mukherjee, D.P., Das, P., Gangopadhyay, A., Chintha, A.R., Kundu, S.: Improved random forest for classification. IEEE Trans. Image Process. **27**(8), 4012–4024 (2018)
10. Sáez, J.A., Luengo, J., Herrera, F.: Evaluating the classifier behavior with noisy data considering performance and robustness: the equalized loss of accuracy measure. Neurocomputing **176**, 26–35 (2016)
11. Schetakis, N., Aghamalyan, D., Boguslavsky, M., Griffin, P.: Binary classifiers for noisy datasets: a comparative study of existing quantum machine learning frameworks and some new approaches. arXiv preprint arXiv:2111.03372 (2021)
12. Song, H., Kim, M., Park, D., Shin, Y., Lee, J.-G.: Learning from noisy labels with deep neural networks: a survey. IEEE Trans. Neural Netw. Learn. Syst. (2022)
13. Wang, L.: Support Vector Machines: Theory and Applications, vol. 177. Springer, Cham (2005)
14. Yang, J., Gong, J., Tang, W., Shen, Y., Liu, C., Gao, J.: Delineation of urban growth boundaries using a patch-based cellular automata model under multiple spatial and socio-economic scenarios. Sustainability **11**(21), 6159 (2019)
15. Zhu, X., Wu, X.: Class noise vs. attribute noise: a quantitative study. Artif. Intell. Rev. **22**, 177–210 (2004)

Optimization Accuracy of Intrusion Detection System Based on Multilayered Neural Network

Chetan Gupta(✉), Amit Kumar, and Neelesh Kumar Jain

Department of CSE, JUET, Raghogarh-Vijaypur, Guna, India
chetangupta.gupta1@gmail.com, {amit.kumar, neelesh.jain}@juet.ac.in

Abstract. As technological capabilities continue to expand at an exponential rate, our reliance on the internet for executing daily activities intensifies, rendering us increasingly susceptible to cyber threats. This augmented dependence on online platforms amplifies our exposure to numerous security vulnerabilities. Consequently, the demand for robust antivirus software or analogous systems capable of identifying and mitigating emerging security risks is escalating. An efficacious solution to this predicament is a system, either hardware or software-based, that can be deployed within a network infrastructure to detect and prevent various forms of intrusions, commonly referred to as an Intrusion Detection System (IDS). This system is instrumental in monitoring network traffic and discerning any anomalies. This study examines an IDS utilizing machine learning and neural networks (ML-NN), which exhibits superior classification accuracy across diverse attack types within the CIC-IDS dataset, surpassing current methodologies. The experimental analysis encompasses both binary and multiclass data classifications, employing optimal evaluation metrics—precision, accuracy, and recall—for the ML-NN approach, considering the specific nature of attack types and suggesting avenues for further investigation. The suggested framework achieves a precision of 99.87%, a recall of 99.89%, and an accuracy of 99.0%, which is 1.07% higher than previous approaches.

Keywords: Neural Network · Machine Learning · Intrusion Detection System · Dos · Probe · R2L · U2R

1 Introduction

Our networks and systems are increasingly susceptible to cyber threats due to the rapid proliferation of internet usage and associated activities. Users often overlook the complexities and inherent risks of internet use. As technological advancements continue, the methods for securing systems and networks must also evolve to enhance their robustness, given the dynamic nature of both domains [1]. While firewalls and antivirus software are pivotal components of network security, they are not infallible and can be subverted by malicious actors. This underscores the indispensable role of intrusion detection systems (IDS) in safeguarding network infrastructures. The inception of IDS can be traced back to

V. B. Gupta et al. (Eds.): IBCD 2024, CCIS 2413, pp. 193–207, 2025.
https://doi.org/10.1007/978-3-031-87511-3_14

1980, and since then, numerous iterations with improved accuracy have been developed [2, 3]. IDS are engineered to monitor network traffic for irregularities. The effectiveness of IDS is augmented through extensive training. It is imperative to distinguish between legitimate user activities and malicious behaviors for accurate intrusion detection. Developing proficient IDS necessitates the formulation and training of a comprehensive rule set against network traffic [4, 5]. An effective IDS is characterized by a high detection rate coupled with a low incidence of false positives. However, the swiftly evolving network environment presents significant challenges for current IDS in identifying novel threats. IDS are generally deployed in proximity to switch nodes, which are secure network junctures within larger networks. Intrusion detection systems are predominantly classified based on Detection Methods and Data Source methodologies [6, 7]. Detection methods are employed to categorize attacks into distinct classes. Misuse detection, also referred to as "signature-based detection," aims to identify and recognize attack patterns. The detection process involves synchronizing historical attack signatures with new data to establish a robust database [8, 9]. A primary challenge in developing detection frameworks is the identification of effective signatures. Benefits include a lower rate of false alarms and accurate identification of intrusion kinds and possible reasons when the origin of a threat is located. However, it also presents drawbacks, including a high rate of missed detections, challenges in identifying stealthy attacks, and the necessity of maintaining a substantial database of signatures [10–12].

Contribution of Research:
This study was driven by the need to improve intrusion detection systems' (IDS) efficacy using novel machine learning and neural network (ML-NN) methodologies. Because cyberattacks are becoming more complicated and varied, traditional methods frequently fail to achieve high categorization precision for a variety of attack types. By creating an IDS that excels in classification accuracy on the CIC-IDS dataset, this research seeks to solve these constraints. The ML-NN approach performed remarkably well, outperforming earlier approaches in terms of accuracy, recall, and precision measures.

Achieving 99.87% precision, 99.89% recall, and 99.0% accuracy, which is 1.07% higher than previous methods, highlights the potential of ML-NN in improving IDS effectiveness. These results encourage further research and development of machine learning models in cyber security, aiming to create more robust and reliable intrusion detection systems capable of effectively countering evolving cyber threats.

Motivation of Research:

1. Enhanced Detection Accuracy: Across a range of attack types, the IDS's use of machine learning and neural networks (ML-NN) considerably increases categorization accuracy. The high accuracy (99.87%) and recall (99.89%) figures show that this results in more dependable identification of both existing and developing cyber threats.
2. Comprehensive Evaluation: To provide an in-depth examination of the IDS's achievement, the research uses two types of binary and multiclass data categories. This provides a more comprehensive security solution by guaranteeing that the system is strong and efficient in detecting a variety of intrusion types.

3. Better Performance Metrics: With an accuracy of 99.0%, the suggested ML-NN framework outperforms current techniques, outperforming them by 1.07%. This demonstrates how well the architecture works in practical situations, improving network security as a whole.

2 CIC-IDS Dataset

The Canadian Institute for Cyber security created the CIC-IDS 2018 dataset, which is a thorough set of network traffic data used for benchmarking and assessing in IDS. It is very flexible for IDS establishment and evaluation since it mimics real-world network settings and supports several attack methods, including brute force, DDoS, penetration, and botnet operations. The dataset provides a comprehensive, historical maintain log of server activity over a period of five business days, with hand labeling to differentiate among legitimate and illicit activity. Its extensive function set, which includes flow-based measurements, cumulative research, and packet-level information, makes it easier to analyses assault trends and behaviors in-depth. CIC-IDS-2018 is open for study and is organized in CSV format for ease of use using machine learning frameworks. This facilitates the repeatability and comparative assessment of IDS methodologies, which in turn spurs experimentation and advances in the field of digital safety. Table 1 shows the number of instance of CIC-IDS dataset.

Table 1. CIC-IDS Dataset

Attack Type	Attack Sub-Type	Number of Instances
Denial of Service (DoS)	DoS Hulk	231,073
	DoS GoldenEye	10,293
	DoS Slowloris	5,796
	DoS Slowhttptest	5,499
Distributed Denial of Service (DDoS)	DDoS	128,027
Brute Force Attacks	SSH-Patator	5,745
	FTP-Patator	7,934
Web Attacks	Web Attack - Brute Force	1,507
	Web Attack - XSS	652
	Web Attack - SQL Injection	21
Infiltration	Infiltration	36
Botnet	Bot	1,966
Heartbleed	Heartbleed	11

The CIC-IDS-2018 dataset must be preprocessed in order for evaluation and applications requiring machine learning to be possible. The collection of data is first imported into pandas Data Frames, where missing rows have to be dropped or properly filled to account for missing values. Label encoding is used to translate data that is categorical, such as assault labels, into numbers. For coherence, numbers are standardized or normalized. In order to improve the performance of the model, characteristics that are

Table 2. Hyper Parameters Detail

Model	ANN
Activation	Relu
Epochs	20
Batch size	32
Metrics	Accuracy, Loss,
Units	64
Optimizer	Adam

Table 3. Comparison of Proposed and Previous Results

Method	Accuracy	Precision	Recall
Existing KNN	93.6%	98%	91%
Existing Fuzzy	91%	-	-
Existing FNN	97.4%	92.5%	86.9%
Existing GRU	97.1%	95.8%	98.7%
Existing Multilayered	98.1%	99.8%	99.8%
Proposed Method	99.0%	99.87%	99.89%

highly associated and unnecessary are removed using the choice of features. After that, the dataset is divided into sets for training and testing, with the group's distributions being balanced using SMOTE methods. Ultimately, the previously processed information is stored for later use, guaranteeing that it is clear, balanced, and appropriate for the construction of reliable security analytics and intrusion detection systems.

3 Literature Review

S. K. B. Sangeetha et al. [1] elucidate that within imbalanced network traffic, malicious cyber-attacks frequently masquerade amidst substantial volumes of normal data. As a result, there are notable degrees of obscurity and concealment in the internet, which makes it more difficult for Network Intrusion Detection Systems (IDS) to continue to identify intrusions accurately and promptly. This work explores the use using deep learning along with artificial intelligence approaches for identifying breaches in unbalanced network activity. To solve the problem of class imbalance, it suggests a novel approach called the Difficult Set Sampling Technique (DSSTE). At first, the imbalanced training set is divided between hard and simple subgroups using the Edited Nearest Neighbour (ENN) method. Then, to lessen the influence of the majority sample in the challenging set are condensed using the K-Means method. The minority sample count is then increased by modifying the constant properties of the minority specimens that are part of the challenging set to produce new instances.

S. Sengan et al. [2] emphasize that proficient and effective malware detection is paramount in the quest to construct secure digital systems. Similar to other domains, malware detection research has witnessed a substantial increase in the utilization of machine learning algorithms. These techniques are applied to various challenging malware datasets. The study reveals that random restarts perform unexpectedly well in comparison to boosting. Only in the most challenging "cold start" scenarios, where training data is significantly limited, does boosting offer sufficient enhancement to justify its higher computational expense during the evaluation phase.

K. Aravindhan et al. [3] concentrate on identifying internal intruders within Host-based Intrusion Detection Systems (HIDS). For business objectives, colleagues may exchange frequently employed account information, which might be abused by hackers to obtain unauthorized entrance to computer system data. The system monitors user activity and extracts System Calls (SC), considering the habitual SC patterns based on user behavior to establish a user profile. Forensic techniques and data mining methods are applied at the SC level of HIDS to detect internal threats. Alongside user login credentials, forensic techniques analyze computer usage patterns against the collected user profile to verify user identity.

In an additional trial [4], the technique attained a 94% precision rate at an outcome level of 0.9. An HIDS prototype for cellphones was created by scientists within the Nokia Research Centre. Observing actions that take place inside a system or internet continuously, looking for indicators of possible problems, and frequently stopping unauthorized usage are all part of intrusion detection. Although a state transition diagram could be created for a series of things, it is insufficient for simulating intricate attack types that can escape the network's detection.

In their research [5], the authors conduct a comparative analysis of various preceding approaches that employ machine learning techniques, classification strategies, clustering methods, matching datasets and other investigative and detection mechanisms. The available datasets and the limitations of previous IDS are also discussed. This study contributes uniquely by advocating for an enhanced autonomous intelligent hybrid IDS model based on advanced machine learning techniques, aimed at reducing false alarm rates while improving accuracy.

The researchers of the study [6] analyses the computer's client's behavioral traits using an 83-dimensional vector to analyze Advanced Persistent Threat (APT) assaults. Every feature in the resulting vector represents a distinct behavior of the user. The system is made to figure out how frequently each behavior occurs for every operation. The gathered data is utilized to build a classification algorithm using the C4.5 decision tree, and every incoming occurrence is compared with this tree to figure out if it is harmful or not. 5.8% of incorrect results and 2.0% of false negatives are shown by the predictive algorithm.

After reviewing the previous studies, the major limitations of IDS are poor detection accuracy of the attack in the real-time dataset, not being able to preprocess the dataset well, and high false alarms. Our research will overcome all these issues.

4 Proposed Methodology

In the proposed hybrid approach, a standard CIC-IDS dataset is used for the training and testing of the model. First, we apply the data preprocessing, in which we normalize and transform the data by removing redundant data. Using the feature selection method, we prepare the training and testing datasets. The Extreme Learning Machine (ELM) is used as a feed-forward neural network to train the model. ELM does not require the assignment of arbitrary numbers for input measurements, predispositions, or hidden element training factors. When it comes to cost and efficacy, ELM performs better than standard techniques. After training the model, we took the testing sample and found that the proposed ML-NN gives better results as compared to the previous technique. Moreover, the commercial capacity demonstrates non-linear differentiability. The featured data is utilized as input for the Back Propagation Neural Network model. The input vectors, along with their associated target vectors, are employed to train the network until it can accurately distinguish, correlate input vectors with specific output vectors, or effectively categories input vectors. This methodology elucidates the identification of features within the noisy or outdated dataset of the CIC IDS (Fig. 1).

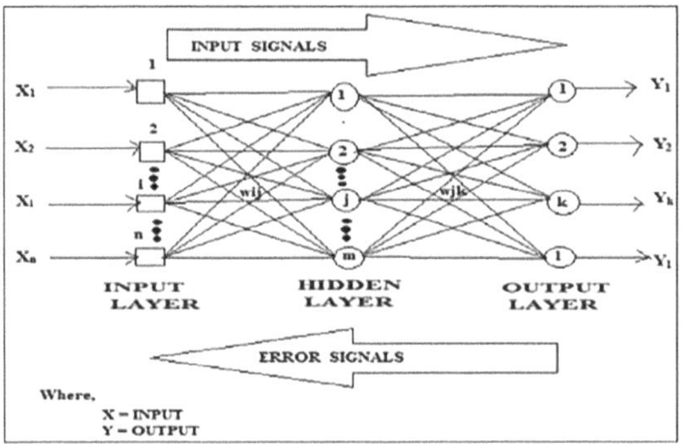

Fig. 1. Three Layers NN

In Fig. 2, the Extreme Learning Machine (ELM) is illustrated as a feed-forward neural network employed for feature enhancement. This network consists of a single hidden layer, which is randomly selected and optimizes the features to a minimal set. By utilizing ELM, the complexity of training is reduced through the use of random values for weights and bias values, which remain fixed. The defining characteristic of ELM is feature minimization, which enhances classification accuracy and improves learning speed. In this model, fixed random weights are assigned to the hidden layer. This method involves a threshold learning machine for feature optimization, specifically a single-layer feed-forward neural network (SLFFNN), where the hidden layer, or feature mapping, in ELM does not require tuning [13, 14].

In this type of calculation, just one or many layers of concealed nodes are used by the Single Layer Feed-Forward Neural Network (SLFFN), which uses a variety of techniques including organisation, statistical regression, aggregation, minimal estimation, contraction, and training features. Most importantly, there is no need to fine-tune

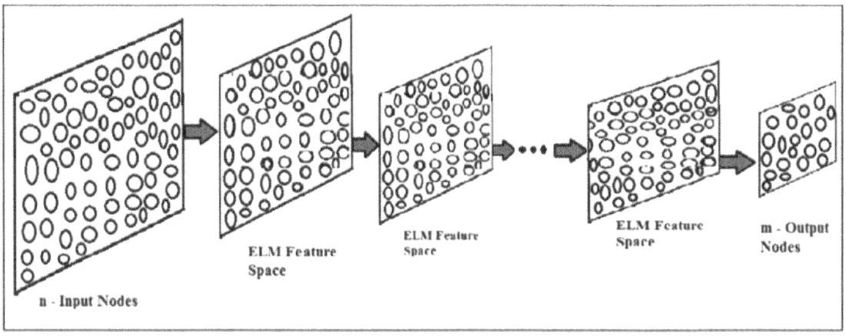

Fig. 2. Feature optimization in the NN working model

the characteristics associated with these concealed nodes, particularly the weights that link inputs to hidden nodes. Such invisible nodes may be inherited by their successors in an unaltered state, or they can be allocated indiscriminately and stay immutable (also known as random projections with quadratic modifications). Usually, the concealed

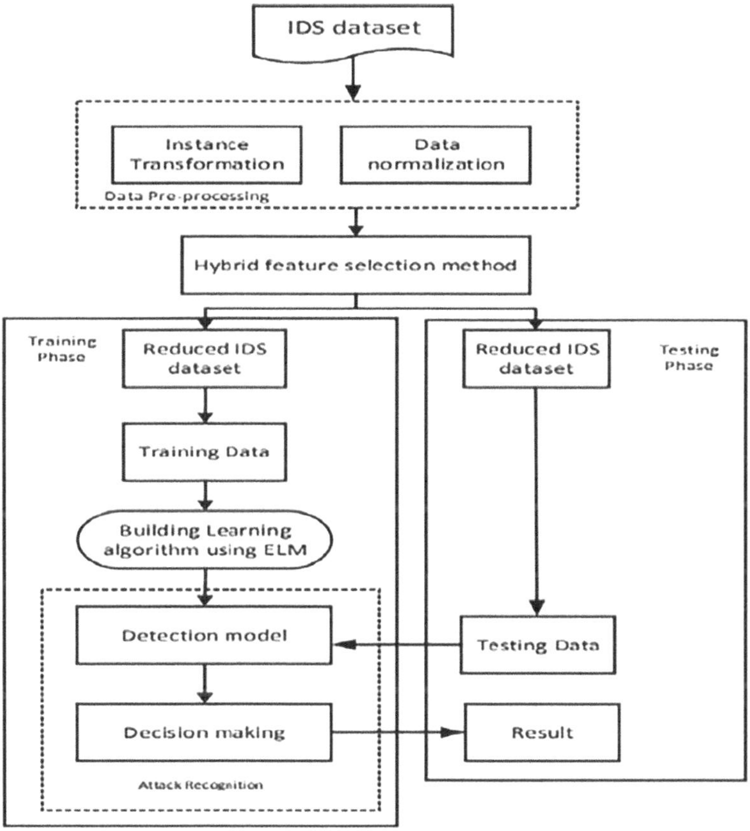

Fig. 3. Flow Chart of propose work

nodes' output weights are obtained in just one step, simplifying how to train into a linear framework. The Fig. 3 shows the overall methodology of the propose work.

4.1 Algorithm

Step 1: Import Libraries

```
import numpy as np
from sklearn.preprocessing import MinMaxScaler
import matplotlib.pyplot as plt
```

Step 2: Make a set of training and test data.
Step 3: Expand the Data

```
scaler = MinMaxScaler()
input_train_scaled =
scaler.fit_transform(input_train)
output_train_scaled =
scaler.fit_transform(output_train)
input_test_scaled =
scaler.fit_transform(input_test)
output_test_scaled =
scaler.fit_transform(output_test)
```

Step 4: Define Neural Network Class
Step 4.1: Define the Initialize method
Step 4.2: Define the Forward Propagation Method
Step 4.3: Define a Backward Propagation Method
Step 4.4: Built a Training Function

```
def train(self, X, y, epochs):
        for epoch in range(epochs):
            o = self.forward(X)
            self.backward(X, y, o)

self.error_list.append(np.abs(self.o_error).mean())
```

Step 4.5: Execute a Program for Training and Assessing the Neural Network Model

```
NN = NeuralNetwork()
NN.train(input_train_scaled, output_train_scaled,
200)
NN.predict(input_pred)
NN.view_error_development()
NN.test_evaluation(input_test_scaled,
output_test_scaled)
```

Step 5: Establish a Prediction Function

```
def predict(self, x_predicted):
        return self.forward(x_predicted).item()
```

Step 4.6: Display the Error Development
Step 4.7: Compute the Degree of Precision and Its Elements

5 Simulation Result

5.1 Simulation Parameter

An IDS performance is shown by its accuracy, which is measured as the ratio of correctly identified anomaly and normal entries to the overall amount of events. The precision indicates the accuracy of its predictions for its targeted class and Recall reveals if model is able to locate every item in its chosen class.

$$Accurancy = \frac{TN + TP}{TN + TP + FN + FP} \tag{1}$$

$$\Pr ecision = \frac{TP}{TP + FP} \tag{2}$$

$$\text{Recall} = \frac{TP}{TP + FN} \tag{3}$$

The Eq. 1, Eq. 2, and Eq. 3 are the simulation parameter to test the model. The efficiency of the deep learning methodologies employed in this investigation [15] is evaluated using a range of standard metrics. Initially, let's elucidate some fundamental terminology: True Positives (TP) was the results of accurately classifying anomaly data as anomalies. The quantity of regular items that are correctly classified as ordinary is captured by True Negatives (TN). Mistakenly flagging regular information as anomalies results in False Positives (FP) [5]. Lastly, False Negatives (FN) pertains to anomaly records that are mistakenly categorized as normal occurrences (Figs. 4 and 5).

5.2 Simulation Result

The proposed methodology involves the following steps:

1. Importing essential libraries.
2. Retrieving and accessing the CIS IDS dataset.
3. Displaying the dataset within a Pandas data frame
1. Preprocessing
   - replace +ve and −ve infinity with NaN
   - drop missing values
   - Implementing binary classification
   - Balancing the data (Under sampling)
2. Perform Exploratory Data Analysis
   - Class distribution
   - Class distribution with equal distribution
3. Data splitting
   Data is divided 80:20, with 80% going towards training and 20% towards testing.
4. Modelling
1. Kernel SVM Classifier
   - Best Accuracy: 99.80%
   - Best Parameters: {'gamma': 1, 'C': 1}
   - Training set Accuracy: 0.999625
   - Testing set Accuracy: 0.9984
2. KNN Classifier
   - Best Accuracy: 99.81%
   - Best Parameters: {'metric': 'manhattan', 'n_neighbors': 6, 'weights': 'distance'}
   - Training set Accuracy: 1.0
   - Testing set Accuracy: 0.9983
3. Decision Tree Classifier
   - Best Accuracy: 99.95%
   - Best Parameters: {'min_samples_split': 3, 'min_samples_leaf': 2, 'max_depth': 10, 'criterion': 'gini'}
   - Training set Accuracy: 0.9999
   - Testing set Accuracy: 0.9992
4. Random Forest Classifier
   - Best Accuracy: 99.95%
   - Best Parameters: {'n_estimators': 50, 'min_samples_split': 10, 'min_samples_leaf': 1, 'max_features': None, 'max_depth': 10}
   - Training set Accuracy: 0.9999
   - Testing set Accuracy: 0.9995

	Unnamed: 0	Dst Port	Protocol	Flow Duration	Tot Fwd Pkts	Tot Bwd Pkts	TotLen Fwd Pkts	TotLen Bwd Pkts	Fwd Pkt Len Max	Fwd Pkt Len Min	...	Fwd Seg Size Min	Active Mean	Active Std	Active Max	Active Min	Idle Mean	Idle S
0	146275	3389	6	6206015	9	11	1213	1948	661	0	...	20	0.000000	0.000000	0	0	0.000000e+00	0.000000e+
1	512109	443	6	60991608	14	14	1211	3396	875	0	...	20	116504.666667	117401.762867	356150	68519	1.000239e+07	1.665183e+
2	807703	53	17	27292	1	1	45	163	45	45	...	8	0.000000	0.000000	0	0	0.000000e+00	0.000000e+
3	491912	443	6	70343424	17	20	1118	5653	258	0		20	527683.500000	386311.526445	800847	254520	3.457024e+07	3.406089e+
4	858679	53	17	137267	2	2	94	214	47	47	...	8	0.000000	0.000000	0	0	0.000000e+00	0.000000e+
...																		
1252841	940974	64678	6	1397	5	2	935	267	935	0		20	0.000000	0.000000	0	0	0.000000e+00	0.000000e+
1252842	45433	51274	6	1	3	0	77	0	46	0		20	0.000000	0.000000	0	0	0.000000e+00	0.000000e+
1252843	912254	80	6	233	2	0	0	0	0	0	...	20	0.000000	0.000000	0	0	0.000000e+00	0.000000e+
1252844	990683	53	17	23818	1	1	34	204	34	34	...	8	0.000000	0.000000	0	0	0.000000e+00	0.000000e+
1252845	576130	80	6	70	2	0	0	0	0	0	...	20	0.000000	0.000000	0	0	0.000000e+00	0.000000e+

1252846 rows × 79 columns

Fig. 4. Data frame of CIS IDS dataset

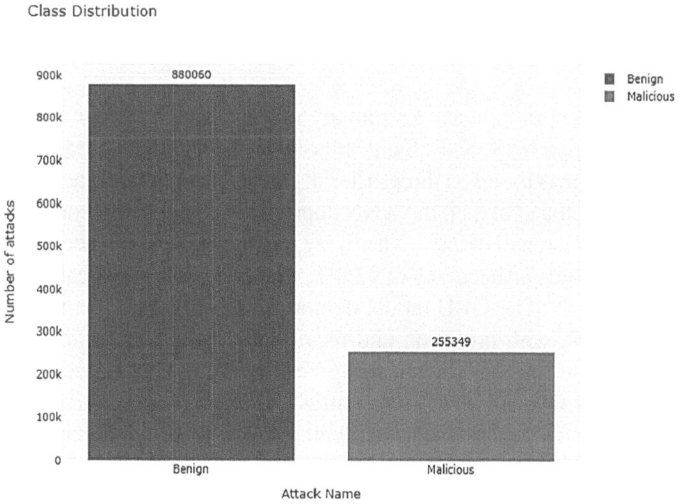

Fig. 5. Number of Attacks

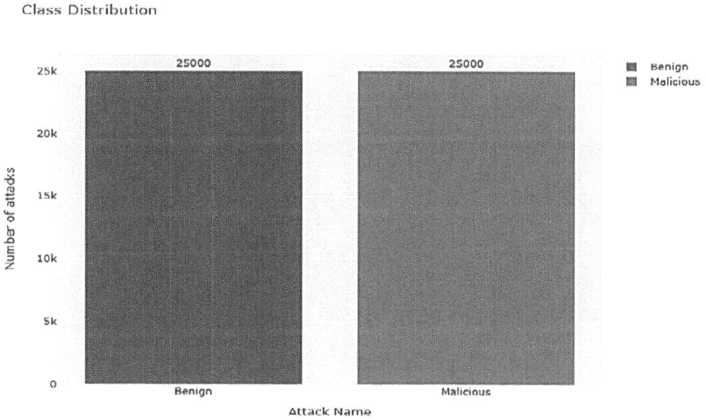

Fig. 6. Class Distribution of Attack

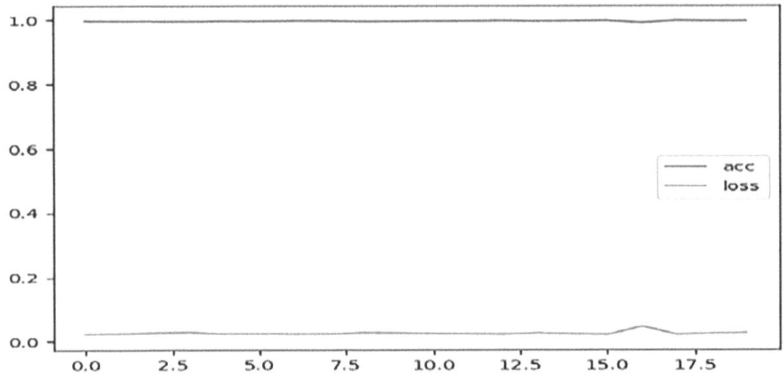

Fig. 7. Accuracy and Loss of CIS IDS Dataset

Table 3 presents a comprehensive summary of the efficiency parameters for several approaches, as discussed by S. K. B. Sangeetha et al. [1], in comparison to the proposed method. The evaluation is based on three criteria: precision, recall, and accuracy. According to S. K. B. Sangeetha et al. [1], the KNN approach achieves an accuracy of 93.6%, a precision of 98%, and a recall of 91%. The fuzzy technique yields an accuracy of 91.0%. The FNN method records an accuracy of 97.4%, with precision and recall rates of 92.5% and 86.9%, respectively. The GRU model demonstrates strong performance, achieving an accuracy of 97.1%, with precision and recall values of 95.8% and 98.7%, respectively. The multilayered model shows strong performance with a precision and recall of 99.8% and an accuracy of 98.1%. In contrast, the proposed method performs even better, achieving an accuracy of 99.0%, a recall of 99.89%, and a precision of 99.87%.

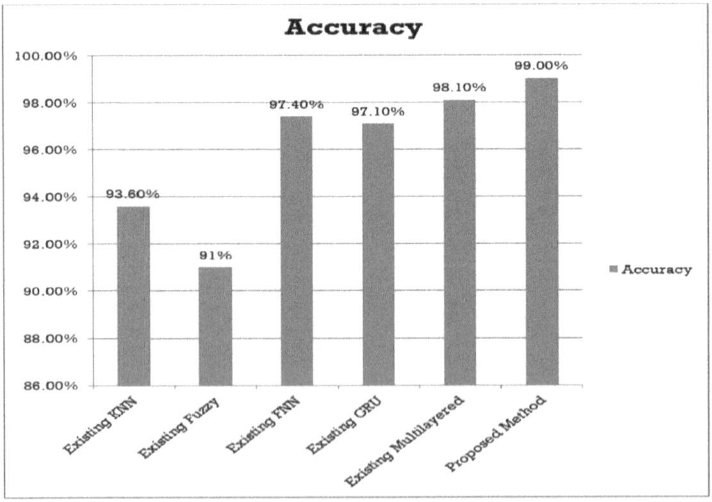

Fig. 8. Comparison of Proposed and Previous Accuracy

Significantly, this marks a noteworthy 1.07% enhancement in accuracy compared to the methodology presented by S. K. B. Sangeetha et al. [1] (Figs. 6 and 7).

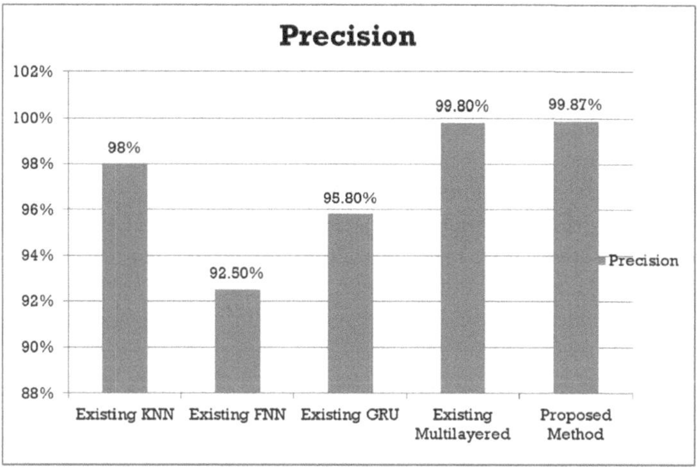

Fig. 9. Comparison of Proposed and Previous Precision

Figures 8, 9, and 10 visually depict the comparative results, providing further insight into the efficacy of the proposed approach. As show in the figure the proposed hybrid technique outperform in all parameters with 99% Accuracy.

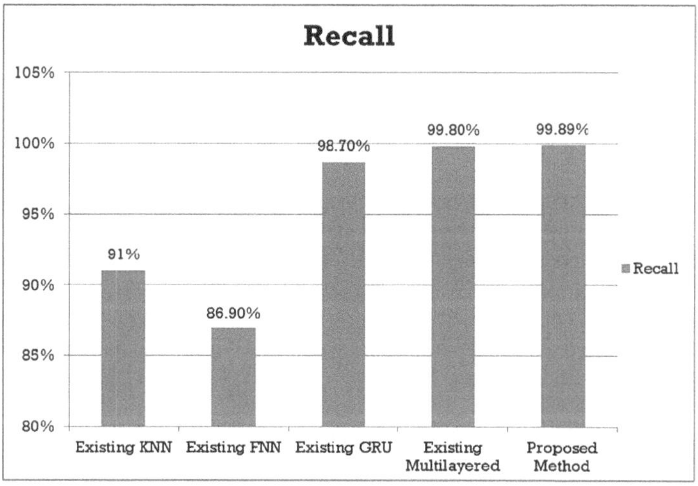

Fig. 10. Comparison of Proposed and Previous Recall

6 Conclusion

Machine learning (ML) techniques are becoming useful tools in the field of detecting malware. Although ML approaches have the potential to increase IDS accuracy, their effectiveness is dependent on several aspects. A minority of these factors encompass the apt selection of functions, the judicious utilization of relevant training and testing datasets, among other pivotal considerations. Optimization of these aspects is paramount for achieving heightened performance levels. However, ML algorithms present certain challenges, such as the potential for misclassification of network data stemming from flawed learning processes. To address these challenges comprehensively, our study introduces and refines an efficient evolutionary strategy grounded in ML-NN principles. This strategy not only ensures precise intrusion detection but also effectively mitigates issues related to over fitting and under fitting, particularly when confronted with vast datasets. This proposed methodology demonstrates remarkable performance metrics, boasting an accuracy rate of 99.0%, recall rate of 99.89%, and precision rate of 99.87%. This represents a significant advancement; showcasing a 1.07% improvement in accuracy compared to preceding research endeavors. In future we use different dataset to test the effectiveness of these proposed approaches. As well as Improvements in AI and machine learning will be used into IDS in the future to improve threat detection and enable interaction with cloud and IoT settings. To further improve IDS capabilities, more automation, threat intelligence, and collaborative security frameworks will be essential.

As a result, the results show that the suggested method is capable of outperforming existing algorithms and competing with them. The suggested selection of characteristics method has significant practical implications. Many fields, including information science, sentiment analysis, etc., can benefit from the combination of these methods. By refining this process, it may be possible to choose the least features that might be the focus of future studies using a new selection strategy. In the future, actual problems like sentiment analysis—which includes cancer detection—may be investigated.

References

1. Sangeetha, S.K.B, Mani, P., Maheshwari, V., Jayagopal, P., Kumar, M.S., Allayear, S.M.: Design and analysis of multilayered neural network-based intrusion detection system in the Internet of Things network. Comput. Intell. Neurosci. **2022**, 9423395 (2022). https://doi.org/10.1155/2022/9423395
2. Sengan, S., Khalaf, O.I., Vidya, S.P., Sharma, D.K., Arokia Jesu Prabhu, L., Hamad, A.A.: Secured and privacy-based ids for healthcare systems on e-medical data using machine learning approach. Int. J. Reliable Qual. E-Healthc. (IJRQEH) **11**(3), 1–11 (2022). https://doi.org/10.4018/IJRQEH.289175
3. Ahsan, R., Shi, W., Ma, X., Croft, W.L.: A comparative analysis of CGAN-based oversampling for anomaly detection. IET Cyber Phys. Syst. Theory Appl. **7**(1), 40–50 (2022). https://doi.org/10.1049/cps2.12019
4. Gupta, C., Kumar, A., Jain, N.K.: An enhanced hybrid intrusion detection based on crow search analysis optimizations and artificial neural network. Wireless Personal Commun. **134**, 43–68 (2024). https://doi.org/10.1007/s11277-024-10880-3

5. Gupta, C., Kumar, A., Jain, N.K.: A detailed analysis on intrusion detection systems, datasets, and challenges. In: Chakraborty, B., Biswas, A., Chakrabarti, A. (eds.) Advances in Data Science and Computing Technologies. ADSC 2022. Lecture Notes in Electrical Engineering, vol. 1056. Springer, Singapore (2023). https://doi.org/10.1007/978-981-99-3656-4_26
6. Manimurugan, S., et al.: Intrusion detection in networks using crow search optimization algorithm with adaptive neuro-fuzzy inference system. Microprocessors and Microsystems. Published by Elsevier (2020). https://doi.org/10.1016/j.micpro.2020.103261
7. Devan, P., Khare, N.: An efficient XGBoost–DNN-based classification model for network intrusion detection system. Neural Comput. Appl. **32**(16), 12499–12514 (2020). https://doi.org/10.1007/s00521-020-04708-x
8. Rajadurai, H., et al.: A stacked ensemble learning model for intrusion detection in wireless network. Springer, London Ltd., part of Springer Nature, Neural Computing and Applications (2020). https://doi.org/10.1007/s00521-020-04986-5
9. Almiani, M., et al.: Deep recurrent neural network for IoT intrusion detection system. Simulation Modelling Practice and Theory. Published by Elsevier (2019). https://doi.org/10.1016/j.simpat.2019.102031
10. Chouhan, N., Khan, A., Khan, H.-U.-R.: Network anomaly detection using channel boosted and residual learning based deep convolutional neural network. Applied Soft Computing (2019). https://doi.org/10.1016/j.asoc.2019.105612/
11. Dongzi, J., Yiqin, L., Jiancheng, Q., Zhe, C., Zhongshu, M.: SwiftIDS: real-time intrusion detection system based on lightGBM and parallel intrusion detection mechanism. Computers & Security (2020). https://doi.org/10.1016/J.COSE.2020.101984
12. Ali, M.H., Al Mohammed, B.A.D., Ismail, A., Zolkipli, M.F.: A new intrusion detection system based on fast learning network and particle Swarm optimization. IEEE Access (2018). https://doi.org/10.1109/ACCESS.2018.2820092
13. Roshan, S., Roshan, S., Miche, Y., Akusok, A., Lendasse, A.: Adaptive and online network intrusion detection system using clustering and extreme learning machines. Journal of the Franklin Institute (2018). https://doi.org/10.1016/J.JFRANKLIN.2017.06.006
14. Vinayakumar, R., Alazab, M., Soman, K.P., Poornachandran, P., Al-Nemrat, A., Venkatraman, S.: Deep learning approach for intelligent intrusion detection system. IEEE Access **7**, 41525–41550 (2019). https://doi.org/10.1109/ACCESS.2019.2895334
15. Atefinia, R., Ahmadi, M.: Network intrusion detection using multi-architectural modular deep neural network. J. Supercomput. **77**, 3571–3593 (2021). https://doi.org/10.1007/s11227-020-03410-y

Leveraging Long-Context Large Language Models for Multi-document Understanding and Summarization in Enterprise Applications

Aditi Godbole[1(✉)], Jabin Geevarghese George[2], and Smita Shandilya[3]

[1] Independent researcher, Seattle, USA
aditi.godbole@ieee.org
[2] Independent researcher, New Jersey, NJ, USA
jabing28@gmail.com
[3] Institute of Advance Computing (Spl. Data Science), SAGE University, Indore, India

Abstract. The rapid increase in unstructured data across various fields has made multi-document comprehension and summarization a critical task. Traditional approaches often fail to capture relevant context, maintain logical consistency, and extract essential information from lengthy documents. This paper explores the use of Long-context Large Language Models (LLMs) for multi-document summarization, demonstrating their exceptional capacity to grasp extensive connections, provide cohesive summaries, and adapt to various industry domains and integration with enterprise applications/systems. The paper discusses the workflow of multi-document summarization for effectively deploying long-context LLMs, supported by case studies in legal applications, enterprise functions such as HR, finance, and sourcing, as well as in the medical and news domains. These case studies show notable enhancements in both efficiency and accuracy. Technical obstacles, such as dataset diversity, model scalability, and ethical considerations like bias mitigation and factual accuracy, are carefully analyzed. Prospective research avenues are suggested to augment the functionalities and applications of long-context LLMs, establishing them as pivotal tools for transforming information processing across diverse sectors and enterprise applications.

Keywords: Large Language Models · Generative AI · Long-context LLM · Multi-document Understanding · Enterprise Applications

1 Introduction

In a multinational corporation, a team of analysts faces the daunting task of summarizing thousands of documents spanning financial reports, market analyses, and internal communications to inform a critical strategic decision. This scenario illustrates the challenge of multi-document summarization in enterprise settings, where the volume and diversity of information can overwhelm traditional analysis methods.

The exponential growth of unstructured text data across various sectors has made document summarization a critical task [1]. Multi-document summarization presents

V. B. Gupta et al. (Eds.): IBCD 2024, CCIS 2413, pp. 208–224, 2025.
https://doi.org/10.1007/978-3-031-87511-3_15

unique challenges due to the need for synthesizing information from diverse sources, which may contain redundant, complementary, or contradictory information across documents [4]. Variations in writing style and level of detail add complexity to the task. Determining the relevance and importance of information from each source is crucial for creating a coherent and comprehensive summary [5].

Traditional document summarization techniques often struggle with redundancy, inconsistency, lack of context understanding, scalability issues for multiple document summarization tasks, inability to capture cross-document relationships, difficulty handling diverse formats, and lack of domain adaptability [6–8]. These limitations highlight the need for more advanced approaches to multi-document summarization.

This paper addresses the following research question: How can long-context Large Language Models (LLMs) be leveraged to improve multi-document understanding and summarization in enterprise applications?

We investigate the use of Long-context LLMs for multi-document summarization, demonstrating their exceptional capacity to grasp extensive connections, provide cohesive summaries, and adapt to various industry domains and integration with enterprise applications/systems [14]. The paper discusses the workflow of multi-document summarization for effectively adopting long-context LLMs, supported by case studies in legal applications, enterprise functions such as HR, finance, and sourcing, as well as in the medical and news domains [46, 49, 53].

By exploring the potential of Long-context LLMs in multi-document summarization, we aim to address the limitations of traditional methods and provide a more efficient and accurate approach to processing large volumes of unstructured data [13, 18]. This research has significant implications for improving information processing across diverse sectors and enterprise applications.

2 Traditional Document Summarization Techniques and Challenges

2.1 Traditional Methods of Document Summarization

Document summarization involves creating a concise version of a document while retaining its key ideas and essential information. The process typically includes several key steps: text analysis to understand document structure and themes, information extraction to identify relevant content, content selection to choose the most important elements, summary generation, and quality evaluation [1].

Traditional approaches to summarization fall into two main categories: extractive and abstractive methods. Extractive summarization selects and arranges existing sentences or phrases from the source document, while abstractive summarization generates new text to capture the core concepts [2].

Extractive techniques often rely on statistical measures of word frequency, sentence position, and other surface-level features to identify important content [1]. More advanced extractive methods use graph-based algorithms to model relationships between sentences and identify central ideas [7]. Machine learning approaches have also been applied to learn patterns for selecting relevant sentences [2].

Abstractive summarization is generally considered more challenging, as it requires language generation capabilities. Early abstractive methods often used templated approaches, filling in extracted information into predefined sentence structures [3]. With the rise of neural networks, sequence-to-sequence models became a popular approach for abstractive summarization [18] (Fig. 1).

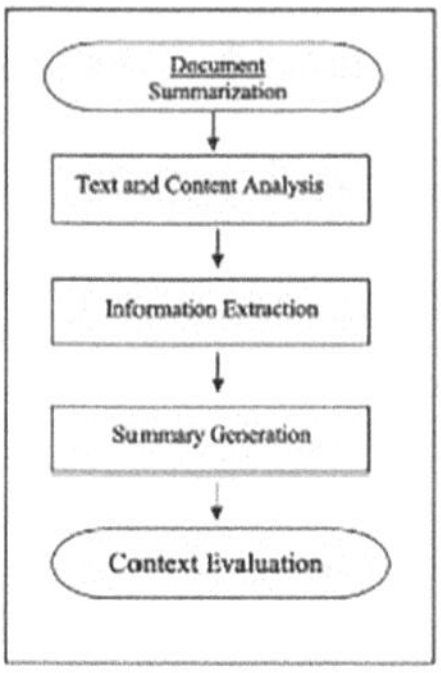

Fig. 1. Traditional Document Summarization Techniques

2.2 Challenges in Multi-document Summarization

While these traditional techniques can be effective for single documents, they face significant challenges when applied to multi-document summarization:

Redundancy: Information is often repeated across multiple source documents, leading to repetitive summaries if not properly managed [4].

Coherence: Extracting sentences from different documents can result in disjointed summaries lacking logical flow [5].

Context preservation: It is challenging to maintain the broader context when combining information from diverse sources [6], leading to summaries that lack focus or miss key points [11].

Scalability: Processing and synthesizing information from many documents increases computational complexity [10]. This challenge persists even with advanced models, as handling very long or numerous documents remains computationally intensive [14].

Cross-document relationships: Capturing connections and contradictions between documents is difficult for methods focused on individual sentences or documents [7].

Domain adaptation: Traditional methods can be limited in their flexibility and adaptability to handle diverse document structures and writing styles [9]. Techniques optimized for one type of document may not generalize well to other domains or writing styles [12]. This challenge extends to ensuring models can handle varied document formats, styles, and topics [59].

Factual consistency: Ensuring that generated summaries remain faithful to the source material is crucial, especially for abstractive methods [66]. This challenge is particularly pronounced in abstractive summarization, where preventing "hallucinations" or factual errors remains an active area of research [65].

Ethical considerations: As summarization techniques become more advanced, mitigating biases present in training data and ensuring fairness in generated summaries becomes increasingly important [63] (Fig. 2).

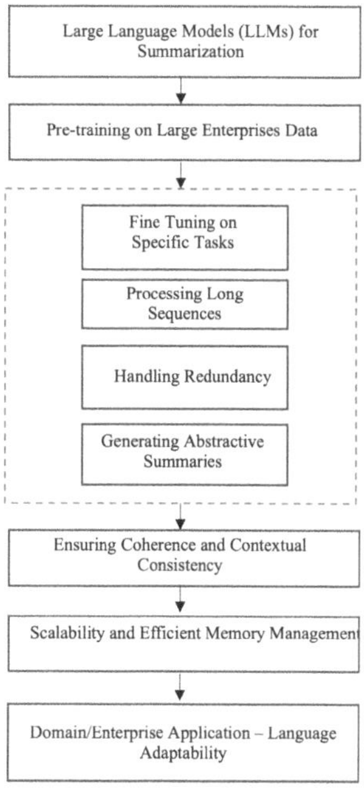

Fig. 2. LLM Workflow for Document Summarization

2.3 Large Language Models for Document Summarization

Large Language Models (LLMs) have emerged as a promising solution to address many of these challenges in multi-document summarization. These models, based on transformer architectures [13], can process and understand much longer sequences of text than previous approaches. This allows them to capture broader context and relationships across multiple documents [14].

Key advantages of LLMs for multi-document summarization include:

Contextual understanding: Self-attention mechanisms allow LLMs to model long-range dependencies and capture document-level context [15].

Redundancy handling: LLMs can identify and consolidate repeated information across sources [16].

coherent and contextually consistent summaries: the hierarchical structure of LLMs allows them to model the inherent structure of documents, which can create more coherent and contextually consistent summaries [17].

Abstractive capabilities: Through pre-training on vast corpora, LLMs develop strong language generation abilities, enabling more natural abstractive summaries [18].

Scalability: Techniques like sparse attention [20] allow LLMs to efficiently process very large inputs.

Transfer learning: LLMs can be fine-tuned for specific summarization tasks while leveraging general language understanding [19, 21].

2.4 Domain-Specific Applications

Researchers have begun exploring the application of LLMs to multi-document summarization in various specialized domains:

Legal: LLMs show promise in summarizing complex legal documents, extracting key arguments and precedents [46]. This can significantly improve efficiency for legal professionals reviewing large case files [47].

Medical: In the medical field, LLMs are being used to synthesize findings from multiple research papers, supporting evidence-based practice [49]. They can also summarize patient records and clinical conversations to aid healthcare providers [52].

News: LLMs enable the aggregation of multiple news sources to provide comprehensive event summaries, potentially reducing bias by incorporating diverse viewpoints [53, 55].

These domain-specific applications highlight the adaptability of LLMs to different types of documents and summarization needs. However, they also underscore the importance of addressing potential biases and ensuring factual accuracy, especially in sensitive domains [62, 65].

Long context understanding within large language models is crucial for document summarization tasks requiring a deep understanding of language semantics, coherence, and context. Long Context LLMs offer a powerful approach to overcome the limitations of traditional methods in multi-document summarization. By capturing long-range dependencies, handling redundancy, generating coherent abstracts, and scaling to large document collections, LLMs have the potential to revolutionize the field of multi-document summarization and enable the creation of more accurate, informative, and user-friendly summaries. In this paper, we describe the application of Long-context LLMs through various case studies.

3 Methodology

A typical multi-document summarization task follows the steps described below.

Model Selection: A Long context LLM such as GPT-4 [22] or Claude 2.1 [23] can be chosen for multi-document summarization task. The final model is selected for its ability to capture long-range dependencies and handle large input sequences and generate coherent and fluent summaries [24]. An LLM's pre-training on diverse datasets allows for effective transfer learning to the multi-document summarization task.

Data preparation: In data preparation step, multiple documents relevant for the summarization task having balanced representation of multiple sources such as news articles, academic papers, and reports [25] are collected to create a comprehensive dataset. The documents are filtered and to remove duplicates, irrelevant content and noise to ensure data quality. For data preprocessing the text is normalized, tokenized, and formatted for input to the LLMs.

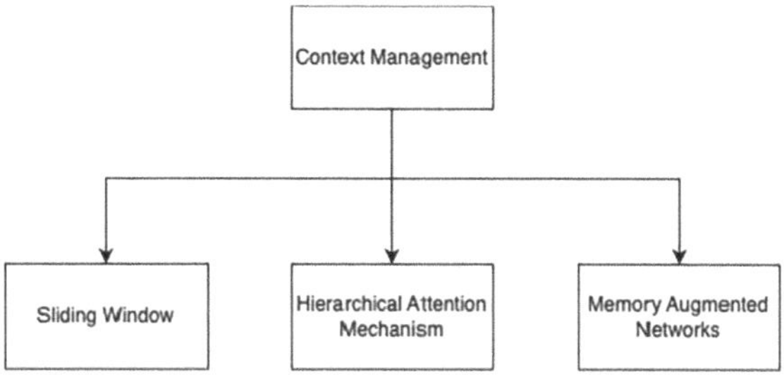

Fig. 3. Context Management Techniques

Context Management: In order, to reduce the complexity of managing longer context we have selected Long-context LLMs, however, even explicit Long-context LLMs may suffer from losing the context when relevant context appears in the middle of a very long text [26], hence managing long contexts is critical for effective summarization. Sliding window, hierarchical attention and use of memory- augmented networks are some of the strategies that are effective. Sliding Window involves dividing the text into overlapping segments to ensure the model captures context across sections. [27]. In Hierarchical Attention Mechanisms layers of attention are implemented to focus on different levels of text (e.g., paragraphs, sentences) for better context retention. [28]. Memory-augmented networks, such as the Differentiable Neural Computer (DNC) [29] and the Memory Attention Network (MAN) [30], are integrated with the LLMs to enable dynamic context retrieval and information storage during the summarization process where it employs external memory structures to dynamically store and retrieve context information, enhancing the model's ability to reference long-range dependencies (Fig. 3).

Information Extraction: This is a crucial step in multi-document summarization, that involves identifying and organizing key pieces of information across multiple documents to generate coherent and comprehensive summaries. Named Entity Recognition (NER), Relation Extraction (RE) and coreference resolution are the techniques most used in Information Extraction step where NER helps to identify and classify entities such as people, organizations, locations, dates, and other important terms within the text and RE assists to identify relationships between entities, such as who did what to whom, when, and where [31]. Coreference Resolution aims to identify, and link mentions of the same entity across different parts of the text or across multiple documents [32]. By applying NER to the input documents, LLM can recognize and extract key entities that are central to the information being summarized [33]. The extracted entities serve as anchors for linking and integrating information across multiple documents. LLMs can utilize RE techniques to uncover the connections and interactions among the extracted entities, providing a deeper understanding of the information structure [34]. Extracting relations helps in establishing the context and coherence of the information being summarized. By applying Coreference Resolution, LLMs can establish connections between related entities and events, even if they are referred to using different expressions [35]. This helps in creating a unified representation of the information and avoids redundancy in the generated summary.

Information Integration: In this step, the extracted entities and relations are used to construct knowledge graphs that capture the interconnections and hierarchical structure of the information [36]. These knowledge graphs aid in maintaining coherence and consistency during summary generation.

Summary Generation: In this steps extractive and abstractive summarization approaches are combined by employing the hybrid approach [37]. Extractive methods are used to identify the most salient sentences, while abstractive methods generate concise and fluent summaries. This approach ensures coherence, consistency, and relevance in the generated summaries: To ensure the quality of the generated summaries, techniques such as coherence modeling [38], consistency checking [39], and relevance scoring [40] are incorporated. These techniques help in maintaining the logical flow, factual accuracy, and pertinence of the summaries to the input documents.

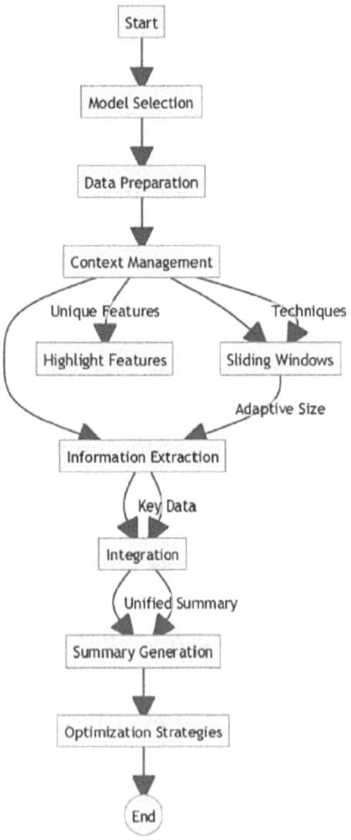

Fig. 4. Workflow Analysis for Leveraging LLMs in Multi-Document Summarization

Optimization Strategies: The pre-trained LLMs are fine-tuned on multi-document summarization datasets using techniques such as transfer learning [41] and domain adaptation [42]. This allows the models to specialize in the specific task and domain of interest. To optimize the performance of the LLMs, techniques such as model compression [43], knowledge distillation [44], and quantization [45] are employed. These techniques help in reducing the computational overhead while maintaining the accuracy of the generated summaries.

The complete methodological workflow integrating all the components discussed above is depicted in (Fig. 4).

4 Applications and Case Studies

In this section we discuss the application and case studies for using long-context large language models (LLMs) for multi-document summarization in the legal domain, medical field, news industry and enterprise application use cases.

4.1 Legal Domain

Problem statement: A legal firm needs to summarize a large collection of legal documents related to a complex corporate litigation case. The documents include court filings, depositions, contracts, and legal precedents spanning thousands of pages.

Using a long-context LLM, the legal team can process and summarize the vast amount of legal information efficiently. The LLM identifies key legal entities, extracts relevant clauses and arguments, and generates a concise summary that captures the essential points of the case [46].

This solution will enhance the efficiency by automating the time-consuming task of summarizing lengthy legal documents, allowing legal professionals to allocate their time and resources more efficiently [47] LLMs can identify and highlight crucial legal details that might be overlooked by human readers, reducing the risk of errors or omissions there by resulting in higher accuracy. The summarized legal information is more easily accessible and understandable for legal professionals, enabling them to quickly grasp the essential points without reading through voluminous documents [40]. Using Long-context LLM for multi document summarization in the legal domain also allows for improved decision making as the summaries generated by LLMs provide lawyers with a comprehensive overview of the case, enabling them to make informed decisions and develop effective legal strategies [48].

4.2 Medical Field

Problem statement: Researchers are conducting a systematic review of medical literature on a specific disease. They need to summarize findings from hundreds of scientific papers to identify trends, compare treatment options, and guide clinical decision-making.

Employing a long-context LLM, the researchers can efficiently process the large corpus of medical literature. The LLM extracts key information such as study objectives, methodologies, results, and conclusions, generating a structured summary of the reviewed papers [49].

Using a long context LLM can allow healthcare researchers and providers stay current with the latest research findings by summarizing relevant medical literature [50].

Summaries generated by LLMs provide a consolidated view of scientific evidence, supporting healthcare researchers and providers in making evidence-based decisions [51]. Healthcare researchers and providers can quickly access the summarized research findings, enabling them to stay updated with the latest medical knowledge without spending extensive time reading full-text articles [52]. by quickly accessing summarized medical information, healthcare providers can make more informed diagnoses, select appropriate treatments, and enhance overall patient care [52].

4.3 News Industry

Problem statement: A news organization wants to create comprehensive summaries of news events by aggregating articles from multiple sources. The goal is to provide readers with a balanced and informative overview of the event.

Utilizing a long-context LLM, the news organization can process articles from various news outlets, identifying key facts, opinions, and perspectives. The LLM generates a coherent summary that combines information from multiple sources, presenting a comprehensive narrative of the event [53]. Multi-document summaries generated by LLMs can provide readers with a broad understanding of news events, reducing the need to read multiple articles [54]. LLMs can incorporate diverse viewpoints from different sources, promoting balanced and unbiased reporting [55]. News organizations can use LLMs to automate the process of summarizing news events, saving time and resources while maintaining high-quality journalism [56].

4.4 Enterprise Applications

Problem statement: A large financial services bank needs to summarize a large collection of documents related to various functions such as HR, finance, sourcing, compliance, and audit to streamline operations and improve decision-making processes.

Utilizing long-context LLMs in enterprise functions allows for the condensation of different document types, resulting in improved efficiency, decision-making, and accuracy throughout the organization. Within HR functions, extensive LLMs are utilized to condense employee performance reviews, training documents, and compliance reports. This offers HR managers a thorough understanding of employee performance and compliance status, eliminating the need to sift through lengthy documents. Within finance functions, LLMs provide valuable support to financial analysts by condensing financial reports, investment analyses, and market research. Analysts can efficiently access crucial insights and make well-informed decisions using summarized financial data.

When it comes to sourcing functions, LLMs with extensive knowledge provide concise summaries of supplier contracts, procurement reports, and market analyses. This assists sourcing managers in making strategic decisions by offering them succinct summaries of procurement-related documents. LLMs play a crucial role in summarizing compliance reports, audit findings, and regulatory documents for compliance and audit functions. This guarantees strict compliance with legal standards and enhances the efficiency of audits by emphasizing important compliance issues and audit findings.

The advantages for enterprise operations can be seen through increased efficiency as it streamlines the process of summarizing lengthy documents, allowing enterprise professionals to save their valuable time.

It offers succinct and pertinent summaries that enable managers to swiftly make well-informed decisions.

These case studies demonstrate the practical applications and benefits of using long-context LLMs for multi-document summarization in various domains. By leveraging the power of LLMs, professionals in the legal domain, medical field, and news industry and enterprises irrespective of their size can efficiently process and summarize large volumes of information, leading to improved decision-making, knowledge sharing, and public understanding.

5 Challenges and Considerations

The application of long-context LLMs to multi-document summarization, while promising, presents several significant challenges that warrant careful consideration. These challenges span technical, ethical, and practical dimensions, each requiring innovative solutions to ensure the effective and responsible use of these powerful models [56]. Technical Consideration.

5.1 Technical Considerations

Multi-document summarization often involves processing datasets with diverse formats, styles, and topics, which can pose challenges for LLMs [59]. LLMs need to effectively handle the complexity and heterogeneity of the input data, including variations in document length, structure, and quality [60] Addressing these challenges requires robust data preprocessing techniques, such as document segmentation, noise reduction, and format normalization [61]. Processing large volumes of documents for multi-document summarization can be computationally intensive, requiring significant resources and time [14]. Techniques such as model compression, distributed computing, and hardware acceleration can be employed to improve the scalability and efficiency of LLMs for multi-document summarization [56].

5.2 Ethical Considerations

The potential for bias in LLMs raises significant ethical concerns. These models may inadvertently perpetuate or amplify existing biases present in their training data, including gender, racial, cultural, or ideological biases [62, 63]. The societal impact of these biases in summarization tasks cannot be overstated, potentially influencing public opinion or decision-making processes in fields such as journalism or policy-making [64].

Privacy concerns are particularly critical when summarizing sensitive documents, especially in domains like healthcare or legal services where confidentiality is of utmost importance [65].

5.3 Ensuring Factual Accuracy and Reliability of Summaries

Generating summaries that are factually accurate and reliable is crucial, especially in domains such as news, legal, and medical [65]. LLMs may sometimes generate summaries that contain inconsistencies, hallucinations, or errors, compromising the reliability of the output [66]. This challenge is particularly pronounced in abstractive summarization, where models generate new text rather than extracting existing sentences.

LLM's performance can degrade when relevant information is positioned in the middle of long input context [68], leading to inconsistent performance, incomplete or inaccurate summaries, and reduced coherence and readability. This issue highlights the trade-offs between abstractive and extractive summarization in terms of factual accuracy and coherence [67].

These challenges can be addressed using techniques such as fact-checking, source attribution, and uncertainty quantification to improve the factual accuracy and reliability of the generated summaries [67]. Rigorous evaluation and analysis of the generated summaries will be crucial to identify and address any performance issues related to the positioning of relevant information in long contexts.

5.4 Emerging Challenges

As the field of multi-document summarization evolves, new challenges are emerging. Multimodal summarization, involving documents with text, images, and other media types, requires models to integrate information across different modalities coherently. Multilingual and cross-lingual summarization present unique challenges in an increasingly globalized world [68].

Developing comprehensive evaluation metrics for summarization quality remains an open challenge [69]. Current metrics often fail to capture nuanced aspects of summary quality, such as coherence, relevance, and faithfulness to the original documents.

The "black box" nature of LLMs raises concerns about explainability and transparency in the summarization process [70]. As these models are increasingly used in critical applications, there is a growing need for methods to interpret and explain their decision-making processes.

Addressing these challenges will require ongoing research and collaboration across disciplines. As we continue to advance the capabilities of long-context LLMs for multi-document summarization, it is crucial to remain mindful of these considerations to ensure the development of effective, ethical, and reliable summarization systems.

6 Conclusion and Future Direction

Long-context large language models (LLMs) have emerged as a powerful tool for multi-document understanding and summarization. This study has demonstrated their significant advantages over traditional methods, including the ability to capture long-range dependencies, handle redundancy effectively, and generate coherent summaries. The application of long-context LLMs for multi-document summarization shows potential to revolutionize information processing and knowledge dissemination across various domains.

Our research, supported by case studies in legal applications, enterprise functions, medical, and news domains, highlights several key findings. Long-context LLMs demonstrate superior ability in synthesizing information across multiple documents and show effectiveness in adapting to various fields, producing relevant and coherent summaries. These models excel at consolidating information from diverse sources, resulting in comprehensive and concise summaries. Importantly, the use of these models led to tangible improvements in decision-making, knowledge sharing, and public understanding of complex information.

However, our study also identified important challenges that require further research. Technical challenges include handling diverse and complex datasets, mitigating performance degradation when crucial information is positioned in the middle of long contexts, and scaling models efficiently for very large document collections. Ethical considerations are equally important, encompassing the need to address biases present in training data, ensure factual accuracy and reliability of generated summaries, and maintain privacy and confidentiality, especially in sensitive domains.

Future studies in multi-document summarization using long-context LLMs should prioritize several important factors. Researchers should focus on incorporating domain-specific knowledge bases and ontologies to improve semantic comprehension and coherence of generated summaries. Applying long-context LLMs to various domains, including financial reports, scientific literature, and social media, will enable the creation of customized summaries for specific industry requirements. Further investigation is needed to uncover the possibilities of LLMs in cross-lingual and multilingual summarization, potentially enhancing information accessibility across linguistic barriers. Developing techniques to improve factual consistency and reliability of generated summaries remains crucial, as does research into methods for handling diverse document formats and styles effectively. Additionally, exploring ways to enhance model scalability for processing very long or numerous documents efficiently will be vital for practical applications.

By addressing these challenges and further improving methodologies, long-context LLMs have the potential to become even more powerful tools for revolutionizing information processing and knowledge sharing in different fields. As research in this field progresses, it is crucial to focus on both improving technical capabilities and addressing ethical considerations. This balanced approach will be key to the effective and responsible use of long-context LLMs in multi-document summarization.

In conclusion, while long-context LLMs show immense promise, their successful application requires continued exploration and advancement. By tackling the identified obstacles and refining current approaches, we can work towards realizing the full potential of these models in transforming how we process and understand large volumes of information across diverse sectors and enterprise applications. The future of multi-document summarization with long-context LLMs is promising, but it demands rigorous research, ethical consideration, and innovative problem-solving to fully harness its capabilities.

References

1. Vishal, G., Lehal, G.S.: A survey of text summarization extractive techniques. J. Emerg. Technol. Web Intell. **2**(3), 258–268 (2010)
2. Allahyari, M., et al.: Text Summarization Techniques: A Brief Survey. ArXiv (2017). arXiv: 1707.02268
3. Gambhir, M., Gupta, V.: Recent automatic text summarization techniques: a survey. Artif. Intell. Rev. **47**(1), 1–66 (2017)
4. Bing, L., Li, P., Liao, Y., Lam, W., Guo, W., Passonneau, R.J.: Abstractive multi-document summarization via phrase selection and merging. In: Proceedings of the 53rd Annual Meeting of the Association for Computational Linguistics and the 7th International Joint Conference on Natural Language Processing [Volume 1: Long Papers], Beijing, China, pp. 1587–1597 (2015). https://doi.org/10.3115/v1/P15-1153
5. Christensen, J., Mausam, M., Soderland, S., Etzioni, O.: Towards coherent multi-document summarization. In: Proceedings of the 2013 Conference of the North American Chapter of the Association for Computational Linguistics: Human Language Technologies, Atlanta, Georgia, pp. 1163–1173 (2013)
6. Chali, Y., Hasan, S.A.: Towards automatic topical question generation. In: Proceedings of the 53rd Annual Meeting of the Association for Computational Linguistics and the 7th International Joint Conference on Natural Language Processing (Volume 1: Long Papers), Beijing, China, pp. 475–485 (2015). https://doi.org/10.3115/v1/P15-1046
7. Parveen, D., Ramsl, H.-M., Strube, M.: Topical coherence for graph-based extractive summarization. In: Proceedings of the 2015 Conference on Empirical Methods in Natural Language Processing, Lisbon, Portugal, pp. 1949–1954 (2015). https://doi.org/10.18653/v1/D15-1226
8. Cao, Z., Wei, F., Li, W., Li, S.: Faithful to the original: fact-aware neural abstractive summarization. In: Proceedings of the Thirty-Second AAAI Conference on Artificial Intelligence and Thirtieth Innovative Applications of Artificial Intelligence Conference and Eighth AAAI Symposium on Educational Advances in Artificial Intelligence [AAAI'18/IAAI'18/EAAI'18], New Orleans, LA, USA, pp. 4784–4791 (2018)
9. Gerani, S., Mehdad, Y., Carenini, G., Ng, R.T., Nejat, B.: Abstractive summarization of product reviews using discourse structure. In: Proceedings of the 2014 Conference on Empirical Methods in Natural Language Processing (EMNLP), Doha, Qatar, pp. 1602–1613 (2014). https://doi.org/10.3115/v1/D14-1168
10. Feigenblat, G., Roitman, H., Boni, O., Konopnicki, D.: Unsupervised query-focused multi-document summarization using the cross entropy method. In: Proceedings of the 40th International ACM SIGIR Conference on Research and Development in Information Retrieval, Tokyo, Japan, pp. 961–964 (2017). https://doi.org/10.1145/3077136.3080690
11. Yasunaga, M., Zhang, R., Meelu, K., Pareek, A., Srinivasan, K., Radev, D.: Graph-based neural multi-document summarization. In: Proceedings of the 21st Conference on Computational Natural Language Learning (CoNLL 2017), Vancouver, Canada, pp. 452–462 (2017). https://doi.org/10.18653/v1/K17-1045
12. Pontes, E.L., Huet, S., Torres-Moreno, J.-M.: A multilingual study of compressive cross-language text summarization. In: Proceedings of the Eleventh International Conference on Language Resources and Evaluation (LREC 2018), Miyazaki, Japan, pp. 4414–4422 (2018). https://aclanthology.org/L18-1696
13. Vaswani, A., et al.: Attention is all you need. In: Guyon, I., et al. (eds.) Advances in Neural Information Processing Systems, vol. 30. Curran Associates, Inc. (2017)
14. Beltagy, I., Peters, M.E., Cohan, A.: Longformer: The Long-Document Transformer. arXiv preprint arXiv:2004.05150. (2020). https://arxiv.org/abs/2004.05150

15. Cheng, J., Dong, L., Lapata, M.: Long short-term memory-networks for machine reading. In: Proceedings of the 2016 Conference on Empirical Methods in Natural Language Processing, Austin, Texas, pp. 551–561 (2016). https://doi.org/10.18653/v1/D16-1053
16. Zhang, J., Zhao, Y., Saleh, M., Liu, P.: PEGASUS: pre-training with extracted gap-sentences for abstractive summarization. In: Proceedings of the 37th International Conference on Machine Learning, vol. 119, pp. 11328–11339 (2020). http://proceedings.mlr.press/v119/zhang20ae.html
17. Yang, Z., Dai, Z., Yang, Y., Carbonell, J., Salakhutdinov, R.R., Le, Q.V.: XLNet: generalized autoregressive pretraining for language understanding. In: Advances in Neural Information Processing Systems, vol. 32, H. Wallach, H. Larochelle, A. Beygelzimer, F. d'Alché-Buc, E. Fox, and R. Garnett, Eds. Curran Associates, Inc., pp. 5753–5763 (2019). https://proceedings.neurips.cc/paper/2019/file/dc6a7e655d7e5840e66733e9ee67cc69-Paper.pdf
18. Lewis, M., et al.: BART: denoising sequence-to-sequence pre-training for natural language generation, translation, and comprehension. In: Proceedings of the 58th Annual Meeting of the Association for Computational Linguistics, Online, pp. 7871–7880 (2020). https://doi.org/10.18653/v1/2020.acl-main.703
19. Liu, Y., Lapata, M.: Text summarization with pretrained encoders. In: Proceedings of the 2019 Conference on Empirical Methods in Natural Language Processing and the 9th International Joint Conference on Natural Language Processing (EMNLP-IJCNLP), Hong Kong, China, pp. 3730–3740 (2019). https://doi.org/10.18653/v1/D19-1387
20. Zaheer, M., et al.: Big Bird: transformers for longer sequences. In: Advances in Neural Information Processing Systems, vol. 33, H. Larochelle, M. Ranzato, R. Hadsell, M. F. Balcan, and H. Lin, Eds. Curran Associates, Inc., pp. 17283–17297 (2020). https://proceedings.neurips.cc/paper/2020/file/c8512d142a2d849725f31a9a7a361ab9-Paper.pdf
21. Ruder, S., Peters, M.E., Swayamdipta, S., Wolf, T.: Transfer learning in natural language processing. In: Proceedings of the 2019 Conference of the North American Chapter of the Association for Computational Linguistics: Tutorials, Minneapolis, Minnesota, pp. 15–18 (2019). https://doi.org/10.18653/v1/N19-5004
22. OpenAI, Achiam, J., et al.: GPT-4 Technical Report. arXiv preprint arXiv:2303.08774 (2024)
23. Anthropic, "Claude 2.1 Release Notes," Anthropic, Apr. 20, 2023. [Online]. Available: https://www.anthropic.com/news/claude-2-1-prompting
24. 2Beltagy, M.E.P., Cohan, A.: Longformer: The Long-Document Transformer. arXiv preprint arXiv:2004.05150 (2020)
25. Yasunaga, M., Zhang, R., Meelu, K., Pareek, A., Srinivasan, K., Radev, D.: Graph-based neural multi-document summarization. In: Proceedings of the 21st Conference on Computational Natural Language Learning [CoNLL 2017], Vancouver, Canada, pp. 452–462 (2017). https://doi.org/10.18653/v1/K17-1045
26. Liu, S., Ding, Y., Liu, C., Hu, W., Shi, Z., Jiang, M.: Long but not Enough: Rethinking Long Context Modeling in Transformers. arXiv preprint arXiv:2305.15003 (2023)
27. Pappagari, R., Zelasko, P., Villalba, J., Carmiel, Y., Dehak, N.: Hierarchical transformers for long document classification. In: Proceedings of the 2019 IEEE Automatic Speech Recognition and Understanding Workshop (ASRU), Singapore, pp. 838–844 (2019). https://doi.org/10.1109/ASRU46091.2019.9003958
28. Yang, Z., Yang, D., Dyer, C., He, X., Smola, A., Hovy, E.: Hierarchical attention networks for document classification. In: Proceedings of the 2016 Conference of the North American Chapter of the Association for Computational Linguistics: Human Language Technologies, San Diego, California, pp. 1480–1489 (2016). https://doi.org/10.18653/v1/N16-1174
29. Graves, A., et al.: Hybrid computing using a neural network with dynamic external memory. Nature **538**(7626), 471–476 (2016). https://doi.org/10.1038/nature20101

30. Singh, V., Verma, R., Shrivastava, M.: Memory attention networks for abstractive summarization. In: Proceedings of the 16th Conference of the European Chapter of the Association for Computational Linguistics: Main Volume, Online, pp. 2177–2187 (2021)
31. Stanovsky, G., Michael, J., Zettlemoyer, L., Dagan, I.: Supervised open information extraction. In: Proceedings of the 2018 Conference of the North American Chapter of the Association for Computational Linguistics: Human Language Technologies, Volume 1 (Long Papers), New Orleans, Louisiana, pp. 885–895 (2018). https://doi.org/10.18653/v1/N18-1081
32. Lee, K., He, L., Lewis, M., Zettlemoyer, L.: End-to-end neural coreference resolution. In: Proceedings of the 2017 Conference on Empirical Methods in Natural Language Processing, Copenhagen, Denmark, pp. 188–197 (2017). https://doi.org/10.18653/v1/D17-1018
33. Luan, Y., Wadden, D., He, L., Shah, A., Ostendorf, M., Hajishirzi, H.: A general framework for information extraction using dynamic span graphs. In: Proceedings of the 2019 Conference of the North American Chapter of the Association for Computational Linguistics: Human Language Technologies, Volume 1 (Long and Short Papers), Minneapolis, Minnesota, pp. 3036–3046 (2019). https://doi.org/10.18653/v1/N19-1308
34. Guu, K., Lee, K., Tung, Z., Pasupat, P., Chang, M.: REALM: Retrieval-Augmented Language Model Pre-Training. arXiv preprint arXiv:2002.08909. (2020). https://arxiv.org/abs/2002.08909
35. Joshi, M., Levy, O., Zettlemoyer, L., Weld, D.: BERT for conference resolution: baselines and analysis. In: Proceedings of the 2019 Conference on Empirical Methods in Natural Language Processing and the 9th International Joint Conference on Natural Language Processing (EMNLP-IJCNLP), Hong Kong, China, pp. 5803–5808 (2019). https://doi.org/10.18653/v1/D19-1588
36. Fan, C.G., Braud, C., Bordes, A.: Using local knowledge graph construction to scale Seq2Seq models to multi-document inputs. In: Proceedings of the 2019 Conference on Empirical Methods in Natural Language Processing and the 9th International Joint Conference on Natural Language Processing (EMNLP-IJCNLP), Hong Kong, China, pp. 4186–4196 (2019). https://doi.org/10.18653/v1/D19-1428
37. See, P.J.L., Manning, C.D.: Get to the point: summarization with pointer-generator networks. In: Proceedings of the 55th Annual Meeting of the Association for Computational Linguistics (Volume 1: Long Papers), Vancouver, Canada, pp. 1073–1083 (2017). https://doi.org/10.18653/v1/P17-1099
38. Xu, J., Gan, X., Cheng, Y., Liu, J.: Discourse-aware neural extractive text summarization. In: Proceedings of the 58th Annual Meeting of the Association for Computational Linguistics, Online, pp. 5021–5031 (2020). https://doi.org/10.18653/v1/2020.acl-main.451
39. Kryscinski, W., McCann, B., Xiong, C., Socher, R.: Evaluating the Factual Consistency of Abstractive Text Summarization. In: Proceedings of the 2020 Conference on Empirical Methods in Natural Language Processing (EMNLP), pp. 9332–9346 (2020). https://doi.org/10.18653/v1/2020.emnlp-main.750
40. Zhong, M., Liu, P., Chen, Y., Wang, D., Qiu, X., Huang, X.: Extractive summarization as text matching. In: Proceedings of the 58th Annual Meeting of the Association for Computational Linguistics, Online, pp. 6197–6208 (2020). https://doi.org/10.18653/v1/2020.acl-main.552
41. Raffel, C., et al.: Exploring the limits of transfer learning with a unified text-to-text transformer. J. Mach. Learn. Res. **21**(140), 1–67 (2020). http://jmlr.org/papers/v21/20-074.html
42. Zhang, X., Wei, F., Zhou, M.: HIBERT: document level pre-training of hierarchical bidirectional transformers for document summarization. In: Proceedings of the 57th Annual Meeting of the Association for Computational Linguistics, Florence, Italy, pp. 5059–5069 (2019). https://doi.org/10.18653/v1/P19-1499
43. Sanh, V., Debut, L., Chaumond, J., Wolf, T.: DistilBERT, a distilled version of BERT: smaller, faster, cheaper and lighter. arXiv preprint arXiv:1910.01108. (2019). https://arxiv.org/abs/1910.01108

44. Hinton, G., Vinyals, O., Dean, J.: Distilling the Knowledge in a Neural Network. arXiv preprint arXiv:1503.02531 (2015). https://arxiv.org/abs/1503.02531
45. Shen, S., et al.: Q-BERT: hessian based ultra low precision quantization of BERT. Proc. AAAI Conf. Artif. Intell. **34**(05), 8815–8821 (2020). https://doi.org/10.1609/aaai.v34i05.6409
46. Bhattacharya, S., Mehta, P., Ghosh, K.: Assisting legal professionals with information extraction. In: Proceedings of the 2019 ACM/IEEE Joint Conference on Digital Libraries (JCDL), Champaign, IL, USA, pp. 329–330 (2019). https://doi.org/10.1109/JCDL.2019.00057
47. Dale, R.: Law and word order: NLP in legal tech. Nat. Lang. Eng. **25**(1), 211–217 (2019). https://doi.org/10.1017/S1351324918000475
48. Huang, X., Zou, J., Tang, J.: Automatic generation of legal case brief by extracting key information from Chinese legal documents. In: Proceedings of the 2021 Conference on Empirical Methods in Natural Language Processing, Online and Punta Cana, Dominican Republic, pp. 6328–6337 (2021). https://aclanthology.org/2021.emnlp-main.510
49. Zhu, Y., Fox, E.B., Obeid, A.J.: TEBM-Net: a template enhanced bidirectional matching network for biomedical literature retrieval and question answering. In: Proceedings of the 44th International ACM SIGIR Conference on Research and Development in Information Retrieval, Virtual Event, Canada, pp. 2555–2559 (2021). https://doi.org/10.1145/3404835.3463133
50. Jin, X., Ding, X., Zhang, W., Tang, J., Qu, J.: Towards accurate and consistent biomedical summarization. In: Proceedings of the 2020 Conference on Empirical Methods in Natural Language Processing: Findings, Online, pp. 4115–4125 (2020). https://doi.org/10.18653/v1/2020.findings-emnlp.373
51. Zhang, L., et al.: Leveraging pretrained models for automatic summarization of doctor-patient conversations. In: Moens, M.F., Huang, X., Specia, L., Yih, S.W.T. (eds.) Findings of the Association for Computational Linguistics: EMNLP 2021, pp. 3693–3712. Association for Computational Linguistics, Punta Cana, Dominican Republic (2021). https://doi.org/10.18653/v1/2021.findings-emnlp.313. Y. Deng, S. Liu, X. Wang, Y. Shen, J. Xie, and H. Ma, "Extracting Structured Information from Clinical Conversations for COVID-19 Diagnosis," in Proceedings of the 2021 Conference on Empirical Methods in Natural Language Processing, Online and Punta Cana, Dominican Republic, 2021, pp. 3109–3121. [Online]. Available: https://aclanthology.org/2021.emnlp-main.246
52. Laban, P., Hsi, A., Canny, J., Hearst, M.A.: The summary loop: learning to write abstractive summaries without examples. In: Proceedings of the 59th Annual Meeting of the Association for Computational Linguistics and the 11th International Joint Conference on Natural Language Processing (Volume 1: Long Papers), Online, pp. 5111–5126 (2021). https://doi.org/10.18653/v1/2021.acl-long.396
53. Gao, Y., Zhu, Y., Zhang, H., Xiao, J., Li, Z., Zhu, J.: Abstractive text summarization by incorporating reader comments. Proc. AAAI Conf. Artif. Intell. **34**(05), 7399–7406 (2020). https://doi.org/10.1609/aaai.v34i05.6228
54. Liu, S., Fa, T., Cui, H., Zheng, K.: Considering diverse information for dialogue summarization. In: Proceedings of the 59th Annual Meeting of the Association for Computational Linguistics and the 11th International Joint Conference on Natural Language Processing: Student Research Workshop, Online, pp. 256–262 (2021). https://doi.org/10.18653/v1/2021.acl-srw.31
55. Bommasani, R., Hudson, D.A., Adeli, E., Altman, R., Arora, S., et al.: On the Opportunities and Risks of Foundation Models. arXiv preprint arXiv:2108.07258 (2022). https://arxiv.org/abs/2108.07258
56. Press, O., Smith, N., Lewis, M.: Train short, test long: Attention with linear biases enables input length extrapolation. In: International Conference on Learning Representations (2022)
57. Ding, Y., et al.: LongRoPE: Extending LLM Context Window Beyond 2 Million Tokens. arXiv preprint arXiv:2402.13753. 2024

58. Liu, Y., Lapata, M., Lan, Y.: Multi-document summarization with diverse formats and styles. arXiv preprint arXiv:2102.12033 (2021)
59. Huang, L., Cao, Y., Jiang, J.: Heterogeneous document summarization with structural regularization. Proc. AAAI Conf. Artif. Intell. **35**(14), 13258–13266 (2021)
60. Zhu, J., Xia, Y., Lapata, M.: Document segmentation for long-form document summarization. In: Proceedings of the 2021 Conference on Empirical Methods in Natural Language Processing, pp. 6584–6594 (2021)
61. Bender, E.M., Gebru, T., McMillan-Major, A., Shmitchell, S.: On the dangers of stochastic parrots: Can language models be too big? In: Proceedings of the 2021 ACM Conference on Fairness, Accountability, and Transparency, pp. 610–623 (2021)
62. Shah, D., Schwartz, H.A., Hovy, D.: Predictive biases in natural language processing models: a conceptual framework and overview. In: Proceedings of the 58th Annual Meeting of the Association for Computational Linguistics, pp. 5248–5264 (2020)
63. Liang, P., Wu, C., Morency, L., Salakhutdinov, R.: Towards understanding and mitigating social biases in language models. In: International Conference on Machine Learning. PMLR, pp. 6565–6576 (2021)
64. Kryscinski, W., McCann, B., Xiong, C., Socher, R.: Evaluating the factual consistency of abstractive text summarization. In: Proceedings of the 2020 Conference on Empirical Methods in Natural Language Processing (EMNLP), pp. 9332–9346 (2020)
65. Maynez, J., Narayan, S., Bohnet, B., McDonald, R.: On faithfulness and factuality in abstractive summarization. In: Proceedings of the 58th Annual Meeting of the Association for Computational Linguistics, pp. 1906–1919 (2020)
66. Falke, T., Ribeiro, L.F.R., Utama, P.A., Dagan, I., Gurevych, I.: Ranking generated summaries by correctness: an interesting but challenging application for natural language inference. In: Proceedings of the 57th Annual Meeting of the Association for Computational Linguistics, pp. 2214–2220 (2019)
67. Li, T., Zhang, G., Do, Q.D., Yue, X., Chen, W.: Long-context LLMs Struggle with Long In-context Learning. arXiv preprint arXiv:2404.02060 (2024)
68. Lakew, S.M., Cettolo, M., Federico, M.: A comparison of transformer and recurrent neural networks on multilingual neural machine translation. In: Proceedings of the 27th International Conference on Computational Linguistics, pp. 641–652 (2018)
69. Krippendorff, K.: Computing Krippendorff's Alpha-Reliability (2011). https://repository.upenn.edu/asc_papers/43
70. Lipton, Z.C.: The mythos of model interpretability. Queue **16**(3), 31–57 (2018)

Transformations in Finance and Accounting: Navigating Through Technological and Regulatory Shifts

Manoj Kumar Vandanapu[1(✉)] and Sivanagaraju Gadiparthi[2]

[1] Corporate Finance Expert, Chicago, IL, USA
manoj.dhs@gmail.com
[2] Independent Researcher, Edison, NJ, USA

Abstract. The finance and accounting industries are experiencing significant transformations driven by technological advancements and evolving regulatory landscapes. This paper explores the impact of technologies such as artificial intelligence (AI), machine learning (ML), blockchain, cryptocurrencies, big data analytics, and cloud computing on accounting standards, financial practices, auditing processes, and reporting frameworks. It also examines recent regulatory changes, including GDPR, SOX, and IFRS, and their implications for data protection, corporate governance, and financial transparency. Through case studies and practical examples, this article provides insights for professionals navigating these dynamic changes and suggests future research directions to further explore these developments.

Keywords: Big Data and Analytics · Artificial Intelligence · Sustainability Reporting

1 Introduction

Finance and accounting are the backbone of any business entity; they provide the basis for the efficient allocation of the organization's financial resources, for the accurate reporting of its financial findings, and for compliance with regulatory requirements [1]. Currently, the fields of financial management and accounting are undergoing disruptive transformations due to rapid technological advancements and evolving regulatory frameworks. These changes significantly impact the financial health, strategic choices, and success of companies across various industries.

The financial management process includes optimizing resource allocation, formulating investment plans, managing risk, and assessing the organization's financial performance. Accounting, on the other hand, involves the recording, classification, and communication of financial transactions to ensure transparent and traceable financial reporting [2]. Proper management of finances and accurate documentation are essential for securing funding and building stakeholder confidence. Analytics provide vital information about a company's profitability, cash flows, and overall financial health, facilitating informed decision-making and strategic planning. Additionally, robust financial and

V. B. Gupta et al. (Eds.): IBCD 2024, CCIS 2413, pp. 225–240, 2025.
https://doi.org/10.1007/978-3-031-87511-3_16

accounting systems are crucial for legal and regulatory compliance, risk management, and protecting the interests of shareholders, creditors, and other stakeholders.

This article examines how technological innovations and regulatory changes are reshaping the finance and accounting sectors. The primary research objectives are:

1. To explore the impact of modern technologies such as artificial intelligence (AI), machine learning (ML), blockchain, cryptocurrencies, big data analytics, and cloud computing on financial and accounting processes. [3]
2. To analyze recent regulatory changes, including the Sarbanes-Oxley Act (SOX), International Financial Reporting Standards (IFRS), and General Data Protection Regulation (GDPR), and their implications for accounting, reporting, and compliance. [3]
3. To understand the shifts in accounting practices, including modifications in international accounting standards, greenhouse gas accounting and reporting, ESG considerations, and auditing and compliance updates.

By addressing these objectives, this article aims to provide insights into the current challenges and opportunities faced by professionals, businesses, and stakeholders in the finance and accounting sectors. Through detailed analysis and case studies, the article will highlight how organizations are adapting to these transformations and strategically positioning themselves in a rapidly changing financial landscape. Recognizing the impact of technological innovation and regulatory changes on finance and accounting is crucial for developing strategies that ensure compliance, foster innovation, and promote sustainable growth in a dynamic global market.

2 Technological Advancements in Finance and Accounting

Finance and accounting have undergone a radical evolution due to the intense pace of technological innovations. Technological advancements in areas including AI, ML, blockchain, cryptocurrencies, big data analytics and cloud computing have significantly altered the financial and accounting work flow, allowing for extra efficiency, transparency and data-driven decision-making opportunities. The impact of technology in finance and accounting has been broad and multi-dimensional in nature. Emergent technologies such as automated processes, intelligent data analysis and secure decentralized systems have transformed traditional techniques, enabling professionals to be more productivity-focused, to use smart information and to adapt to the constantly changing business environment. Figure 1 below shows the current technological advancements in finance and accounting [26]. Specific advances are explained below.

2.1 Machine Learning and Artificial Intelligence

Machine learning and Artificial intelligence have come out as giant changers in the finance and accounting industries [4, 5]. These innovations can process enormous amounts of data, detect market trends and even predict future events very reliably. AI and ML is applied in finance for tasks such as credit risk evaluation, fraud detection, algorithmic trading, and investment portfolio optimization [6]. In accounting, solutions are

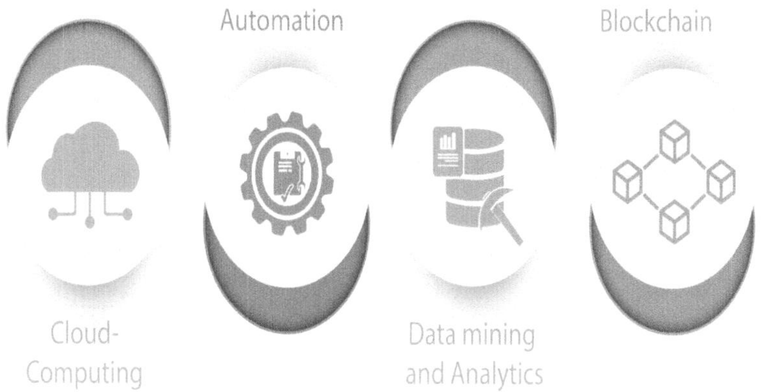

Fig. 1. Technological Advancements in Finance and Accounting [26]

primarily used to eliminate repetitive data inputs, reconcile processes, and audit tasks, which decreases error and speeds up operations.

2.2 Blockchain and Cryptocurrencies

The advent of block chain technology and crypto currency now displays a new financial system that has seen a decentralized and transparent way of conducting transactions. As a property of blockchain, attributes such as immutability, transparency, and security have shown ways for innovative financial transactions, smart contracts, and reliable record-keeping systems [7]. Cryptocurrencies, like Bitcoin, have appeared as digital alternatives to fiat currencies, ostensibly upending the traditional currency order and allowing for borderless and secure transactions.

2.3 Big Data and Analytics

The accounting and finance industry gather and process vast amounts of data, which de facto makes it almost impossible to survive in the market without employing big data analytics services. Through the use of sophisticated analytics tools, companies may process financial data, discover patterns, develop investment approaches, make decisions concerning risk management, and improve operational efficiency [8]. Predictive analytics can also assist in projecting future performance, which facilitates proactive decision-making and strategic planning.

From Fig. 2, with the development of social networks, artificial intelligence, Internet of Things, are made up of a vast array of sensors and gadgets, big data is only going to become more important. Three variables are used to measure data: variety, volume, and speed. More information is available than ever before—often in real time. This deluge of information is meaningless and ineffective until it is analyzed. Nevertheless, the big data analytics methodology looks at language, statistics, and text using machine learning to uncover previously undiscovered insights. It is possible to mine every data source for insights and forecasts.

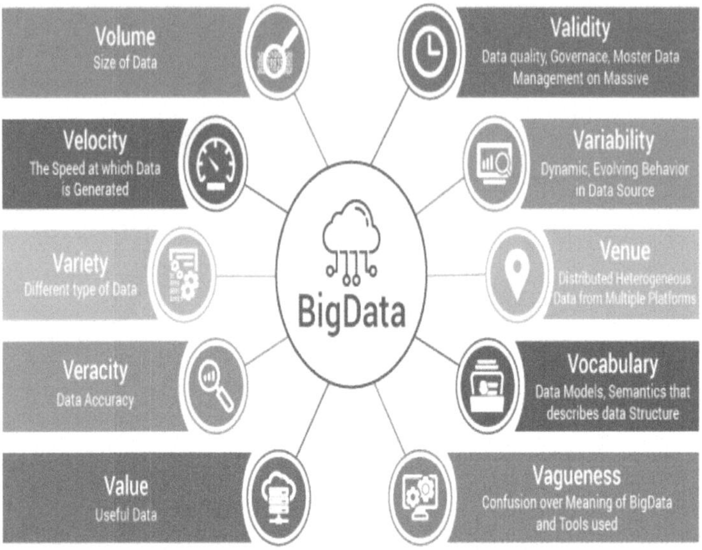

Fig. 2. Representation of big data and analytics [27]

2.4 Cloud Computing

Cloud computing is a game changer in the way financial and accounting data is stored, retrieved and managed [9, 26]. Through cloud-based solutions, organizations can be more confident about data security, they can work even better together and access information from any point in real-time at any time. Cloud-based accounting software systems and financial management tools are currently very much in fashion everywhere, offering scalability, cost efficiency, and a smooth interface with other business applications, among many other benefits.

2.4.1 Case Studies

The actualization of the influence of these technological achievements is also portrayed through the examination of real-life scenarios. JPMorgan Chase implemented AI & ML tools to accelerate trading operations, which consequently lowered the cost and increased the speed adequately [10]. Besides, Deloitte, a recognized accounting firm, has adopted blockchain in auditing and accounting, which elevates transparency and security. American Express has led the way in big data analytics adoption, it has enabled the firm to derive significant insights into customer spending trends, fraud detection and targeted marketing, thus enhancing the clients' satisfaction and revenue growth [11]. On the other hand, the Salesforce and Workday companies have successfully shifted to cloud-based financial and accounting services that empower their clients with real-time data, which can also enable them to work collaboratively and ensure security and flexible contracts. These case studies show real-life situations where finance and accounting forward-thinking companies about technology excel at its operational efficiency, better data-based decision-making, increased security, and adaptability to market conditions.

However, the rate of technological advancement is moving at an unprecedented speed. Therefore, finance and accounting professionals are obliged to keep abreast of the latest technological developments and be ready to incorporate and implement them in their practices. In this way, they will be able to get ahead in business by using modern technology to encourage innovation and remain successful in the increasingly digital world where data reigns (Fig. 3).

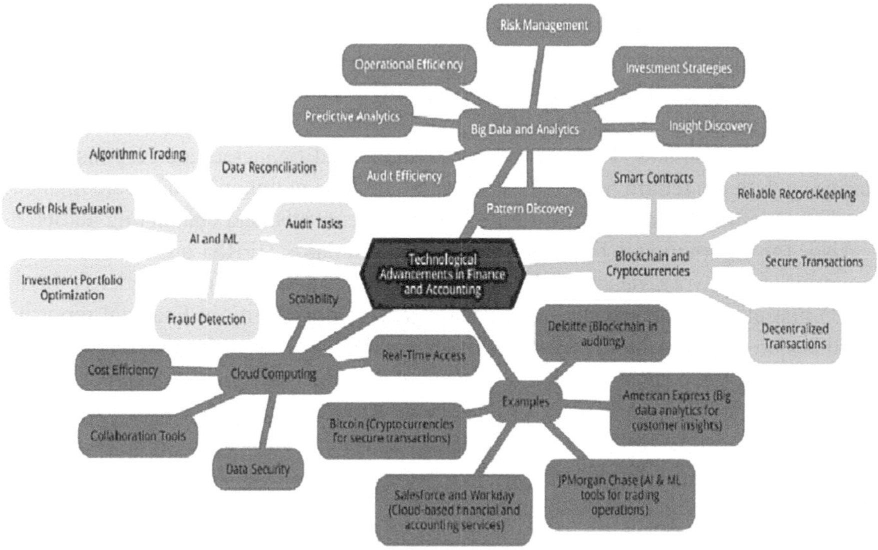

Fig. 3. Mind Map Illustrating the Impact of Technological Advancements on Finance and Accounting

3 Regulatory Changes Impacting Finance and Accounting

The finance and accounting sectors are exposed to a complex network of regulations in which clarity and protection of consumer rights, as well as the stability of the financial system, are preserved. Notably, strong regulatory reforms have been implemented internationally up to date, with the financial accounting and reporting conditions being greatly affected and equipped with increased monitoring demands. The reasons for these regulatory movements are blended, very often involving the rate of financial scandals, the level of data privacy and security measures, uplifting corporate governance quality, as well as the efforts to have higher standardization and comparability in the financial reporting approach. The global business environment has consistently evolved into an interconnected economic model, consequently making the process of maneuvering through these regulatory alterations a pivotal function that businesses take as a credential. One of the most impactful steps of regulation in this context is maybe the General Data Protection Regulation (GDPR) adopted by the European Union in 2018 [12]. The

GDPR is a 'general data protection law,' which shall be comprehensive legislation, and the most important objective of which is to empower individuals to control their personal data and enforce the strict rules for organizations using such data. But these provisions of regulation bring about more serious consequences for finance and accounting professionals, for they are often dealing with discreet financial data and personal information [12]. The GDPR states data protection standards in a robust manner and thus requires entities to obtain consent from data subjects and take actions towards ensuring the secure management and storage of personal data. Additionally, the Sarbanes-Oxley Act (SOX), another landmark regulation, is a 2002 United States legislation that was enacted after corporate accounting scandals happened. SOX aims to strengthen corporate governance, reporting, and, as regards financial statement audits, its independence [13]. It creates the most robust control mechanisms, both for the internal staff and for financial disclosures and accounting practices. Professional accountants and financiers are responsible for complying with the requirements of SOX, which include maintaining accurate financial records, implementing effective systems of internal controls, and conducting audits.

Also, the International Financial Reporting Standards (IFRS) are a standardized accounting framework designed by the International Accounting Standards Board (IASB) that allows consistency, transparency and comparability in financial reporting [14]. It is also quite common for nations to opt for IFRS or follow the path of converting it, which has notable consequences for financial statement preparation and accounting software. Finance and accounting professionals should keep pace with current IFRS requirements and ensure their companies are up-to-date with these policies in order to enable smooth cross-border transactions and attract overseas investors. The regulatory changes caused the aforementioned complex dynamics in accounting practices and financial statements. Consequently, it has led to heightened transparency and strict audit processes to prevent fraud within the organization, which entails the implementation of a detailed internal control system and documentation as well as an audit. This has forced the implementation of the latest technological means, including data analytics and report automation, so as to execute the compliance requirements and increase the accuracy and reliability of the information in the financial sphere. Accounting reporting regulations also have implications for how financial statements are reported. In particular, IFRS has put forward new accounting standards for revenue recognition, leases and financial instruments, thus leading organizations through the process of redefining their accounting policies and, in the worst cases, re-stating their financial statements [15]. These changes have consequences for financial analysis, decision-making, and stakeholder communication, which are very important. On the same note, recent amendments would underline the role of corporate governance and ethical behavior in the workings of companies. Today, finance and accounting professionals are tasked with creating and executing efficient internal control systems that foster fairness in their workplace and ensure consistency and transparency in their reporting [16]. This has eventually translated to more attention being given to training, compliance monitoring and setting up impeccable governance structures. Following such regulations may be difficult since, in most cases, it involves significant resources, high-level expertise and restructuring energy in companies. While complying with the rules will avert such harsh sanctions, a breach of the rules is associated with reputational damage and a loss of stakeholder confidence. In this case, finance and accounting experts have to heavily rely on staying informed on the latest regulatory changes, continuously evaluating their organization's adherence to these modified regulations, and taking action to remain fully compliant with the regulatory developments. In the advent of these regulatory changes, the organization shall be based on prevention and not correction methods, which will result in a culture of compliance and ethical behavior. While transitioning to these regulations may be uncertain, by embedding technology in the compliance processes, the accounting profession will successfully reduce the risk and attain a competitive advantage through increased transparency, reliability, and trust among stakeholders.

3.1 Recent Developments and Ethical Implications

Recent regulatory changes, including the California Consumer Privacy Act (CCPA) and updates to the GDPR, reflect ongoing efforts to enhance global data protection and privacy standards, requiring continuous adaptation by finance and accounting professionals. The rapid integration of advanced technologies such as AI, blockchain, and cryptocurrencies in finance introduces ethical considerations related to data privacy, cybersecurity, and transparency. While AI improves efficiency, it can also introduce biases and opacity in decision-making. Blockchain and cryptocurrencies pose challenges for regulatory compliance and financial transparency, necessitating new frameworks to mitigate risks like fraud and money laundering. These evolving regulatory landscapes and ethical implications highlight the need for finance and accounting professionals to stay informed, adaptable, and committed to maintaining high standards of integrity and transparency.

4 Shifts in Accounting and Financial Practices

In respect to dynamic technological advancements as well as regulatory changes, accounting and financial habits have been triggered by transformational trends. The changing patterns highlight the emerging needs of the companies, the stakeholders, and the world economy; therefore, the set of rules on accounting standards, reporting frameworks, is to be changed accordingly, too.

Accounting Standards and Practices: Accounting rules and practices is subject to constant change and adaptation in order to keep businesses afloat in ever-changing surroundings. The merger of accounting standards is the one remarkable trend leading towards the adoption and use of the international-computerized compiled IFRS for the purpose of providing similar and consistent financial records in different regions globally. The issuance of IFRS has compelled companies to re-write their accounting policies, commit to new recognition and measurement norms, and take-up revised disclosure regulations [15]. Furthermore, accounting bodies and standard-setters are currently engaging in the exciting area of tackling up-coming topics such as accounting for digital assets, revenue recognition from cloud computing arrangements, and the treatment of lease contracts. Such action not only disturbs the conventional manner of financial statement preparation, analysis, and decision making in them but also reverberates the way these companies operate.

Sustainability and ESG Reporting: The trend toward sustainability and the reporting of Environmental, Social, and Governance (ESG) criteria has accelerated in recent years. [17]. The actors within (investors, regulators, the general public and alike) tend to be capable of complete transparency when it comes to an organization's ecological performance, social responsibility and governance operations. Consequently, finance and accounting professionals should integrate the ESG factors into their reporting process, create metrics to measure and disclose their performance under this framework, and guarantee that the data is provided in a reliable way [17]. Such a move on the part of corporate organizations toward ESG reporting has particularly paved the way for new reporting rules and standards, e.g., GRI and SASB guidelines. These standards require businesses to perform social and environmental assessments, and governance updates, which they should then use to incorporate this information when developing strategies.

Global Economic Shifts: The global business environment is characterized by continuous restructuring, where such issues as geopolitical confrontations, market intricacies, technological innovations, consumer preferences, and others have significant impact. This economic phenomenon is having far-reaching effect on virtually every aspect of financial institutions, requiring them to implement new strategies that lead to the adoption of new operational systems. For example, the coming into effect of emerging markets and the general shift of economic power from the developed world to developing markets have seen businesses respond with a great change of investment strategies, a redesign of their supply chain, and a shifting of their financial reporting practices to address the differences in regulatory environments as well as market conditions [18]. As well, the most important issue arises concerning the development of a digital economy along with a novel concept of platform-based business models that determine the new criteria for revenue recognition, asset evaluation, and tax rules.

Auditing and Compliance Practices: A rise in law increased compliance and control technologies has been an effect of the regulatory changes and technological advancements mentioned above. Using all the new digital technology, conventional auditing has been augmented by the integration of data analytics, continuous monitoring, and automated testing to be more efficient and comprehensive. In contrast to the past, when auditors manually analyzed financial data, nowadays, auditors are using technology to analyze huge financial data sets, detect existing risks and highlight abnormalities, and dig deep into an organization's financial records to know if compliance policies are being followed. This has caused auditing to move to a continuous approach based on continuous risks rather than infrequent, sample-based audits.

Definitely, the widespread use of cloud-based accounting systems and real-time data access have fostered remote auditing practices and constant monitoring of financial transactions [19]. Such a fact has been helpful in enabling the auditors to provide immediate feedback and suggestions, which has in turn strengthened the importance of compliance and risk management processes. Furthermore, the regulatory compliance mandatory procedures have also experienced alterations to incorporate the intricate aspects associated with changes such as GDPR and IFRS. Organizations are enacting strong governance frameworks, data privacy and security mechanisms, and robust training programs to meet these regulations. Besides, the duties of compliance officers and risk managers have been viewed more and more at a higher level since they are the ones who deal with the complexity of the regulatory requirement freeholders and protect the organisation's interest considerations. This environment, with ever changing conditions, requires finance and accounting professionals to become quick and flexible. While adoption of these practices might entail continuous learning, cross-functional teamwork, and the use of advanced digital technology, it will be very important for the success of digital transformation processes. This allows companies to not only comply with the requirements but also gain an edge over competitors by increasing transparency, risk mitigation, and trust among stakeholders. Technological advancements and regulatory changes are becoming more influential on financial and accounting operations, which is revealed in these two case studies of businesses that have passed through significant evolutions.

4.1 Case Study 1: Blockchain Technology Integration by Walmart

Walmart, the significant international retailer, has been a pioneer in leveraging blockchain technology to transform its supply chain management and accounting practices. In collaboration with IBM, Walmart implemented a blockchain-enabled system in 2017 to trace food products from farm to store using a traceable digital ledger system [20]. Previously, the supply chain process was labor-intensive, relying heavily on manual data entry and paper records, which made tracking products throughout their journey challenging and inefficient.

The blockchain approach revolutionized this process by enhancing transparency and efficiency in tracing food item origins. Each step of the supply chain—from harvesting to transportation and processing—is recorded on the blockchain, creating a permanent and decentralized ledger. This system ensures food safety and quality control while providing real-time access to accurate data on stock, product origins, and account history. As a result, Walmart can trace the origins of contaminated food products in seconds, compared to the weeks it previously took [21]. This rapid traceability significantly reduces health risks and financial losses associated with food recalls.

The blockchain system has also facilitated quick information sharing among suppliers, distributors, retailers, and consumers, minimizing manual reconciliations and improving the accuracy of financial reporting. Figure 4 illustrates Walmart's blockchain technology integration. The digital transformation has led to substantial cost savings and streamlined business operations, showcasing the effectiveness of blockchain in enhancing supply chain transparency and efficiency.

Moreover, the integration of blockchain technology has provided Walmart with additional benefits. By ensuring data integrity and security, the blockchain system has bolstered consumer trust and confidence in Walmart's products. The system's immutability feature prevents unauthorized data alterations, ensuring that all transactions are verifiable and tamper-proof. This level of transparency has also enabled Walmart to meet stringent regulatory requirements more efficiently, thereby enhancing compliance with food safety standards and other regulations.

The implementation of blockchain technology at Walmart exemplifies how innovative digital solutions can address longstanding challenges in supply chain management. It highlights the potential for other industries to adopt similar technologies to improve traceability, efficiency, and transparency in their operations. Through this case study, it is evident that blockchain technology not only enhances operational processes but also provides significant financial and strategic advantages, positioning companies like Walmart at the forefront of digital transformation in the retail industry.

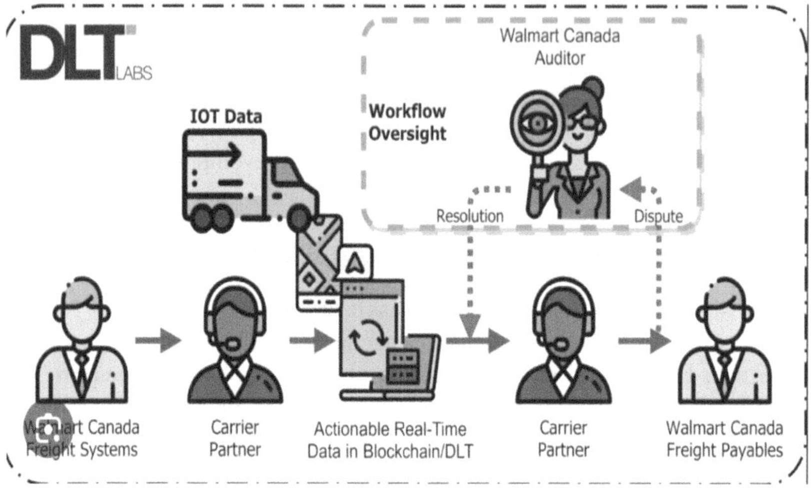

Fig. 4. Walmart's Block Chain Technology

4.2 Case Study 2: KPMG's Implementation of IFRS 16 Leases Standard

KPMG, one of the Big Four accounting firms, has established a reputation for assisting clients with the complexities of the IFRS 16 lease standard. This standard requires companies to recognize most lease contracts on their balance sheets, significantly altering financial ratios, debt covenants, and key financial figures [22]. This change impacts industries with substantial leasing activities, such as retail, transportation, and real estate.

KPMG's approach leverages advanced data analytics, automation, and the latest technology solutions to provide comprehensive assistance during the transition process. The KPMG IFRS 16 solution encompasses operations involving lease data, from initial data extraction to detailed financial impact analysis and the creation of implementation strategies. By collaborating with clients, KPMG develops tailored business cases, manages lease portfolios, and formulates specific accounting and reporting practices [23].

4.2.1 Analysis and Outcomes

Initial Data Extraction and Financial Impact Analysis: KPMG begins by extracting lease data from various sources, ensuring accurate capture and categorization. Advanced data analytics tools streamline this process, reducing manual effort and increasing accuracy. The financial impact analysis evaluates how the new standard affects financial statements, helping clients anticipate changes in financial ratios and debt covenants.

Implementation Strategy and Ongoing Support: KPMG develops customized implementation strategies, considering each client's unique context. This includes detailed plans for transitioning to the new standard, ensuring compliance, and optimizing financial reporting practices. KPMG provides continuous support through regular updates, training, and consultations, addressing any emerging issues and ensuring ongoing compliance.

Enhanced Financial Reporting and Decision-Making: The adoption of IFRS 16, facilitated by KPMG's expertise, results in more transparent and comprehensive financial reporting. Recognizing lease liabilities on the balance sheet allows companies to present a clearer picture of their financial obligations, aiding stakeholders in making informed decisions and enhancing investor confidence.

Industry-Wide Implications: KPMG's implementation of IFRS 16 has significant implications across various industries. For example, in the retail sector, companies achieve greater accuracy in financial reporting and improve strategic planning processes. In transportation and real estate, recognizing lease liabilities leads to more precise asset management and investment strategies.

Broader Impact

KPMG's successful implementation of IFRS 16 demonstrates the importance of integrating advanced technologies and aligning with emerging standards to modernize financial operations. This approach adds value, enhances transparency, and builds stakeholder trust. Future research should explore the ongoing impacts of IFRS 16 and further technological advancements to streamline compliance and enhance financial reporting practices.

In conclusion, KPMG's work with IFRS 16 not only helps clients achieve compliance but also positions them for long-term success by fostering transparency, informed decision-making, and strategic agility.

5 Challenges and Opportunities

The modifications that are evoked by modern technology and regulatory slippages in the finance and accounting disciplines will lead to both difficulties and opportunities for the professionals in that market who are adapting to the fast-changing world.

5.1 Challenges

Keeping pace with rapid technological change: Finance and accounting systems' evolution follows exponential progress, thus, professionals in these areas need to learn to deal with newly-ensued platforms and tech innovations. This necessitates constant education, picking up new competencies, and being ready for and welcoming change. In line with this, refusing to embrace these innovations could result in waste, disruption of work streams, and eventually a setback to the competition.

i. Managing data privacy and cybersecurity risks: Based on the fact that the use of digital technologies is much more widespread and their purpose for data is complex, the continued challenge is the protection of data and the safeguarding of cybersecurity [25]. This is why compliance with GDPR regulations and the proper implementation of robust security measures are suitable in terms of resilience against data leaks, financial losses and the associated risks to the company's reputation.
ii. Adapting to evolving regulatory frameworks: The regulatory landscape rapidly and frequently changes with new laws, standards and reporting requirements. Financing and accounting professionals must not forget about these changes and make certain that their organizations are in complete possession of them. As a rule, such expenses include both resource allocation, staff up-training, and major investments into the construction and repair of required installations.
iii. Integrating new technologies with legacy systems: Through our work at various organizations, I have seen this problem to be a big challenge, and we have to work hard to ensure it does not interrupt or exhaust existing legacy systems and processes. Interoperability may be deteriorated by this, which in turn will cause data isolation, cause inefficiency, and hamper the possibilities of deriving technology benefits to the fullest.
iv. Talent acquisition and retention: As the demand for high-skill professionals with expertise in the areas of data analytics, cyber security, and regulatory compliance, grows, organizations may be likely to face the problem of the attraction and retention of top talent in these specific fields.

5.2 Opportunities

a) Increased operational efficiency: Integration of technologies like automation, artificial intelligence, and cloud computing into finance and accounting professionals' work helps in removing physical processes, resulting in reductions in manual effort, and better operation efficiency, which in, turn saves costs and increases productivity [24].
b) Enhanced data-driven decision-making: Nowadays, finance and accounting professionals can use modern data analytics and business intelligence tools that assist in gaining insights about financial data, detecting trends and patterns in data, and making faster and better decisions regarding investment strategies, risk management, and resource allocation, all of which rely on the use of data.
c) Improved transparency and accountability: The upcoming technologies like blockchain and advanced bookkeeping schemes are the leading focuses for greater transparency and accountability in financial reporting, which would create a reliable environment and easy cross-border payments.
d) New service offerings and revenue streams: Changing finance and accounting fields set new barriers for service development and revenue growth. Indeed, that is a reason why services like aiding in regulatory compliance, cybersecurity, or sustainability reporting are good opportunities in business.
e) Collaboration and knowledge sharing: The digital turnover of finance and accounting is the ground where accountants collaborate more, exchange knowledge and learn, enabling them to draw on each other's experience, share best practices and encourage innovation in the industry.

5.3 Future Trends

Several trends and projections in the accounting and finance industries become apparent as we move towards the future:

i. Continued integration of emerging technologies: Technologies including blockchain, artificial intelligence and quantum computers are to be up-to-date and advanced, and in consequence, financial and accounting processes will become more efficient, secure, and data analysis in real-time will be achieved for better decisions [24].
ii. Rise of digital currencies and decentralized finance: The direct consequence of the digital currencies' and DeFi platforms' adoption will be an increased speed of change, that will make the former financial systems look hopelessly outdated and demand new models for accounting and regulation.
iii. Emphasis on sustainability and ESG reporting: The ESG element will gain more attention as the stakeholders' expectations, legal restrictions, and the need to decrease possible risks of environmental and societal nature deal with it.
iv. Continued regulatory evolution: The authorities will continue to promulgate standards and measures to mitigate new risks, the impact of technological evolution, and global economic fluctuations. This will help professionals with finance and accounting expertise keep pace with the changes by being compliant.
v. Talent development and upskilling: Given that the financial and accounting systems are changing constantly, organizations must build great learning and retraining programs as well as ensure that their professionals develop the needed technological, analytical and regulatory skillsets. Embracing such challenges and taking advantage of the technological and regulatory changes as steppingstones toward their considering themselves as strategic partners by helping the organizations drive innovation, mitigate risk and chart the course toward success and sustainability.

6 Conclusion

The finance and accounting sectors are undergoing significant transformations driven by rapidly advancing technologies and evolving regulatory frameworks. This paper has explored these changes, focusing on key technological advancements such as artificial intelligence, blockchain, big data analytics, and cloud computing, alongside critical legislative developments like GDPR, SOX, and IFRS. Our analysis has highlighted how these innovations have reshaped accounting methods, financial reporting, and operational procedures, revealing both the challenges and opportunities they present.

Practical implications of these transformations include the necessity for finance and accounting professionals to continuously adapt to new technologies and regulatory changes. This involves developing new skills, strategies, and frameworks to effectively integrate cutting-edge technologies with existing systems. Organizations must prioritize talent development programs that foster a growth mindset, teamwork, and continuous knowledge acquisition to stay competitive. Addressing issues like data privacy, cybersecurity, and regulatory compliance is essential for building trust and ensuring seamless transitions.

Looking forward, future research should explore deeper into the long-term impacts of emerging technologies such as quantum computing and decentralized finance on traditional financial practices. There is also a need to explore the expanding focus on sustainability and ESG reporting, driven by stakeholder demands and environmental considerations. Understanding how these factors influence financial decision-making and reporting will be crucial for developing robust and sustainable business practices.

In conclusion, the roles of finance and accounting professionals are evolving beyond traditional duties, positioning them as strategic business partners essential for organizational success. By embracing these changes and overcoming associated challenges, they can drive innovation, mitigate risks, and contribute significantly to the overall prosperity of their industries. Adapting to this dynamic landscape will not only enhance their professional capabilities but also ensure the long-term resilience and sustainability of their organizations.

Declarations:.

Conflicts of Interest. The authors declare that they have no conflict of interest. The manuscript was written through contributions of all authors. All authors have given approval to the final version of the manuscript. The author has no financial or proprietary interests in any material discussed in this article.

Ethical Approval. The article has no research involving human participants and/or animals.

Funding. No funding is applicable.

References

1. Kenton, W.: Financial Accounting. Investopedia (2023). https://www.investopedia.com/terms/f/financialaccounting.asp
2. Lip, G.: Financial Accounting. Corporate Finance Institute (2023). https://corporatefinanceinstitute.com/resources/accounting/financial-accounting/
3. OECD. Artificial Intelligence, Machine Learning and Big Data in Finance Opportunities. Challenges and Implications for Policy Makers (2021). https://www.oecd.org/finance/financial-markets/Artificial-intelligence-machine-learning-big-data-in-finance.pdf
4. Marr, B.: The 6 Biggest Technology Trends In Accounting And Finance. Forbes (2020). https://www.forbes.com/sites/bernardmarr/2020/07/27/the-6-biggest-technology-trends-in-accounting-and-finance/?sh=6340ef933c7e (accessed May 07, 2024)
5. Aspire Systems. AI is playing a crucial role in accounting and finance. www.aspiresys.com (2024). https://www.aspiresys.com/artificial-intelligence-in-finance-and-accounting/
6. Jindal, I.: AI and ML in Finance: How Technology is Revolutionizing the Financial Industry. Tars Blog (2023). https://www.hellotars.com/blog/ai-and-ml-in-finance-how-technology-is-revolutionizing-the-financial-industry/. Accessed 07 May 2024
7. Javaid, M., Haleem, A., Singh, R.P., Suman, R., Khan, S.: A review of blockchain technology applications for financial services. BenchCouncil Trans. Benchmarks, Stand. Evaluations **2**(3), 100073 (2022). https://www.sciencedirect.com/science/article/pii/S2772485922000606
8. Penn, L.P.S.: 5 key reasons why data analytics is important to business | Penn LPS Online. lpsonline.sas.upenn.edu (2022). https://lpsonline.sas.upenn.edu/features/5-key-reasons-why-data-analytics-important-business

9. Stander, B.: Cloud Accounting Vs. Traditional Accounting. thrivecfo.co.za (2023). https://thrivecfo.co.za/cloud-accounting-vs-traditional-accounting/. Accessed 07 May 2024
10. PYMNTS. JPMorgan Chase Unveils AI-Powered Tool for Thematic Investing. PYMNTS.com (2024). https://www.pymnts.com/news/artificial-intelligence/2024/jpmorgan-chase-unveils-ai-powered-tool-thematic-investing/. Accessed 07 May 2024
11. Llano, M.: American Express: Using Big Data to Prevent Fraud. Digital Innovation and Transformation (2022). https://d3.harvard.edu/platform-digit/submission/american-express-using-big-data-to-prevent-fraud/
12. Hoofnagle, C.J., Sloot, B.V.D., Borgesius, F.Z.: The European union general data protection regulation: what it is and what it means. Inf. Commun. Technol. Law **28**(1), 65–98 (2019). https://doi.org/10.1080/13600834.2019.1573501
13. Blokhin, A.: The Impact of the Sarbanes-Oxley Act of 2002. Investopedia (2022). https://www.investopedia.com/ask/answers/052815/what-impact-did-sarbanesoxley-act-have-corporate-governance-united-states.asp#:~:text=The%20Sarbanes%2DOxley%20Act%20of%202002%20was%20passed%20by%20Congress
14. Deloitte. International Accounting Standards Board (IASB). Iasplus.com (2019). https://www.iasplus.com/en/resources/ifrsf/iasb-ifrs-ic/iasb
15. IFRS. IFRS. Ifrs.org (2017). https://www.ifrs.org/issued-standards/list-of-standards/ias-8-accounting-policies-changes-in-accounting-estimates-and-errors/
16. Huang, W.: Internal Controls and Internal Audit. Built on Value, pp. 373–415 (2019). https://doi.org/10.1007/978-981-13-7507-1_15
17. Barbosa, A., da Silva, M.C.B.C., da Silva, L.B., Morioka, S.N., de Souza, V.F.: Integration of environmental, social, and governance (ESG) criteria: their impacts on corporate sustainability performance. Hum. Soc. Sci. Commun. **10**(1), 1–18 (2023). https://doi.org/10.1057/s41599-023-01919-0
18. Fernandez-Arias, N., Musso, A., Osorio-Buitron, C., Popescu, A.: Emerging Markets Are Exercising Greater Global Sway. IMF (2024). https://www.imf.org/en/Blogs/Articles/2024/04/09/emerging-markets-are-exercising-greater-global-sway
19. Cloud Computing for Accountants: Embracing Digital Transformation. www.vintti.com (2024). https://www.vintti.com/blog/cloud-computing-for-accountants-embracing-digital-transformation/
20. Sristy, A.: Blockchain in the food supply chain - What does the future look like?. Blockchain in the food supply chain - What does the future look like? (2021). https://tech.walmart.com/content/walmart-global-tech/en_us/blog/post/blockchain-in-the-food-supply-chain.html
21. Hyperledger. How Walmart brought unprecedented transparency to the food supply chain with Hyperledger Fabric. www.hyperledger.org (2024). https://www.hyperledger.org/case-studies/walmart-case-study#:~:text=%E2%80%9CUsing%20the%20IBM%20Food%20Trust
22. O'Donovan, B.: IFRS 16 – An overview - KPMG Global. KPMG (2023). https://kpmg.com/xx/en/home/insights/2021/03/ifrs-handbook-leases-lease-accounting-overview-ifrs16.html
23. KPMG Services to Help Clients Realize the Full Value of Technology Business Management KPMG -Combining Leadership in Tax, Audit, and IT Advisory Financial Resources Technology Portfolio Business Demand TBM Strategy & Roadmap Sustained Value Optimization Transparency TBM Journey -Pathway to IT Value Optimization Stages in the TBM Journey TBM Optimization Domains Managing the TBM Journey & Realizing the Value Value Measurement and Management Organization & Behavioral Change Management Program and Risk Management 5 Key KPMG Services That Help Apptio Customers Achieve TBM Excellence. Accessed 07 May 2024. https://assets.kpmg.com/content/dam/kpmg/pdf/2015/09/tbm-readiness.pdf
24. Rubin, L.: Accounting and Finance Trends for 2024 - Why it's a Breakout Year for Finance Professionals and Data Enthusiasts www.linkedin.com (2024). https://www.linkedin.com/pulse/accounting-finance-trends-2024-why-its-breakout-year-lance-rubin-q7h8c/

25. Quach, S., Thaichon, P., Martin, K.D., Weaven, S., Palmatier, R.W.: Digital technologies: tensions in privacy and data. J. Acad. Mark. Sci. **50**(1), 1299–1323 (2022). https://doi.org/10.1007/s11747-022-00845-y
26. Panhalkar, K.: Technology Change in the Accounting Industry in 2023. technology-counter.com (2020). https://technologycounter.com/blog/technology-change-in-accounting-industry
27. Dekate, T.: The Origin of Big Data Analytics. Analytics Vidhya (2022). https://www.analyticsvidhya.com/blog/2022/09/the-origin-of-big-data-analytics/
28. 44722676 - Online Store. superostmk.live. https://superostmk.live/product_details/44722676.html. Accessed 07 May 2024

Author Index

V. B. Gupta et al. (Eds.): IBCD 2024, CCIS 2413, p. 241, 2025.
https://doi.org/10.1007/978-3-031-87511-3

The manufacturer's authorised representative in the EU is Springer Nature Customer Service Centre GmbH, Europaplatz 3, 69115 Heidelberg, Germany. If you have any concerns regarding our products, please contact ProductSafety@springernature.com

Printed and bound by CPI Group (UK) Ltd, Croydon, CR0 4YY
01/10/2026
02225908-0005